AMERICAN UMPIRE

AMERICAN UMPIRE

Elizabeth Cobbs Hoffman

HARVARD UNIVERSITY PRESS
Cambridge, Massachusetts
London, England
2013

Publication of this book has been supported through the generous provisions
of the Maurice and Lula Bradley Smith Memorial Fund.

Library of Congress Cataloging-in-Publication Data

Cobbs Hoffman, Elizabeth.
American umpire / Elizabeth Cobbs Hoffman.
p. cm.
Includes bibliographical references and index.
ISBN 978-0-674-05547-6 (hardcover : alk. paper)
1. United States—Foreign relations. 2. International relations.
3. International organization. 4. World politics. I. Title.
E183.7.C595 2013
327.73—dc23   2012027905

For the world in all its glory and tragedy,
and for my brothers and sisters—
Don, Viki, Robert, Joseph, Moira, and Sally

Contents

Introduction

*Or, A Cautionary Tale of How the World
Changed after 1776*

Amid brutal mortar fire, lightning-fast air raids, and fierce hand-to-hand combat embroiling troops from four countries, the Egyptian siege defied every stereotype of the Cold War. Britain used its veto to overturn American peace resolutions in the United Nations Security Council. The Soviet Union vowed cooperation with the U.S. Sixth Fleet. India, Saudi Arabia, Indonesia, Canada, and numerous other countries feverishly but fruitlessly offered advice, while the Soviet-American bloc stood poised against the Anglo-French-Israeli alliance.[1]

The stakes were high. They varied by country, but concerns common to both participants and onlookers included the principle of national sovereignty, the openness of world waterways, the right of self-defense, compensation for confiscated property, and access to crucial commodities of every type, including oil. Virtually every nation on the planet wanted and needed all of these things.[2]

In the topsy-turvy Suez Canal Crisis of 1956, which would decide Egypt's fundamental right to rule its own territory, the United States had limited resources, minimal financial investment, and zero authority. It exercised no direct control over its wayward best allies. It enjoyed little clout with the angry local government and had clumsily helped to provoke the crisis by denying Egypt a high-profile, previously promised, much-desired loan. The UN was divided and had delegated no responsibility. Yet the United States was the wealthiest nation on the planet, with the best-equipped military force. If any one player could halt the melee, rule on the dispute, and force the offending parties to retire from the field, it would be the United States of America.

Remarkably, it was willing to do so, at the risk of reputation, friendship, and material resources.

President Dwight D. Eisenhower had personally commanded the Allied invasion across the English Channel that defended bombed-out Britain and liberated occupied France from the Nazis twelve years earlier. In 1951, as NATO's first commanding officer, easygoing "Ike" had cooperated more closely with Europe's leaders and common soldiers than any president in two centuries. But in 1956 he used the financial resources at his disposal to force America's closest friends to back down.[3] Egypt's attackers withdrew and the canal came under full local control. Gamal Abdel Nasser triumphed. Arab dignity and Egyptian sovereignty were reinforced. The principles of national independence and compensation for seized assets were sustained. Britain was forced to accept the painful limits of storied family ties, and France decided to develop an atomic bomb to ensure its future autonomy from Washington, D.C.

America had violated the spirit, if not the letter, of international rules by exercising an unscripted authority that arose from sheer wealth—and it had become a little more entangled in the troubled Middle East in the process. All the outcomes were imperfect. Nonetheless, once Eisenhower achieved his objectives, punitive measures were dropped and the world went on with a collective sigh of relief.

This book attempts to explain dynamics at work below the surface of events like the 1956 Suez Crisis, underpinning the modern world itself. Circumstances in Egypt were a tiny piece of a much larger puzzle. How did emerging nation-states like Egypt, with weak armies and paltry treasuries, stand up successfully to the kinds of empires that had ruled the globe since time immemorial? Why did world opinion matter, and why did it almost unanimously side with a man as verbally aggressive and unpleasant as President Nasser, who described other nations as stooges and bloodsuckers? Why did President Eisenhower intervene in a conflict 5,700 miles away, when not a single American life was on the line?

The story begins with the 1776 birth of the United States but embraces a history that transcends any one country. Thomas Paine, the passionate, poetic, politically reckless son of an English corset maker, declared in colonial Philadelphia that Americans had it in their power "to begin the world over again."[3] What Paine could not see from the self-described City of Brotherly Love was that the world was already remaking itself on a grand scale, and at a rapid pace. He correctly predicted that the former British colonists would play an extraordinary role in this transformation, but external events shaped Americans just as much as Americans shaped events.

The Western values that the United States was later sometimes accused of pushing onto an unwilling, culturally different world were, in fact, global ones that led to a new world order. The United States acted as an *umperial* power in this new order. Although umpire is not a perfect metaphor, it describes the U.S. function in global affairs more accurately than the outdated but widely used term "empire." It also illumines the historical costs, consequences, and contradictions of such a role.

The Peace of Westphalia, the agreement in 1648 that ended the Thirty Years' War in Europe, laid the foundation. Starting around 1648, quickening in 1776, and culminating in 1991 with the break up of the Soviet Union, the world of monarchies and empires dissolved. Over the course of three centuries, the dominant system of human political organization—dating back further than the pharaohs—was irrevocably replaced by a world of nation-states. The majority of them were republics, defined roughly as countries governed by commoners rather than monarchs. Nearly all of these nations became democracies, or at least pretended to majority rule. (Pretense is important, for it indicates what people think the world wants to see and reveals unwritten standards.) Almost uniformly, the nations of the world eventually adopted free-market, capitalist economies. Although cultural and religious diversity endured, the broad patterns of political and economic life converged in an altogether new mold that did away with empires.

The United States was the pivot of this worldwide transformation, having been first to show it was possible for a disparate group of people to proclaim a republic and will their state into existence. It was a "new species," as British philosopher Edmund Burke observed at the end of the eighteenth century. In the following two centuries the species proliferated. Half the nations in today's world began with declarations of independence that were inspired, at least in part, by the first such proclamation in 1776.[4] No external force made this happen. In fact, peoples like the Vietnamese and Algerians founded nations against epic outside resistance. Others who demanded popular sovereignty faced massive internal resistance, such as Libyans in 2011.

What this shows is that some aspirations, like the desire for local autonomy or democratic government, can become global—or "go native"—very quickly. Historian Dipesh Chakrabarty argues that political practices first associated with Western Europe are "now everybody's heritage."[5] In the course of a couple centuries, peoples all over the world came to view the nation-state as the only worthwhile type of political community. Like the invention of the wheel in Mesopotamia or the hybridization of corn in Mesoamerica, geographical origin did not greatly matter in the long run. Humans passed tools and ideas from person to person, nation to nation. By the time President Nasser insisted upon Egypt's right to control *all* its own territory in 1956, empires like Britain's had lost the argument.

A tectonic shift in economic organization went along with this political metamorphosis. Here, too, many of the changes that gradually overtook almost all peoples were observable first in the United States. Early on, the United States dropped the mercantilist tradition whereby emperors, kings, or parliaments granted specific economic privileges (such as fiefdoms or proprietary charters) to members of the aristocracy. In 1811, starved for goods by Napoleon Bonaparte's wars, New York State passed the world's first general incorporation law to encourage manufacturing. After that, any group of people meeting certain minimal standards could form their own legal corporation.[6] They no longer had to seek the privilege of commercial existence, such as that granted by the British and Dutch governments to their East Indian trading companies. First in New York, but then throughout the United States, businesses acquired the right to self-definition.

Unsurprisingly, economic and political ideas dovetailed. Both emphasized citizen initiative. The nation that was self-made encouraged self-made men. For ease of reference, we might call the system that arose democratic capitalism: "democratic" because the people were sovereign, not a titled elite, and "capitalist" because most wealth was generated, deployed, and owned by individuals, not government.

Yet it does not make sense to stop at this rather general definition. The dissimilarities between societies are sometimes so striking that it can be hard to see the underlying characteristics that unify them in a single historical system. If one follows the news, the United States, China, and Iran appear diametrically opposed and fundamentally unalike. But they have been influenced by the same powerful ideas that swept the world in recent centuries. All, for example, are republics—the first one becoming so in the eighteenth century, the latter two during the twentieth century. All give wide latitude to private wealth and corporate initiative.

So it is important to probe deeper to find the underlying characteristics that make democratic capitalism adaptable to widely differing cultural contexts. Doing so reveals three key practices. These practices, which reflect social values, explain the thinking patterns that allowed disparate societies to apply a general model to their particular circumstances, much as different Neolithic peoples adapted the concept of agriculture to their own latitude and terrain. They explain why the human story took the turns that it did between 1648 and the present, and why dissimilar peoples made similar choices out of their own self-interest. They show why one of the most commonly held scholarly assumptions of our day—that the United States is a kind of empire—is not simply improbable but false.

But first, a caveat.

Historians do not normally try to derive general principles from messy human affairs. We emphasize contingency, complexity, and the unanticipated. Knowing how conflicted most people are, and how easily plans go awry, we are suspicious of explanations that make history seem predetermined. In the nineteenth century, a number of thinkers believed it was possible to discover general laws that predicted change over time, to which "details" like genocide could be appended. The most famous was Karl Marx. Subsequent events showed that the classless society that Marx believed inevitable was not fated at all.

Few principles apply all the time. But it is nonetheless helpful to identify general forces underlying modern history, so long as they can be concretely documented and we accept that they do not account for all that happened in the past or guarantee what happens next. As events like 9/11 and the banking collapse of 2008 suggest, progress is neither inevitable nor unsullied, and it may be reversed. History always lurks around the corner, ready to mug the unsuspecting. Nuclear destruction, environmental degradation, and ideological fanaticism still pose basic threats to human existence. Each generation confronts its own dangers. To observe that democratic capitalism prevailed is not to say that it is the final or best system, as others may yet emerge. There is no triumphal or comforting "end of history."[7]

But the new academic field of world history encourages us to look for broad patterns that are visible if we step back far enough to see them. When sketched realistically, these patterns help us see the confluence of ideas, events, and practices that gave us the world we experience—a world in which some nation-states have much greater size, power, and wealth than others, but none is an empire. In it, this book suggests, Washington sometimes exerts a unique, controversial, and (probably) temporary authority that arises from America's particular historical experience, but in defense of values that have become common. In other words, the United States does not merely impose on others what George Kennan once famously dismissed as America's provincial (and dangerously delusional) "moralistic-legalistic" view of international life.[8]

English poet John Donne wrote, "No man is an island . . . ; every man is a piece of the continent, a part of the main." So it is with nations. Scholars often begin by asking what makes American history different. Yet similarities are equally important. They explain why nation-states cooperate even when not coerced.

Leaders attract followers when what they say touches an inner chord—when the listener feels that the speaker shares his aspirations. America's leadership has been potent because it has resonated with communal patterns of thinking and desire. Had the aspirations to freedom, prosperity, and security been American alone, the United States would never have had power enough to overcome the contrary intentions and actions of people in distant climes.

In recounting the tale of foreign relations from 1776 to the present, this book teases out three goals or practices that gradually transcended ancient differences and pushed *both* the United States and the rest of the world in the direction of democratic capitalism. These are *access* to opportunity, *arbitration* of disputes, and *transparency* in government and business. Such terms do not have the emotive appeal (or historical baggage) of "life, liberty, and . . . happiness," but perhaps partly for that reason they may help us better understand how these broad trends worked in a variety of cultural contexts.

Although the new trends did not emerge full-blown, they can be glimpsed more consistently over time in the welter of events, even though buffeted by countertrends. Adoption of access, arbitration, and transparency has been terribly uneven and occurred on what might be called a sliding scale. At the opening of the twenty-first century, Chinese autocrats still limited Internet access in their country, Somali warlords rejected arbitration, and corrupt grandees everywhere opposed transparency. Some individuals and groups resisted the dominant trends and did their best to undermine them. But the new practices could be justified according to the precepts of most traditions and religions, and all three became universally influential. While they were not made in America, the U.S. example and U.S. foreign policy helped speed the trends along. Evolutionary biologist Richard Dawkins calls such phenomena "memes": ideas, practices, or customs that "propagate themselves in the meme pool by leaping from brain to brain via a process which, in the broad sense, can be called imitation."[9]

Of course, new ideas are not inherently, consistently, or eternally superior to older ones. These particular practices attracted adherence because they were better than other contemporary alternatives for meeting basic goals. Many nations came to embrace access, arbitration, and transparency for the same reasons that Americans did: they served their material interests and cultural preferences.

By *access,* I mean the modern propensity to believe (albeit selectively) that people should have entrée to opportunity at almost all levels. There is an instinctive assumption that open social systems are superior to those that are closed. They not only seem to function better, but they also appear fairer because—as most contemporary societies at least profess to believe—"all men are created equal." The spread of access can be seen in the worldwide expansion of democracy over a period of three centuries. One example would be the widening ripple of suffrage. In the United States, propertied white men gained the vote first, then the white male poor, then black men, then women, then adults between the ages of eighteen and twenty-one. Another example would be the steady increase in the number of democratic nations, despite periodic retrenchments such as those in the 1930s and 1960s.[10] Compared with preceding centuries, access to power has widened steadily across the globe. Democracy is its political expression.

Access finds economic expression as well, such as in the trend toward open competition in markets of all types, for individuals as well as nation-states. Domestic examples would include U.S. civil service regulations against nepotism, designed to prevent family monopolies, and the Sherman Antitrust Act of 1890, designed to prevent corporate monopolies. An international example would be the World Trade Organization, founded in 1995 to facilitate nations' opening their internal marketplaces to one another. Examples abound in the history of individual countries as well. Britain was the preeminent champion of free trade during the nineteenth and early twentieth centuries, exemplified by its reversal of the restrictive "Corn Laws" in 1846, which had previously shut out cheap imported grains. The United Kingdom initially did more than the United States to advance the trend toward open international exchange.

The growing commitment to access has also been expressed in foreign policy. A key example is the largely symbolic Open Door Policy of 1900. This was a pronouncement by U.S. secretary of state John Hay (in his youth one of Abraham Lincoln's two presidential aides) that the Japanese and Europeans should not colonize China and close its markets to their competitors. All foreigners should have equal access, it proclaimed, and China should retain sovereignty. In 1978, China revitalized this approach by declaring its own "Opening Up" policy (Kai Fang) to encourage foreign trade and investment. That year, the theory that access is vital to prosperity was effectively Sinicized.[11]

The second practice, *arbitration,* has been reflected in a growing preference for economic sanctions, transnational regulation, and diplomacy over physical violence. Arbitration is defined here to include bilateral and multilateral negotiations as well as conflict resolution processes in which an outside party makes a final determination that is imposed on the disputants with their acquiescence (ready or grudging). The preference for arbitration shaped the American constitutional republic after 1787, with the federal government acting as umpire over the states and over corporations that crossed state lines. When they pleaded for passage of the U.S. Constitution, revolutionaries like Alexander Hamilton and James Madison were driven by the conviction that only a strong federation, guided by some central body, would forestall the kinds of conflict that periodically decimated Europe. Both fear and hope fueled their sense of urgency. A national government would mediate interstate conflicts while providing a structure for useful cooperation. Hamilton confessed to a "trembling anxiety" for its success.[12] Almost two centuries later, the goal of arbitration shaped the structure of the United Nations, which outlawed war and created procedures for negotiating international disputes. As this book explains, the aim of avoiding physical violence between nation-states created the need for an umpire precisely because there was no empire.

Naturally enough, arbitration sometimes disappoints. Force remains a potent tool to which nations still resort, though increasingly within a sanctioned framework of collective security. Indeed, this has been true even within the United States. For example, legislative compromises contained a schism within the United States for half a century, but they failed in 1860. In the devastating secession crisis that followed Abraham Lincoln's election, the federal government turned to violence to enforce its will. The reunited nation that arose from the ashes of the Civil War had more steel in its spine. Again the tools of compromise were taken up, and since 1865 the nation has avoided another rupture—just as Europe has mostly eschewed physical conflict since the formation of the United Nations in 1945. In the past century and more, war has declined in legitimacy, replaced by a belief in the viability and necessity of arbitration.

The third practice, *transparency*, changed the ways that people communicated. Over time, the United States and a growing circle of nations came to accept that transparency in their economic and political dealings was more useful than secrecy. To some extent transparency was subordinate to access and arbitration, or at least it served them, since the two other objectives depended on a free flow of information. Power structures and economic opportunities could be accessible only if transparent. So, for example, a plethora of laws in the economic arena required honest reporting by corporations in the belief that buyers and sellers of stocks and bonds should have equal access to important news. In domestic politics, the majority of nations embraced written constitutions to make rules visible and changeable, and in international relations it became standard practice to publicly reveal the content of treaties. Transparency reflected the idea that power should be exercised in the open, where it could be judged, and knowledge should be unfettered. As political scientist Yaron Ezrahi has written, "The belief that the citizens gaze at the government and that the government makes its actions visible to the citizen is, then, fundamental to the democratic process of government."[13]

Today, transparency is nearly a universal demand, though inconsistently achieved. In 1985 Mikhail Gorbachev kicked off his great internal reform of Soviet communism with the policy he called *glasnost*, translated as openness or transparency. In 1993, Transparency International was formed in Germany. A citizens' organization with chapters in more than ninety countries, its sole purpose is to reveal government corruption, in the belief that exposure is the first step toward stamping out behavior that weakens public morality and saps resources. In 2010, entrepreneurs in India founded the website Ipaidabribe.com to help average citizens expose government graft, and other nations began copying it within a year, from the Republic of Kenya to the Kingdom of Bhutan.[14] When totalitarian regimes marshal all their resources to oppose transparency, they now find it almost impossible to do so for any length of time because of the Internet. Changes in communications technology have hastened a trend sparked initially by ideological considerations. Not surprisingly, humans created devices that both served their goals and reinforced them.[15]

On the first full day of his presidency, Barack Obama announced he, too, would improve transparency so that citizens could better know their government. As the WikiLeaks controversy showed in 2010, even democratic governments are subject to the spiral of transparency, quickened by new technologies.

The assumption that transparency is essential to improving society is not a modern idea, however. We glimpse it in the 1777 Articles of Confederation that required the Constitutional Congress to publish a monthly journal of its proceedings, and in the British practice after 1803 of releasing the texts of parliamentary debates. Americans enshrined free speech in their 1791 Bill of Rights. The French had done so in their Declaration of the Rights of Man and the Citizen two years earlier. In his Farewell Address, George Washington reminded his countrymen that even between nations, "Honesty is always the best policy." In 1861, Abraham Lincoln made perhaps the single most important contribution to transparency of any world leader by initiating the first program to release secret diplomatic correspondence. Between 1910 and 1997, ten additional nations followed suit, routinely washing their dirty laundry in public.[16] The vast majority of countries still do not do this, but their own citizens increasingly criticize government opacity.

Although people sometimes thought of access, arbitration, and transparency in ideological terms, these were pragmatic choices that gradually acquired the flavor of "best practices," from Mumbai to Montevideo. They found early expression in American government, but the United States was not as exceptional as is often assumed. The nation was part of an evolving human community in which societies continuously swapped goods and technologies. It was one of a group of interconnected, competitive nations, some a thousand years older, which organically developed the goals and practices that resulted in the new world order. This means that the United States was less unique than popularly imagined, but more important as a bellwether. To credit America with inventing the new world order would be like crediting one society with the invention of engineering. Such widespread and transformative practices evolved in bits and pieces to further the universal goal of survival.

Some authors believe that the world system functions as it does almost entirely because of American pressure. The import of this book's assertions, if they are true, is that access, arbitration, and transparency have achieved enough momentum to transcend their point of origin and the efforts of any one nation. Indeed, these three practices became complementary and self-sustaining, despite paradoxes that vexed implementation and conflicts that defied solution. They spread because their beneficial effects outweighed their negative ones. They enhanced peace and prosperity in most places where they were implemented. By the end of the twentieth century, people generally lived longer and better, even though poverty, bad weather, and human misdeeds kept journalists as busy as ever. (Being better off does not necessarily mean being well off; sometimes the world is plain awful.) Empires had disappeared, replaced by autonomous countries. Nation-states provided a sense of identity and self-determination that most people valued as the globe became more crowded. And despite war—a failing our species may never entirely overcome—life expectancy gained dramatically on every single continent, rising from an average of thirty-six years in 1900 to sixty-seven in the year 2002. In a few countries, life expectancy zoomed past eighty.

The last half of the twentieth century also witnessed greater global economic development than any other period since humans first inhabited the earth. Economic historians call the years from 1950 to 1973 history's Golden Age, and the following three decades rank as the second most affluent period on record.[17] This growth occurred because democratic capitalism drove material progress and facilitated enough peace and cooperation for humanity to flourish.

This is not the only way that history could have happened, but it is the way it did. It resulted from conscious striving on the part of billions of people to improve life. Three thousand years ago, the Greek slave Aesop told the fable of an ant and a grasshopper. The grasshopper lived for the day, enjoying the balmy weather and lush grass of spring and summer, while the ant toiled relentlessly to store hard nuggets of grain that would sustain him through the winter. The "moral of the story"—the phrase that Aesop bequeathed to popular memory—was that humans should learn from the ants.

Surprisingly, they did. Much of the progress since 1648 was planned—not in the sense that anyone knew the outcome, and not that different ethnic groups coordinated goals. But humans acted more or less purposefully. Scientists toiled to unravel the mysteries of biology, farmers sought ways to grow more food, manufacturers strove to make products more plentiful, migrants searched for better places to raise their families, and governments devised strategies to improve security. Overall, despite periodic cataclysms, humanity multiplied like Aesop's ants. Access, arbitration, and transparency shaped this process.

This is not to imply that democratic capitalism was any panacea. While more functional than other contemporary systems, it nonetheless had some obvious failings. For example, the complexity and fluidity of modern society created multiple opportunities for corruption. In the United States, under both Democratic and Republican administrations, processes like deregulation resulted in such catastrophes as the mortgage-banking meltdown of 2008. Insider trading, political collusion, individual greed, partisan selfishness, and outright fraud at the highest social levels sometimes made a mockery of transparency and fair dealing. Worldwide, the opening decades of the twenty-first century saw the virulent resurgence of some of humanity's oldest troubles, from wars of religion to maritime piracy. The United States reeled from the most violent foreign assault ever launched at its civilian population, and retaliated by making war on a dictator unconnected with the plot. The daily news is enough to make one think that the world is an appalling, irredeemable place.

Nonetheless, a historical view—the long view—suggests something different. Despite all that could and did go wrong, democratic capitalism introduced useful new practices that gained traction over time. It also brought down the world order known as empire.

Like most terms of ancient origin, "empire" has multiple meanings. In common parlance, one may speak metaphorically of a local appliance dealer creating a "washing machine empire," or some Madison Avenue mogul building a "media empire." But in history, "empire" originally designated two ubiquitous types of government that incorporated and commanded obedience from people who generally did not wish to yield it and who continued to seek political release after their annexation.

The oldest type was that which subordinated multiple ethnic groups in a contiguous territory, like the Mongol, Ottoman, Roman, and Aztec Empires, as well as more recent ones like the Soviet Union. The second, newer type of empire was one that ruled multiple peoples from afar in scattered colonies, like those of the British, Dutch, French, and Spanish, sometimes called saltwater empires. Both of these types were actual empires, not merely metaphorical ones. The United States initiated the second kind of empire when it took over the Philippines in 1898.[18] The American government commanded obedience from Filipinos, who were denied the rights of U.S. citizenship, sought to break away, and eventually did achieve separate status.[19]

Yet 1898 to 1946 was the one and only period in which the United States sustained an empire, even though it and other American republics had a long history of suppressing native peoples and fighting one another for favorable boundaries. The U.S. Congress moved to cancel America's membership in the imperialist club by passing the Philippine Autonomy Act of 1916, followed by the Philippine Independence Act of 1934. After this, there was little talk of a U.S. empire until the second decade of the Cold War, when self-doubt began to set in over the damage to American integrity from fighting that murky battle. Consequently, three new, rather looser definitions of "empire" arose.

The first equated economic prowess with imperialism. Historian William Appleman Williams pioneered this interpretation in the late 1950s, calling the United States an Open Door empire. Like the magical cloth in Hans Christian Anderson's fable "The Emperor's New Clothes," this empire was invisible. It existed on no map but was presumed to exist because of American commercial dominance. This argument equated entry into foreign markets with exploitation, and assumed that a reduction in trade barriers inherently diminished the sovereignty of whichever country was less industrially developed, making it into a virtual (but not formal) colony.[20] The Vietnam War gave verve to Williams's argument, which became the basis for widespread historical revisionism during the 1960s and 1970s.

Time gradually dulled the cutting edge of this argument, but historical depictions of the United States as an empire surfaced anew with the end of the Cold War and became ubiquitous in the wake of September 11, 2001. Some books portrayed the empire as benign, but the majority portrayed it as malignant. Many adopted the trade-dominance model since there was no territorial or legal entity at which to point. Scholars based their claims of U.S. imperialism on the rise of the United States to economic preeminence in the twentieth century, assuming there was simply little other way to account fully for American wealth and influence.

In addition to the trade-dominance model as a definition of empire, a second new definition arose from studies of nineteenth century American expansionism. The rapid, often ruthless enlargement of the United States across Indian, Spanish, British, and Mexican territory appeared to offer conclusive proof of American imperialism, dressed up as Manifest Destiny. A third theory of empire was grounded in the military interventionism of the United States. The thinking here was that any nation that intervenes consistently in others' internal affairs is, ipso facto, an empire—especially when the more powerful nation maintains military bases in the other countries.[21] (Yet other scholars simply asserted "the empire" as a given, requiring no proof at all but merely in need of "deconstructing" to reveal its race, class, and gender biases. These scholars sought to document the American Empire's "everyday life."[22])

The weight of all these assertions might seem insuperable. But there is ready evidence that throws doubt on all three claims: that America's wealth reveals a pattern of imperial control; that continental expansion resulted in a landed, multiethnic realm; and that having military bases around the world constitutes an imperial force. The purpose of this book is to sift through the evidence and place it alongside global trends between 1648 and the present. Comparing the American experience with that of other nations is essential to establishing context and proportion, the historian's best defense against presentism, or the tendency to let contemporary events get in the way of seeing the past. Before doing so, however, it may be helpful to introduce a few of the discordant facts that rub uncomfortably against the regnant interpretations—and that prompted this inquiry.

Take, for example, the argument that Americans' extensive investments in foreign countries prove that the United States is an empire, and that an industrial economy inherently bests a less-developed one in any negotiation. This allegation sounds intuitively correct, but in 2010 the United States had a lower per capita income than numerous European nations and two Middle Eastern ones. People of forty-nine other nationalities lived longer than Americans.[23] How did the United States rank seventeenth in income, and fiftieth in life expectancy, if it ruled the world and set the terms of transaction? Were the denizens of imperial Athens, Amsterdam, London, Machu Picchu, Persepolis, Paris, or Rome that far behind the peoples they dominated at the height of their power?

Imperialism is supposed to be driven by material interests, but by this thumbnail measurement, Americans either do not possess an empire or are extraordinarily inept at exploiting it. Some historians make the latter claim, but this is certainly at odds with the Yankee reputation for driving a hard bargain. Also, if an empire is required to produce wealth, why did the U.S. economy flourish spectacularly for more than 100 years before the nation assumed its supposed worldwide reign—before the Open Door Policy, before America's imperialist fling in 1898, before the first doughboy hit the shores of France, and before the invention of the International Monetary Fund?

Or take the claim that the United States built an empire during its nineteenth-century expansion to the Pacific Ocean. Some scholars believe that America has been an empire at least since 1803, when it purchased Louisiana from Napoleon Bonaparte.[24] After that, the United States negotiated treaties with Spain for Florida, and with Britain for Oregon. It forced Indian nations at gunpoint to relinquish their lands, and conquered Mexico and Hawaii.[25] According to this interpretation of events, the United States gradually assumed the shape of a continental, landed empire analogous to the Russian, Inca, Chinese, and Austro-Hungarian. It incorporated subordinate nationalities into a giant, mostly contiguous empire.

This definition sounds sensible, but simple comparisons reveal its inadequacy as well. Consider Chile, which elbowed aside the Spanish Empire and then used its army to expand northward at the expense of Peru and Bolivia, and southward at the expense of native peoples. Was Chile an empire? Were Argentina, Australia, Brazil, and Canada empires too, since they also evolved by dispossessing indigenous inhabitants and sometimes other nation-states? We generally do not call countries like these empires because of an implicit distinction between imperialism and nationalism that perhaps ought to be made explicit. Landed empires like those of Rome or ancient Egypt treated the peoples they incorporated as subjects. Argentina, Australia, Brazil, Canada, and Chile are comprised of citizens. These nations chose the same path as America's founders, who embarked in 1776 upon "the world's first experiment in popular government over an extended area."[26] Although formed opportunistically in ways we would condemn today, they were not empires because they eventually granted citizenship to all residents on a basis of legal equality, and peoples who had been absorbed stopped trying to escape the nation's sovereignty.

Most modern nation-states exhibited a coercive side in their formative stages. They corralled heterogeneous populations, harnessed them in a common economy, and enforced a lingua franca—whether Castilian in Spain, Hindi in India, Mandarin in China, or Spanish in Peru. They resisted secession and imposed law. The earliest nation-states created and defended their own sovereignty. (Today many nation-states have had sovereignty handed to them.) But these countries also committed themselves to treating all of their citizens with the same due process. The United States and its fellow republics were nation-states, each with its glaring faults and hypocrisies, but not empires. For the most part, people wanted to be in them.

Finally, if we accept that military bases on foreign shores should be equated with imperialism, why do so many other countries welcome them? Why do international disasters, whether foreign invasions or domestic genocides, invariably seem to raise the question both at home and abroad, "Where are the Marines?" Observers of today's complex world are confronted by the undeniable and often distressing fact that the United States plays a relatively unique role as the nation with the greatest power to determine outcomes in international conflicts. The fact that it is the "go-to" nation in times of trouble certainly raises legitimate questions about why it is necessary, and if it is advisable, for any one nation to play such a large role. But it does not automatically prove empire, for the simple reason that numerous foreign nations, notoriously jealous of their sovereignty, have actively encouraged the United States to act as guarantor.

Belgium, Britain, France, Luxembourg, and the Netherlands were first to do so. In 1948, they initiated NATO, the North Atlantic Treaty Organization. Its purpose, as the first NATO secretary-general famously quipped, was "to keep the Russians out, the Americans in, and the Germans down." In 2007, the greatest concentration of American bases abroad was still in Europe.[27] If its allies did not trust the United States, it seems logical that they would cancel the treaties that authorize foreign encampments. They would expel the occupier.

Indeed allied nations have sometimes cancelled U.S. base agreements. But they have done so with an ease inconceivable in any empire. In 1967, France asked the U.S. to evacuate eleven air bases, which America did while maintaining perfectly amicable relations with its historic (indeed, original) ally. In 1992, the Philippines asked the United States to close its naval base at Subic Bay, which it did, and in 2003, Saudi Arabia requested the removal of all protective troops stationed on its national territory. In 2009, both Japan and Kyrgyzstan made noises about withdrawing base privileges, though they stopped short of making formal requests. Local populations have sometimes wished their leaders would expel the foreigners, especially when individual soldiers have committed heinous crimes or acted the part of "ugly Americans." Yet such requests have been exceptional. If body language is any indication at all, host governments have been remarkably sanguine about the military harmlessness of the United States, despite the size of its guns. They have treated the United States as a guest they could ask to leave.[28]

In place of these theories of empire, this book introduces an alternative hypothesis: that the United States acted not as an empire in modern foreign relations, but as a kind of *umpire,* to compel acquiescence as necessary with rules that had earned broad legitimacy. After each such intervention, as in the Suez Canal Crisis of 1956, the United States retreated to its position as a single nation-state, with no on-going administrative power outside its territory.

"Umpire" is an imperfect metaphor, but it fits reality more closely than "empire." It reasonably approximates the ways in which the United States periodically brought action to a halt, exacted a penalty, and then tried to get out of the way to allow competition to resume. What made the American role controversial was that it was also a player, and therefore never completely above the game.

Yet the growing international trend toward arbitration of disputes meant that if the United States did not already exist, it would have had to be invented. In fact, it was. The nation's founders were first to use the term "umpire." In the words of Alexander Hamilton (repeated by John Jay, Thomas Jefferson, and James Madison), the proposed federal government would act as an "umpire or common judge to interpose between the contending parties" in cases of commercial or territorial conflicts between the states.[29]

Committed to a policy of arbitration over force in international affairs, the founders recognized that state governments would sometimes be unable to achieve compromise quickly enough to respond to urgent problems, as proved by the six chaotic years between the War of Independence and George Washington's first administration. The problems created by the Articles of Confederation foreshadowed the challenges we see today with respect to institutions like the United Nations. Ideally, the UN should act as an umpire, but too often it lacks the coherence and independent resources necessary to the task.

The Continental Congress had no powers of taxation or enforcement. The nation-states that comprised it were envious of one another's wealth and territory. Faced with threats from within and without, the authors of the Constitution made the federal government an arbiter. This may explain Americans' propensity to believe some ultimate authority is necessary in relations between states (foreign and domestic), and their willingness, after two world wars, to exercise that function on an ad hoc basis. This book explores the possibility that the United States gravitated toward the role of referee in the international arena partly because of its own historical experiences of *domestic* conflict. In the clinch, federal authority has been wheeled out to crush state nonconformity. (Enforcing desegregation in the 1960s is but one example). Yet the federal goal has been coordination of the states, not their subjugation.

Historically speaking, there may be a subtle parallel in international relations. After 1945, whenever the United States and its allies spotted a particularly egregious violation of the spirit or letter of the post–World War II order, the United States intervened to quash nonconformity. America was not atypical in its "Western" values (which originated on the cusp of Asia and Europe) but in its willingness to enforce new global norms.

This role created significant economic benefits for American citizens and corporations, though prosperity was shared by many other nations as well. It brought security benefits, too. As Canadian minister of defense Peter MacKay noted in 2012, the first time that NATO ever came to the military aid of a member nation was on behalf of the United States after 9/11.[30] But the umpire role also carried substantial costs in blood, treasure, and identity that generally were not shared by others that benefited significantly under the new global order. Umpires sometimes make wrong calls. On a baseball diamond, the consequences are trivial; in foreign policy they can be tragic. Umpiring has been a pricey responsibility.

How the United States might cease playing umpire is not obvious. The trends toward access, arbitration, and transparency have not yielded an idyllic world. Violent, divisive conflicts remain. Holding the proverbial tiger by the tail, the U.S. government has been loath to let go. Perhaps by examining how the American role developed, this book will encourage other trustworthy nations to do more policing and the United States to do less—as occurred during the Libyan crisis of 2011, when France and Britain took the lead.[31]

Scholars sometimes soften the classic definition of imperialism by calling the United States an "empire by invitation" or a "hegemon"—hegemony being a situation in which the top nation is so powerful that "no other power, or combination of powers, can prevail against it."[32] But neither label accurately accounts for the subtle dynamics of the past century. When a nation as new, remote, and weak as Kyrgyzstan can order a country as powerful and pushy as the United States to withdraw a strategic air base, as it threatened to do in 2009, we must recognize that the world order of today is as different from past systems as the Neolithic was from the Paleolithic. Farming replaced foraging just as decisively as nations replaced empires—even though past and present remained connected by threads of continuity.[33]

This is not a purely academic matter. Inexact historical arguments can have dire, real-world consequences. The global critique of imperialism is long-standing, but it has taken a wicked twist in recent decades. In 1979, for example, the chief Iranian interrogator of imprisoned American hostages had studied at the University of California, Berkeley, where he encountered the fiery hometown rhetoric that denounced the U.S. government as "tyrannical," "racist," and "imperialist."[34] He and a generation of religious extremists conveniently appended these well-meaning self-criticisms to their own grievances—some with a solid historical foundation, such as U.S. involvement in the 1953 Iranian coup d'état.

Since the time of the 1979 hostage crisis, doctors, soldiers, diplomats, tourists, businessmen, and journalists have been kidnapped, disappeared, tortured, shot, and even decapitated, partly because their irate captors believed all Americans to be part of a malignant imperialist plot. Heads have literally rolled. The ivory tower overlooks the street, and American academics have a sober responsibility to make sure that incriminations of their country and fellow citizens are made only to the extent warranted.

Most of the scholarship on the United States is produced in the United States. People around the world take seriously what we say about ourselves. Scholar Philip Zelikow, executive director of the 9/11 Commission, observes that the empire "metaphor is tempting, but vicious."[35] Indeed, the events of 9/11 teach that words must be as precise as possible, for they can become like slippery knives. An umpire accused of being an empire may bleed out, to everyone's detriment.

The United States is no paragon of virtue and has almost invariably fallen short of its rhetoric and aspirations. American citizens are sometimes embarrassingly boastful and ambitious, calling their country "the greatest nation in the world," as if all others do not have the same pride or cannot overhear. Like other great powers, Washington has sometimes acted like a bully as well. The U.S. government can be callous, foolish, and self-serving in the extreme—all of which should be unsurprising given human nature. This does not make it an empire, nor does it mean that America's highest ideals are hollow illusions. It is naive to assume that ideals are incompletely realized because people do not genuinely believe in them. Ideals are like laws: behavioral codes that are violated constantly but still important, influential, and indicative. Without them, we have no compass.

Much has changed since the end of empires. The practices of access, arbitration, and transparency have taken hold around the globe. They can be uprooted, of course, but for now they broadly define the imperfect, evolving, disorderly new world order. It is to the birth of this system that we now turn.

I

To Compel Acquiescence

Or, How Federalism Replaced Empire with
Umpire, 1648–1789

In a peculiar way, Americans' first foreign alliances—and thus their first foreign relations—were with one another. After the colonies collectively declared independence, each wrote and adopted a separate constitution. They knew they would have to stick together to resist Britain's fearsome opposition, so they also passed the Articles of Confederation. This document created a permanent body to replace the emergency assemblies that had been called in 1774 and 1775 as the First and Second Continental Congresses. The resulting federation could make recommendations to the sovereign states but had no power over them or their citizens. It could not impose one penny in taxes, or regulate one item of commerce. It had no executive or judiciary. Any change to its charter required the unanimous approval of the member states. They were more like thirteen countries than one.[1]

It took seven bloody years for the thirteen states to achieve their independence. But once the revolutionaries climbed that peak they saw another range of obstacles stretching out before them. Within a few short years, the states combined forces even more firmly and placed what they called a "general government" over their heads. To achieve this they wrestled with age-old tensions between nation and empire: how to maintain state autonomy while reaping the advantages of belonging to a larger confederacy.

In 1789, they cobbled together the valuable traits they saw in both nations and empires, creating a hybrid. They fashioned a republic of republics. At the top was an elected government that could act, when necessary, as an "umpire" between political contestants and "compel acquiescence"—to use their terms. It was not an empire for the reason that participant states joined voluntarily and ruled collaboratively. They were not victors or victims of conquest. This atypical, often awkward arrangement gave Americans experience with the notion that one might have dual citizenship in both the state and nation, and that one government could yield to a more powerful one above it without losing dignity. The prerogatives that the federal government ultimately assumed—to reach across state borders to punish or protect individuals, and even to overrule the laws of states themselves—were the subject of ongoing controversy. They evolved gradually. Some of the founders did not get as powerful a central government as they initially wished for (and later regretted, in the case of James Madison). But passage of the Constitution propelled the federal government down the road toward "umpire."

Europe then had nothing comparable. No higher authority could discipline the governments of, say, England or France, or arrest its citizens for a crime. Indeed, for more than a century, since 1648, Europeans had emphatically rejected any authority superior to the nation-state. Consequently, Americans developed a different feel for sovereignty from that of their cousins across the Atlantic. They became willing to grant at least some powers to an overarching government. Interventionism across state borders, in extremis, became acceptable. Each generation became more accustomed to the arrangement. By the end of the first century, they even spoke of themselves differently: as *the* United States, not *these* United States.

The American constitutional experiment was a fork in the road. In the far future, this path led to the United Nations and the European Union. But to a greater extent than the nations that joined these later bodies, perhaps because of their longer historical experience with dual sovereignty, Americans came to accept the exercise of a higher power as sometimes "necessary and proper." They recognized the importance of an umpire, first for themselves in their domestic arrangements, and then in their international relationships.

Although it is natural to fix U.S. history on a grid marked by milestones like the founding of Jamestown or the Revolution, this can be like walking into the middle of a conversation. As historian Daniel Rodgers observes: "Every serious reader of the past instinctively knows . . . that nations lie enmeshed in each others' history. Even the most isolated of nation-states is a semipermeable container, washed over by forces originating far beyond its shores."[2] The new world system in which the United States arose, and where it was initially an anomaly, began with the Reformation. This religious cataclysm fundamentally redefined the relationship among the existing European nations, making them absolutely autonomous from one another. It led them to reject any kind of outside supervision. To understand how this happened, and its significance for the American story, we must step back at least briefly into the dim and distant past.

Hunched over his desk in the dusty Roman province of Palestine, the old man worried that he was inadequate to the task of eulogizing the dead. He felt voiceless, knowing they could not hear his words. His pen seemed "rusty" and even his writing tablet wore "a sad look." Heathens and brigands had brought down the vibrant empire in whose marble libraries he had come of age. "For twenty years and more," Saint Jerome wrote his friend Heliodorus in 396 CE, "Roman blood has been spilt every day between Constantinople and the Julian Alps." All that his generation knew had "been laid waste, pillaged, and plundered." Commoners and aristocrats alike had been tormented, mocked, raped, enslaved, and slain. "Grief and lamentation are everywhere, and the image of death in its many forms."[3]

Jerome's cry from the heart was the first of many recorded during the nine centuries of Europe's Dark Ages, when invaders and thieves made people quake in their homes and fear venturing beyond locked town gates. After Rome's ruin, violence and pestilence stalked the land. Innocents were not safe even on distant shores, protected by the wide moat of the fierce Atlantic, or barricaded in castles on high hills. When one wave of invaders receded, another took its place. In 787, the seaborne Vikings made their first raids on England, blazing a path of destruction that took them from Scandinavia to Jerusalem, slaying defenders where they stood, looting homes, ravaging women, burning churches, and trampling holy men "like dung in the street."[4] Beginning in 1237, the Mongols swept on thundering hooves across Russia, then Hungary, then Bulgaria—while simultaneously pillaging imperial China at the other end of Asia. Then came the conquering Ottoman Turks. In 1453 they captured Constantinople, the capitol of ancient Christianity. Twice they chased Europeans to the gates of Vienna.

In these bleak centuries, the idea of empire elicited longing rather than scorn. Europeans looked back on Rome as the ideal society. Then, stern legionnaires had curbed wanton killing. The roads, bridges, walls, and aqueducts of antiquity stood firm, rather than in tumbled ruins. When the Vandals reduced the Western classical heritage to rubble, they headed a roster of

names that connoted chaos. At the start of the modern era, around the time
Christopher Columbus sailed into the West Indies, Europeans remembered
the Pax Romana as a time of human unity, when empire had been "the guarantor of glory and of safety."[5]

Religious faith reinforced this nostalgia. In the ancient world, *orbis chris-
tianus* and *orbis romanus* were intertwined.[6] The empire of men and the empire of God appeared to mesh seamlessly. The identity of Christ and the
temporal emperor blurred: both were the King of Kings, one in heaven, the
other on earth. Once the Roman state ceased to operate, the Latin pope assumed the mantle of kingmaker. In 800 CE, he recognized the Frankish
ruler Charlemagne as emperor of the Holy Roman Empire. Charlemagne
began the reign that eventually passed to Otto the Great and encompassed
much of central Europe. Until the Reformation, Latin Christianity was Europe's official religion, with the pope claiming ultimate authority (often in-
effectively) on any number or matters, from the marriage of royals to the
division of the continents discovered by Columbus. But a general *pax* remained elusive. The pope's ability to quell internal strife or halt external attack was extremely limited. The more powerful monarchs of Europe also
resisted his authority, and some discordant voices (like that of poet Dante
Alighieri) questioned whether secular and religious authority might be better separated.[7]

Then came the Reformation begun by Martin Luther in 1517, which broke
Europe into pieces and gave birth to the nation-state. It dispelled forever the
aspiration to unite all Christendom under a single, benevolent emperor.[8] It
took more than a century for the full catastrophe to become apparent, co-
inciding with the first European settlements in the Western Hemisphere.
Between 1517 and 1648, civil and international conflict roiled the Old World.
Protestants vied bitterly with Catholics for the eternal souls and earthly
treasure claimed by the church. The rupture of the Christian empire under
papal supervision produced the Schmalkaldic War, the Eighty Years' War,
the Spanish Armada, the English Civil War, the French Civil War, the Thirty
Years' War, and numerous other bloody battles, large and small. Roman over-
sight became associated with oppression by foreigners, rather than protection
and salvation. Europeans finally rejected empire emphatically, turning their
backs on the past.

Henry VIII of England, the hotheaded, heir-obsessed Tudor king, was
among the first to declare his nation unbeholden to the pope or any other

temporal authority. He appropriated the word "empire," previously used to describe a system of linguistically dissimilar, noncontiguous peoples under an outside authority, and claimed it instead for his own nation as a coherent and autonomous assemblage. In Henry's usage, the word meant country. And so his 1533 declaration of independence (the Act of Restraint in Appeals) read: "This realm of England is an empire . . . without restraint or provocation to any foreign prices or potentates of the world." Here, stood on its head, "empire" meant that England ruled itself. As late as 1860, Englishmen equated "empire" with the United Kingdom alone and not its overseas possessions.[9]

Although the king's famous difficulties with siring a male heir prompted his break with Rome's papal authority, Henry Tudor's 1533 pronouncement touched a deep chord in the island population's sense of itself as distinct from continental Europeans. Parliament passed the Act of Restraint handily. The following year, the Act of Supremacy declared Henry "the only supreme head in earth of the Church of England," and claimed for him all the privileges pertaining to "the imperial crown." (One of which, conveniently, was the power to divorce aging Catharine of Aragon and wed comely Anne Boleyn.)

Internecine warfare and ruthless royal intrigue plagued Great Britain for most of the following two centuries, but the claim stuck. The king became head of the church, and the island of Great Britain became an "empire" unto itself, eventually uniting all the kingdoms within—some of them forcibly. Citizens had no further appeal on legal matters to any higher authority outside the country—namely, the pope. The realms of England, Wales, Scotland, and Ireland gradually came under a single central government as the United Kingdom. Despite internal diversity and outbreaks of rebellion, they were one state.

In Europe itself, wracked by religious schism, the first plank for peace was laid in Augsburg, the ancient Bavarian town built by Roman troops at the woodsy confluence of the Lech and Wertach Rivers. There in 1555, after more than a thousand years of Latin orthodoxy, Holy Roman Emperor Charles V granted the principle *cuius regio, eius religio* ("whose region, his religion") to the Lutheran princes of Germany. Roughly translated, this meant the faith of the ruler would prevail within his territory. It was a stunning concession to political and religious freedom for European monarchs, after centuries of papal supervision. Of course, the common people themselves had no such freedom, being required to follow the faith of their local rulers.[10]

But the temptation to squelch heresy in a neighbor's backyard proved too strong for some to resist. King Philip II of Spain, heir of Charles V, brushed aside his father's dictum of *cuius regio, eius religio*. Less battle-weary than Charles, Philip II was determined not to lose western Europe to Protestantism. As he wrote his ambassador to Rome, "You may assure His Holiness, that rather than suffer the least damage to religion and the service of God, I would lose all my states and an hundred lives, if I had them; for I do not propose nor desire to be the ruler of heretics."[11]

In 1588 Phillip launched the Spanish Armada against England in an effort to tow it back into the Catholic fold. Elizabeth I successfully repelled his attack—aided by a providential storm that drove Philip's fleet onto the rocks, saved Britain, and made the Virgin Queen into England's greatest monarch. The Spanish king simultaneously warred against his Protestant subjects in the Netherlands to make them conform, touching off a conflict there that burned for eighty years and resulted in Dutch independence. Predating a very similar American declaration by two centuries, the Dutch proclaimed in 1581 that when a monarch "oppresses" the people, infringes upon "their ancient customs and privileges," and treats them tyrannically, they "may not only disallow his authority, but legally proceed to the choice of another prince for their defense."[12] King Philip exhibited little awareness of the full consequences of his actions, but his battles against the English and Dutch eventually exhausted the colossal fortune in silver and gold that Spain had wrested from the Aztecs and Incas only decades earlier.

Elsewhere, domestic tyrants implemented *cuius regio, eius religio* with a vengeance that made local self-determination hardly kinder than foreign imposition. In Trier, the oldest of all German cities, the local Catholic archbishop expelled the Protestants, then the Jews, and eventually torched 368 people as witches.[13] And he was not the most merciless figure in the campaigns of religious cleansing designed to re-Catholicize dissidents, or to make Catholics into good Protestants. In the Republic of Ireland, Puritan Oliver Cromwell is reviled to this day as a genocidal maniac for the massacre of those stubborn Catholic Celts he called "barbarous wretches."

The most infamous of all internecine feuds during the Reformation was the Thirty Years' War. At least one-quarter of central Europe's population died between 1618 and 1648, many killed with the new gunpowder weapons that enabled professional armies to fight more efficiently. In German-speaking areas, warfare destroyed a third of all homes. Peasants in the region suffered from robbery, murder, and starvation with horrifying regularity. Some were slaughtered where they stood, while others disappeared into the forests. Brutal punishments were used to torture captives, including the "Swedish drink"—pouring excrement down the victim's throat.[14] Famine and bubonic plague, let loose by the dislocations of war, took perhaps the greatest toll. Six to seven million German civilians perished. It took more than a century for European populations to recover and begin growing again.[15]

When peace came, it brought the first inklings of the new world order—and set the stage for American history. The Reformation's warring parties finally sat down to history's inaugural European peace congress in 1643, about the same time that the Dutch started constructing Manhattan's first stone church. The participants in the peace congress were so deeply divided and suspicious of one another that they refused to occupy the same buildings. Delegates from the leading Protestant nations met in the Westphalian town of Osnabrück, while Catholic representatives convened in Münster, thirty miles away. The 150 official delegations that attended these awkward proceedings took five years to arrive at a compromise. But they created the mold for international, secular negotiations among interested parties that wished to solve problems of war and peace—and initiated the trend toward arbitration.[16] In 1648 they officially abandoned the hope of a single Christian empire and confirmed the legitimacy of multitudinous, independent states wherein the sovereign alone chose the national religion. No pope, umpire, or empire would exercise decisive power over them.

Indeed, freedom of religion became the litmus test of sovereignty itself. States could be considered truly independent and equal, free from any international control, only if their rulers had the uncontested right to decide such basic matters as the faith of the realm. The Thirty Years' War had been unprecedented for violence. The Peace of Westphalia, as the separate agreements signed at Osnabrück and Münster came to be called, enshrined an equally unprecedented international order.[17]

Although some European nations did not participate in the meetings, the premises of the peace gradually assumed the air of sacrosanct legitimacy, like that once equated with the idea of a transnational Christian imperium. Whereas many Europeans previously associated security with the inclusive embrace of a strong empire or universal church, after the Reformation's bloodbath, security became identified with impermeable, unbridgeable, hermetically sealed national borders. (Of course, no border ever was, or can be, hermetically sealed in practice, but the Peace of Westphalia made them so in principle.) The scorching pain of conflict over religion was burned into Europeans' collective memory, making them instinctively reluctant afterward to intervene in one another's domestic decisions. It was a sane compromise between saving a brother's soul and minding one's own business.

In the following century, philosophers tried to make sense of these changes. With the medieval church's political authority at an end, they articulated a substitute: the secular "law of nations." It was a Swiss lawyer, Emer de Vattel, who came up with the clearest and most influential formulation (as Alexander Hamilton later pointed out to George Washington).[18] In 1758, Vattel literally wrote the book, *The Law of Nations,* which spelled out the implications of the Peace of Westphalia. Jurists, politicians, revolutionaries, and heads of government looked to Vattel as the most competent authority on the subject.

According to Vattel, the Westphalian system had three key tenets: first, states had a fundamental right of self-determination; second, all states were legally equal; and third, no state could interfere in the internal affairs of another, because to do so would violate territorial integrity. *Within* societies, Vattel said, there must be "an authority capable of commanding all the members . . . and of compelling those who should refuse to obey." But *between* nations, such an idea was tyranny. Every sovereign state, to be a state, must "possess an absolute independence."[19]

Yet how was the law of nations itself to be enforced, if the law eliminated the papal enforcer? For enforcement, European governments embraced what they called the "balance of power." This was an informal system of shifting alliances that kept any state from becoming so strong that it could impose its suzerainty and religion on others. Any nation that tried to dominate would face opposition from a temporary coalition of otherwise independent states. None—at least in theory, and if the balance held—could become an empire. An especially critical consideration at the time was the relative strength of the Protestant and Catholic coalitions. As a Dutch merchant observed, his nation supported "England as the bulwark of the Protestant Religion and the most important Weight in the Ballance of Power in Europe against France."[20]

England was not an empire or hegemon over the other Protestant countries, but emerged as the leader of a bloc.

There was an unspoken caveat in all of this. No state could be said to exist a priori. If a nation could not or did not defend itself, it might well be incorporated into the realm of another. Lands left lying unattended were subject to the dictum of "finders, keepers." Sovereignty was earned, never given. It belonged only to nations with sufficient brute force to command their own population and defend their turf from outsiders. If the rulers of a given territory lacked competence, they and their people would suffer conquest and not a single neighbor would weep. Nature abhors a vacuum.

Poland met this fate. From 1652 to 1791, jealous nobles used the *liberum veto* to curb the power of the central government. This procedural statute of the Polish legislature, or Sejm, allowed a single member to dissolve the assembly at will and nullify all acts passed during a session. A requirement of unanimity rather than majority rule made consensual government a farce. Absolutism looked good in comparison. As a result, surrounding powers divvied up Poland a piece at a time until it disappeared from the map in 1795. (It reappeared 125 years later by international fiat, when norms changed yet again and sovereignty, rather surprisingly, became an entitlement.)

This ironclad but unspoken understanding of the law of nations also applied to states, tribes, and clans outside the Continent. European nations acted as if such nations did not exist unless they could defend militarily whatever claims they cared to make.[21] Thus, Japan earned tacit acceptance as a full-fledged member of the Westphalian system of states only by defeating China in 1895 and trouncing Russia in 1905. Of course, the Europeans' assumptions were not unique, but rather the expression of human experience across the millennia. Those who could not defend themselves were subject to colonization or expulsion, as the Roman emperor Hadrian infamously showed the Jews in 135 CE. It had always been so, on every continent. No one proposed anything different, since that would be to suggest the impossible or absurd.

Still, the Peace of Westphalia established new rules of play for the countries of Europe, eliminating interference in one another's domestic affairs as a potential source of conflict. After a traumatic century of fratricide, Europeans accepted the hands-off pledge that ended the wars of the Reformation. The shock of total war had given them a gut regard for the principle of absolute autonomy in domestic affairs.

The peace agreement did not necessarily imply how nations would organize themselves internally. In fact, by upholding *cuius regio, eius religio,* the peace of 1648 might easily be taken for a vindication of absolutism. Louis XIV of France, the self-described Sun King, was then a mere boy of ten. But the famous boast attributed to him, "I am the state!" fit the ethos of the age in which a single man might determine his entire nation's religious allegiance. In Britain, however, the Reformation opened a new age that gave more power to the people than ever before. This, too, helped define America's revolutionary generation and the choices it confronted and made.

In England, internal wars over religion led to a fast and furious game of dynastic ping-pong between Catholic and Protestant claimants to the crown. From the reign of reformist Henry VIII (1509–1547) to the reign of Catholic James II (1685–1688), England witnessed a parade of monarchs with competing visions of the domestic religious character of the United Kingdom. When Parliament disappointed, the king dissolved it. Charles I, who many believed was too tolerant of Catholics, ruled for eleven years without calling a single session of the legislature. He was eventually beheaded for his refusal to accept curbs on monarchical power.

Indeed, rejection of Catholicism gradually became twinned with a rejection of absolutism in Britain, though not of monarchy per se. The last Catholic king of England, James II, fled the island in 1688, replaced by his Protestant daughter Mary and her husband, "Dutch William," the Prince of Orange. William and Mary were made king and queen in exchange for agreeing to a Bill of Rights. With this bill, Parliament forever barred Roman Catholics from the throne of England, abolished the crown's right to suspend the legislature or its laws, limited the uses of the army in peacetime, required free elections and free speech in Parliament, and prohibited the monarch from levying taxes without legislative approval.[22]

The philosopher John Locke, exiled and hunted for treason under James II, justified these changes by citing what he called the "natural right" of the reasoning individual, namely, the right to life, liberty, and property. Locke denied that kings had any divine mandate. Instead, he described government as a civil contract in which ruled obeyed ruler in exchange for security and freedom. If the sovereign reneged on those entitlements, he (or she) violated the contract. The people then had a right and duty to bring the monarch down, forcibly if necessary. They "might as often and as innocently change their Governours as they do their Physicians."[23]

Locke's statements echoed the Dutch declaration of independence from Spain and anticipated the words of Thomas Jefferson. But as Barbara Tuchman observes, "This is not to suggest that Jefferson [or Locke] plagiarized America's most important document, but rather that men's instinct for liberty, and belief in the people's right to depose a ruler who has governed unjustly, travels in deep common channels."[24] Another way of putting this is that Locke and Jefferson were part of a slowly emerging consensus about human rights, stimulated by the Reformation, that would eventually become global. Locke penned and refined *Two Treatises of Government* during the turbulent years in which James II was enthroned and deposed, William and Mary were installed, and Parliament approved the Bill of Rights. Although Locke wrote in the language of eternal, philosophical truths, his essay was a defense of contemporary events.

The wars of religion nurtured new ideas about the fundamental nature of both states and empires. Fearful of Catholic monarchs who might impose their religious beliefs on the populace, the Protestant majority in Britain turned *cuius regio, eius religio* around. The people would decide the religion of their ruler, who would never again be Catholic. The nation belonged to the people. Of course, these political changes had implications far beyond religion, but that is where the matter started. Encapsulated today in the phrase "popular sovereignty" (as opposed to divine right), these new beliefs slowly but unmistakably seeped into the European aquifer.

Although the English Civil War enhanced the power of the legislature, Britain retained a hereditary monarch. Parliamentary elections typically featured only a single candidate. Those empowered to vote were a tiny elite, probably well under 5 percent of the population.[25] Yet because more absolute forms of monarchy remained the rule around the globe, the British model appeared remarkably liberal in contrast. Persons claiming royal blood, or what the Chinese called the mandate of heaven, managed governments from Japan to Peru, as they had since time immemorial.

The Reformation had lasting consequences for North America: it prompted the settlement of New England and set the stage for the colonies' later rebellion. The religious wars pushed thousands of dissenters out of Britain after

1620 and across the sea in search of safe haven. Separatists, Puritans, Baptists, Quakers, and Jews emigrated to what seemed a howling wilderness in order to attain religious self-determination and take a stand on the rights of Parliament. This experience became so central to their national identity that many Americans still imagine that the Pilgrims arrived in Plymouth before African slaves arrived in Jamestown—even though slaves arrived a year earlier. The dissenters also brought with them an instinctive grasp of the Westphalian principle: no state was inferior to another, and no outside power had the right to impose its religion. Nations had to guard their autonomy or risk losing precious liberties.

For all these reasons, English migrants who arrived in the northeastern colonies were strongly conscious of striking out into the perilous unknown on behalf of causes greater than themselves. This consciousness made them a peculiar subset of the Anglo-European population: concentrated in their moral fervor and personal intrepidity. The starvation and disease that killed half of those who sailed on the *Mayflower* became part of their lore of risk taking and survival against the odds.[26] This lore included the dangers of misunderstandings with Indians, the perilous "seasoning" that killed 80 percent of all immigrants to Jamestown before 1625, and the utter disappearance of every person in the Roanoke Colony—including the aptly named Virginia Dare, the first daughter born to English parents who had dared the wilds. For good or ill, their efforts would be an example to others.

The words of Massachusetts's first governor—"We shall be as a City upon a Hill, the eyes of all people are upon us"—are commonly interpreted as an example of incipient American arrogance.[27] But John Winthrop intended just the opposite: to encourage humility. He was reminding his followers in 1630 that failure was a distinct possibility, and would be very public indeed. "We shall be made a story and a by-word throughout the world. . . . We shall shame the faces of many of God's worthy servants."[28]

Yet the early settlers thrived after the first ghastly winters, and they passed on to the next generation a sense of grievance against the political systems that had forced them out. Those migrants who broke with England when Charles I dissolved Parliament in 1630 left at the height of the Thirty Years' War (to which Britain sent a smattering of troops), and avoided altogether the English Civil War that followed. The Glorious Revolution of 1688 eventually resolved many of the questions that had pushed them overseas. Thus, the gains in parliamentary power after 1688 were especially near and dear to the hearts of colonists. For the next few generations they took immense pride in being Englishmen of a "New England," literally and figuratively, and having been among the first to defy monarchical absolutism in their own way.

Imagine, therefore, their distress during the Stamp Act Crisis in the 1760s, when it first became apparent that Parliament did not consider colonists entitled "to all the inherent rights and liberties of his [Majesty's] natural born subjects within the kingdom of Great Britain."[29] The leagues of blue Atlantic separating the Thames and the Chesapeake apparently validated the imposition of precisely those abuses that the Glorious Revolution had obliterated back home: standing armies to repress the people in peacetime, taxation without representation, interference with the judiciary, dismissal of public assemblies.

The colonists found that petitions to King George III were worse than useless. His responses merely confirmed that the sovereign who stood between them and Parliament was naught but a "sullen-tempered Pharaoh of England" who held colonists in contempt. Americans initially revolted to uphold the English constitution rather than defy it.[30] They did not see themselves as inventing a new ideology but as defending what the Glorious Revolution had supposedly wrought for all Englishmen. When it became clear that the king differed in his interpretation of their legal rights, the thirteen colonies of the North American coastline gradually came to see their interests as different from the British government's and more similar to one another's. In 1776, they declared, "These United Colonies are, and of Right ought to be Free and Independent states." The most unusual step they took was to dispense altogether with monarchy and proclaim themselves republics.

Of course, because of the Peace of Westphalia, there was no supranational authority to rule on the legitimacy of their new status. Here was another consequence of the Reformation. The revolutionaries had asserted a God-given natural right, but there was no burning bush (or pope) to intone yea or nay. English critics called the notion of "self-evident" truths—such as the right of rebellion—an "absurdity, in which the thing to be proved is all along taken for granted."[31] Acknowledgment by foreign nations, at first individually and then collectively, was the disgruntled colonists' only hope. To achieve recognition of their independence, they bound themselves to one another in a "firm league of friendship," much as the Republic of the Seven United Netherlands had done a century earlier in order to expel the Spanish.[32]

Indeed, the Articles of Confederation and Perpetual Union preserved the essential autonomy of each former colony. They created a union that was, in David Hendrickson's words, "a species of international cooperation."[33] The revolutionaries did not assume, as we so casually do today, that an American state was akin to a province, inferior to the nation. Instead, they equated their own governments with those of post-Westphalian Europe, each separate, distinct, and strictly autonomous in internal matters. When Thomas Jefferson penned *Notes on the State of Virginia* for friends in Europe in 1781, for example, his mentions of "my country" typically referenced Virginia proper.[34] Significantly, the revolutionaries called their gathering a congress, not a parliament, since a parliament was a domestic body. "Congress" was then purely a diplomatic term to describe an assembly of nations, such as the convocation at Westphalia.[35] And so, at the outset, Americans blended mechanisms of foreign relations with domestic governance.

Thus it was natural that when the thirteen colonies combined forces to repel Great Britain, the second article of their founding document resolved that: "Each state retains its sovereignty, freedom, and independence, and every power, jurisdiction, and right, which is not by this Confederation expressly delegated to the United States, in Congress assembled." Regardless of size or population, each had one vote on matters pertaining to the business or cooperative defense of the whole.[36] They granted one another's citizens "free ingress and regress to and from any other State" and "all the privileges of trade and commerce" therein. They further prohibited two or more states from signing separate treaties between them without the consent of the others. Although they formed an army under a unified command, each state had the responsibility of funding its own militia and retained the right to defend itself by land or sea if invaded. In other words, they granted one another mutual courtesies without giving up internal sovereignty. Fundamentally, they established a commercial union and a mutual security guarantee, committing themselves "to assist each other" against all outside attacks "on account of religion, sovereignty, trade," or anything else.

In their separate domestic affairs and as a league, the former colonies pledged themselves to republicanism, meaning government without hereditary rulers. As they looked around them, they believed republicanism was the best of bad choices, though it had a terrible historical reputation for corruptibility and early mortality. Nonetheless, they preferred representative government to monarchy, which they had experienced as tyrannical, and to "pure democracy," which they and their European contemporaries thought a spectacle of "turbulence and contention . . . incompatible with personal security or the rights of property."[37]

Unfortunately, there were no really good role models. Only the Dutch appeared to have a viable republic, the United Provinces of the Netherlands, barely a hundred years old. Leading citizens of seven semi-independent provinces met in town councils (the common people could not vote), and each province had one vote in the States-General, the national assembly. The provincial government also elected the stadtholder, a nobleman who coordinated national defense, ran the meetings of the States-General, and intervened as necessary to settle disputes. But the Dutch Republic was essentially aristocratic and suffered from the same dysfunctional structure that stymied Poland under the *liberum veto*. All motions in the States-General had to be unanimous. This made their coalition less cohesive than was optimal, increasing its vulnerability to domestic turbulence and external aggression. As James Madison observed, jealousies among the sovereign provinces exposed them to "the most fatal inconveniences."[38] The Dutch Republic was also quite elitist in temperament, with the wealthy there holding power even more closely than those in Great Britain, which had open debates and hundreds of elected members in the House of Commons. Despite the Netherlands' mercantile wealth, beggars were forced to toil in workhouses and the poor rarely ate meat. The Dutch Republic bore a certain similarity to the Venetian Republic, also ruled by a closed coterie of noble families and presided over by an elected magistrate, the doge. Republican government at the state level—but with no stadtholder or doge—seemed to best fit American circumstances.

The United States of America thus took halting steps toward forms of government that combined the best elements of what they could see in others. They were halting because the revolutionaries found it far easier to declare their separate independences than to fashion a workable alliance with one another. In fact, it took *five full years* for the states to ratify the Articles of Confederation. The war was nearly over before the last recalcitrant member signed. In a hard bargain over western real estate, Maryland held out long past the epic winter at Valley Forge—and the frightening occupations of New York, Philadelphia, and Savannah—in order to persuade Virginia to sweeten the alliance by ceding some land. Not even the horror of war and the threat of hanging for treason could clinch the deal. Unanimity was hard won. After that, it took an additional three years for the ad hoc league to achieve its collective independence, made good by the so-called Paris Peace Treaty of 1783 between England and the United States.

Once independence was achieved, the challenges of acting cooperatively became even greater. The states soon found that the provisions governing their relations were too loose for effective coordination. Like European countries, their economic and political interests frequently clashed. They were thirteen different republics, each with its own constitution, administration, and militia. Any and all decisions concerning their common affairs, from the mundane to the extraordinary, had to pass through a fractious, unicameral Congress that in theory could adjourn at any time, for up to six months each year. Every state had the power to recall its delegation at will, though none did.

Meanwhile, bilateral relations among the states were equally tortured. State governments relied on tariffs for revenue. Within a couple of years of independence, each was slapping taxes on goods that crossed state borders. Mercantile New York was a principal offender, as was Connecticut, which placed a 5 percent duty on numerous items "imported" from its neighbors. Massachusetts, New Jersey, Rhode Island, and Vermont reacted angrily to taxes against which they had little power of retaliation and that made their products more expensive and thus harder to sell. By 1785, most tariffs within the confederation were aimed not at external competitors like Great Britain, but at rival sister states.[39]

The problems were evident to no one more than George Washington, the retired military leader who had given the colonies their victory. He had planned to enjoy his remaining years at his pastoral overlook on the broad Potomac. The troops had sent him off with tears and huzzahs. He had said good-bye to governing anything but his own plantation. But the failings of the Confederacy—which proved unable to collect revenue, pay its foreign debt, or resolve tariff feuds—were apparent even from his rural retreat. Washington's generation had made a revolution, but not a government. "We are either a united people under one head, and for federal purposes; or we are thirteen independent sovereignties, eternally counteracting each other," Washington wrote in 1785 to James McHenry, a Scotch-Irish physician who had served in the general's small so-called family of adjutants during the war. How could the United States effectively defend or represent itself in the world, the general worried, when "we are one nation today, & thirteen tomorrow"?[40] The new country needed some kind of higher authority to settle the states' competing claims. It needed an umpire.

The defeated British gloated over the Confederation's incompetence. They treated U.S. minister John Adams with ill-disguised contempt. "An ambassador from America! Good heavens what a sound!" sneered one London newspaper. The London government refused to appoint an opposite number to America, eschewing normal diplomatic reciprocity. As one wag queried, should Whitehall send one minister to the Continental Congress, or thirteen? Meanwhile, brazen Redcoats continued to occupy seven of their old forts on U.S. land in the northwest. Four years had flown by since victory at Yorktown, and yet the British still had not withdrawn their troops from American soil. And who was going to make them leave? The Continental Congress did not have a functional army, most of its men having gone into retirement along with George Washington. When Minister John Adams asked the British government to evacuate American territory, the letter he mailed—just across London—went unanswered for three months, after which the request was simply denied.[41] If the United States could not defend its/their Westphalian sovereignty, it/they would not enjoy the perquisites. Was the United States a singular entity, or a plural one?

The Spanish Empire also bullied the United States with little fear for the consequences. In 1784 Spain closed the mouth of the Mississippi River to American ships. The United States had no recourse. What navy or army would enforce American claims to the right of passage on an international waterway? The cash-poor Congress had sold its last naval ship to a private buyer in 1785. The army had shrunk to 700 soldiers.[42] States that did not border the Mississippi were hardly eager to hazard their militias or spend their own limited funds to liberate the river for the benefit of other governments. New Yorker John Jay, asked by Congress to reason with Spain, found that the best deal he could wangle was the right to trade in Spanish colonial ports, if Americans promised to stay off the Mississippi. To those looking or heading west, Jay's willingness to even entertain such an insulting offer was treachery. Others were willing to grant Jay's good intentions but feared that such a compromise would lead westerners to secede from the union. And who, Thomas Jefferson asked rhetorically, would be willing to "cut the throats of their own brothers and sons" to make them stay?[43]

Yet it was already too late to prevent outbreaks of violence. Vigilantism struck Massachusetts in the summer of 1786 and lasted eight months before it was put down. Like many other states, Massachusetts struggled to pay its debts from the Revolution. Coupled with the former colonies' banishment from British markets, Revolutionary War debts had plunged the economy into a depression. Beginning in July 1786, in hundreds of town meetings, residents vented their anger at the Boston-dominated state government. They accused legislators of being even more corrupt than George III (the definition of corruption, of course, according to their anti-English prejudices). They scorned the constitution penned by the illustrious John Adams only a decade earlier, and pledged to suppress the "tyrannical government in the Massachu-setts State."[44] Angry citizens demanded abolition of the elite upper house, or senate, along with the common courts, which they believed had no legitimacy. Former officers of the Continental Army led the armed rebels. Calling themselves Regulators, throngs of up to a thousand men (bigger than the entire army of the United States) intimidated judges and blocked courthouse doors in Massachusetts towns like Concord, Northampton, Great Barrington, Worcester, and Pelham.

Mechanisms for stopping the revolt proved inadequate. The government had no means of defending itself from within. When Governor James Bowdoin called out the state militia, virtually no one showed. Out of 92,000 militiamen on the state rolls—obligated by law to assist their government—only 100 initially responded. The Continental Congress had little power to assist Massachusetts, though three months into the uprising it finally voted to add 1,340 soldiers to the nation's 700-man army. Since other states had almost nothing to gain from helping New England with its problems, Congress proposed getting half of the troops from Massachusetts itself. But Massachusetts needed outside assistance precisely because it was unable to recruit enough men. Baron von Steuben, the Prussian who had trained Washington's men during their freezing encampment at Valley Forge, revealed outsiders' confusion over the exact nature of the American coalition when he queried why Massachusetts needed "foreign" (meaning federal) support to bolster its government. Meanwhile, the rebellion spread, eventually targeting the federal stockpile of weapons at Springfield. Desperate, Governor Bowdoin finally employed a mercenary army of 4,400 men, financed by wealthy Bostonians. In February 1787, the governor's hirelings caught up with the Regulators, arresting Daniel Shays and thirteen other leaders for treason.[45]

The former revolutionaries held divergent opinions on Shays's Rebellion, as it came to be called. Thomas Jefferson, then living a comfortable life as

America's first postindependence representative to France, opined that "a little rebellion now and then is a good thing." He hoped from afar that state governments would be "mild in their punishment of rebellions, as not to discourage them too much."[46] But most leaders were deeply alarmed. Some, including former firebrand Samuel Adams, argued for swift executions to contain the growing chaos. The normally sedate George Washington was apoplectic. "I am really mortified beyond expression," he wrote David Humphreys, a Connecticut man and trusted former aide during the Revolution. Americans' conduct had confirmed "the predictions of our transatlantic foe," that the United States would be unable to rule itself effectively. To fellow Virginian Henry Lee, Jr., he confessed, "I am lost in amazement." The slow, inept response to either the real or imagined grievances of the rebels offered "melancholy proof of what our transatlantic foe have predicted; . . . that mankind left to themselves are unfit for their own government." To fellow general Henry Knox, Washington wrote during the troubles, "Good God! who besides a tory could have foreseen, or a Briton predicted them!"[47]

By the mid-1780s, the competence of the Continental Congress had ebbed to such a low-water mark that it was routinely mocked at home and abroad. Congress had trouble generating a quorum, a failure that Washington thought "disgraceful, in a very high degree," as he told Thomas Jefferson. Even ratification of the Treaty of Paris, liberating Americans from George III, had to be delayed until enough delegates showed up to hold a meeting. Lacking authority to impose direct taxes, Congress had to count on the goodwill of state legislatures for its meager budget. Yet the states were inconsistent in paying their obligations. Sometimes a state would withhold funds out of pique if another did something of which it didn't approve. New Jersey, for example, refused to pay its bill to Congress until New York cooperated in ratifying a new tax proposal.[48] In notes to himself on the "vices" of the Articles, James Madison observed that the United States suffered from the same funding problem that had afflicted every "similar confederacy" in world history. The states' failure to comply with federal requisitions, in both peace and war, was the natural result of their "independent authority."[49]

A sideshow now that the Revolution was over, Congress had to beg for extensions from foreign bankers, unable to repay the debts it (and the individual states) had incurred in fighting the British. Many citizens had little sympathy. The Revolution had reinforced their distrust of authority. An aversion toward all forms of central power took root, blooming into an

antiestablishment ethos that made effective leadership more and more prob-
lematic. Some Americans genuinely believed that, as one citizen said, "if
permanent Funds are given to Congress, the aristocratical Influence, which
predominates in more than a major part of the United States, will fully establish an arbitrary [monarchical] government."[50] Revolt had become a habit. In
the words of British philosopher Edmund Burke, Americans were quick to
scent tyranny on any "tainted breeze." George Washington warned that under
the circumstances, uprisings born of false suspicions would "like snow-balls,
gather strength as they roll, if there is no opposition in the way to divide &
crumble them."[51]

At the urging of his young neighbor James Madison, the former general
thus agreed to come out of retirement. In May 1787, Washington attended
the Philadelphia convention called in order to revise the defective Articles of
Confederation.

The proceedings were confidential, to minimize outside interference and
protect the delegates' freedom to speak candidly. But the demand for transparency was becoming engrained and assuming a life of its own. To those not
invited, confidentiality seemed a cloak for conspiracy. Meetings of the Continental Congress before, during, and after the Revolutionary War had also
occurred behind closed doors, yet their proceedings were published monthly,
while decision making was still in progress. The reticence in 1787 to air the
debates of the Philadelphia convention prior to revealing its finished product
now seemed unreasonable. Mercy Otis Warren, a well-known playwright
and close friend of John Adams, noted from a firsthand perspective that "it
was thought by some, who had been recently informed of the secret transactions of the convention at Philadelphia, that the greatest happiness of the
greatest number was not the principal object of their contemplations, when
they ordered their doors to be locked, their members inhibited from all com-
munication abroad, and when proposals were made that their journals should
be burnt, lest their consultations and debates should be viewed by the scruti-
nizing eye of a free people."[52]

Yet as controversial as the proceedings were, and as rickety as the Confederation had become, what is most remarkable is the degree of cooperation
that the revolutionaries were willing to consider. After the Peace of Westphalia, European governments rejected *any* limits on their internal freedom of
action, and they competed constantly for territory. In contrast, despite contentious discussions over how much sovereignty to cede, representatives to

the convention in 1787 drafted a constitution for a "general" or "federal" government. They entertained proposals for a type of "umpire" to guide compromise.

This was not an easy process. Rhode Island had refused to send a representative to the Constitutional Convention, so opposed was it to giving Congress any additional powers. Other states sent delegates who felt much the same. New York's representatives (with the singular exception of Alexander Hamilton) objected to any proposal that led to "the consolidation of the United States into one government"—revealing that in their eyes the United States was not a single country, but merely a coalition (a "they" rather than an "it").[53] Across the long, hot, humid Philadelphia summer, the delegates debated the future structure of a general government that not everyone agreed ought to exist.

Diminutive, bookish James Madison, often called the Father of the Constitution, was one of the participants most ambitious for its powers (at least until he became leader of the opposition during George Washington's first administration). Madison hoped that the new government would have a blanket veto: "A negative *in all cases whatsoever* on the legislative acts of the States, as heretofore exercised by the Kingly prerogative." Madison was not arguing for a king, but for what he explicitly called a "dispassionate umpire in disputes"—a higher government to which the states would send representatives and that would, in an ambiguous sense, rule over them. Here Madison was wrestling with the conflict between post-Westphalian autonomy and imperial-level coordination. America needed parts of Roman government and parts of Tudor government. The "individual independence of the States is utterly irreconcilable" with their functionality as "an aggregate sovereignty," he wrote George Washington at Mount Vernon, but neither did anyone want "consolidation of the whole into one simple republic." So, as he explained to both Washington and Edmund Randolph, "I have sought some middle ground."[54]

Other delegates at the Constitutional Convention in Philadelphia thought even this middle ground was too close to tyranny, and they voted seven states to three against Madison's proposal to create a veto. However, they did devise a Supreme Court, which left the door open for judicial review of state laws to ensure compliance with the national constitution.[55] In essence, the court would exercise a veto over state laws when necessary. In the end, after a seventeen-week marathon, the weary delegates placed their signatures on a document that also provided for an elected chief executive (the president) and a bicameral legislature. The Senate would give equal representation to every state (preserving the Westphalian principle that *all sovereign states are equal*), while the House of Representatives would give local delegations greater or lesser weight in relation to population size. If passed, the proposal would bind the separate states more tightly than ever before, inexorably diminishing their sovereignty in order to elevate the national authority.

Acceptance of a national government was far from assured. Federalists and Anti-Federalists drew swords against one another in Albany, New York, where opponents burned the proposed Constitution.[56] In fierce arguments that buffeted ratification in each state, proponents and detractors drew on nearly every precedent of government from ancient times to the Revolutionary War. Prodigiously learned, they employed all they knew of classical and contemporary systems to debate best practices for self-government.

With the facility of town gossips reliving local events, Federalists and Anti-Federalists batted around the Lycian and Achaean Leagues, the Amphictyonic Council (and the Lacedaemon attempt to subvert it), the confederacies of Switzerland and the Netherlands, the foolishness of Carthage, the aspirations of the Holy Roman Emperor, and the unity and perfidy of Great Britain. At stake, they recognized, was "whether societies of men are really capable or not of establishing good government from reflection and choice, or whether they are forever destined to depend for their political constitution on accident and force."[57] That is, they entertained the idea of government as a rational plan.

The thorniest detail of this plan was how to respect state sovereignty while creating an authority higher than the states to ensure cooperative action or resolve trenchant conflicts. Opponents deemed this nothing more than sophistry: sovereignty could not be divided. They had read their Vattel on the law of nations. A state could not stand above another state. The whole point of sovereignty was the *absolute control* over all matters of internal governance that it gave the possessor.

The debate had roots in the colonial experience, as well, when colonial representatives first considered placing a "general government" over their head to interface more effectively with the outside world, especially the British Empire. Scholar Alison LaCroix notes that a "metropolitan power vacuum" helped spur earlier attempts at coordinating separate sovereignties, including the Albany Plan of 1754. Even then, however, colonists were not anxious to dilute local control, and they rejected the plan.[58]

In 1787, those in favor of the new Constitution tried to finesse the obvious contradiction. The musings of French political theorists, whose philosophies had never been tested by reality, offered the Federalists "a happy combination of authority and ambiguity," in the words of historian Peter Onuf. Indeed, the founders ignored the mismatch between theory and practice by discussing sovereignty as little as possible.[59] Federalists painted a benevolent face on the hoped-for higher government. James Madison used the term "compound republic," and emphasized a division of powers balanced against one another to prevent tyranny. Tellingly, the founders sometimes called the proposed general government an umpire, other times an empire.

Then as now, "empire" was an elusive term. The founding generation used it casually, but always to indicate the thirteen states acting cooperatively. When George Washington retired at the end of the Revolutionary War, the citizens of Richmond welcomed him back to the bosom of his "native country" (Virginia) while thanking him for his exertions on behalf of the "Empire" (the United States). In conversations about where to establish a permanent capital, General Washington called the proposed home of congress the "seat of Empire."[60] Before the Constitutional Convention, when it seemed John Jay was willing to exchange the use of the Mississippi for access to Spain's colonial ports, James Madison was outraged that the New Yorker would barter away "the interests of one part of the empire" to serve the interests of yet another.[61]

But whenever the founders used the term "empire," they clearly viewed their experimental union as different in kind from all preceding empires. It would borrow from Rome in that it would coordinate and protect, but its members would join voluntarily and rule democratically. It would have no hereditary aristocracy, nor any subjects who were not also full citizens. (Of course, they conveniently ignored the hypocrisy in their treatment of slaves, Indians, and women, who obtained full civil rights only much later.) It would differ from Rome by eschewing conquest. Under the Northwest Ordinance of 1787, the original thirteen had already declined to keep any superior voting privileges for themselves if joined by new members. They again rejected special privileges for themselves at the Constitutional Convention. Unlike empires of old, the American union would defend the rights and integrity of individual states, rather than robbing them. Yet, akin to Henry VIII's England, America would also be, in some ways, one country—an "empire unto itself." As Alexander Hamilton averred, it would be "an empire in many respects the most interesting in the world." The revolutionary United States was not alone in thinking of itself this way. When Haiti declared independence from France just a few years later, the new Caribbean nation also described itself as an "empire of liberty."[62]

Advocates for the new constitution argued that a central government with sovereignty over the whole people and power to corral the states was the only alternative to anarchy and perhaps even foreign or civil war. Under the generous terms of the Treaty of Paris, which also granted independence, England had ceded the vast lands west of the Allegheny Mountains to the United States. The former colonies doubled in size at the stroke of a pen in 1783. The combined territory of the thirteen instantly became nearly as big as all of Western Europe, and thus too massive for informal cooperation. (Ten additional states would later be formed out of the unexpected territorial windfall.)

Even critics who questioned the proposed constitution were sometimes willing to concede that "a federal government is the only one that can preserve the liberties and secure the happiness of the inhabitants of such an extensive empire as the United States."[63] Notably, in their first version of this particular document, Pennsylvania Anti-Federalists used the term "empire." In the final draft, they substituted the word "country." As this and other examples demonstrate, terms like "empire," "nation," and "country" were beginning to merge as the aggregated states explored closer ties. Americans gradually conflated their meanings, making them synonyms for unified government.

The founders also freely used the term "umpire," found in the writings of Washington, Jefferson, Madison, Hamilton, Jay, and others with reference to the proposed federal government. Although the traditional English sport of cricket then employed umpires, what the founders meant was a decisive power in politics. The term dated to the Middle Ages, from the Middle French word *nonper*, meaning without *(non)* peer *(per)*. An umpire was someone with the power to resolve disputes between contending parties. An umpire stood apart and was supposed to be an impartial higher authority with no stake in the outcome—an odd man out, so to speak. Umpires could even be coercive. In 1718, English poet Nicholas Rowe lyrically wrote that, in battle, "The Sword is now the Umpire to decide." But James Madison's allusion was more typical: what better "umpires could be desired by two violent factions," he wrote, than peaceful representatives in congress from states "not heated by the local flame?"[64] Empire and umpire thus had overlapping meanings, as a metaphor for a supreme decision-making power above sovereign states.

The proposed government elicited intense opposition. Critics of the newly drafted Constitution pointed out that the Philadelphia convention had far exceeded its mandate. Delegates had been charged with improving the Confederation, not replacing it. They had overstepped their authority. "We are wandering on the great ocean of human affairs," the eloquent, electric Patrick Henry protested at the Virginia ratification meeting. "The federal convention ought to have amended the old system; for this purpose they were solely delegated."[65]

The essential contrast was that between a consensual federation of small, contiguous states, and "one great consolidated empire," Patrick Henry argued. He observed that the proposed Constitution began, "We, the people." Had it been true to the purpose for which it was devised, the new document should have begun "We, the States." Insightfully, Henry remarked that the proposed "consolidated government" followed no clear precedent: "Is this a monarchy like England," he asked, "a compact between prince and people," or is it "a confederacy like Holland, an association of a number of independent states, each of which retain its individual sovereignty?" The proposal was "radical." Why, it meant revolution, protested the man who a dozen years earlier had demanded, "Give me liberty, or give me death!"[66]

The states were not being asked to surrender themselves *wholly* to rule by a central body, but Patrick Henry correctly perceived that the boundaries between federal and state authority were indeed blurring. Federal laws might trump state laws when the two conflicted. The general government could potentially reach across sovereign borders to arrest individuals and ensure local compliance with the Constitution. This was indeed the goal.

The battle for ratification in New York, where Anti-Federalists dominated, inspired the fullest, most famous defense of the proposed Constitution. Alexander Hamilton, George Washington's twenty-two-year-old aide-de-camp during the Revolution, organized the massive literary effort. He, John Jay, and James Madison coauthored a series of essays written under the single name Publius. (Publius was a Roman first name meaning "public" in Latin.

Today we might say "John Q. Public.") As proposed, the Constitution would be "the supreme Law of the Land" (Article VI, Clause 2). In disputes between the states, John Jay wrote, the general government would be "the umpire" that would "decide between them and compel acquiescence."[67] Without a federal constitution, the states might otherwise end up warring against one another whenever boundary disputes and commercial rivalries frayed anxious nerves to the breaking point.

Alexander Hamilton painted a graver picture yet, drawing upon the sad story of "the petty republics of Greece and Italy." To modern ears he might have been describing the phenomenon of Balkanization: "We shall be driven to the alternative either of taking refuge at once in the arms of monarchy, or of splitting ourselves into an infinity of little, jealous, clashing, tumultuous commonwealths, the wretched nurseries of unceasing discord and the miserable objects of universal pity or contempt."[68] Hamilton pointed to the ancient, bloody competition between Britain and France—implying that someday two or more of the former colonies might find themselves in a similar rivalry. Neighboring countries, in competition for natural resources that did not respect boundaries, were "naturally enemies of each other."[69] Even Athens and Sparta, allied against the Persians up through the victory at Salamis, became competitors afterward and eventually foes. In one of their few joint essays, Hamilton and Madison observed in *Federalist* 18, that the two Greek rivals ultimately "did each another infinitely more mischief than they had suffered from Xerxes."[70]

In *Federalist* 1 and 7, Hamilton argued that "nothing less than the existence" of the thirteen-member union hung on ratification of the Constitution. If it was rejected, in time the thirteen governments would inevitably clash, he wrote, as neighbors always do, over territory, commerce, and the selfish, opposed interests of their citizens. Joined together as one "empire"—a republic of republics, though—they would thwart the attempts of their foreign enemies to "divide et impera" (divide and command). The federal government would be an "umpire or common judge to interpose between the contending parties" whenever disputes arose, Hamilton wrote, echoing John Jay. A long-standing, bitter debate between Connecticut and Pennsylvania over territory, only recently resolved, showed the potential for violent disagreements. A central government would best defend the states from outside aggression and bullying while simultaneously preventing a "War between the States."[71]

Perhaps it is only human to paint a straw-man portrait of one's opponent that he would not recognize as himself. Time and again in the *Federalist Papers*, Hamilton, Jay, and Madison refer to those who "whispered in . . . private circles" that the "thirteen States are of too great extent for any general system."[72] These opponents supposedly argued that the former colonies should "divide themselves into three or four nations"—regional confederacies of states that had more in common with one another.[73] Each of the first eight *Federalist* essays refers to this outlook of the opposition. Anti-Federalists meanwhile protested that they proposed no such dismemberment of the union. Indeed, they were tired of those who put this argument in their mouths. It was a mere "hobgoblin," one proclaimed, invented by "the deranged brain of Publius, a New York writer."[74] Federalists, of course, suffered from equally false portrayals by their enemies, most notably that they were aspiring tyrants who wanted to revive monarchy.

But the Federalists' obsessive defense of an "extended Republic" merits renewed attention. Some modern scholars have suggested that the Founders were indeed planning an expansive empire that might one day dominate the hemisphere or even the world, akin to Rome.[75] This was actually the reverse of their concerns. Hamilton, Madison, and Jay used gallons of ink to justify the idea of an "extended empire" because they worried that the *original* thirteen states, enlarged by the 1783 peace treaty with Britain, already comprised a territory too vast for republican government. Far from conspiring to tyrannize or expand, they wanted to avoid disintegration. They wanted to save the United States from the fate of Poland. Doing that appeared to require contemplating the unthinkable: resuscitating some elements of "empire"— meaning, an external authority capable of bringing states to heel when absolutely necessary.

Truthfully, disunion *was* implicit in at least some Anti-Federalist arguments, which called an "extensive empire . . . a misfortune to be deprecated," implying that the massive territory should not be governed as one entity. A "Maryland Farmer" who published several tracts criticizing the Constitution (probably a war veteran who attended the Philadelphia convention on behalf of Maryland but opposed the final document) argued that an extensive empire would concentrate wealth and power, to Americans' misfortune. A general government would encourage the building of an "overgrown, luxurious, and effeminate capital," like Rome, which would become a target for covetous enemies. Even Europeans had learned this lesson, the writer pointed out. "The balance of power has long engaged the attention of all the European world, in order to avoid the horrid evils of a general government."[76] Separate sovereignties had been a guarantee against outside oppression ever since the Peace of Westphalia. A general, and thus imperial, government should be avoided at all costs.

In *Federalist* 13, Alexander Hamilton challenged the implication that the enlarged American territory would have to be subdivided if government was to remain responsive to local concerns, revealing his worry that disunion was nigh. "The ideas of men who speculate upon the dismemberment of the empire seem generally turned towards three confederacies—one consisting of the four Northern, another of the four Middle, and a third of the five Southern States," he wrote. Conflicts within the Confederation during the 1780s did, in fact, tend to have a sectional flavor. John Jay experienced this during his attempts to resolve problems with Spain over the Mississippi. Southern delegates routinely accused Jay of sacrificing navigation of the Mississippi for the benefit of northeastern commercial interests.[77] Southerners' alarm was not surprising. In fact, the eight northernmost states approved Jay's proposal, though they lacked the ninth vote required by the Articles to pass any formal treaty. Division into separate confederacies to defend local interests was a real possibility. The idea of a large, but thoroughly republican nation apparently needed justification, or three-headed Publius would not have returned to it again and again.

In *Federalist* 14, James Madison reasoned that the newly expanded territory of the United States really wasn't *that* big, "not a great deal larger than Germany" or "Poland before the last dismemberment."[78] (The example of Poland, whose last and fatal dismemberment came only seven years later, would have been chilling to readers.) In *Federalist* 5, John Jay pointed out that size had its advantages, citing the example of Great Britain, whose peoples "were for ages divided into three, and . . . [consequently] almost constantly embroiled in quarrels and wars." Enemies took advantage of their disunity until the island kingdoms pooled their resources for defense. Instead of three small navies, Great Britain had one large navy, the most powerful in the world. Instead of three militias under independent command, it had one effective army. But if the "constituent parts of the British Empire" were redivided into independent governments, he wrote, soon each would "dwindle into comparative insignificance."[79] Jay noted that Queen Anne had made this very argument in her 1706 plea to the Scottish Parliament to join with England.

But any comparisons with Britain could be dicey, since this was precisely what the Anti-Federalists most feared: reversion to English ways. Even passing references to Britain's positive qualities typically provoked scornful denunciations or sidelong glances. When James Wilson, a delegate to the Constitutional Convention from Pennsylvania, first moved that the executive consist of a single person, a pregnant silence greeted his proposal. Americans had been meeting in congresses for twelve years, each with a temporary president—himself a member of congress elected for only one year—who chaired the meeting. A separate executive branch, with a powerful individual over it, inevitably reminded the delegates of the king they had fought an eight-year war to cast off.[80] No framer wished to be tagged with that vilest of epithets, "monarchist."

James Madison contributed a different argument, drawing on Scottish philosopher David Hume to cleanse and rehabilitate some elements of large, Roman-scale government.[81] A big republic would provide greater assurances of liberty for its citizens than a small one. A direct, *pure* democracy, he said, had to be tiny so that all of its people could meet "and administer the government in person." In that situation, ruinous factionalism could be avoided only "by giving to every citizen the same opinions, the same passions, and the same interests." In a large, *representative* democracy, a republic, the government could easily be extended over a much greater area. It would also better guarantee individual liberty.

"Extend the sphere and you take in a greater variety of parties and interests," Madison asserted; "you make it less probable that a majority of the whole will have a common motive to invade the rights of other citizens." An extensive republic, he suggested, might at last rescue the idea of popular government from "the opprobrium under which it has so long labored." Up to this point, both ancient and modern commentators had associated democracy with mob rule. The United States might set an example of popular government that would finally prove it worthy of "the esteem and adoption of mankind."[82] It would square the circle: protecting the individual states' Westphalian sovereignty while creating a sovereign over them.

The Federalists made good arguments and they won their point. Among the populace, there were many who understood, as one man wrote to the *Poughkeepsie Country Journal,* that the union needed "a firmer cement" if it was to achieve "respect abroad, and tranquility at home."[83] But it was a close race. The Constitution cleared the New York convention by only three votes, and Massachusetts by nineteen votes. In September 1788, the Continental Congress elected to put the new Constitution into operation once eleven of the thirteen states had ratified the document. North Carolina and Rhode Island did not join the United States until months after George Washington's inauguration in March 1789. Under the old Articles of Confederation, every state had to agree to any change before it could be implemented. But under the Constitution, states could be outvoted—and their only choice was either to submit or refuse to participate in the new nation. Each measure to strengthen the federal government seemed to weaken local government, at a time when "my country" still meant one's state.

The central lesson of the Reformation peace process—that sovereignty must be absolute, that it should *not* be shared with some overarching, transnational entity that claimed superior judgment—retained a powerful hold on the European and American imagination. No one wanted to relive the horror of the religious wars. But at the same time, the U.S. Constitution was based implicitly on a weakening, or at least a modification, of Emer de Vattel's *Law of Nations*. It created an authority "capable of giving commands, prescribing laws, and compelling those who refuse to obey."[84] Vattel had held that within any country there could be only one jurisdiction, but in the United States there were both state and national jurisdictions. This unprecedented compromise defied the entire European political tradition since the Peace of Westphalia.[85] The oddity of the American experience was that at a time when the states of Europe had backed away from any supranational authority, the states of North America were voluntarily creating one.

Americans muddled "empire," "umpire," "state," and "nation" so that they could have government both ways: sovereignty at the state level to maintain their freedom from distant rulers, combined with a superior sovereign to compel peaceable coordination. It was not a program for future expansion but one to deal with expansion retroactively. James Madison and Thomas Jefferson would be among the first to challenge the authority of the United States government in following years. The Civil War would try the full extent of its power. Yet the founders did not mean "empire" in the way it is sometimes employed today in reference to the founders' vision. They aimed at *internal* coherence, not at dominance over populations beyond America's political boundaries.[86]

Although it is easily forgotten centuries later, the original thirteen states were most internationalistic not with respect to foreign countries but with respect to relations among themselves.[87] The trust they gradually and grudgingly extended to one another was extraordinary. It was soon sorely tested.

2

Umpire Attacked

*Or, How the French Revolution Created
the American Party System, 1789–1800*

George Washington was not a timid man. As a young colonel in 1754, long before the Revolution, he had delighted in making a stand against France on behalf of Britain: clearing away the forest underbrush to better see the enemy and preparing the open field as one might a drawing room for a dance. From the exposed position in which he and his men returned the enemy's barrage, he wrote his brother afterward, "I heard Bulletts whistle and believe me there was something charming in the sound."[1]

But when the eleven states then bound under the Constitution elected him president thirty-five years later, the aging general departed Mount Vernon feeling like "a culprit who is going to the place of his execution," he confided to his old comrade Henry Knox. With his best brown suit packed for the occasion, its eagle-embossed buttons bright, the once-brazen commander set off for the first inaugural "with a mind oppressed with more anxious and painful sensations than I have words to express."[2]

Why was Washington apprehensive? Although he did not explain himself further to Henry Knox, perhaps because the challenges seemed obvious, Washington must have intuited that it would be far harder to create a permanent government than it was to win a war, especially amid rivals who did not always make themselves plain on the political battlefield. Washington's premonitions were borne out. Early on, the United States struggled against two forces that threatened to end the experiment before it had hardly begun. First, a wave of revolution swept the Atlantic rim, partly as a consequence of America's war for independence. Second, domestic factionalism grew more heated with every year over how much power the new federal government should exercise, especially in light of the dangers emanating from abroad. Fear of foreign bogeymen—some real—drove the founders into opposite corners. It created America's two-party system and sharpened tensions over the scope of federal power, or "umperialism," if you will.

Outside threats demanded an immediate response, but the choices were complicated. The founders disagreed about which great power had more to offer the United States: revolutionary France or industrializing England. Friends found themselves fighting over the oars to the ship of state. Their disagreements hastened the first serious experiments with arbitration: that is, using incentives and sanctions to avoid physical violence. The effort failed and war broke out in 1812, but the idea had staying power. In the following two hundred years, Americans continued to wrestle with techniques of negotiation, trying to get them right. This period helped enshrine the notion that arbitration, coupled with economic pressure, was the proper approach for resolving international conflict. It also showed that sanctions could hurt the umpire as much as the brawling parties, sometimes even more immediately.

Revolution in France precipitated the external dangers and internal disputes. Only five days after George Washington touched his lips to the Bible in front of a cheering inaugural crowd on New York's Wall Street, the decorous Estates-General of France met for the first time in 175 years. They convened in an ornate pavilion just outside the royal palace at Versailles. This gathering of 1,201 representatives from the three estates (the nobility, the clergy, and the people) became the opening salvo of the French Revolution. Within weeks, the anger and resentments of centuries spiraled out of control. The common people demanded access to the political process and power over their own lives and country.

For the ensuing twenty-six years, until the redoubtable Napoleon Bonaparte met defeat at the Battle of Waterloo, the Atlantic world was rocked by continual turmoil. The French pulled down their own government, guillotined Louis XVI and Marie Antoinette, slaughtered the aristocracy and clergy, invaded and conquered much of Europe, and touched off rebellions throughout Central and South America that gave the United States nearly a dozen sibling republics. They also killed many of their own leaders. As Georges Danton remarked when he himself fell victim to the violence he had orchestrated, "The Revolution devours its children." It was Europe's most alarming event between the 1648 Peace of Westphalia and the World War of 1914.

Throughout, the fledgling American government constantly risked being crushed between the titans of Europe. Eventually it did go to war, against the United Kingdom a second (and last) time.

The coterie that joined forces to write and ratify the Constitution cracked under the strain. The federal structure had been devised largely to enable the nation to defend itself against outside dangers, but no one foresaw just how quickly such dangers would materialize. Despite the new president's pleas for cooperation, the former revolutionaries split. Old companions came to hate one another, each convinced that the other was betraying the spirit of 1776. Base accusations and malicious gossip destroyed the peace of mind of Washington, Adams, Jefferson, Madison, and many others during the nation's early years.

From today's remove, the founders seem incredibly self-confident. But they were riddled with doubts. Republicanism seemed so breakable. They began to suspect one another. Remarkably, given what happened elsewhere, the founders shunned physical violence to solve their disputes—with the exception of the duel in which Vice President Aaron Burr killed Alexander Hamilton.[3] The nation escaped the vindictive terror that soaked the sand of Paris's Place de la Révolution in blood, yet the spirit of fraternity nonetheless foundered on the reef of foreign relations.

Not surprisingly, the first presidents tried to devise a foreign policy that reflected their revolutionary values. They disagreed on how this should be done. International threats—magnified by the distance from Europe like shadows on a wall—sharpened their disputes. Because both sides of the political divide were committed to an enlightened diplomacy, they would not have recognized the bifurcation between realism and idealism that historians later perceived. They disagreed over what was practical, though they made the error (common among revolutionaries) of mistaking their differences of opinion about tactics for something deeper and more ominous. Washington is best remembered for setting out in his Farewell Address what he called the Great Rule, the policy of neutrality and nonentanglement. Washington also advocated what we now call transparency: "For in public, as in private life, I am persuaded that honesty will forever be found to be the best policy."[4] Like arbitration, transparency was a device that the revolutionaries valued as both efficacious and moral.

Of them all, Thomas Jefferson had the clearest vision of a new, nontraditional way to achieve international peace. Economic incentives, he believed, were the key means to a better world in which nations would negotiate their differences. The United States might set a "precious example," Jefferson speculated to James Madison, if it were able to demonstrate "that nations may be brought to do justice by appeals to their interests as well as by appeals to arms."[5] Jefferson and his followers borrowed this hypothesis from European thinkers and hoped that Americans would pioneer in its proof. Access to trade would be intertwined with the negotiation of political differences to achieve both prosperity and peace. Open markets would be used to reward friends. Trade restrictions would be used to punish enemies. The Jeffersonians did not look upon the profit motive with quite the cynicism of readers today, many influenced either by corporate malfeasance or by Karl Marx's nineteenth-century critique of capitalism (latent, but enduring). To Jefferson's generation, odd as it may sound to modern ears, trade carried the potential of moral transformation.

In the short run, however, economic pressure failed completely. Americans exaggerated, or simply did not comprehend, the real value of their trade to others. Jefferson placed the United States on the path toward a calamitous war and Madison marched the country into it. Public anger almost produced the rupture into regional confederacies of which Publius had warned, and international events after 1789 severely strained the bonds among the former revolutionaries. The federal union held, but the extent of its integrative or coercive power vis-à-vis the states remained an open question.

Despite bitter partisanship, the precedent of prerevolutionary days—when Americans first used boycotts to seek redress—was kept alive. Perhaps *because* of partisanship, each side was spurred to fight harder for its ideals: Federalists for an organized, prosperous, well-defended state based on contemporary realities, Republicans for their vision of international goodwill. Together, they created an unusually dynamic nation and nurtured new global trends. Over the next hundred years, the federal government periodically took up trade as an instrument of coercion, beginning with the third president. Each time, it tried to create incentives for foreigners to yield to American demands. The attempt often backfired, particularly because the United States sometimes made the mistake of pointing the gun at its own head. Yet the idea gradually gained traction, and it evolved in the twentieth century into the international practice of economic sanctions as an instrument of arbitration, first under the League of Nations and then the United Nations.

These developments were far in the unseen future, however. America's initial attempts to use economic suasion failed. On the brink of ruin, the government eventually scrapped them. Here, as in many other cases, developments outside the United States established the parameters of possibility.

The founders' first policies toward nations outside their thirteen-member coalition derived from the European Enlightenment. Every member of the revolutionary generation was born during that remarkable, century-long flowering of hope in human potential. Heartened by the Scientific Revolution—which produced such spectacular thinkers and inventors as Copernicus, Galileo, Descartes, van Leeuwenhoek, Newton, and America's own Benjamin Franklin—Enlightenment writers believed that the laws of the social world could be discovered just like the laws of the physical universe. Politics and society could be improved by rational study. The Enlightenment had adherents throughout Europe, but it was in eighteenth-century France that the "philosophes" most fully imagined and articulated new ideals of intergovernmental relations. In France was born the idea of using economic tools to resolve political problems and avoid physical violence, soon copied by Americans.[6]

Above all, the philosophes were pacifists. They thought that war, waged at the expense of the people for the benefit of the elite, was almost always immoral. And, unlike realists from Niccolò Machiavelli onward, they believed that states had an obligation to be moral. They rejected the old doctrine of raison d'état, which they called "power politics" or "the old policy," as inherently destabilizing and corrupt because it cynically (and inaccurately) assumed that the interest of each nation was opposed to those of its neighbors. The philosophes also derided double-dealing and state secrecy, or nontransparency. As one writer put it, old-style European diplomacy was "an obscure art which hides itself in the folds of deceit, which fears to let itself be seen and believes it can succeed only in the darkness of mystery."[7] Raison d'état inevitably tempted monarchs to enlarge their domains at the expense of neighboring states whenever they could get away with it. Each bit of territory added a lump to one side of the scale or the other. The philosophes detested this application of "balance of power" and criticized the race for colonies as an outcome of the desire to monopolize both trade and territory.[8]

Among the philosophes, it was a subgroup known as the physiocrats that most fully described the alternative to power politics. Their ideas deeply influenced American attitudes. The physiocrats called their proposal the "economic policy," referring to the establishment of unrestricted trade between nations. Not only would this enrich all parties, they posited, but even more important, it would give countries an incentive to stay on good terms. The physiocrats believed that merchants, unlike kings and generals, instinctively understood that war was counterproductive. It disrupted business and robbed the treasury. It must always be the last resort.

This supposition derived from commonsense experience. The trader was a citizen of the world, whether Russian, Dutch, Arab, English, or Chinese. He or she served everyone, not just a single nation. Trade thrived because the interests of nations were inherently compatible, not opposed. Only monarchs made the error of believing in eternal rivalry, which suited their political interests vis-à-vis their own people. Year-round access to Indian cotton, Irish linen, Jamaican sugar, Arabian coffee, African cocoa, English wheat, Scandinavian pine, Chinese silk, and Mexican silver proved to any commoner (and every buyer) that the world was a better and brighter place thanks to traders. Commerce bound nations in a common society.[9]

How, then, should government treat merchants? "Leave us alone," industrialists are reputed to have told Jean-Baptist Colbert, the mercantilist controller-general of France. The French phrase *laissez faire* ("allow to do") became associated with physiocratic doctrine. Led by François Quesnay, the royal physician to Louis XV, and then Anne-Robert-Jacques Turgot, chief minister of finance to the next king, Louis XVI, the physiocrats were in a position to be heard. Their ideas ran counter to the prevailing system of beggar-thy-neighbor mercantilism, but slowly gained momentum. In 1786, France and England signed an unprecedented commercial agreement that lowered trade barriers and guaranteed the rights of the citizens of either country while they were residing in the other. Three years later, however, revolution overtook and dashed these gestures toward free trade. War with England ended the treaty, and the French government remained in constant turmoil for a quarter of a century, unable to execute any coherent economic policy.[10]

Similar ideas about open access flowed from the pen of David Hume, the Scottish laird and lifelong bachelor who spent much of his adulthood traveling between England and Europe. Hume argued that mercantilist policies made enemies unnecessarily, premised as the policies were on the idea that one nation's profit was another's loss. If nations lowered their barriers and dispensed with what he called "this narrow and malignant opinion," trade would increase and everyone would profit. Peace among nations would be more attainable. Physical violence would decline. Hume asserted in his 1752 essay "Of Jealousy of Trade" that "not only as a man, but as a British subject, I pray for the flourishing commerce of Germany, Spain, Italy, and even France itself. . . . Great Britain, and all those nations, would flourish more, did their sovereigns and ministers adopt such enlarged and benevolent sentiments towards each other."[11] He defended the existence of altruism as deriving from empathy. It was fundamental to human nature, Hume observed, to laugh when others laughed and grieve when they grieved. Humankind did not have to live in perpetual enmity.

The bourgeoning middle class in Europe paved the way for these theories on the superior morality of merchants. Tradesmen, small manufacturers, shippers, and other social climbers felt entitled to more economic elbow room. As their influence grew, they hammered away at the trade restrictions imposed by royals and aristocrats. The philosophes' way of thinking was congenial to them. It supplied the middle class with a moral justification for their personal ambitions. Through homely trade, war would be abolished.[12] This simple but powerful assumption—that trade promoted peace and power politics fomented war—was woven into the American Revolution.

Thomas Paine's *Common Sense* contained one of the earliest assertions of what eventually became preferred policy. America's "plan is commerce," he wrote in 1776, "and that, well attended to, will secure us the peace and friendship of all Europe; because it is the interest of all Europe to have America a free port." An independent United States, he confidently asserted, could simply opt out of the European balance of power. Only as an appendage of England—a "make-weight in the scale of British politics"—did it attract the hostility of powerful nations like France.[13] A giant entrepôt, the United States would become a welcoming crossroads for world trade.

John Adams, the portly, irascible New Englander who flopped between optimism and pessimism about man's potential to get along, also initially hoped to use free trade as a carrot. Like Paine, he was determined to avoid any entangling political ties—since that was the traditional tool of benighted European diplomacy. Two months after the 1776 publication of *Common Sense,* Adams warned the country's first emissary to France, Silas

Deane, not to seek any potentially corrupting political alliance. In notes to himself during the tumultuous run-up to open warfare against Britain, Adams wrote that the only treaties the United States could safely sign would allow solely "a commercial connection." Under no circumstances should Americans allow French troops to aid them.[14]

Shortly before declaring independence, the Second Continental Congress appointed John Adams head of a committee to devise a template, or "Model Treaty," for all future alliances of the United States. Congress hoped and expected that France would be first to sign. Here was the chance to put a new kind of diplomacy into practice, something that Europe's coffeehouse thinkers had yet to do. Adams's draft showed the influence of the physiocrats but took their ideas even further. He proposed that merchants of both countries be allowed to act as if borders did not exist.

In Adams's scheme, the citizens and companies of one country would be treated as citizens of the other in matters of commerce. Frenchmen in the United States, and Americans in France, would "enjoy all the other Rights, Liberties, Priviledges, Immunities and Exemptions in Trade, Navigation and Commerce . . . which the said Natives, or Companies enjoy."[15] Any tax or restriction placed on the citizen of one country would be placed on the citizen of its trading partner, and not a penny more. Tradesmen might come and go in perfect harmony and with equal rights, on the same basis as they would among the thirteen former colonies. The Continental Congress approved the novel suggestion that gave workaday form to the loftiest implications of the physiocrats' free-trade ideas. It had no precedent in English or French law.[16]

Their plan approximated what is today called "national treatment." It is the principle of equal access that was implemented among cooperating nations almost two centuries later, under the 1947 General Agreement on Tariffs and Trade. But in 1776, it was so far in front of existing practice that the revolutionaries recognized that the French monarchy was likely to reject it. Congress consequently authorized its diplomats "to relax the Demands of the United States" if they proved impracticable. Emissaries were told to request most-favored-nation status as an alternative. This was a less generous principle, but one with precedents in bilateral commercial treaties signed by England, France, Spain, and the Netherlands in 1713. "Most favored nation" meant that France and the United States would grant to each other's inhabitants any trade privileges that they gave any other *foreigner* (which typically were few).[17]

What is remarkable is that the newborn United States, even before winning its independence, sought such an outlandishly liberal trade agreement. Equally shocking was how little Americans were willing to offer in return. The proposed treaty on which all others would be modeled gave only the incentive of unhindered access to U.S. markets, previously closed to France by Britain's Navigation Acts, even though the mere act of recognizing the United States would expose the ancient monarchy to mortal hazards. The more savvy members of Congress, including John Adams, realized that the only reason for the French king to sign a treaty with the otherwise non-existent United States would be to weaken its historic enemy, Britain. George III was bound to retaliate with a declaration of war. The Model Treaty showed no cognizance of these risks and offered only the most liberal form of free trade in compensation. It embodied physiocratic theory but, as Felix Gilbert notes, was "entirely alien to the spirit of the diplomatic practice of the time."[18]

Congress soon found that France wanted military guarantees before siding openly with the rebels and had no interest whatsoever in treating American citizens like its own. The United States would have to share any danger that it asked France to undertake. Two years into the Revolutionary War, Americans were frantic for assistance. The Redcoats had chased George Washington out of New York and across New Jersey, and occupied the American capitol at Philadelphia. The American negotiating team in France set aside the unique precepts of the Model Treaty. In 1778 they signed two treaties with Louis XVI, very different from the proposed model, one of which was a Treaty of Alliance that pledged mutual military defense and stooped so low as to countenance Gallic designs on British colonies in the West Indies.[19] The second was a Treaty of Amity and Commerce in which the two nations granted one another most-favored-nation status (rather than national treatment), and guaranteed the rights of neutrals during times of war. With independence at stake, the revolutionaries dropped their pacifist attempt to ground international relations on the rock of free trade.

It was well that they did. French loans to the revolutionaries eventually reached eighteen million livres.[20] The first French officers came in 1777, followed by troops that lent moral and physical support to the besieged Americans. The young Marquis de Lafayette, whom George Washington treated as a son and Alexander Hamilton loved as a brother, came to symbolize French joy in America's triumphs and the leap of the Enlightenment across the Atlantic. At the decisive Battle of Yorktown in Virginia, the fair-haired, twenty-four-year-old Lafayette took responsibility for positioning 7,000 American troops of the Continental Army and blocking the maneuvers of Cornwallis while awaiting Washington's rendezvous.

On his arrival at Yorktown, George Washington consulted the older and more experienced French commander, Count de Rochambeau, on military strategy. French engineers showed American infantrymen how to dig the trenches that allowed U.S. artillery to inch progressively closer to the entrapped British army. French ground troops nearly equaled Americans in number. Without their arms, reinforced by twenty-four ships of the line and thousands of seamen off the coast, the Revolution would have been lost.[21] To achieve victory, the revolutionaries tacitly accepted the ethos of the Westphalian system into which the United States had no choice but to fit itself. In this system, each state had to exploit the balance of power and defend militarily its right to exist. The fundamental assumption of Vattel's law of international relations was that the first duty of any nation was self-preservation.[22] World reform would wait—at least until 1789.

It was under a single, federal constitution that the United States was finally in a position to barter the combined trade of the thirteen former colonies for concessions in the outside world. After the final break with England in 1783, U.S. ships were excluded from British colonial ports in the Western Hemisphere. Those colonies, especially the sugar islands of the West Indies, were Americas' nearest and oldest trading partners and the pivot of the lucrative trade triangle involving Africa. Excluding U.S. "bottoms," meaning merchant ships, was perfectly reasonable from a British point of view. The former colonies had become alien by choice. Why should they have any access to the wealthy marketplaces of the empire they had quit?[23] Britain opened its home ports to the United States (with duties and prohibitions on selected goods) but resolutely closed its colonial ones. For many Americans, this was symbolic of continued British obstinacy and selfishness—though to many Britons it proved exactly the same about Americans, who arrogantly demanded the same historic trade privileges despite the changed relationship on which the upstarts themselves had insisted.

On April 8, 1789, during the very first session of Congress under the Constitution and even before Washington's inauguration, James Madison took up the cudgel of trade retaliation. The word "boycott," coined by the mid-nineteenth-century Irish, did not yet exist, but Americans knew the tactic well. They had been the first to use it in a species of international conflict during prerevolutionary struggles over the Sugar Act, the Tea Act, and other British measures. Madison had fought for the Constitution partly to ensure that the United States would be unified enough to take up this weapon again. Denied a seat in the Senate by Virginians still annoyed at the passage of the federal Constitution, Madison's stamina and intellectual talent quickly made him a leader in the House.

There he proposed "tonnage duties" with both discriminatory and revenue-raising intent. American vessels bringing in foreign goods would pay an import tax of nine cents on the ton. The proceeds would fill a purse from which the government could sustain itself and repay creditors. Ships from countries that had most-favored-nation treaties with the United States, like France, would pay thirty cents. (Had France granted U.S. merchants national treatment, its ships could have paid nine cents.) Those nations that refused to sign a bilateral commercial treaty would pay fifty cents on the ton. Here Madison meant the United Kingdom, of course, and said so explicitly: "a discrimination ought to be made, and ought to operate particularly on Great Britain."[24]

Madison was certain that Parliament and George III would capitulate to pressure if Congress applied it. Like many citizens at the time, he was convinced that England's "addiction" to luxury and its dependence on cheap foreign food to feed its oppressed working class would compel it to open all its markets in order to palliate America and exchange goods on the most favorable terms possible. He also believed that the United States could withstand any trade war that Britain chose to pick. Madison and like-minded supporters thought that the United States imported only "superfluities" from Britain, meaning unnecessary manufactures that Thomas Jefferson called "gee-gaws." From America, Britain received food and raw materials, or "necessaries"—or so they believed.

But when Parliament closed the West Indies to the United States after 1783, British shipping boomed from the lack of American competition. The islands remained well supplied with basic goods imported in British bottoms. Yet Madison still entertained no doubts. As he stressed vehemently during congressional debate, "I am not afraid of suffering in the contest [with Britain]; her interests can be wounded almost mortally, while ours are invulnerable." Madison also rejected the idea of any justice in Britain's sovereign decisions, charging "she has bound us in commercial manacles, and very nearly defeated the object of our independence."[25]

British audiences, especially Tories, had little inclination to grovel. Their attitudes after the Revolution were colored by anger at what they viewed as American impertinence, unappreciativeness, degeneracy, and betrayal. They saw little reason or need to placate the ingrates. Many Britons were convinced that America's people lacked patriotism and its government was foolish and immature. It was not to be feared.[26]

Madison and his followers planned to convince the British otherwise, using restrictive tariffs as a tool of negotiation. Notably, however, the Republicans did not advocate permanent trade barriers. "Liberty of trade" made every person "a citizen of the whole society of mankind," Madison jotted in notes for a 1789 speech to Congress. It reduced discord "by abolishing the causes of external violence and making it [the] interest of all to maintain the peace of all."[27]

Madison was not a mercantilist who wanted a closed door in order to protect the infant American economy. Like the physiocrats, Madison believed quite the opposite. A high tariff need only be temporary, since the British government was sure to capitulate. Once this occurred, restrictions would be unnecessary because commerce would finally be free to flow in its "natural channels."[28] In fact, the Virginian's fertile imagination went even further: "Suppose all the world under one Govt—provinces of one empire," Madison wrote. "Free intercourse" would promote "mutual advantage."[29] This usage of "empire" suggests a nonexploitive millennium—a society of equals with a supervisory federation at the top. One might say it echoed Immanuel Kant's 1795 proposal for a "Perpetual Peace," had Madison's sketch not predated the Prussian philosopher's famous essay by six years.

To his surprise, Madison found that the majority in Congress did not share his enthusiasm. Instead, they rejected his punitive tariffs three times: in 1789, 1790, and 1794. Congress refused to use federal power for the purpose for which it had been created: swift retaliation against the foreign countries that had bullied the United States under the weak Articles of Confederation. For Madison and his friend Thomas Jefferson, Congress's rejection of the tariffs was a mystery with only one logical explanation. Betrayal.[30]

In reality, Madison's opponents were hardly infused with evil motives. New Yorker John Lawrence spoke for the congressional majority when he argued that the new nation simply could not bear the consequences of a commercial war with Britain. If England retaliated by imposing its own stiff tariffs, then exports like tobacco, rice, corn, and salted fish would rot on American wharves. Farmers would sink into subsistence and stop cultivating export crops. The nation would cease to grow. "Once destroy this spring of industry," Lawrence argued, "and your country totters to ruin."[31]

Madison's suspicions deepened as it became clear that the leading opponent to battling Britain was Alexander Hamilton. Madison's collaborator on the *Federalist Papers* had jumped into the new federal government with both feet and quickly raced ahead of nearly everyone's expectations as to what government might do. Hamilton's esprit, drive, and nimble intelligence made him a formidable champion for his ideas. Madison and Hamilton each had reason to suspect the other of reneging on principles they earlier held in common. Madison seemed to turn his back on federal initiative vis-à-vis the states, while Hamilton turned his back on union for the purpose of foiling Great Britain.

Only a year earlier, Hamilton had written in *Federalist* 11 "Suppose, for instance, we had a government in America, capable of excluding Great Britain (with whom we have at present no treaty of commerce) from all our ports; what would be the probable operation of this step upon her politics?"[32] But as the nation's first secretary of the treasury, Hamilton took an entirely different tone. For reasons of expediency, he strongly opposed trade discrimination. Britain was America's primary customer. The United States sold twice as many goods to Britain as to France, and purchased five times as many imports from her.[33] Trade with England had enormous momentum because of the historic relationship, shared language, and consumer preferences. (Even Jefferson once defended his purchase of a superior-quality British harness over a French one as being "not from a love of the English but a love of myself."[34]) Almost the entire income of the federal government—and thus whatever resources it had with which to retire old debts and promote future development—came from fees on imports and exports. A sudden drop in foreign trade would bankrupt Congress and Washington's administration, which collected no taxes from citizens on personal income.

Hamilton recognized that a trade war would stunt U.S. growth while little affecting British prosperity. Britain had a more diversified economy. The best the United States could hope for was to catch up. In his 1792 "Report on Manufactures," Hamilton urged Congress to promote industrial development. He preferred government "bounties" to protective tariffs but was willing to experiment with both incentives and tariffs to get the new national economy onto firmer ground.[35] Hamilton went so far as to help organize a Society for Establishing Useful Manufactures, which built America's first cotton-spinning mill. Typical of his hard-driving style, the omnipresent treasury secretary recruited British textile specialists (industrial spies) to set up the factory. He even picked the site for their enterprise, at a New Jersey waterfall where he, Washington, and the effervescent Marquis de Lafayette once picnicked during the Revolution.[36]

Bilingual in French and English, and raised on the Danish island of Saint Croix in the West Indies, Hamilton had had a wider and rougher life experience than any of the other principal founders. Orphaned at age thirteen—without a dime in his pocket and stained by illegitimacy—Hamilton had been apprenticed to a West Indian shipping firm. A quick study at anything to which he applied his attention, he was soon given responsibility for freight, accounts, and international pricing. Only a few years later, after coming to America, Hamilton became George Washington's "principal and most confidential aide" (in the general's words), and personally witnessed the grave provisioning problems caused by the Continental Congress's insolvency. He initially attributed Madison's unbending championship of trade retaliation in 1789 to the fact that, while the Virginian was "uncorrupted and incorruptible," he was "very little acquainted with the world."[37]

Madison saw Hamilton quite differently. Both he and Thomas Jefferson concluded that Hamilton's tactical unwillingness to challenge Britain bespoke a dangerous fondness for monarchy. The Virginians abhorred Hamilton's manufacturing schemes, fearing that the spread of wage labor would recreate British class divisions in the new nation. (Neither, of course, balked at chattel slavery.) In this, they echoed an ongoing debate within the Enlightenment about whether or not complex manufacturing, with its specialization of labor, inherently led to vice, poverty, and social stratification. The Jeffersonians followed the thinking of Jean-Jacques Rousseau, who argued that "man" in his more natural, rustic state, making his own simple clothing and living largely off the land, was more virtuous and thus more capable of self-government than an urban worker dependent on wages and warehouses.

In contrast, the Hamiltonians reflected the influence of David Hume and Adam Smith, who defended commercial growth as salutary in advanced societies. These British spokesmen for manufacturing acknowledged the negative consequences that sometimes resulted. Indeed, they were more forthright about the downside of industrialization for factory workers than the Jeffersonians were about the downside of agricultural life for Southern laborers, mostly slaves.[38]

The Jeffersonians argued that Hamilton's vigorous advocacy of manufacturing would put American yeomen on the road to ruin. They also opposed Hamilton's proposal for a national bank, believing that the Constitution had given the federal government no such creative powers. When supporters responded that the Constitution's "necessary and proper" clause gave government the authority to respond to any important national need, the man who had once advocated a federal veto over *any* state law altered course. Madison became a strict constructionist of the Constitution and an advocate of narrow federal powers. Jefferson, despite his position as secretary of state under Washington, was also not reconciled to a strong central government. Only the individual, sovereign states had the authority to create banks, he believed. When a "*foreign* legislature," as Jefferson chillingly called the U.S. Congress in 1792, impinged on this right, anyone cooperating with this "foreign legislature" (he repeated) should be judged by the state courts as "guilty of high treason and suffer death accordingly."[39]

To Madison and Jefferson, each step Hamilton took proved that the treasury secretary was trying to recreate an aristocracy. They took perverse solace in a brief 1792 panic that resulted in a run on government securities. It demonstrated, so they believed, that Hamilton's schemes encouraged greedy spongers and were thus inimical to a virtuous republic. With her keen eye trained on national politics, Abigail Adams privately observed: "The southern members are determined to ruin the Secretary of the Treasury, destroy all his well-built systems, [and] if possible give a fatal stab to the funding system."[40]

By this point Hamilton was well aware that Madison and Jefferson had grown "personally unfriendly" and were convinced he was trying to destroy the new nation for which he and Washington had both had horses shot out from under them—risking life and limb for years on end during the Revolution. (Neither Madison nor Jefferson ever served in battle.) Hamilton was especially mystified by Madison's "extraordinary" turnabout since, as he told a former fellow officer in Virginia, "I know for a certainty it was a primary article of his Creed that the real danger in our system was the subversion of National authority by the preponderancy of the State Governments." Hamilton began to attribute the Jeffersonians' animosity to an "unsound and dangerous" partiality toward everything French. In the unashamedly gendered discourse of the times, he described his opponents as blinded by a "womanish attachment to France and a womanish resentment against Great Britain."[41]

Hamilton's comment reflects the extent to which foreign policy considerations began to shadow domestic disagreements. Nothing split the founding generation more deeply than its perceptions of the conflict between France and Britain. Turmoil in Europe complicated every dispute the young nation had with the great powers and exposed it constantly to fresh hazards. In their reactions to the revolutionary violence that wracked France, former friends found themselves divided as if by a cleaver. Political factions turned into political parties. Washington ruefully observed, "I had no conceptions that parties would, or even could go, the length I have been witness to." Jefferson concurred that polite discourse among "gentlemen of different politics" had come to an end. "Men who have been intimate all their lives cross the streets to avoid meeting, and turn their heads another way, lest they should be obliged to touch their hats."[42]

The distant spectacle across the sea assumed the character of a morality tale in which audience members became deeply, emotionally involved, and from which they drew diametrically opposed lessons. To Jeffersonians, France acted the part of America and Britain acted its old role as arch villain, subverting liberty wherever the downtrodden took to arms in self-defense. To Federalists, Britain was defender of the peace, especially after Napoleon Bonaparte conquered much of Europe. French fanaticism made a parody of republican government, they believed. It undermined the good in France's own revolution and could easily, if it spread, destabilize the American experiment. If that should happen, Hamilton warned, "one may as well preach moderation to the Winds as to our zealots." The survival of the infant American government rested on the fragile cooperation of its leaders, and yet, he noted, "statesmen are but men and far more actuated by their passions than they ought to be."[43]

By the second national election, in 1792, when Jefferson and Hamilton could still bear to be in each other's presence in Washington's cabinet, all members of America's revolutionary generation were well aware of the disastrous decline of government in France, then three years into its revolution.

Gouverneur Morris of New York, who had replaced Thomas Jefferson as America's representative in Paris, was an eyewitness to the atrocities. As he scribbled to his predecessor, in a single week "of uncheck'd Murders . . . thousands have perishd in this City." The mere accusation of counterrevolution was enough to result in grotesque lynchings. Although only one woman had been killed that week, Morris noted, "she was beheaded and embowelled, the Head and Entrails were paraded on pikes thro the Street and the Body dragged after them."[44] William Short, Jefferson's friend and former secretary, wrote that the Parisian streets were literally "red with blood" from the work of "those mad and corrupted people in France who under the name of liberty have destroyed their own government."[45]

Jefferson was disappointed in William Short's reports. He confessed, "The tone of your letters had for some time given me pain, on account of the extreme warmth with which they censured the proceedings of the Jacobins of France." The arrest and mortal peril of the Marquis de Lafayette, Count de Rochambeau, and many others who had served America valiantly at Yorktown prompted the further comment: "My own affections have been deeply wounded by some of the martyrs to this cause, but rather than it should have failed, I would have seen half the earth desolated. Were there but an Adam and an Eve left in every country, and left free, it would be better than as it now is. I have expressed to you my sentiments, because they are really those of 99 in an hundred of our citizens."[46]

Jefferson was correct in his assessment of American feeling. Jacobin fever was catching. There were many in the States who agreed that radical excesses were necessary and deserved. France's antiaristocratic turn deepened antiauthoritarian sentiments like those expressed in Shays's Rebellion. Insufficient ardor for France was equated with support for Britain, which was equated with betrayal of America. Hamilton, of course, became an early target. The secretary of the treasury was "averse to liberty" and had "calculated to undermine and demolish the republic," Jefferson told President Washington in September 1792.[47] John Adams, who warned that "Dragons' teeth have been sown in France and will come up as monsters," also attracted suspicion. Even the president, whose "want of confidence" in the French Revolution depressed Jefferson, was suspect.[48] Unwilling to concede that the Hero of Valley Forge might honestly disagree with them for valid reasons, Jefferson and Madison increasingly described the general as the enfeebled dupe of a conniving Hamilton. Venomous whispers eventually ended the personal relationship between the two Republicans and their widely revered Mount Vernon neighbor.

Both the international and domestic climates worsened after the wet, cold morning of January 21, 1793, when Louis XVI, dressed in a simple shirt, was guillotined in front of a cheering throng of Parisians. After news of the execution reached the young nation whose revolution the king had funded and defended in 1776, Philip Freneau's *National Gazette* ran the unsympathetic headline: "Louis Capet has lost his caput." Anyone critical of the act betrayed "a strong remaining attachment to royalty" or belonged to "a monarchical junto," the newspaper claimed.[49] Meanwhile, France declared war on England and the Netherlands, having earlier declared war against Austria for abetting exiled aristocrats.

President Washington immediately pronounced U.S. neutrality, though some questioned his authority to do so, since only Congress had the power to declare war and thus, presumably, its opposite. Secretary of State Jefferson viewed France as the victim in the pan-European war, and hoped Congress might respond with an economic boycott, excluding "from our ports all the manufactures, produce, vessels and subjects of the nations committing this aggression." He advocated economic coercion as the safest and most honorable resort in foreign relations. Denying belligerent nations the dollars they might earn in American markets would "introduce between nations another umpire than arms. It would relieve us too," he added casually, "from the risks and the horrors of cutting throats."[50] The "umpire," to borrow Jefferson's word, would use marketplace sanctions as preferable to muskets.

The following month, Jefferson made his single most important contribution as secretary of state, establishing the de facto rule of recognition. The United States, he argued to President Washington, was honor bound to receive republican France's new minister and fulfill all commitments formerly made to Louis XVI. The king's death in no way diminished American treaty obligations, since the United States had pledged itself to France and thus the French people by the Treaties of Alliance and Commerce of 1778. Although Hamilton disagreed that the United States was still obligated to defend its ally militarily, the treasury secretary concurred that the new minister should be welcomed, since every "nation has a right, in its own discretion, to change its form of government—to abolish one, and substitute another."[51]

This de facto rule required acknowledging the credentials of whatever government held power, regardless of how it got there. The rule remained standard American policy up until Woodrow Wilson's presidency. Notably, Jefferson himself made the single nineteenth-century exception to this rule when he refused as president to recognize the government of Haiti, which had come to power by overthrowing slavery. (Abraham Lincoln became the first president to accept a minister from the island nation.)

The de facto rule was the last thing on which Jefferson and Hamilton agreed. In December 1793, Secretary of State Jefferson fired his final broadside across the deck of Congress. Every single nation of Europe engaged in trade discrimination, he reported. Yet the United States wanted commerce "relieved from all it's [sic] shackles in all parts of the world." America preferred to obtain free trade through friendly negotiation, but when that failed, Jefferson urged, "it behooves us to protect our Citizens, their Commerce and Navigation, by Counter-prohibitions, Duties, and Regulations. . . . Free commerce and navigation are not to be given in exchange for Restrictions, and Vexations: nor are they likely to produce a relaxation of them."[52] Two weeks later Jefferson resigned from Washington's cabinet, quitting the battle within the administration and leaving the field in Congress to his bosom friend, James Madison.

Internal discord worsened in tandem with the European war. Despite its best efforts between 1789 and 1794, Washington's administration had been unable to reach a trade agreement with Britain. It still needed to resolve old issues such as the continued British occupation of forts on American soil and U.S. exclusion from the West Indies, as well as new demands arising from the Anglo-French feud. One of these new issues was President Washington's hope that Britain would leniently interpret a long-standing rule that forbade *in wartime* any trade that mercantilism made *illegal in peacetime*. A profitable new trade with France depended on this interpretation.

France's merchant marine was fully occupied in supporting its navy. Normally excluded from French colonial ports by mercantilist laws, American shippers sought to replace the French vessels that usually brought goods back and forth between the mother country and its colonies. This wartime "carrying trade," as it was called, was immensely lucrative for neutral shippers. With a smaller navy and merchant marine than Britain, France had greater need for neutral carriers in wartime. Also, by the terms of its original treaty with America, France had obligated itself in 1778 to abide by the legal formulation "free ships make free goods." This was a principle that the seafaring Dutch had championed for more than a hundred years and managed to introduce into several bilateral treaties. It allowed a neutral nation to carry all the goods of its ally's enemy except contraband (that is, military supplies). Traditionally, even an enemy's civilian goods were liable to confiscation wherever found. But "free ships" made "free goods," rendering an enemy's civilian property "free" (protected) when shipped under the flag of a "free" (neutral) vessel. The Franco-American treaty of 1778 thus allowed the United States to supply France's enemy, Britain. George Washington wanted Britain to allow the United States to do the same for France.

But Britain was unwilling to grant this leniency. Since the United Kingdom had no commercial treaty with the United States, it had no obligation whatsoever to honor liberal provisions to which it had never agreed. Why should Britain allow Americans to help France when it had a giant navy to stop them?

This was not just a hypothetical question. Short of cash, both France and Britain temporarily opened their Caribbean ports to American merchants in early 1794. Fully half of the U.S. commercial fleet was enticed southward, where it loaded up on goods from both nations. Then, in the first week of March, British warships swooped down and arrested 250 American vessels found in French ports or carrying French property to markets abroad. They forced the merchantmen into British and Dutch ports, and kept 150 ships as legal spoils of war. (The legality of these actions was decided by hastily arranged "prize courts"—judges who ruled on merchant seizures in times of war, and "condemned" cargoes or ships found in violation of international precedents regarding contraband or colonial trade.) Insult was added to injury when one judge lectured a group of stranded, dispossessed American mariners, saying they were "Bad men, supplying the wants of Bad Men in a Bad Cause."[53]

The American public howled for retribution. On George Washington's request, Congress approved a provisional embargo that prevented foreign and domestic merchant ships from entering or leaving American ports for two months.[54] American ships would be out of harm's way, and European merchantmen might feel the pinch. Republicans tried to engineer a stricter prohibition aimed solely at Britain, but Vice President John Adams cast the tie-breaking vote against the bill.[55] Washington also dispatched John Jay to London to try once again to obtain a commercial treaty or, at the least, redress for the most recent events. He then requisitioned the very first U.S. warship under the Constitution, appealing to Congress's new power to "provide and maintain a navy."

John Jay, one of the three faces of the former Publius, was a sophisticated New York lawyer with significant experience in previous negotiations with Spain, England, and France. But he had little leverage. Britain's war with its historic rival had become all consuming. Measured against that struggle, American desires counted for little. Britain intended to use every legal provision at its disposal to hurt France, including that which prohibited the kinds of trade during wartime that mercantilism restricted during peacetime. Nonetheless, Jay was able to win several important concessions from the British, including withdrawal of the Redcoats at last from their occupation of forts in the American northwest, limited access to the British West Indies for American shippers, and most-favored-nation status in British home ports. (Most-favored-nation privileges did not amount to much during wartime, since trade was already so compromised.) Jay also won agreement to an arbitration commission of three people to peaceably resolve a boundary dispute with Canada. Both countries would appoint representatives, to whose findings they pledged to submit.

In exchange for these privileges, Jay withdrew the American demand for "free ships make free goods" and agreed to swallow British restrictions on neutrals' rights for the duration of the war with France, plus two years. Commercial retaliation and discriminatory tariffs imposed by Congress— threatened by James Madison for six years—were finally off the table. Britain would compensate Americans $10 million for the ships it had already seized but would retaliate without apology for any further trading with France. These terms should not have been surprising. London officials could hardly relinquish their most effective economic weapon against France (cutting it off from colonial suppliers). And without a navy, the United States could not coerce them.[56]

A compromise that looks reasonable by the light of today felt insufferable to Americans at the time. Although Jay's Treaty, as it was called, sent the last Redcoat packing and averted a potential war over ship seizures, President Washington recognized that domestic audiences would consider it a disaster. He delayed submitting the treaty to the Senate in hopes of finding an optimal moment to present the bitter terms, and then asked the senators to debate them in secret. (When pressed by events, even George Washington was not above bending the new rules of transparency.) Congress passed the measure with the bare minimum of votes required, almost entirely out of respect for the general. In a remarkable display of physical courage, former artillery captain Alexander Hamilton defended the treaty in an impromptu speech to an unruly crowd of 500 protestors in New York, but was forced to retreat when people began throwing stones, one of which hit him in the face. Protest rallies in Boston, Philadelphia, Baltimore, and Charleston hung the "damned arch traitor" John Jay in effigy, and on the Fourth of July, towns and villages across America flew the flag at half-mast.[57]

In Virginia, Jefferson passed along the rumor that a preoccupied president had given up the helm to traitors: "Our part of the country is in considerable fermentation," he wrote. "They say that while all hands were below deck mending sails, splicing ropes, and every one at his own business, and the captain in the cabbin attending to his log-book and chart, a rogue of a pilot [Hamilton] has run them into an enemy's port.—But metaphor apart, there is much dissatisfaction with Mr. Jay and his treaty."[58]

Jay's Treaty, and the Alien and Sedition Acts that came later in the decade in response to virulent factionalism and French meddling, prompted the first serious assertions of state autonomy from the federal union. Thomas Jefferson secretly authored the Kentucky Resolutions of 1798, and James Madison anonymously penned the Virginia Resolution that passed on Christmas Eve the same year. Both bills proclaimed the inalienable sovereignty of the states. The United States was naught but a coalition, or "compact," devised for "special purposes." And so, Jefferson claimed, "as in all other cases of compact among powers having no common judge, each party has an equal right to judge for itself . . . of infractions." In other words, the federal government was *not* a "common judge" or umpire with sovereignty over the states. The individual states might cancel any federal laws that were predicated on powers not specifically delegated by the Constitution. Jefferson called this veto the state's "natural right" of "nullification."[59] Madison more obliquely called it the state's duty "to interpose itself," especially if the federal government tried to fuse the states "into one sovereignty."[60] Neither Kentucky nor Virginia tried to nullify specific laws at this point, but they declared their right to do so.

Disgruntled Americans were not the only ones outraged by Jay's Treaty. Frenchmen balked as well. Because Louis XVI had previously granted extravagant neutrals' rights to the United States, the new Anglo-American commercial agreement put revolutionary France at a grave disadvantage. When the United States agreed not to challenge English raids on neutral commerce going to France, America's former ally took it as gross ingratitude for the money, arms, and blood that France had poured into America's revolution.[61] One can hardly blame them for feeling betrayed.

But blame them Americans did, when France unilaterally renounced its obligations under the revolutionary-era Treaty of Amity and Commerce and retaliated by seizing more than 300 unarmed U.S. merchant ships in the six months following the signing of the Jay Treaty. President Washington and his successor, John Adams, stepped up their warship program. Congress created a permanent Department of the Navy in 1798, followed by official establishment of the Marine Corps. The government launched its first three frigates in May that year (including the USS *Constitution,* still afloat today in Boston harbor), and President Adams obtained congressional authorization for an additional two dozen. By then, the United States was waist deep in the so-called Quasi-War with France, during which it captured more than eighty-five French vessels. Adams remained stubbornly coolheaded, however, and finally negotiated a settlement that peacefully terminated the Treaty of Amity and Commerce with France in 1800.

Foreign relations fatefully split the founders. Hamilton ultimately lost his life. Although Jefferson was later depicted cheek to cheek with Washington on Mount Rushmore, he ruined their friendship with his rumormongering. In the last two years of Washington's life, the general ceased corresponding with the fellow Virginian he began calling *"that man."* When Washington passed away, Jefferson declined to attend the memorial service for America's first president.[62] The French Revolution had fatefully transformed the American Revolution and helped to crystallize a party system.

Thomas Jefferson beat John Adams in the fourth contest for the presidency shortly thereafter, helped by the Federalists' internal disagreement over Adams's unpopular compromise. Opposed in principle to a blue-water navy, anxious to shrink the national debt, and hoping to reverse the expansion of government power under the first two chief executives, a new Republican majority in Congress authorized Jefferson to sell, scrap, or moth-ball the new naval vessels. From 42 warships, the U.S. Navy shrank to only 6 ships in the water. Great Britain, in contrast, had 864 vessels, including 180 massive "ships of the line." Benjamin Stoddert, the first naval secretary, left office with Adams. Gone was the defense barrier that Stoddert hoped would "prevent the squadrons of a strong maritime enemy from penetrating into American waters."[63]

Jefferson suffered no doubts about the wisdom of this course. Secure at last, America would now pioneer the new norms of international relations of which Enlightenment thinkers had long dreamed. Yet the volatility of Europe made such innovations particularly challenging between 1800 and 1815. To achieve almost any of Jefferson's goals, the federal government needed extraordinary powers vis-à-vis the states: precisely what the lanky Virginian had long abhorred.

3

Another Umpire than Arms

Or, How Economic Sanctions Became
a Tool of Foreign Relations, 1800–1815

When he took office, Thomas Jefferson sought to heal at least some of the wounds of the preceding decade, declaring at his inauguration (which John Adams pointedly skipped), "We are all republicans: we are all federalists." Jefferson was fortunate to look out upon an international environment that was temporarily less complicated than that confronted by either of his predecessors—at least for the United States. Gone was the liberal, revolutionary-era treaty of 1778 with France. In its place was the uncomfortable but practical modus vivendi that John Jay had shaped with Great Britain.

The new president believed that the United States finally had its international competitors right where it wanted them. They would have to yield to the logic of the marketplace and grant Americans the terms they had long sought. As he put it, "Our commerce is so valuable to them that they will be glad to purchase it when the only price we ask is to do us justice."[1] What Jefferson meant by justice was generous, self-sacrificing treatment toward neutral American merchants during wartime, and full access during peacetime to European colonial markets in the West Indies and elsewhere. Unfortunately these two goals were as likely as pie in the sky during what historians have since called the Age of Revolutions.[2] Nonetheless, Jefferson grasped the tool of economic coercion for his party, and it became the basis of a distinctly Republican foreign policy.[3] Even if belligerents initially refused to play along, they would eventually see that it was in their economic interest to compromise—or so he thought.

Jefferson called his policy "peaceable coercion." It was not a uniquely Jeffersonian tactic; the colonists had used it in their earlier sugar and tea boycotts. Nor was it necessarily an American tactic, as "peaceable coercions . . . are in the power of every nation," Jefferson wrote in 1801. They were a tool even the weak might wield. But economic duress became identified with the third president because he projected it onto a larger stage, and with greater consequences, than anyone else. These measures expressed Jefferson's imaginative groping toward a new ideal of arbitration. Sanctions like embargoes and discriminatory tariffs were an alternative to war. They created incentives for negotiation by making war unprofitable.

The policy recognized that both sellers and consumers had much to gain from open international markets, and that they would pressure governments to make whatever political concessions were necessary to keep goods flowing. Economic sanctions adopted by the legislature were also transparent: they candidly announced government goals and demanded an equally public response by other nations. Within days of his inauguration, Jefferson expressed confidence that with "the return of republican ascendancy" under his administration, the government finally had in its hands "the means of peaceable coercion" to bring "freedom to the ocean."[4]

The ideas were transformative. In the long run, they pointed humanity in new directions. In the short run, they led to a ruinous war that just missed splitting the nation in two.

Up to this point, America had been relatively lucky. War without quarter had ensnared nearly every nation of Europe and spilled over into South America. In 1797, when Napoleon Bonaparte first devised plans for the invasion of the British Isles, he commented to Foreign Minister Talleyrand that they needed merely to "destroy England [and] Europe is at our feet."[5] By Jefferson's 1801 inaugural, the French Republic was well on its way to becoming the Napoleonic Empire, surrounded by conquered states and intimidated allies from Spain to Scandinavia. Napoleon had defeated armies fielded by Italy, Austria, Russia, Prussia, Egypt, Spain, the Dutch Republic, and the Ottoman Empire. He became a virtual dictator as first consul, and within a few years crowned himself emperor, conclusively ending France's first experiment with republican, nonmonarchical government. In time, nearly a million Frenchmen died for Napoleon's ambitions.[6]

Jefferson's enthusiasm for France waned, though as late as 1802 he described Napoleonic France as "our natural friend" whose "growth . . . we viewed as our own, her misfortunes ours."[7] At no point during the Napoleonic Wars did the president and his party falter in their belief that Britain was America's (indeed, the world's) primary enemy. Jefferson's overweening Anglophobia convinced him that the United Kingdom was simply using Napoleon's aggression as an excuse to strangle America in its cradle. Jefferson refused to see a rational fear of Napoleon in England's actions and attributed them instead to jealousy of America's national aspirations.[8] Every British measure to deprive the French dictator of resources was primarily intended to harm America, the president believed, and only secondarily France. In other words, the European catastrophe was really about the United States.

During Jefferson's first administration, however, the nation benefitted significantly from continental disasters. The president had little need to implement the economic coercions he was primed to deploy. In 1800, Napoleon tricked Spain out of its colony of Louisiana by promising to exchange it for holdings in Europe that the first consul never actually relinquished. Napoleon planned to use North America as a supply depot for the French sugar colony of Saint-Domingue (later called Haiti), and then reestablish a strong empire west of the Mississippi. (France had previously lost Louisiana to Spain as a consequence of the Seven Years' War, which ended in 1763.) Within three years, however, a successful slave rebellion resulted in Haitian independence and rendered Louisiana both useless and indefensible. In a surprise move, Napoleon offered to sell the vast western lands to the United States. Thrilled at the opportunity to purchase Louisiana for the pittance of $15 million (three cents per acre), Jefferson set aside his constitutional scruples against expansive federal powers. Striking the bargain, he added almost 83,000 square miles to America's agricultural domain. This well served Jefferson's political philosophy, as he had earlier expressed it to Madison, because the new territory ensured that "our governments will remain virtuous for many centuries; as long as they are chiefly agricultural." Louisiana meant that Americans would not be "piled upon one another in large cities, as in Europe."[9]

Bonaparte's motivation was more Machiavellian. Calculating to the nth degree, he later explained, "I would have given it to them for nothing, for . . . I could not have protected it and the English would have taken it."[10] Bonaparte worried little about the new prowess with which the acquisition of Louisiana might endow the United States. Jefferson's nation would eventually break apart anyway, Napoleon believed, owing to internal rivalries. Con-

federations like the United States that styled themselves "perpetual," he remarked in 1803, "only last till one of the contracting parties finds it to its
interest to break them." England was France's only real obstacle to world
mastery, and for the time being, America was a useful makeweight against
the ancient opponent. As the first consul commented on transferring Louisiana, "This accession of territory . . . strengthens for ever the power of the
United States; and I have just given to England a maritime rival, that will
sooner or later humble her pride."[11]

The fierce European wars also benefitted the United States by stimulating
a dramatic expansion in agricultural exports and the carrying trade, despite
attempts by the belligerents to put neutral suppliers out of business. Between
the outbreak of the Anglo-French War in 1793 and the start of Jefferson's first
administration, the sale of American products abroad and earnings from
neutral shipping nearly quadrupled. The value of U.S. exports went from $26
million per year to $93 million. Lulls in fighting diminished profits. During
the short-lived Peace of Amiens (March 1802 to May 1803), U.S. exports
plunged almost by half (from $93 million in 1801 down to $51 million in
1802).[12] With the resumption of war, France and England both eagerly reem-
ployed the United States as a neutral carrier. They also used their navies to
seize any American ships they could get their hands on: denying contraband
to each other and preventing any colonial trade that was illegal in peacetime,
and thus subject to confiscation in wartime. But the risks to American shipping were worthwhile overall. Highly profitable cargoes that got through
well made up for those seized.

During his first administration, Jefferson thus found it expedient to tolerate violations of neutrals' rights. He held back on the retaliatory measures he
and Madison had long championed. If the government now implemented
new discriminatory tariffs against Britain, Treasury Secretary Albert Gallatin cautioned the president in 1805, "every measure of retaliation which we
may adopt, however well calculated for that object, will diminish the revenue."[13] Republican "small government" principles prohibited most forms of
internal taxation, so the administration was forced to rely heavily on tariffs to
meet the government's expenses. Retaliatory taxes on imports to punish
Great Britain would also discourage the consumption of said imports, diminishing tariff revenues. Federal income would decline. So, like Washington and Adams, Jefferson found himself making the most of an uncomfortable situation.

That is, until the explosive international climate changed again. In 1805, a flotilla under British admiral Horatio Nelson finally shattered Bonaparte's navy. In battling the French for twelve years, the unflagging five-foot-six Nelson had lost an arm and an eye, and then, off Spain's Cape Trafalgar, finally lost his life when a French sniper entwined high in the rigging of an enemy ship shot down at him from the crosstrees. Yet Nelson died fulfilled. At Trafalgar he extinguished Napoleon's long-standing plan of a cross-channel invasion. Relieved but still wary, the English took no chances and continued building stone fortifications called Martello towers (still visible today) along the coastlines of Great Britain, Canada, and Ireland, to watch for sails from the Continent. Fatefully, Nelson's victory also swept the Atlantic virtually clean of French frigates and merchantmen, freeing Britain to crack down harder on American neutral trade.

The consequence of Trafalgar was a stalemate. Britain became paramount at sea, France paramount on land. This drove both Britain and France to intensify economic warfare as a supplement to the clash of arms. In May 1806, Britain declared a blockade against all territory under Napoleon's control, which was most of Western Europe. Blockade was an old form of warfare designed to starve an enemy and prey on neutral shipping. Any vessel caught trying to breach a blockade was subject to legal condemnation under accepted prize-court rules. There was plenty of incentive for English sailors to enforce the rule, as every man on board got a cut of the cash from confiscated goods and ships. For the first time in the war, which had been going on for thirteen years, American products were effectively closed off from European markets.

Napoleon retaliated in November 1806 with the Continental System. This system combined a sham or "paper" blockade of the British Isles (which Bonaparte could hardly enforce, given his depleted navy) with something even more ambitious. Napoleon required economic integration within his empire, compelling subordinate nations to participate in a closed, coordinated system that in theory pooled resources for regional development. French historian Louis Bergernon calls the Continental System a "one way common market," since its real purpose was to serve France alone. British goods were excluded from Europe, to deprive the United Kingdom of income as well as protect French manufactures that lagged technologically. Other Europeans were forced to buy French goods despite their relative costliness. Bilateral treaties, forced on other states, effectively treated them as colonies under mercantilist restrictions. For example, the system required Italy to send its raw silk to Lyons, France, and to import finished fabric from French weavers rather than from the Swiss textile producers that many preferred.[14]

The belligerents' use of economic weapons as a form of warfare was inventive. They took the limited tool of port blockade and expanded it into a flat embargo of the other's entire international trade, meaning all exports and imports. England tried to deny Napoleon access to the world (including the United States, Asia, Latin America, and France's own colonial markets), while France tried to deny all of the European continent to Britain. Embargo in this form was an act of war calculated to clinch the opponent's military capitulation, not an act of neutrality designed to prevent or stop physical violence.

President Jefferson and Secretary of State James Madison vehemently denounced these unprecedented restrictions. They rejected the Europeans' legal right to confiscate noncontraband goods from shippers that were caught crossing the new lines of blockade. According to international precedent, a blockade was valid only when patrolling warships physically obstructed the mouth of a given harbor, such as Le Havre on the Seine or Southampton on the Thames. A government could not simply post warships in mid-Atlantic shipping lanes (determined by ocean currents and trade winds), and then seize neutral merchants hundreds or thousands of miles from their final destination. Yet this is precisely what the belligerents now proposed to do. Empowered by Nelson's devastation of the French Navy, Great Britain was in a better position than France to carry out these obnoxious rules and deprive the enemy. American exports continued to climb profitably because of extreme wartime shortages and demands, reaching $101 million in 1806, but a greater and greater percentage of goods went to Britain, which of course allowed neutral ships to reach London. Revolutionary France, beloved by Jefferson, received less and less.

And there was worse. Britain persisted in measures that effectively denied the sovereignty of the United States. Under new laws called Orders in Council, Parliament and the Royal Navy acted as if U.S. citizens were subject to their whim. In 1795, John Jay had managed to get Britain to back down on its occupation of American soil. But neither he nor any other U.S. negotiator had ever been able to convince the United Kingdom to refrain from randomly stopping U.S. merchant ships to "impress" sailors it claimed were deserters from the British Navy, whether they were or not. Britain used press-gangs extensively at home between 1775 and 1815 to meet military manpower needs, as the nation could not rely solely on voluntary service. Men were drafted off the streets and out of pubs. With the Royal Navy's growing mastery of the seas, impressment of British males became increasingly frequent on the open ocean and in foreign ports as well.

This inability to fend off British impressment was not just a matter of wounded pride for the United States. Any nation that could not defend its boundaries and citizens had no right to exist, under the Westphalian system. There was no pope, empire, or transnational authority to sustain such an entitlement. Newly fledged, the American eagle had urgent cause to demand that England refrain from seizing its citizens and dragooning them into service. In this dangerous and competitive world, weak nations were prey. Between 1803 and 1812, more than 6,000 sailors were taken off U.S. ships at gunpoint.[15]

Britain had equal cause to continue impressment, however, as Jefferson and many others well knew. The United States had pushed its export trade to dizzying heights with the help of British tars. As early as 1793, the English home secretary estimated that "one half of the Crews which navigate the American merchant ships are British seaman."[16] American pay was better, discipline more relaxed, and duties less dangerous than on royal men-of-war. Desertion from Britain and immigration to America were two sides of the same coin. The United States claimed that anyone could become an American, and port authorities sold certificates of U.S. citizenship for thirty-seven dollars—slightly more than a month's wages for an able seaman.[17] The British subscribed to the widespread, customary definition of citizenship as a function of birthplace, a definition that gave government the right to call up citizens for service in wartime. The United States, however, chose to adopt a free and easy process for naturalization that gave individuals the right of self-definition, and it refused to cooperate in the extradition of deserters. When an American negotiator tentatively offered such cooperation in 1804 to stem growing animosity, his British counterpart questioned whether the federal government even had the authority to induce states to turn over sailors wanted for questioning.[18]

The truth was that the Jefferson administration, despite its vehement self-righteousness, had little interest in resolving the problem in an equitable manner. In early 1807, President Jefferson asked Treasury Secretary Albert Gallatin what it would cost the United States to turn away British seamen.

Gallatin undertook a survey concerning "the whole number of our seaman and the proportion of British subjects among them." He found the number so high (approaching 50 percent) that he advised the president not to offer Whitehall a quid pro quo. Any promise not to employ British sailors "would materially damage our navigation, much more than any restrictions . . . they could lay upon our commerce," Gallatin wrote President Jefferson. Ending impressment was simply not worth the commercial "sacrifice."[19]

This was a dangerous game. Had Jefferson acknowledged that impressment and trade harassment were reasonable gambles for the unusual profits of wartime trade, as the Federalists in effect had done by signing Jay's humiliating but prudent treaty, the brutal War of 1812 might have been avoided. But the Republican government was reluctant to admit it would compromise citizens' safety in order to sustain the lucrative carrying trade. Instead, Jefferson disingenuously insisted that Britain was entirely at fault. It was politic as well as gratifying for Jefferson to believe that Britain's Orders in Council were designed primarily to undermine the United States, not to hurt France and defend England's own people. His followers concurred. The British were "disturbers and destroyers of nations, [who] burn with infuriated rage toward us and fasten on our neutrality as the pretext for depredation," charged the Tammany Society of New York, a Republican club.[20]

When friends questioned the wisdom of hitching American peace to wartime profits, Jefferson sometimes reacted with preachy, anti-British venom.[21] But he also believed in the inherent morality of neutral trade rights. Indeed, time vindicated his values: neutral trade rights were subsequently written into international law over the next two centuries. Jefferson's defensiveness probably stemmed mostly from his recognition of the potential folly of adhering to these principles when other nations had not yet adopted them. Yet he was unable to think of any better way to start on the road to a distant goal. One choice was "to stand with respect to Europe precisely on the footing of China," Jefferson wrote early in his career, referring to China's policy of forbidding its citizens to engage in international trade or travel. In other words, the nation could avoid foreign wars by avoiding foreigners. Yet Americans had a "decided taste for navigation and commerce" that rendered this impossible, Jefferson noted. They wished to throw "open all the doors of commerce" worldwide. As there was "no great probability that Europe will do this," Jefferson remarked, "I suppose we shall be obliged to adopt a system which may shackle them in our ports as they do us in theirs."[22]

The fatal clash between the world as Jefferson wanted it and the world as it was came in 1807. On June 22, the United States' warship USS *Chesapeake* was out to sea, readying itself for a long Mediterranean voyage, when it sighted the sails of His Majesty's Ship *Leopard* ten miles off the low Virginia coastline. The American commodore chose to keep the men at their tasks and not beat to quarters, despite standard practice at the approach of another nation's vessel. On board were four sailors from the Royal Navy who had jumped ship in Norfolk, Virginia: three Americans who had previously volunteered for the Royal Navy (including two African Americans) and one sailor of British birth. HMS *Leopard* sent a boat with an officer to request that the USS *Chesapeake* muster its men and allow a search.

By definition, naval ships are an extension of a nation's territory. Yielding to an inspection under duress would have been equivalent to granting the Redcoats one more chance to occupy New York. Commodore James Barron refused the demand and quietly gave the order, too late, for his men to clear the cluttered decks, load their empty cannons, and brace themselves for battle. Before the Americans could properly prepare, HMS *Leopard* launched its broadsides, killing three men outright and disabling eighteen. The wounded Commodore Barron now offered his surrender, but the British captain declined to accept it, boarded the *Chesapeake,* and took the four deserters. A British court-martial two months later decided to hang the British sailor and give the three American deserters a suspended sentence of 500 lashes apiece.[23]

Impressing seamen off private merchant ships was one thing, but disabling a U.S. naval warship quite another. The American public erupted in fury. Residents of Norfolk bashed water casks meant for British ships, and 4,000 residents marched behind the coffin of the last *Chesapeake* defender who died of his wounds. New Yorkers sabotaged a British ship in Manhattan's harbor, and Philadelphians sawed the rudder off an English merchantman and paraded it before the residence of the British consul. Up and down the Eastern Seaboard, spontaneous rallies urged residents to prepare for invasion and war. Jefferson expelled the British Navy from American waters. Secretary of State Madison registered a protest through James Monroe, then U.S. minister in London: "The immunity of a National ship of war from every species and purpose of search on the high seas, has never been contested by any nation."[24]

Jefferson's anger initially led him to welcome war with Britain as an opportunity to "settle the old and the new."[25] He was not alone. Feelings ran especially high around the anniversary of independence in July. The president compared American sentiments with the wrath felt at the time of Lexington and Concord. Albert Gallatin wrote a friend that, should war come, "We will be poorer, both as a nation and as a government," but such a conflict might awaken "nobler feelings and habits than avarice and luxury . . . to prevent our degenerating, like the Hollanders, into a nation of mere calculators." But it would cost. Gallatin reckoned on a budgetary shortfall of several million, to be borrowed from private banks.[26] Gallatin's comment about the Dutch showed how far the Republicans had drifted from the position of the physiocrats, to whom calculating merchants exhibited just the right attitude—allowing economic disincentives to douse hot tempers.

The summer passed without a war. British ships stayed away from American shores as Jefferson requested, although he and his cabinet spent the majority of July analyzing strategies of attack and defense. The nation now had only a miniscule army, and the state militias were unreliable. Nonetheless, Jefferson itched to retaliate. His hand was restrained partly by the knowledge that more than 2,500 U.S. merchant ships were then away at sea, with commercial cargoes valued at more than $100 million. They were sitting ducks for British guns if the president declared war. He needed to wait for them to sail home. As summer waned into autumn, Gallatin recommended restraint. U.S. ports were unfortified and there were no plans for remedying this state of affairs. If New York, New Orleans, or Charleston fell to the enemy, the treasury secretary pointed out to Jefferson, "The executive especially would be particularly liable to censure for having urged immediate war whilst so unprepared against the attack." Only Federalist "anglomen" would benefit.[27] Meanwhile, both Paris and London tightened their systems of trade exclusion.

If ever a time called for experiments in peaceable coercion, this was it. Even before the *Chesapeake* incident, Elbridge Gerry of Massachusetts pointed out to Madison the potential utility of a general embargo of American trade—cutting the nation off from a world gone mad until either Europe came to its senses or the United States girded itself properly for war.[28] Other friends also urged Jefferson to announce an embargo, an idea that had been in the air for decades.[29] Desperate for American supplies and for American help with shuttling colonial goods, the British and French would capitulate immediately, they believed. One correspondent wrote, "We have only to Shut our ports & *remain firm*—the *People* of *England* would do the rest . . . and *compel* the [Prime] Minister to open our ports at *any price,* or they would Massacre him."[30]

On December 18, 1807, President Jefferson asked Congress to seal off the nation. Americans would be prohibited from exporting any goods whatsoever. Foreign ships loaded with outbound cargo in U.S. ports could depart with what they had already taken on board, but nothing more. Any U.S. merchant who wished to transport goods up or down the coast would have to post a bond guaranteeing that the cargo would stay within the country. If it ended up elsewhere, the merchant would forfeit his deposit, worth twice as much as ship and cargo combined.[31] Under Jefferson's new law, Americans could receive the world's goods, but they could not send out any of their own. Congress passed the embargo almost without debate. Oddly, the only people that the law coerced were Americans themselves.

The dirty work of enforcement fell to Secretary of the Treasury Albert Gallatin, the cabinet member least enthusiastic about the measure. War itself would be preferable to a lengthy embargo, he had advised Jefferson. "Governmental prohibitions do always more mischief than had been calculated," he reminded America's chief barker for limited government, "and it is not without much hesitation that a statesman should hazard to regulate the concerns of individuals as if he could do it better than themselves."[32] Nonetheless, it was Gallatin's responsibility to implement trade laws and prevent smuggling. He made a supreme effort in the months that followed. Ironically, it was the murdered Alexander Hamilton who had made enforcement possible by organizing the Revenue Cutter Service (later renamed the U.S. Coast Guard). Its assignment was "to guard Revenue laws from all infractions, or breaches, either upon the coasts or within the bays, or upon the rivers and other waters of the United States, previous to the anchoring of vessels within the harbors for which they are respectively destined."[33]

From December 1807 until March 1809, when Jefferson left office, the administration stoutly maintained its controversial embargo. Congress's swift ratification showed an initially exuberant patriotism, and there were many expressions of popular support for a foreign policy in line with pacifist ideals. The legislature of New Hampshire declared, "We will suffer any privations rather than submit to degradation, and will cooperate with the General Government in all its measures." The legislature of Pennsylvania similarly resolved "that we consider the embargo a wise, pacific and patriotic measure, called for in the best interests of the nation . . . without a resort to the horrors and desolations of war, so repugnant to the feelings of humanity and the principles of free government."[34]

But the grinding reality of a nearly complete cessation of trade led to endemic smuggling. The embargo swiftly became the low point of Jefferson's eight years in office. Agricultural cargoes from the Southern and middle states continued to make their way north to international transshipment points in New England, or south to Amelia Island off Spanish Florida. Gallatin required governors to issue permits for interstate trade in amounts not to exceed the precise quantity required by residents, but found governors applying elastic definitions of need. Permits to sell to other states were traded outright on the docks at Alexandria, Virginia, and elsewhere, with cargoes ending up on their way to England instead.[35] Other traders sailed under cover of darkness without filing bond and secretly rendezvoused with British ships that took the goods to Halifax, Nova Scotia, or other British ports on the Great Lakes or in the Caribbean. Some exporters were even bolder. An armed mob on the wharf at Newburyport, Massachusetts, prevented customs officers from interfering with one ship that sailed in broad daylight. At Oswego, New York, open insurrection required the governor to dispatch the militia.[36]

Gallatin was pessimistic. "The embargo is now defeated," he told Jefferson in August 1808, "by open violations, by vessels sailing without any clearances whatsoever; an evil which, under the existing law, we cannot oppose in any way but by cruisers."[37] Jefferson had to call out the remnants of the very navy he had previously scuppered. Republican governor James Sullivan of Massachusetts warned the president that the embargo was wrecking support for the party. Petitions from rural towns poured into Boston, and the state legislature formally protested in February 1809: "Commerce has been one of the chief employments of the people of New England, from the first settlement of the country. . . . Governments have hardly ever succeeded in changing the habits of a great people; and most certainly in a free country it cannot be attempted with any prospect of success."[38] The export figures for the United States proved the point. Foreign trade fell from $108 million in 1807 to $22 million in 1808. Jefferson could severely restrict U.S. trade, but he could not stop it dead.[39]

Public anger brought assassination threats, including one from a man trying to feed six children "in a starving condition" with no hope of work on the idled wharves. He warned Jefferson: "If you don't take off the embargo . . .

you will be shott. . . . You are one of the greatest tirants in the whole world. You are wurs than Bonaparte." A man from Boston began his letter with the salutation, "You Infernal Villain." The "damned Embargo" had led to his son's death from malnutrition. Yet another correspondent, a self-supporting widow, asked for pity on her and her "Helpless orphans." They were "starved" of work and sustenance by "the imbargo."[40]

Undaunted, Jefferson strengthened enforcement against what he called the "numerous and bold evasions . . . principally under cover of the coasting trade."[41] In March 1808 the ban was widened to include trade overland to either Spanish Florida or Canada (taking the matter beyond the question of neutrals' rights at sea). By the next year, the penalty against violators approached six times the value of ship and cargo. In January 1809, Congress passed its most draconian enforcement act yet, allowing seizure of any cargo if a customs official suspected the slightest wrongdoing, and authorizing the president to use the army, navy, and state militias to enforce federal law against individual American citizens. Residents of the third ward of New York filed a protest against these measures, and especially against the caprice shown by revenue officers. "The city of New York [the island of Manhattan] receives its supplies of provisions and necessaries by boats and water craft," they reminded Congress. "We presume New York is the only city on earth, where, according to a public and formal law, the public may be starved at the mere will of a single individual."[42] Ironically, the Republican administration, strictly opposed to creative interpretations of federal prerogatives, had extended its powers far beyond anything dreamed by Alexander Hamilton.[43]

Although the extent to which the embargo squeezed France and Britain is unclear, it certainly did not cause Napoleon to modify his Continental System or Britain to revoke its Orders in Council. When Jefferson left office in 1809, Congress dropped the fifteen-month embargo against foreign trade by Americans. It substituted instead the Non-Intercourse Act against trade by Britain and France. Any ship of either nation that entered a U.S. port would be seized and condemned as prize. Americans were free to trade once again, but at their own risk. Congress authorized President Madison to drop the ban against whichever of the two belligerents revised its restrictive statutes first and promised to honor American neutral rights. When this did not work, new legislation in 1810 known as "Macon's Bill" extended trade rights to both Britain and France, but with the proviso that if one of them relented on economic restrictions, the other would be cut off. Ever wily, Napoleon

Bonaparte sensed his opportunity and now swore to drop all French measures, although he never did so in practice.

President Madison took the bait and early in 1811 reinstated the ban on British imports. A year later, citing the long history of impressment, "spilt American blood" on the *Chesapeake,* and British incitement of Indians, Madison asked Congress to declare war. The measure passed seventy-nine to forty-nine in the House, and nineteen to thirteen in the Senate. The war that followed climaxed in the 1814 burning of Washington, D.C., by Redcoats, and the 1815 slaughter of British infantry on a forsaken battlefield outside of New Orleans. American prisoners of war rotted in English jails until the middle of 1815, months after the war had ended.[44]

The War of 1812 was the United States' most unpopular and divisive foreign war, bar none. The army was unable to recruit even half the soldiers authorized by Congress. Republicans failed to pass a conscription bill. To prohibit smuggling, Madison approved a new embargo even more stringent than Jefferson's, allowing no coastal trade whatsoever, even between states of the union. Exports shrank from $108 million in 1807 to barely $7 million in 1814, compounding the nation's debts and throwing even more people out of work.[45] Long critical of Hamilton's First Bank of the United States, President Madison had allowed its charter to expire the year before the war started. Most of the nation's private banks refused to purchase war bonds, and the government nearly went bankrupt at a critical moment. Many thought Madison had trained his guns on the wrong enemy. In the words of Harrison Gray Otis, a moderate Federalist living in Boston, "The most intelligent and respectable men in the country . . . tremble for the fate of Britain, and consider her . . . as the Bulwark for the liberties of this country and mankind."[46] Others employed arguments used earlier by Jefferson and Madison. The federal government, they said, had usurped powers "never granted to the United States, but belonging more clearly to the several states."[47]

Talk of sedition spread. The threat of secession worried Madison constantly, according to Maryland attorney William Wirt. The president's "heart and mind were painfully full of the subject." Madison had little familiarity with New England, having visited it only once in his lifetime, and had to rely on reports from Republican correspondents to gauge the changing temper of the North.[48] The news was discouraging. Federalist John Lowell of Massachusetts published a popular pamphlet in 1812 called *Mr. Madison's War.* A patrician and well-known philanthropist, Lowell advocated the division of the United States. He charged that the Republican Party had violated "the great original compact." Federalist newspapers in Boston concurred that New England should ponder its choices without obligation to "a compact which has long ceased to exist." Massachusetts governor Caleb Strong sent an emissary to explore a separate peace with Britain.[49]

Protest was strong at the grassroots level as well. Town meetings across Massachusetts called for redress. "The National Government," the towns-people of Wendell complained, exhibited "a direct tendency to the Establish-ment of an Absolute tyranny over these States."[50] Calls for nullification and secession now came from the North rather than from the South, and finally prompted delegations from Massachusetts, Connecticut, Vermont, New Hampshire, and Rhode Island to meet in secret at Hartford in December 1814. Moderate Federalists dominated the meeting. Disunion was kept out of consideration, but participants demanded the states' right to mount their own military defense. They also proposed seven new amendments to the U.S. Constitution, including elimination of the infamous three-fifths clause by which the Southern states had boosted their population numbers (counting each slave as three-fifths of a human) and thereby their seats in Congress. The so-called Hartford Convention vowed to consider stronger measures if Madison ignored its counsel.

Before this could happen, however, the War of 1812 came to an abrupt end. The United States and Great Britain negotiated a peace treaty in Bel-gium that ended the conflict early in 1815, and Napoleon's defeat at Waterloo in June dissipated the continental issues that had provoked impressment and blockade. Domestic divisions quieted. Popular memory of the "disloyal" Hartford Convention damaged and eventually killed the Federalist Party. Constitutional government had weathered its first secession crisis.

Jefferson's policy of peaceable coercion failed to avert international strife. It postponed war, but arguably there would have been no clash if the United States had not tried to force the belligerents to modify their tactics or if it had been willing to forsake the services of British mariners. Moreover, Jefferson misapplied physiocratic doctrine. The Napoleonic Wars profited the United States every year that it remained neutral. Not until 1835, twenty-seven years after the embargo, did U.S. exports meet and exceed the level they reached in 1807, when Jefferson began his policy of peaceable coercion.[51] According to physiocratic theory, Jefferson and Madison would have brushed insult aside if they had been merchants, and peace would have held. This is precisely what the mercantile interests in New England wanted, which led to their near mutiny when the government insisted upon upholding Republican "honor." The British government faced similar challenges from its own commercial classes for robbing Liverpool of American trade and throwing factory laborers out of work across England and Scotland.[52] The physiocrats were correct that politicians would let pride and passion tempt them into war, ignoring economic self-interest. It would be tempting to view Jefferson's experiment as thoroughly quixotic if economic coercion were not such a prominent tool in foreign relations today.

Jefferson and Madison found that economic sanctions could easily hurt the user. They began by pointing the gun at the wrong target—American exporters—expecting them to embrace self-sacrifice. Furthermore, Jefferson did not act with integrity in regard to impressment. He demanded that other nations forgo material advantages without holding the United States to the same standard. Both presidents then allowed prejudice against one of the belligerents to overwhelm their judgment, when they could have held both French and English feet to the slow fire of nonimportation. In the end, Jefferson and Madison proved that a democracy could stand up to outside pressure and defend its own borders—leading many to call the War of 1812 the "Second American Revolution"—but they had risked unmitigated disaster in the process.[53]

Such conditions would not always apply. The United States was most remarkable at this juncture for pushing economic sanctions into the international limelight. Jefferson showed a willingness to go to daring extremes in defense of larger goals that had germinated in Europe but taken root across the Atlantic. The first goal was to ensure open access to foreign markets in both peace and war. Access during peacetime meant abolishing mercantilist doctrine and lowering tariffs. Access during wartime meant guaranteeing neutrals' rights. President Jefferson's second goal was to achieve change through negotiation. Bilateral trade treaties were a start. As Jefferson had previously suggested to Congress: "Would even a single Nation begin with the United States this System of free Commerce, it would be advisable to begin it with that nation; since it is one by one only, that it can be extended to all."[54] In time, economic sanctions would become the first resort in both trade and military wars.

Other ambitious nations in the Atlantic world had already experimented with similar techniques. In 1713, the bilateral Treaties of Utrecht first introduced the notion of most favored nation, intended to place downward pressure on tariff barriers in peacetime. The Russians, Danes, and Swedes maintained an ad hoc League of Armed Neutrality in the 1780s to defend the principle of "free ships." The rebellious thirteen colonies had begun by throwing their market doors open to the world, as did the Spanish-American colonies that proclaimed independence a few decades later.

New ideas were a fungible international currency: swapped, borrowed, traded, and used. Napoleon Bonaparte, captive and exiled at the remote edges of the Atlantic world on windswept Saint Helena, recognized their power as greater than any army or navy. Upon receiving flowers from a tearful common sailor eager to meet the little corporal who once defeated generals, Napoleon remarked: "What is the power of imagination! What it cannot do to men! . . . Yes, imagination rules the world!"[55]

Progress was not a straight line and it sometimes doubled back. The United States was not the first, nor always the firmest champion of free trade against mercantilism and closed imperial systems. After 1815, England took up the cause with much greater energy and efficacy than the United States, which adopted new protective tariffs. But the overall trends toward open markets and economic sanctions—forms of access and arbitration—were clearly visible in the history of the early republic.

4

A Rowboat in the Wake of a Battleship

*Or, How America Flagged the Continent
and Federal Power Triumphed, 1815–1865*

William Mumford, a forty-one-year-old veteran of the Mexican-American War and the father of three, watched in anger as the determined crew of the USS *Pocahontas* scaled the Confederate Mint in New Orleans on the spring morning of April 26, 1862. Above the handsome brick facade and Greek Revival columns, the proud standard of the State of Louisiana fluttered in the breeze off the Mississippi. Within moments, the blue-uniformed sailors tore down the state emblem, replacing it with the tenth flag to be hoisted over Louisiana. The invaders pointed to their gunship anchored behind the levee and warned a snarling mob that the *Pocahontas* would fire on anyone who dared to remove the Stars and Stripes.

But Mumford had already started climbing. Dodging grapeshot and exploding bricks, he and six others mounted the roof, seized the Union flag, and dragged the hated symbol to the street. From there Mumford carried the banner to City Hall. Along the way, bystanders begged for swatches until the cloth was reduced to a tiny rag that the veteran tucked proudly in his buttonhole. Yet rebel victory was brief. Spurning all pleas for clemency, General Benjamin Butler of the Union Army had Mumford hanged a month later for "resistance to the lawful authority of the Government of the United States."[1]

The Union flag atop the New Orleans Mint capped a process under way since 1519, when Iberian navigators first claimed the Mississippi Delta for the king of Spain. In the next century, French explorer Robert de LaSalle canoed the 2,300-mile length of the river with the help of native peoples, usurping and naming the entire Mississippi region "Louisiana," for the Sun King of France. After that, official sovereignty exchanged hands eight more times—from

Spain to France to Britain to the United States, and so on—until the Union Army established supremacy by force of arms. The tussle on the roof in April 1862 finally resolved two long-standing questions. Which country would dominate the North American continent, and, would the federal government indeed act as umpire if the states reached a critical impasse?

These questions took center stage in the nineteenth century. Done fighting one another after the Napoleonic Wars ended in 1815, the great European empires overspread Africa, Asia, and Oceania during the century that followed. Within just a few decades, aided by steam engines and new antimalaria drugs like quinine, the major powers established colonies from Congo to Fiji. Wherever a competitor seemed likely to establish a foothold, a race ensued. Europeans took with them a cultural practice of drawing fixed boundaries on maps, started after the Treaty of Westphalia, when Sweden and Brandenburg set the first modern border with a row of stones. Exact lines gradually replaced nebulous frontiers as empires vied to define their domains, or their power over space.[2]

Newly independent republics in the Americas were doing the same on a smaller scale, seeking borders that they also considered favorable and defensible vis-à-vis rivals. After 1811, the Viceroyalty of the Río de La Plata became Argentina, Bolivia, Uruguay, and Paraguay. In 1830, Gran Colombia fractured into Ecuador, Venezuela, and Nueva Granada. In 1823, Guatemala, El Salvador, Honduras, Nicaragua, and Costa Rica broke apart from the Mexican Empire and formed the United Provinces of Central America. In 1838 they divided again, into the five countries they are today. Texans sought separation from Mexico in 1836, and achieved it. Yucatecans sought separation in 1840 but failed.[3] And in 1865, the eleven states of the Confederacy lost their own bid for independence.

Nationalism was still in its infancy. Yucatecans did not accept that they should feel like "Mexicans" and remain loyal. Native Americans did not accept that they were "Indians" and should act compassionately toward other tribes to elicit unity. Residents of New Orleans certainly did not see themselves as "Americans" in 1862. The "imagined communities" suggested by political scientist Benedict Anderson were not yet fully imagined. But times were changing. The very process of defending or capturing border zones tended to reinforce a sense of shared identity among those who stood arm in arm. And the idea began to spread, as British liberal John Stuart Mill expressed it, that "boundaries of government should coincide in the main with those of nationalities." Sentiments of national solidarity—taken for granted today—were then just coming into existence.[4]

Within this fluid environment, new technologies made every state and tribe more vulnerable and visible to its rivals than ever before. None had a choice but to respond. Telegraphs told people of new lands. Steamships and railroads took them there. Some willingly, some literally in chains, millions of Africans, Europeans, and Asians migrated from their native shores to new nations and colonies around the world. Their presence placed unremitting pressure on indigenous inhabitants. Settlers meanwhile forged ahead of government, defying it to stop them.

Native peoples fiercely resisted these incursions and in some cases some achieved temporary dominance. Seizing upon foreign imports like the horse and rifle, they beat local opponents while also holding Europeans at bay. In most cases, however, the natives fell back steadily, outnumbered and outgunned. It is also unlikely—given time and the right tools—that native populations would have eschewed conquest or coercive nation-building themselves. As a Tlaxcalan would have known about an Aztec, or a Pawnee about a Sioux, native peoples could also be expansive.[5]

Americans called this process Manifest Destiny. It was the local moniker for an international phenomenon. The nineteenth century saw an epic race between nation-states and empires to "flag" every bit of the globe and establish their claims. Both exercised coercive power over residents, as all governments do. They sometimes overran and incorporated minority populations that would have preferred to remain separate, and they resisted secession once formed. But a crucial difference between nation-states and empires was that the former relied chiefly on the voluntary allegiance of the majority population and the latter on long-term forced association.

Journalist John L. O'Sullivan coined the term Manifest Destiny in 1845, and historians have long used it to describe nineteenth-century expansion. Many scholars employ O'Sullivan's phrase as a synonym for empire. But the United States was, if anything, anti-imperial. Cunning and ambitious, it was no more an empire than Mexico, a republic that also subdued natives and tried to impose rule on secessionist provinces.

Like other peoples during this period, Americans were often openly racist toward rivals whom they considered "lesser." Indeed, racism bloomed as nationalism heated up. While many surviving members of the revolutionary generation scorned these new, pernicious pretensions, younger leaders often embraced the doctrine that only "whites" had it in their blood to achieve representative government or to develop the continent. Racists used doctrines like polygenesis to dispossess Indians, justify the extension of slavery, and seize lands that others proved unable to defend.[6]

Events on the ground encouraged such arrogance. The United States' comparatively strong internal organization made it an effective competitor. The nation expanded westward in giant leaps, doubling in size for the second time following the purchase of Louisiana in 1803. Then, in 1821, Secretary of State John Quincy Adams negotiated the Adams-Onís Treaty, which codified the vague boundary of Louisiana and extended it to the Pacific Ocean. War with Mexico and the acquisition of Alaska followed. The United States accomplished six of its seven formal territorial acquisitions by diplomacy or purchase, and one by outright conquest. Native peoples suffered, regardless of how the land was formally acquired. Nonetheless, despite scholarly depictions of American expansion as particularly violent, this ratio of negotiation to war suggests instead a preference for horse-trading over shoot-outs.[7]

To describe this process is not to applaud it. As railroads and steamships shrank the globe, states typically expanded their borders until they hit another well-organized state. Native peoples lost sovereignty across the Western Hemisphere. Spain did not even sign treaties with indigenous nations, since treaties imply legal parity, although Spanish viceroys accepted the authority of Indian nobles to discipline their own villagers. The successor nations of Latin America continued these policies. In Canada, Britain signed treaties with Indian nations, but as in the United States, these negotiations also gradually pushed native peoples off their land to make way for settlers.[8]

The same process played out on other continents. In the Antipodes, the British Crown initially recognized local sovereignty—and even encouraged the United Tribes of New Zealand to adopt a national flag in 1834—but then convinced the Maori chiefs to sign their sovereignty over to the Empire. (One motivation was competition with France, which appeared ready to encroach.) In yet another formulation, Britain settled Australia as a penal colony for its criminal class, many of them rural workers pushed into the cities by "enclosure," the gradual conversion of common pasture into private property. (Enclosure in England can be seen as a domestic form of flagging.) Once former prisoners shucked their chains, they and their descendants gradually obtained land titles with no regard at all to indigenous tenants. Indeed, for the next two centuries, courts treated Aboriginal lands as *terra nullius* (unowned earth).[9] Unable to defend their sovereignty, native Australians were pushed to the margins, without treaties or even reservations until the late nineteenth century. Like Poles in 1795, they were disinherited under the unwritten dictum of the regnant international system. Only those independently equipped to defend their borders militarily could claim the prerogatives of statehood. New technologies and the lack of any international law, authority, or umpire turned the nineteenth century into a free-for-all.

The United States was an avid, successful entrant in the competition for land, yet it neither set the rules nor fired the starting pistol. Americans thought it manifest that they would beat other contenders. They also took it as an article of faith that the triumph of republican nation-states like the United States and Argentina was preferable to the further extension of monarchical empires such as England's and Spain's. Revolutionaries elsewhere in the Americas agreed with them. Leaders like Venezuela's Simón Bolívar, Chile's Bernardo O'Higgins, and Mexico's José Morelos were spectacularly optimistic about a bright future for "free men" everywhere under new, republican governments.[10]

Thus, although the United States was unremarkable in trying to obtain as much territory as possible, it was at the forefront of the movement to ensure that republics governed those lands. The United States shared this aim not only with other countries in the Western Hemisphere but also with Great Britain—ironically, then on the way to becoming the largest empire the world had ever seen. Republicanism widened access to foreign markets by disengaging colonies like Peru from mercantilist imperial powers like Spain. This benefitted Britain economically, although its long constitutional tradition also spurred an undercurrent of sympathy for those bucking absolutism.[11]

In contrast, European aristocrats looked askance at this spread of democratic ideology. They had little interest in granting the populace greater access to the political process and hoped republicanism might yet be discredited. European middle-class reformers like the Italian Giuseppe Mazzini and Hungarian Lajos Kossuth hoped just the opposite: that the democracies would multiply.[12] At stake was not just who would control which turf but whether the world would be organized into nation-states or empires.

Territorial competition was not the only form of expansion that characterized this period. Industrialization and new transportation technologies also fostered the dramatic expansion of trade networks between 1815 and 1865. Speedier ships brought far-flung peoples into more frequent contact. This exacerbated questions about the responsibilities of states toward foreign visitors, especially merchants. Industrializing countries with maritime capabilities pushed for access to the markets of nations traditionally closed to outsiders. Although their approaches differed, both Britain and the United States led efforts to "open" Asia to traders in this period.

Indeed, after the War of 1812, Britons and Americans found many of their policies to be unexpectedly synchronized as they responded to similar stimuli. Neither fully trusted the motives of the other and both were wary of cooperation, especially Americans, who had less power to implement their goals. Consequently, the United States was more often a follower than a leader, although it pretended not to be, taking advantage of British initiatives while aping an independent stance. In the antebellum era, the United States was exactly what Secretary of State John Quincy Adams said it ought not to be: a tagalong. Yet there remained an important distinction between the two nations. The American federal government was not an empire in which some states were subordinate to others or to the metropole, such as Australia then was to England. Also, its power to "compel acquiescence" within its own borders—a key requisite of statehood—was still untested. Up until the fight that decided which flag would fly over the New Orleans Mint, the United States itself was not yet clearly a single nation.

Thus, during this period, alongside nearly identical British trends, the United States devised the Monroe Doctrine to defend republicanism in the Americas, intervened in Japan to expand foreign trade, and grew territorially at the expense of native peoples. The policies toward Latin America and Asia had few consequences for the internal cohesion of the United States. In contrast, its foreign policy of westward expansion sundered the Union and led to the deaths of approximately 700,000 men. The Civil War also completed America's metamorphosis into a modern nation-state, but one with an unusual characteristic: supportive of separate state identities, yet willing in extremis to cross borders for the sake of higher principle. *These* United States became *the* United States.

President James Monroe's cabinet debated the matter of cooperation with Britain for more than three hours on the sleepy afternoon of November 7,

1823. In the end, the fifth president was still undecided. Most cabinet members were inclined to accept the United Kingdom's invitation to join in opposing recolonization of Latin America by Europe. The offer was an extraordinary compliment coming from the victor of Waterloo. For the first time in its brief history, the United States was being asked to sign on to a high-level international diktat. George Canning, foreign secretary of the United Kingdom and America's former adversary, courted Washington's opinion.

Only the U.S. secretary of state, John Quincy Adams, disagreed. He shrewdly waited until others had vented their enthusiasm and then appealed to every politician's soft spot: vanity. Britain wanted to deter France and Spain from forcibly reimposing imperial control over the breakaway Latin republics. This was splendid. Adams himself had acerbically lectured Britain's minister in Washington that "the whole system of modern colonization is an abuse of government and it is time that it should come to an end."[13] But America ought to proudly issue its own preemptive declaration, he said, rather than rowing behind the Royal Navy. "It would be more candid, as well as more dignified," Adams observed, "to avow our principles explicitly to Russia and France than to come in as a cock-boat in the wake of a British man-of-war."[14] Actually, it would have been more candid for the United States to acknowledge that the whole idea of a public protest had been England's from the start.

By the end of the long afternoon, Monroe was nearly persuaded. The president certainly did not wish to be seen as deferring to the United Kingdom, not after the United States had just lost 2,200 men defending its honor on land and sea in the War of 1812. Not after the carpenters and painters had just finished restoring the burned-out shell of the White House, torched by British troops in 1814. But with the weight of the country on his shoulders, Monroe remained anxious that Spain, France, and Russia might send as many as 10,000 troops to quell republicanism in the Americas.[15] He could not quite bring himself to adopt Adams's breezy self-confidence. Britain was the only country equipped to stop the menacing European powers. Prudence counseled acceptance of its offer.

Foreign Secretary George Canning had floated the idea of coordinated action the previous summer as a tidy solution to a ticklish situation. Central and South America had been in turmoil since 1808, when Napoleon Bonaparte ousted the king of Spain and installed his brother Joseph on the throne. Status-conscious Creoles in the Americas led the struggle for independence from the beleaguered empire. They already resented the superciliousness of *peninsulares,* immigrants from the Iberian peninsula who were entitled to greater political privileges as a birthright, and they were certainly not going to be bossed by a mere French puppet as well. Then, at the tail end of the Napoleonic Wars, King Ferdinand VII recaptured the Spanish crown. But it was too late to stop separatist movements that had gotten a taste of autonomy. By 1820, victory was a foregone conclusion nearly everywhere, including in Argentina, Chile, Colombia, Mexico, and Peru. Every rebellious Spanish colony eventually declared a republic, and England forged a bustling, postcolonial trade from Acapulco to Asunción.

Spain refused to recognize the independence of even one of the new nations, however. It was determined to reimpose political control and economic exclusion. The empire had an impressive ally in the Holy Alliance, a coalition of Russia, Prussia, Austria, and France. This cabal hoped to rein in all the disturbing ideas unleashed by the American and French Revolutions. It pledged itself to the full restoration of absolutist, Christian monarchy. To the Holy Alliance, democracy equaled anarchy, heresy, bloodshed, and revolution. Even English constitutionalism was suspect, since it limited the divine right of kings.[16]

Britain refused to join the conservative alliance. Canning's influential predecessor, Lord Castlereagh, had written in 1820 that His Majesty's goal in the preceding quarter-century had been "liberation of a great proportion of the Continent of Europe from the Military Domination of France." Castlereagh could not agree with continental Europe's new determination to stamp out constitutionalism altogether. The world had changed. Britain opposed the French Revolution because of its "Military Character," the foreign secretary wrote, rather than because of its "Democratic Principles."[17] But after Napoleon's defeat, the Holy Alliance wanted more. In 1823 it began marshaling forces to corral Ferdinand's former colonies and put down republicanism on the far side of the Atlantic. Britain decided to protest.

That task fell unexpectedly to George Canning. Born in poverty and raised by a beautiful widow who scandalously took to the stage to support her child, the brilliant Canning was abruptly elevated to the post of foreign secretary after the depressed, politically unpopular Castlereagh—who had wounded Canning in a duel a decade earlier—slit his own throat with a letter opener. (British politics rarely disappointed for drama.) Poor Castlereagh, engineer of the alliance against Napoleon, had not fully merited the criticisms of liberals, who accused him of cozying up to foreign despots and blithely crushing the British working class. Few critics were more caustic than the poet Percy Bysshe Shelley, who wrote in 1819, "I met Murder on the way—, He had a mask like Castlereagh." Few were more callous than Lord Byron, who scribbled after the foreign secretary's suicide:

> Posterity will ne'er survey
> A nobler grave than this:
> Here lie the bones of Castlereagh:
> Stop, traveller, and piss.[18]

In contrast, George Canning had a knack for making practical choices sound idealistic, sparing him the opprobrium directed at his predecessor. Canning also initiated a trend of greater transparency, making it a point to communicate directly with the public. This endeared him to reformers while annoying traditionalists. As one of the latter observed, Canning's public "speechifying and discussing the intentions of the Gov't were ridiculous . . . quite a new system among us . . . which excites great indignation."[19] Yet Canning's approach to foreign policy otherwise paralleled Castlereagh's. It dovetailed as well with many tenets of American foreign policy.[20]

British policymakers argued for nonintervention in other countries' internal affairs. Entwinement in ambiguous and intractable foreign disputes could easily damage national interests. Interventionism also violated the well-established principle that states must scrupulously refrain from "interfering by force in the internal affairs of another," except when faced with "direct and imminent danger."[21] In addition, with the Napoleonic Wars behind them, Britons reasserted a preference for free trade and foreign markets leveraged open by most-favored-nation treaties. Although the United Kingdom retained a monarch, and thus rejected republicanism for itself, the trend toward nonaristocratic government in the Western Hemisphere held a certain attraction for His Majesty's ministers.

The republics of the New World rejected closed mercantile systems when they cut their ties with monarchy, and they opened their markets to international trade on declaring independence. The United States also continued to press for access to the British West Indies, adding to the momentum behind freer trade.[22] With its pioneer industrial complex and flourishing merchant marine, Britain stood to gain significantly from the death of mercantilism. Once doors were unlocked in the Americas, England had a practical interest in keeping them that way. It was even willing to reciprocate. Beginning in 1822, Britain started repealing the restrictive Navigation Acts that had so angered the American colonists before their revolution. In 1846, Britain opened its domestic markets to foreign grain imports by repealing the protectionist Corn Laws. By 1854, His Majesty's government had completely reversed its navigation policies and ancient import restrictions in favor of free trade.

Nonentanglement and open doors were not the only points of convergence between the United States and England. Britons' willingness to tolerate republicanism in the name of nonintervention led to explicit adoption of the de facto rule of recognition. One did not have to like everything about a government to accept its credentials. (In fact, one might cordially revile said government.) Spain's ongoing intransigence toward the renegade republics could not be tolerated forever. "The Separation of the Spanish colonies from Spain has neither been our work, nor our wish," Canning told His Most Catholic Majesty. "But out of that separation grew a state of things." It was absurd as well as "monstrous" to go on treating established governments in Central and South America as "Pirates and Outlaws."[23]

The United States had extended recognition to the Latin Americans a year earlier, becoming the first nation to do so, on the presupposition that acknowledgment of a new foreign government depended not on "its justice, but on its actual establishment," as Congress put it.[24] Governments might rise or fall. The question was whether they exercised control over their own people and borders. If citizens tacitly accepted a government, outsiders must accept it as well. It was stable control that established legitimacy, not divine right. Britain now agreed with this policy but wanted to make sure that the last great threat to Latin Americans' full sovereignty had been checked before granting overt recognition. This was where the United States came in.

In August 1823, George Canning shocked the U.S. minister to Great Britain, Richard Rush, by asking that the U.S. government join in opposing the designs of the Holy Alliance. Canning further suggested that both their nations disavow any intent to seize the Spanish king's former possessions for themselves, to prove their honorable intentions. Aware of Canning's earlier reputation for strident anti-Americanism, Richard Rush immediately sent to President Monroe for instructions. Rush would have been even more amazed had he known that Canning was already taking steps. While still awaiting Monroe's decision, Canning told a French emissary in October 1823 that the United States had far more right to be consulted on Western Hemisphere affairs than Austria or Prussia, and should be included in future international negotiations. As British historians have noted, "Europe was horrified and astounded by Canning's proposal to invite a Republic to share the deliberations of Kings."[25]

Monroe's November 7 cabinet meeting saw the first debate of Canning's proposal. Secretary of War John C. Calhoun voiced his strong support for a joint declaration and mutual disavowal of territorial ambitions. England could easily outcompete the United States in any land grab. Here was a chance to box the British Empire into a corner, the South Carolinian argued.

John Quincy Adams disagreed with Calhoun. While the United States entertained "no intention of seizing" Spain's former territories by force, Adams pointed out, it should not foreclose the possibility that provinces like Cuba or Texas might "exercise their primitive [natural] rights, and solicit a union with us."[26] They would never elect to rejoin a monarchical empire, but they might consider a coalition of equals. Adams had been in and out of European capitals ever since his father, John, now so elderly that he had to be helped across a room, first took him as an eleven-year-old boy to France, in 1778. John Quincy Adams was the least likely person in Washington to swoon at Canning's courtship. He argued that America had little to gain from any joint declaration and something to lose: freedom of action.

Adams raised another problem that the United States might also solve if it issued an independent proclamation instead of signing on to Britain's. While the Holy Alliance glowered at Latin America, Russia was inching down the western coast of North America. Danish navigator Vitus Bering, sailing for Peter the Great, had discovered the western edge of North America and staked the first Russian claims there almost a century earlier. The Romanov Dynasty was now getting serious about settlement. In 1812 it established Fort Ross (derived from "Rus," the ancient name for Russia), an agricultural colony north of San Francisco, then the upper limit of Spanish settlement. In 1821, Czar Alexander I went further and issued an edict barring all foreigners from the coastline north of 51 degrees (Vancouver Island).

This ukase, or imperial decree, contradicted British territorial claims and American maritime practices, particularly those of the Yankee traders who supplied goods to Russian trappers in Alaska in exchange for furs to sell to China. Yet the czar decreed that thenceforth the "whole of the north-west coast of America . . . is exclusively granted to Russian subjects. . . . It is therefore prohibited to all foreign vessels not only to land on the coasts and islands belonging to Russia as stated above, but also, to approach them within less than 100 Italian miles."[27] Any foreign vessel in violation was subject to unremunerated confiscation. John Quincy Adams was as concerned about Russian ambitions as he was about the Holy Alliance. America needed a policy to counter them, unless it wished to concede the entire Northwest to the Romanovs.

Yet President Monroe remained unconvinced that America could go it alone, without English help. Despondent about the Latin American republics' chances for survival, he sought further advice from his two predecessors. In retirement on their verdant plantations south of the newly built capitol, Jefferson and Madison had softened in their instinctive animosity toward Britain. The aging revolutionaries now encouraged James Monroe to accept Canning's offer. John C. Calhoun also pressed the president, lest the nations of the Southern Hemisphere become victims of infanticide.

Privately convinced that Secretary of War Calhoun was "perfectly moon-struck" with fear of the Holy Alliance, Adams objected again at a subsequent cabinet meeting on November 15. The secretary of state countered that the Holy Alliance could not possibly prevail in the long run. And, if the Europeans could quash the nascent governments as easily as Calhoun believed, it was not the place of the United States to commit American "lives and fortunes in a ship which he declares the very rats have abandoned."[28]

Adams was a genius at argument. (He also did not have very high regard for Southerners, whom he described as a mixture of "principles and prejudices, . . . wisdom and Quixotism, which has done some good and much mischief to the Union."[29]) By the end of November, Adams had won the debate. Monroe decided that the United States would make its own pronouncement, drafted by the secretary of state. This declaration would check the ambitions of both the Holy Alliance and Russia, and signal American autonomy from Britain.

In the annual address that the fifth president sent Congress on December 3, Monroe announced, without forewarning George Canning, that the United States would oppose any attempt to colonize or recolonize even the smallest piece of the Western Hemisphere. The Atlantic Ocean would be the dividing line between two types of government: republican on one side, monarchical on the other. The United States also reasserted its strict neutrality on European questions, including a movement by Greeks to obtain national self-determination. It could only be a well-wisher to republicanism and liberty on the far side of the Atlantic. With regard to the American republics, however, it would consider "any interposition for the purpose of oppressing them . . . as the manifestation of an unfriendly disposition towards the United States." That is, Americans would challenge European colonization anywhere in the Western Hemisphere "as dangerous to our peace and safety."[30]

The president's annual message soon entered popular memory as an iconic principle of foreign relations and a uniquely American initiative. What became known as the Monroe Doctrine was the nation's first public stand on a controversy that did not immediately touch its own citizens or territory, thereby modifying George Washington's rule "to have as little *political* connection as possible" with "any portion of the foreign world."[31]

Canning was not amused. The foreign secretary wrote to friends that American egotism was true to form. He immediately released the substance of conversations he had already had with the French ambassador, the duc de Polignac, two months before Monroe's declaration. Canning had explicitly warned Polignac against interfering on behalf of Spain in the New World. Britain's vast navy hovered behind him, ready with all its physical might. France accepted Canning's ultimatum, expressed in the so-called Polignac Memorandum. A year and a half later, the foreign secretary granted official recognition to Spain's former colonies. "We have called a new world into existence to redress the balance of the old," Canning told Parliament in 1825, implicitly taking credit for the independence that revolutionaries had purchased with 600,000 lives in Mexico and Central America alone.[32]

Despite its imperialism elsewhere, British maneuvers were not entirely unsurprising given the United Kingdom's economic interests and unusual political structure. Britain's domestic system blended constitutionalism with monarchy, and it now purported to balance monarchy in one sphere against democracy in the other. Each would be defended. Fractured, imperfect, and incomplete, popular sovereignty had taken over half the globe—and within the space of a handful of decades. No great power imposed these ideas. Instead, peoples fired by the common heritage of the Reformation and Enlightenment grasped them for themselves. They wanted nation-states, and they wanted access to political power within them.

Britain and the United States had arrived autonomously at a similar policy: an Anglo-American protectorate for republicanism. But the implementation was all Canning's. Whatever concessions the Holy Alliance granted Britain, it certainly did not accord the same respect to the United States, which had virtually no military establishment and no inclination for genuine defense of the hemisphere.

Russian and Austrian officials expressed their disdain at American pretensions, but it was a French newspaper that crafted the most artful put-down. "Mr. Monroe, who is not a sovereign, has assumed in his message the tone of a powerful monarch, whose armies and fleets are ready to march at the first signal," the editors observed. Yet, they continued, "Mr. Monroe is the temporary President of a Republic situated on the east coast of North America. This republic is bounded on the south by the possessions of the King of Spain, and on the north by those of the King of England. Its independence was recognized only forty years ago; by what right then would the two Americas today be under its immediate sway from Hudson's Bay to Cape Horn?"[33] While grateful to Monroe, the other American republics also recognized that any effective action would come from Britain. Simón Bolívar even worried about getting too close to the United States, lest this partiality alienate the British, who were "omnipotent and because of this terrifying."[34]

The competitive world system in which the United States came to maturity demanded that states solidify their borders against other potential contenders for land. To fail to do so was to risk destruction. Yet on top of this foundation, the United States, Great Britain, and the Latin American republics began adding new structures of popular sovereignty and republicanism. They began fashioning a new world system from the old.

The American and British governments soon found their policies coincided on Asia as well, as they edged toward a consensus on the value of routinized access to foreign markets. Separately and together, they took measures that drew China and Japan deeply into global trade for the first time. Italian navigator Christopher Columbus had braved the unknown ocean to find the unique products of the so-called Orient, inadvertently locating the Western Hemisphere. After the nation's founding, freed of mercantilist constraints and cut off from the British West Indies, Americans eagerly expanded this trade. In 1784, the American vessel *Empress of China* sailed from New York, initiating the exchange of furs, ginseng, and tobacco for silk, tea, and fine porcelain so distinctive it was called simply "china."

Yet Britain dominated the Asia trade. In 1789, sixty-one of the eighty-six foreign ships in Canton Harbor were English.[35] There would have been more if the Qing Dynasty had not strictly limited the number of foreigners for four centuries. China first closed its doors in 1433, a few decades before Europeans developed the sailing expertise necessary to round Africa and sail into the Indian Ocean. The Tokugawa shogunate, the ruling family of Japan, adopted similar laws in 1638. During the years that Western rivalries sped scientific and military development, the most advanced nations of Asia largely forbade contact with the outside world, prohibiting citizens from traveling and foreigners from visiting. The Japanese called it *sakoku,* meaning "locked country." In *Moby Dick,* former whaler Herman Melville expressed the average seaman's view of Japan in 1851, calling it "that double-bolted land."[36]

Asian governments had little interest in anything outside their borders. China considered itself the Middle Kingdom, to which "barbarians" were subordinate. Since the 1648 Peace of Westphalia, Western governments had devised elaborate diplomatic protocols to symbolize legal equality between "opposite numbers." But China clung to its superiority. It rejected the exchange of ambassadors since that implied parity, and insisted that visiting foreigners perform the kowtow to show obeisance, which meant prostrating oneself on the floor and touching one's head to the ground nine times.

Success bred this conceit. For nearly two millennia, China had sustained a coherent government. Enlightened agricultural policies and advanced infrastructure had made it the most populous country on earth. The Chinese had invented cast iron, gunpowder, porcelain, paper, and the compass. They were the sole suppliers of England's favorite beverage, tea. Few peoples were as prosperous or resourceful. Adam Smith acknowledged in *The Wealth of Nations* in 1776 that, "China is a much richer country than any part of Europe."[37] Unbeknownst to the Chinese, however, the technology gap was closing rapidly. With the quickening of the Industrial Revolution in England and the United States after 1815, the Middle Kingdom was headed toward the margins.

China condescended to a minimal trade. Exercising its sovereign rights, it commanded that all foreign ships go through the port of Canton, located seventy miles up the Pearl River Delta, across from the island of Hong Kong. Without any national tariff structure (since foreign trade was considered superfluous to growth), local officials charged fees and extorted bribes according to whim. There were more than sixty unofficial "taxes" to be paid between the mouth of the delta and the port of Canton.[38] Once upriver, foreigners were required to stay in "factories" (a "factor" was the agent or representative of a foreign company), to shield local people from polluting outside influences. The Dutch, Swedish, French, English, Spanish, Danish, and Americans each had their own building in a restricted communal compound.[39]

Japanese trade law was even harsher. The shogun allowed exchanges only with the Chinese, at a small, artificial island in the bay of Nagasaki, supplemented by one or two Dutch ships annually. From the Dutch they imported a few European newspapers and books to help government ministers keep tabs on the Western world. Citizens were forbidden to travel. Japanese sailors shipwrecked on foreign shores were not permitted to return home, lest they bring infectious "forbidden thoughts" with them, especially the teachings of Christianity, which the ruling family abhorred. Foreigners who made the mistake of landing without permission were threatened with beheading and sometimes held captive in open-air cages for months, until they could be deported from Nagasaki. This was particularly alarming to New Englanders, who by then operated the world's largest whaling industry and frequently fished in the waters of the Pacific off Asian shores.[40]

As the emerging economic powerhouse, Britain had an even greater interest than the United States in pressuring the Chinese government toward more hospitable practices. In 1759, 1793, and 1816, the English sent envoys to the Forbidden City, the imperial palace in Beijing, to try to obtain better terms. The Chinese emperor rebuffed all three missions. In 1833, relations became tenser when the British Parliament dissolved the East India Company's monopoly on private trade. A measure that created greater economic equality among Englishmen was seen as threatening by the Chinese. The Qing government preferred foreigners to be under tight control. The emperor foresaw new difficulties as the number of merchants increased, multiplying providers of the one foreign product for which the otherwise self-sufficient Chinese market had shown high demand: opium.

The East India Company was the world's largest purveyor of opium, a product illegal in China but then legal in Britain, India, and the United

States. Exercising strict quality control, the East India Company made opium into India's largest export. For decades the company had quietly relied on unlicensed third parties (British, American, and East Indian) to smuggle its wares into the Middle Kingdom.[41] This allowed the company, which imported legal goods to China, to pretend that it was in compliance with local ordinances.

But corruption was endemic in the Chinese government. Officials at all levels colluded in the import of high-grade foreign opium, which then passed through domestic sales networks to customers. An increase in the number of British companies allowed to trade in the Orient threatened to swamp China with what the imperial government called "foreign mud." China had a wealthy leisure class, and its growing addiction to opium allowed the British to indulge their own very expensive, but much less debilitating passion for tea.[42]

American and British merchants meanwhile resented the various Chinese trade restrictions, and not just those on opium. They continued to press their governments to intervene on their behalf, especially on the matter of uniform tariffs. Merchants were willing to pay higher fees if they no longer had to pay multiple bribes as well. Tensions between Westerners and Chinese officials came to a boil in the late 1830s. The Chinese government had noticed a growing imbalance in its ledgers: opium purchases finally outweighed sales of tea. For the first time in its history, China had a trade deficit. Imperial silver reserves declined and inflation soared. Financial disaster threatened. The emperor's advisors suggested making the use, import, and sale of opium punishable by death. An imperial high commissioner was given power to investigate and stop the trade.

Lin Zexu, a zealous fifty-four-year-old magistrate who considered opium an unmitigated evil, took his responsibility seriously. He arrived at the foreign traders' factories in March 1839, at the head of a flotilla of black junks emblazoned with gold Chinese lettering. When the barbarians proved uncooperative, Lin sealed off the enclave, trapping the occupants and cutting them off from their food suppliers and local staffs. The foreigners finally handed over 20,283 chests of British-owned opium cakes. Lin publicly burned the pyramid of contraband on the beach, a process that took twenty-three days. Traders in the American, French, and Dutch factories pledged to stop selling the drug, but the British withdrew in anger. Emotions escalated. A drunken British sailor killed a Chinese villager and English officials refused to turn him over to local officials for punishment. Britain finally agreed to stop the opium trade, but it refused to countenance China's demand for the immediate execution of smugglers. War broke out.[43]

American merchants who had been trapped in Canton petitioned the U.S. Congress for assistance. "We have no wish to see a revival of the opium trade," they stated, but they objected to the "detention of the persons, ships, and property of those who are entirely disconnected from the obnoxious trade." They wanted Washington to appeal to the imperial government for fixed tariffs, the right to conduct commercial relations on the same basis that "exists between all friendly powers," and a guarantee "against the occurrence of similar arbitrary acts." They requested no overt intervention but suggested a frightening show of collective determination. So far as the merchants were concerned, the mere appearance of a joint squadron of U.S., French, and British ships off the coast of China would, "without bloodshed," convince the Chinese Empire to be more reasonable.[44]

The British had fewer qualms and a larger navy. London dispatched wooden steamships and an iron gunboat. The Chinese emperor rejected British demands and vowed instead to "annihilate them all so that we can show our Heaven-sent superiority." The Royal Navy captured Hong Kong and Canton in 1841. The next year, its gunboats penetrated the Yangtze River as far as the Grand Canal, the ancient manmade waterway linking Beijing with southern rice-growing provinces. Never having seen steamships, Lin Zexu described the vessels as "wheeled vehicles which use the heads of flame to drive machines, cruising very fast."[45]

According to Qing annals, American and French merchants approached imperial officials on three occasions to offer support against the British, who had blockaded the entire coast of China, interrupting trade and exposing all foreigners to harm. They were properly "obsequious to China," and "hereditary enemies of England," a court scribe observed.[46] But the emperor spurned assistance, and after local officials inadvertently killed several Americans in a night attack on the factories in March 1841, American offers were not renewed. The French persisted, however, even offering to build vessels for the Chinese, but to no avail. Once the Chinese capital was in the sights of English cannons, the Qing Dynasty was finally forced to surrender.

The 1842 Treaty of Nanking gave Britain the island of Hong Kong and the right to trade and reside at five Chinese ports. Tariff rates were fixed at a low 5 percent, and the emperor accepted the humiliating clause that China's import taxes could be revised only by mutual agreement. The treaty also granted Britain extraterritoriality, that is, the privilege of punishing its own private citizens for crimes committed abroad. This practice had roots in Ottoman-European relations. Within what the Ottomans called the "millet" system, they allowed distinct religious groups inside their realm to adjudicate the crimes of coreligionists. This system of legal pluralism took on a foreign dimension under the so-called capitulations that the Ottoman Empire bestowed voluntarily on European allies at the height of its power in the sixteenth century. Under these treaties, non-Muslim foreigners also obtained the privilege of being judged for their crimes by a European representative. The capitulations provided trade privileges as well, that Europeans agreed to strictly reciprocate. Over time, however, as the Ottoman Empire weakened and European power grew, the privileges became more and more lopsided.[47]

In China, extraterritoriality blended European diplomatic custom with a kind of millet system for foreign citizens. Traditionally, only ambassadorial staffs had immunity from local law. But under extraterritoriality, foreign civilians in China gained immunity as well, while Chinese travelers abroad did not. This contributed to the later characterization of the Nanking accord and others that followed as the Unequal Treaties. Historian Immanuel Hsü notes that they earned this label because "they were not negotiated by nations treating each other as equals but were imposed on China after a war, and because they encroached upon China's sovereign rights . . . which reduced China to semicolonial status."[48] Ironically, however, the treaties also resulted partly from China's initial reluctance to consider any treaties whatsoever, since it viewed all other nations as inferior. It did not wish to be equal.

Remarkably, the British did not seek a closed sphere in their trade with China, nor did they take any territory other than Hong Kong. Breaking with previous patterns of European colonization, including their own, they negotiated most-favored-nation status and the principle of equal commercial opportunity for all foreigners. None would have greater access than another. Whatever ports China chose to open—and the emperor "chose" to open ten others after the Second Opium War against Britain (1856–1860)— they would treat all outsiders equally. No European empire could impose a closed, mercantilist system. Chinese commentators called this the open-door principle.[49]

The United States and other nations with no hand in the fighting nonetheless took advantage of the results. The United States was first to send a formal emissary, Caleb Cushing, to ask for everything granted the British. The Chinese sensed an opportunity to divide the barbarians at their gates. Even while under siege, a Chinese official had written: "The American barbarians at Canton have always been peaceable, not obstinate like the English barbarians." He further noted that there was jealousy between the two, and that if the Americans received preferential favor, "the English barbarians will certainly not take it lying down." But Chinese officialdom's hope that foreigners might fight among themselves did not come to pass. Instead, French and American merchants pressed their cases individually. The foreigners complained that since they had not been treacherous and bullying like the English, why should China treat them all with the same hostility? Even before Cushing arrived in 1844, the emperor's advisors conceded that it made little sense to deny the tractable Americans (and French) those privileges already granted the British.[50]

U.S. Secretary of State Daniel Webster left observance of the irksome kowtow to Minister Cushing's discretion, but urged him to avoid appearances of "inferiority on the part of your Government, or any thing less than perfect independence of all Nations." In the subsequent 1844 Treaty of Wanghia, Cushing obtained most-favored-nation status, meaning that Americans would receive any privileges extended to other foreigners. He also negotiated another, more unusual concession. American visitors could purchase Chinese books and hire scholars "to teach any of the languages of the [Qing] Empire," something previously forbidden. In other words, Cushing sought access not only to Chinese markets, but also to Chinese thought and culture.[51] Soon thereafter, French, Belgian, Swedish, and Norwegian emissaries negotiated similar accords. To the Chinese elite, such agreements were uniformly mortifying. One high official, who had previously boasted that he would "pull out the nerves of the foreigners to make whips for his horses," committed suicide.[52]

The United States followed opportunistically after the British in China. But in Japan twelve years later, Washington took the initiative in a fainter, more peaceable imitation of London's policy. After 1815, whaling had brought Americans into repeated conflict with Japanese law. Before kerosene became popular later in the century, whale oil was the best illuminant for domestic oil lamps and the primary lubricant for the new machinery of the Industrial Revolution.[53] Nantucket whaling ships were the oil tankers of their day, and crews hunted the mammals round the world. The Japanese archipelago, consisting of thousands of islands slung across 1,300 miles of the Pacific Ocean, was for mariners a potential source of much-needed food, fresh water, and shelter from storms.

The United States was not the only concerned foreign nation. After 1804 the Russian navy made several rough attempts to force Japan to open its doors. In 1808, a desperate ship of the British Royal Navy finally obtained food and water in Nagasaki by threatening to sink all Japanese ships in the harbor. In 1837, the unarmed American merchant ship *Morrison* tried twice to repatriate seven Japanese castaways who had washed up on the Oregon coast during a storm, but imperial gunfire forced the *Morrison* to sail away without accomplishing its mission.

In 1845, a whaling ship rescued and successfully repatriated twenty-two Japanese subjects from a sinking junk, but even this good deed did not go unpunished. When Commodore James Biddle of the USS *Columbus* subsequently tried to negotiate a rapprochement, a Japanese sailor struck him on the head after inviting him aboard a local vessel. The imperial coastguard then towed Biddle's becalmed sailing ships out to sea. Two years later, in 1849, the USS *Preble* visited Nagasaki to argue for the release of fourteen marooned Americans, one of whom had been imprisoned for four years. Forbidden to anchor, and told that it was against Japanese law to provide copies of Japanese law, the ship's captain prevailed only after promising to leave the minute he took the prisoners on board.[54]

Indeed, the Japanese would communicate willingly only with the Dutch, whom they granted the right to keep a small factory in Nagasaki harbor. To sustain this privilege, the Dutch were periodically required to travel under escort to the capitol city of Edo (Tokyo). There, in the words of Samuel Eliot Morison, they were expected "to approach the Shogun across the audience Hall of a Hundred Mats crawling on their bellies—no small feat for a Dutch merchant—and then put on a song-and-dance act and play drunk, to amuse his highness."[55]

In 1851, both the Russian and American governments decided to press harder. Steamships now plied the globe. They were propelled not by the ubiquitous wind but by coal, which had to be stored or purchased at scattered locations. The U.S. Navy gave Commodore Matthew Perry, a veteran navigator of all five oceans except the Pacific, the assignment of persuading the Japanese government to treat marooned American sailors kindly and to allow their ships to buy coal, water, and other provisions.

The Americans hoped to achieve this without force. They preferred arbitration, and had little means to conduct war. In 1837 the United States ranked eighth in navies of the world, behind Turkey and Egypt. But Washington also viewed its motives and methods as distinct from the European powers. It sought neither converts nor colonies. Perry was told to emphasize that the U.S. government, "unlike those of every other Christian country, does not interfere with the religion of its own people, much less with that of the other nations." Americans and Britons spoke the same language, so the Japanese might naturally confuse U.S. citizens with the English, "of whose conquests in the east, and recent invasion of China, they have probably heard." But the two peoples were different. Perry was told to emphasize that "the United States are connected with no government in Europe."[56]

Perry's instructions emphasized sweet reason. Steamships now meant that Japan and the United States were only a twenty-day sail apart. Open access to markets and mutual cooperation made sense. Americans rescued Japanese sailors whenever possible, and treated them humanely; they wanted the same in return. Americans also desired peace, but how could friendship exist if Japan persisted in treating "the people of this country as if they were her enemies?" A local tradition that may have been wise before the advent of steamships and global commerce had become "unwise and impracticable now that intercourse between the two countries is so much more easy and rapid than it formerly was." But Perry's instructions also echoed the advice of American merchants in Canton: set forth logical arguments and second them with "some imposing manifestation of power." Perry was ordered to show forbearance even if treated discourteously, but to warn the Japanese that if they continued to act "cruelly" toward shipwrecked Americans, "they will be severely chastised."[57] The potential for violent retaliation underscored polite requests for better relations, as was customary between foreign nations at the time.

Matthew Perry was the son of a naval captain who had fought in the War of Independence and the plain younger brother of handsome Oliver Perry, who achieved naval fame during War of 1812 when he reported, "We have met the enemy and they are ours." A New Englander, Matthew supported slave emancipation and had volunteered for the cruise to establish Liberia years earlier. He was now almost sixty years old, but with dark hair still so luxuriant that novelist Nathaniel Hawthorne mistook it for a wig. Perry had promoted the steam-driven navy, and he was meticulous and hardy even for a seaman. He carefully planned what became his most important mission. For the cruise to Japan, Perry read the memoir of a Russian captain who had been shipwrecked and held prisoner for years, and the chronicle of a physician formerly attached to the Dutch at Nagasaki. He spent six months collecting the latest marvels to impress and seduce his potential hosts, including clocks, farm implements, a daguerreotype camera, a Morse telegraph, and a quarter-size railroad train and track. Perry's chief assignment: to deliver a letter from President Millard Fillmore to the emperor of Japan.[58]

The squadron sailed from New York Harbor in October 1852, with onlookers waving their handkerchiefs and a band playing "Hail, Columbia." It made landfall in Hong Kong in early April and caught sight of Mount Fuji on July 8, 1853. Perry entered the port of Edo with two wooden sailing ships and two steamers. He intentionally bypassed Nagasaki, unwilling to enter by the backdoor customarily showed Westerners. The dense black smoke of the steamers and their amazing ability to sail directly into the wind surprised local inhabitants, who dubbed them "Black Ships." Numerous junks swam out to meet the foreigners, surrounding the American fleet. A tense diplomacy ensued, with both sides testing the resolve of the other. Well aware of the Japanese reputation for a strict social hierarchy, Perry insisted on meeting with officials equal in rank. American sailors eyeballed the port's earthen fortifications, a style not seen in the West for almost two centuries and incapable even of crossfire. They were "unsatisfactory defenses, easy to overpower," a German immigrant on the U.S. crew observed.[59]

The Japanese finally granted permission for the ships to anchor in a small inlet, which they ringed with 150 junks. Onshore, an eight-foot-high curtain of black cloth stretched for two miles, cloaking the town. Five to seven thousand Japanese soldiers holding muskets and two swords apiece stood ready, with cannons of ancient vintage at the head of the assembly. The Americans were outnumbered more than ten to one in unknown territory. Taking courage, they came ashore with martial symbolism of their own. Perry marched behind a red-jacketed marine band, flanked by two particularly tall African American seamen whom he had chosen to bear the U.S. flag. Four companies of well-armed marines and sailors completed the complement of 400 troops.

Understandably, each side saw the other as tricky, difficult, threatening, and barbarian. Aware that some Europeans had previously acceded to a form of kowtow, Perry and his men strode into the gathering, refusing to crawl or touch their heads to the ground. "How different our behavior [was] from that of the Russians and the Dutch . . . and how egregious we alien barbarians must have seemed," observed William Heine, the German-born sailor. But the governor had anticipated Perry, and sagaciously invited the commodore and other officers to sit on chairs as tall as his own.[60]

They conversed in Dutch through translators. Perry delivered Fillmore's letter. The governor accepted it for consideration and Perry said he would return the following year for an answer. Formal dialogue at an end, the Japanese surprised the sailors and officers by inviting them back for a party the next day. There, savory foods served on dishes of exceptional artistry were accompanied by copious amounts of alcohol and tobacco, which "made everyone happy." Young Japanese attendees peppered the common sailors with questions, including: "Is it true that anyone can go to California and find gold?" and "How long did it take to get here?" To general hilarity, several merry gallants donned the Americans' coats and hats. According to William Heine, the generosity and informal friendliness of the Japanese "touched my comrades and me, each and every one of us."[61]

Japanese first impressions were not as sanguine, at least among high officials. Perry's intrusion inflamed a debate that had been smoldering for several years. Japanese officials knew about the Opium Wars. Some were convinced that Japan would be better off negotiating access on its own terms, rather than waiting to be overwhelmed. They had also heard about America's victory over Mexico in 1848, and worried that the barbarians' intentions were less benign than they were being portrayed. At least a few reformers chafed at the restrictions on learning and personal advancement imposed by the isolationist policy of the Tokugawa Shogunate. They counseled acceptance of a changing world.

The government weighed its goals carefully. Defense was paramount, and no one believed that relations with the outside could ever be truly harmonious. One proponent of granting President Fillmore's request noted, "There is a saying that when one is besieged in a castle, to raise the drawbridge is to imprison oneself." Japan would be safer, he argued, if it opened the bridge to avert hostilities and then, "after some time has elapsed, gain a complete victory." The nation could procure its own steam vessels in the guise of trade, but for "the secret purpose of training a navy." Through an open door, the Japanese could go out and not merely let foreigners in, as the Chinese had done.[62]

The counterargument had an even steelier edge. Japan "must never choose the path of peace," one member of the Tokugawa dynasty repeatedly emphasized. Not only would such a policy anger the spirits and defile the population, but Perry's "arrogant and discourteous" behavior constituted "the greatest disgrace we have suffered since the dawn of our history."[63] The shogunate was unprepared for war, its armaments were inadequate, and its prestige was at stake. Americans were simply too dangerous to be admitted. If they came, so would other foreigners.

In the end, the Japanese concluded it was more strategic to grant Perry's requests than deny them. Opportunities for economic and military development would widen with a more open policy. Access would make the nation stronger. The government also preferred to deal with America than with Britain, at least at first. The shogunate decided that U.S. ships would be allowed to purchase provisions, castaways would be protected, and Japan would grant Americans any privileges they might later extend to other foreign governments. When Perry returned in February 1854, this time with seven vessels, Japan signed the Treaty of Kanagawa, its first with any nation. Europeans swiftly obtained comparable treaties. In 1856, the first U.S. consul took up residence in the town of Shimoda, cultivating Japanese trust despite what Britain's emissary called the "perpetual menace of massacre."[64] Hostile gangs killed seven foreign diplomats before attitudes softened further and Japan fully embraced contact with the outside world.

Methods affected outcomes. Britain chose physical violence in China, and the local government chose to ignore what it could learn from the West. China became less stable and prosperous in subsequent decades. The Americans used persuasion in Japan, and the local government adopted new practices for its own purposes. Japan became a world power within forty years. Japanese and American methods more closely anticipated the patterns of the future than did those of the other two countries. All of them, however, were headed toward a more accessible, less controllable world.

Foreign policy often has deep and unintended domestic consequences. As we have seen, European countries typically added to their domain in the nineteenth century by accumulating colonies overseas. The United States grew by enlarging its home territory, and newly acquired lands entered on a basis of political equality. This made expansion a more intimate, proximate, and destabilizing affair than it was for Europeans. It also exacerbated Americans' most painful internal contradiction and led to civil war.

The founders had put on hold the one issue they knew had the potential to destroy their coalition. The Constitutional Congress placated slaveholding states by adopting the three-fifths clause. Those "bound to service" counted thereby as three-fifths of a person, allowing populous Southern states to boost their Congressional representation. (No one wanted the word "slave" in a declaration about the "Blessings of Liberty.") This uncomfortable but durable compromise held for seventy years. Had the United States not grown beyond the original thirteen colonies, it may well have held for another seventy.

Slavery was dynamite wedged under bedrock American values. No American president, or candidate for president, ever suggested touching it in the Old South. It was expansion that triggered the Civil War, not slavery per se. And it was the Civil War, in turn, that established the full authority of the federal government and at last consolidated what were then thirty-four potential rivals into a single, unitary nation.

From 1783 to 1848, each addition of territory reintroduced the irritating question: Would slavery be extended to virgin lands or not? Whether fairly or ill-gotten, whom would the gains benefit? The original territory of the United States had been divided long before. The South walked away from the Constitutional Convention satisfied with its share of land and power. But the windfalls of the Revolution, the Louisiana Purchase, the Adams-Onís Treaty, and the Mexican-American War changed all this. Every major acquisition raised the stakes and required some new compromise between the contenders. Each fresh debate exacerbated old tensions, until they became maddening. When it was apparent that the balance of power had shifted permanently, Southerners wanted out. Manifest Destiny thus helped kill 700,000 Americans in a fratricidal war.[65] Swept along by the flood tides of the era, many nation-states expanded during the nineteenth century. Few paid as high a price.

The very first compromise was so effortless that it hardly seemed like one at all. At the close of the Revolution, Britain ceded 233 million additional acres west of the Appalachian Mountain Range (approximately 10 percent of the nation's territory today, or an area the size of modern Germany, France, and Sweden).[66] This prompted the founders to make several pivotal choices consistent with their republican ideology.

Passed under the old Articles of Confederation, the Northwest Ordinance of 1787 was anti-imperial. It provided that new states would be formed out of these lands. The thirteen former colonies would not merely aggrandize their holdings. Furthermore, the ordinance mandated that new states would enter on an absolutely "equal footing with the original States"—though they would also be required to stay in the Union. New members would "forever remain a part of this Confederacy of the United States of America." Unlike the original thirteen states, which had had to break with the British to defend their constitutional equality, the new territories in the West could look forward to being received as equals automatically.[67]

The ordinance also forbade slavery north and west of the Ohio River: "There shall be neither slavery nor involuntary servitude in the said territory." Although some settlers illegally imported human chattel, the Continental Congress established the precedent that forced labor and new land should not go together, at least in theory, at least in the north.

If all this sounds intentional, it was not. The ordinance was drafted haphazardly and passed with virtually no debate. Lobbyists for the Ohio Land Company pressed the Continental Congress to act quickly so that more than five million acres could be subdivided and sold. Squatters were already pouring through the Cumberland Gap into Kentucky, headed for Ohio. Income from authorized sales would profit middlemen as well as the government, generating revenue to reduce debts left over from the Revolution. Territorial governments could also strengthen military defenses. British Redcoats still loomed on the Canadian boundary.[68] Well-organized tribes like the Iroquois remained a powerful threat, at least so long as they could exploit European rivalries. Expediting settlement of the Ohio River Valley had much to commend it, from a strategic point of view.

But snap decisions often reveal underlying values and automatic assumptions. The slave states voted unanimously to approve the Northwest Ordinance. They did so for complex reasons, including a belief that restrictions on slavery elsewhere would give them an economic edge. Congressman William Grayson of Virginia told James Madison that Southerners voted for the ordinance to prevent the northward spread of tobacco and indigo, and thus to preserve the Southern monopoly in those markets. Also, the ordinance did not pertain below the Ohio River, and it required the return of slaves who escaped to the North.[69]

Yet antislavery sentiment was woven into the fabric of the ordinance, like a faint pattern visible only at a distance. Thomas Jefferson drafted the first version in 1784. He proposed limits on slavery's spread not merely for economic reasons, but also because "the fate of millions unborn" was at stake.[70] Many leaders of the Upper South hoped that slavery would gradually die out, and a precious few even freed their property, as George Washington famously did upon his death. Jefferson's 1784 draft failed, but a similar, less sweeping version was approved without comment in 1787. It had little immediate effect because the national government possessed few enforcement powers and no inclination to use them on this issue. Yet the ordinance took hold in mythology. In later arguments against slavery, Daniel Webster, Thomas Hart Benton, Samuel P. Chase, and Abraham Lincoln all made references to the precedent of 1787. Although the road proved long, the ordinance placed slavery in the United States on the path to extinction.[71]

The Northwest Ordinance was the last easy compromise on the foreign policy of expansion. In 1819, the United States faced a new set of choices when Secretary of State John Quincy Adams concluded negotiations to define the boundaries of Louisiana, purchased sixteen years prior. Louisiana was America's single largest acquisition, representing approximately 23 percent of its final land area. But the borders were vague, and it was only after 1815 that world events calmed enough for the United States to insist on some final definition of what it had gotten for its money. With Napoleon out of the picture, it was Spain that had to contend with American ambitions, since its colony of Mexico neighbored Louisiana. Also at issue was Florida, which had bounced from Spain to Britain in 1763, and back to Spain twenty years later. Spain possessed Florida but occupied it lightly. Americans coveted the exhausted empire's last stretch of sand on the North Atlantic seaboard.

John Quincy Adams was perhaps the shrewdest man ever to negotiate on behalf of the United States. He exploited contemporary events at every turn, including an unauthorized invasion into Spanish territory by impetuous General Andrew Jackson, who was on the trail of Indians.[72] (When President Monroe consulted his neighbor Thomas Jefferson on the advisability of appointing Jackson to a diplomatic post, the ex-president exclaimed, "Why, good God! He would breed you a quarrel before he had been there a month!"[73]) Spain's grip on Florida had been weakening for years and the U.S. secretary of state sought to loosen it further.

Don Luis de Onís faced Adams across the bargaining table. An astute, aristocratic man, Onís also entertained ambitious hopes. Indeed, he was authorized to trade Florida (43 million acres) for all of Louisiana (523 million acres). John Quincy Adams was not about to accept such a poor bargain, of course, but Spain's bold offer suggests the malleability of New World boundaries and the opportunism driving both countries. The negotiations took two years. Don Luis de Onís tried to drum up support from England and France against the "scandalous ambition of this Republic," lest it take Canada, Cuba, and Mexico.[74] But at that particular moment other Europeans had little interest in rescuing the hapless Spanish Empire, then falling apart in giant chunks. As nation-states took hold across the hemisphere, Adams's position gradually strengthened.

In 1819, Onís and Adams redrew the map of the continent. In exchange for a favorable boundary at Texas (then the northernmost region of Mexico) and payment of assorted Iberian debts, Onís signed Florida over to the United States along with a new Louisiana border that went clear to the Pacific Ocean. Lewis and Clark had trekked to the mouth of the Columbia River more than a decade earlier, but across lands to which the United States had no clear title. Now the Louisiana Purchase ended at the foaming surf of the Oregon coastline.

Once again the question arose: How would the nation dispose of these new riches? Into whose hands would they be delivered: slaveholders or free labor?

John Quincy Adams despaired about the lack of any great congressional champion for the antislavery cause. He fumed in his diary: "Oh, if but one man could arise with a genius capable of . . . communicating those eternal truths that belong to this question, to lay bare in all its nakedness that outrage upon the goodness of God, human slavery, now is the time, and this is the occasion, upon which such a man would perform the duties of an angel upon earth!"[75] But a few powerful speakers did make themselves heard, including Congressman James Tallmadge, a forty-one-year-old lawyer from New York and veteran of the War of 1812. On Saturday, February 13, the week before the Adams-Onís Treaty was signed in Washington, Tallmadge proposed that slavery be outlawed in any states formed inside the new boundaries of the Louisiana Purchase.

A frenzied debate ensued that went on for more than a year. Opponents in Congress pointed out that the general government had "no right to prescribe to any State the details of its government, any further than that it should be republican." A state could not choose monarchical rule, but it could do anything else it pleased. Such were the provisions of the Constitution and the definition of state sovereignty.

Tallmadge replied that he had no wish to "intermeddle" or require abolition in any one of the original states. There, he conceded, "I submit to an evil which we cannot safely remedy." But newly acquired territory was another matter. Moral obligation compelled a different course.

An angry Georgian took to his feet. "You have kindled a fire which all the waters of the ocean cannot put out, which seas of blood can only extinguish," Representative William Cobb scolded Tallmadge.

The New Yorker shot back: "If a dissolution of the Union must take place, let it be so! If civil war, which gentlemen so much threaten, must come, I can only say, let it come!"[76]

Henry Clay of Kentucky, a slave owner and speaker of the House, was so unnerved that he predicted that within five years—"shocking" as it was to contemplate—"the Union would be divided into three distinct confederacies."[77] Nonetheless, Clay worked hard with other moderate Southerners to head off disunion. The Missouri Compromise, which he shepherded through Congress, established an explicit sectional balance for the first time. In January 1820, there were eleven slave states and eleven free states. The compromise admitted Missouri as a slave state in exchange for Maine, which was free, creating the expectation that all future states would board the American ark in pairs. Even more important, the compromise drew a line in the dirt. Other than for the one-time exception of Missouri, no state formed out of the Louisiana Purchase above parallel 36°30′ north could allow slavery. Once again Congress banned the peculiar institution in new territory, this time anywhere above the boundary originally surveyed for Britain by Mason and Dixon.

Although it averted immediate disaster, the Missouri Compromise of 1820 left anxiety in its wake. Previously euphoric at the expansion he had wrought with a pen, Adams now gloomily confessed: "Since the Missouri debate, I considered the continuance of the Union for any length of time as very precarious, and entertained serious doubts whether Louisiana and slavery would not ultimately break us up." Thomas Jefferson, age seventy-seven, expressed "terror" the following month. The Missouri Compromise was a fire bell in the night. "A geographical line . . . once conceived and held up to the angry passions of men, will never be obliterated," he foresaw. "Every new irritation will mark it deeper and deeper."[78]

Indeed, the Missouri Compromise stimulated a new proslavery defense. Whereas prominent planters had previously bemoaned the institution as antithetical to republicanism, opinions now shifted and Southerners rallied. Charles Pinckney of Virginia, a framer of the Constitution, spoke for his brethren. "The great body of slaves are happier in their present position than they could be in any other," he asserted defiantly in 1820, "and the man or men who attempt to give them freedom would be their greatest enemies."[79]

For the next thirty years, the Missouri Compromise did its work, however. New states entered in pairs routinely. National and local sovereignties coexisted with relative ease. The power of the executive umpire was still untried, except on one occasion, during the 1832 Nullification Crisis.

Fed up with taxes, South Carolinians resurrected the concept of nullification in an attempt to flout federal authority over tariffs. John C. Calhoun led the charge, drawing on the Virginia and Kentucky Resolutions penned by Madison and Jefferson three decades earlier. Never one to stand idly by when his authority was questioned, President Andrew Jackson asked Congress for permission to send troops into South Carolina. He reputedly told one congressman that if South Carolina's nonsense led to the shedding of one drop of blood in defiance of the federal government, "I will hang the first man of them I can get my hands on to the first tree I can find."[80] The so-called Force Bill gave Jackson everything he wanted. South Carolina backed down, acceding peaceably to federal authority.

On other occasions, Jackson conveniently pleaded federal impotence. When Georgia trampled on the property and civil rights of Native Americans in 1830, Jackson declined to enforce the decisions of the Supreme Court, which had overruled Georgia law. "As individuals we may entertain and express our opinions of their acts, but as a Government we have as little right to control them [the states] as we have to prescribe laws for other nations," the president told Congress. Jackson simply did not wish to risk internal strife merely to protect natives. Indeed, he praised the federal Indian Removal Act of 1830 for putting "an end to all possible danger of collision between the authorities of the General and State Governments on account of the Indians."[81] For a time at least, the only danger was to the Indians, forced to walk the unsparing "Trail of Tears" that led out of Georgia to federal territory across the Mississippi. American nationalism brutally robbed the peaceable natives of their ancient homelands.

Despite Jackson's efforts to finesse the tensions of dual sovereignty, the states continued on a collision course. The Missouri Compromise might have kept the nation together longer if foreign policy had not produced another great burst of growth. War with Mexico in 1846 resulted in the nation's third largest acquisition. Another 334 million acres, 15 percent of the nation's territory today, came into the Union. The former lands of Mexico occasioned two last-ditch compromises between the states, but these unraveled in turn, precipitating the greatest disaster in American history. Britain peaceably abolished slavery in the 1830s. The United States managed to do so only at a horrific cost in lives.

Barely six months after Spain ratified the Adams-Onís Treaty, the Iberian empire lost all the territory that Don Luis had worked so hard to demarcate. Even though Madrid did not accept the fact until 1836, Mexico became independent in August 1821. Unfortunately, the government of the United Mexican States (Estados Unidos Mexicanos) was notoriously unstable, suffering forty-eight turnovers of the national executive between 1825 and 1855. Mexico's war of independence had cost hundreds of thousands of lives, and economic recuperation proceeded haltingly. All of this made foreign negotiations nearly impossible when conflicts arose. Mexico's internal chaos fed American worries that its neighbor was poised to become the dupe of its archenemy, Great Britain. A growing sense of racial superiority, mixed with anti-Catholicism, completed the picture of Yankee attitudes toward America's struggling neighbor.

The diplomatic wrangle that resulted in the Mexican-American War began over Texas. Spain and then Mexico had encouraged immigrants to settle there in the 1820s to provide a buffer against the expanding Comanche Empire.[82] They hoped to better secure the territory, which had attracted little population from Mexico's interior because of the formidable Indian presence. Encouraged by rock-bottom land prices and confident in their fighting ability, American settlers flocked to Texas, largely ignoring the requirement that they convert to Catholicism. Their numbers soon frightened the Mexican government. More Americans arrived in one decade than Spain had settled in three centuries. Mexico City banned further immigration in 1830 and more strongly asserted its restrictions on Protestantism and slavery. The settlers sent Stephen Austin to Mexico City to petition for relaxation of these terms, or at least for Mexican statehood for Texas, then merely a province of the State of Coahuila. After some initial conversations, however, Austin was thrown into a former prison of the Spanish Inquisition, where he endured solitary confinement for three months.[83]

In 1834 events became even more complicated when General Antônio Lopez de Santa Anna dissolved the Mexican Congress, suspended the nation's wobbly constitution, and dispatched troops northward to chasten the presumptuous gringos as well as other Mexicans in rebellion against the general's coup. Recognizing the futility of negotiations with the new dictatorial government, the Texans declared and then won their independence in 1836. Citizens of the "Free and Sovereign" states of Yucatán and Zacatecas undertook similar measures, though without success.[84]

The Texans immediately sought foreign diplomatic recognition. Fearful of provoking Mexico, President Andrew Jackson delayed employing Jefferson's *de facto* principle until the last day of his administration in 1837, a year following Texas's independence. France subsequently recognized Texas as an autonomous nation-state in 1839, and Britain in 1840. Mexico remained unreconciled, however, much as Spain had resisted Mexico's own secession two decades earlier. Santa Anna tried again in 1842 to suppress the rebels. In 1844, England tried unsuccessfully to persuade the Mexican government to accept the facts on the ground, partly to establish Texas as a counterweight to growing U.S. power.

Under an ongoing threat of Mexican invasion, Texas petitioned three times to join the Union. Not until 1845, nine years later, did the U.S. Congress agree to the proposition, and then only by a slim margin. Unwilling to countenance Texas's independence, nor its unification with the United States, Mexico broke diplomatic relations four days later. The United States sent an ambassador to negotiate the impasse. John Slidell waited in Mexico City for four months in hopes of meeting with President Mariano Paredes, an army general who had recently taken over the government. But President Paredes refused to receive Slidell, who wanted to negotiate a new U.S.-Mexico border at Texas as well as the possible purchase of California. The newspaper *El Tiempo* scorned the requests of the "colossus with feet of clay."[85] Of course, such intransigence was perfectly within Mexico's rights as a sovereign nation, but its strategy was not well calculated to defend the nation's interests through adroit diplomacy. Within months, the neighbors were at war.

All this took place in the context of the nineteenth-century struggle among states and empires over territory. The United States showed a decided preference for arbitration. On three occasions it attempted to persuade Mexico, known to be insolvent, to sell all or part of sparsely populated California. Why not another Louisiana-style purchase? Washington also feared that the land might otherwise go to Britain and panicked whenever it seemed that Mexico might sell California to the United Kingdom in preference to America, or that the English would merely invade southward from their position in Vancouver. Should arbitration fail, at least some Americans entertained visions of fighting for California. "It would be worth a war of twenty years to prevent England acquiring it," one U.S. diplomat argued. The Mexican representative to Great Britain did, indeed, propose settling English citizens in California (as it had earlier settled American migrants in Texas), partly to induce the Royal Navy to station protective warships off the coast.[86]

Coincidentally, the Americans and British were in dispute at the very same time over lands in the northwest, haggling over where to draw the border of Oregon, which they had jointly (and peaceably) occupied pending a final settlement. For a time, pugnacious President James K. Polk insisted on a boundary well above Vancouver Island: "54°40'—or Fight!" Policymakers in Washington, anxious to obtain a large share of whatever riches might be up for grabs, were paranoid about the possibility that Britain might eventually squeeze them on two sides, north and south of where the Adams-Onís line touched the Pacific. Britain tried to allay American fears about California while pressing its own ambitious demands in Oregon, but the U.S. government hardly trusted London. Greed, fear, and international rivalry fueled Manifest Destiny in an era of explosive, worldwide expansionism that flagged the last ill-defended territories.

America's war with Mexico was brief. Santa Anna fired the first shots in April 1846, but only after Polk had ordered troops to the disputed boundary of Texas. The United States then invaded, conquering California and Mexico down to its capital city. Whigs in Congress, including a young Abraham Lincoln, deplored Polk's aggression as wholly unnecessary and utterly rapacious. Mexico had no obligation to receive an American ambassador or sell any part of its territory.

Even the State Department official whom Polk sent to negotiate a peace treaty balked at the president's harsh demands. In negotiations at the town of Guadalupe Hidalgo, overlooking the ancient capitol of the Aztecs and the modern capitol of Mexico, Nicholas Trist asked for *less* territory than instructed by President Polk. A former law student under Thomas Jefferson who had married the third president's granddaughter, Trist later commented that the 1848 Treaty of Guadalupe Hidalgo "was a thing for every right-minded American to be ashamed of, and I *was* . . . most cordially and intensely ashamed of it." Ulysses S. Grant made a similar admission: "I do not think there ever was a more wicked war than that waged by the United States in Mexico. I thought so at the time, when I was a youngster, only I had not moral courage enough to resign."[87]

Mexico was forced at gunpoint to cede more than a third of its land for the paltry consideration of $15 million. The "only advantage" in the otherwise disastrous agreement, admitted Mexico's minister to the United States, was a promise contained in Article 11 that the U.S. Army would henceforth prevent Indian raids into Mexican territory. In preceding decades, the disorganized central government had been nearly helpless to stop the widespread theft of horses and cattle by Comanches and Apaches, and the abduction of women and children as slaves. Locals collaborated widely with American troops during the war in exchange for protection.[88]

Mexico's loss was otherwise unmitigated. In a stroke of continuing bad luck for America's southern neighbor, James Marshall discovered gold at Sutter's Mill in the Sierra Nevada that same year, unexpectedly enriching the new owners of California.

Yet the conflict was far from unique. The abrupt collapse of Spanish colonialism had created a power vacuum across the hemisphere. From 1821 to 1935, twenty-one border wars broke out among the various American republics. Most were motivated by "simple geopolitical competition," according to Miguel Centeno.[89] In 1821, for example, Haiti invaded the Dominican Republic. It took two decades for the Dominicans to successfully reclaim independence. In 1864, Brazil and Argentina took half of Paraguay, which they divided between themselves. In the latter conflict, 60 percent of the Paraguayan population (including nearly every adult male) perished.[90]

In 1879, following a lengthy impasse during which Chile attempted to negotiate a border dispute—while vowing to keep its "gunpowder dry"—Chilean troops invaded northward. At the expense of Peru and Bolivia, Chile increased its territory by one-third and acquired a monopoly on the world's supply of nitrates, a primary chemical in bombs and fertilizer. As the foreign minister stated baldly in 1880, "Chile's security required territorial expansion."[91] Soon thereafter, Chilean troops conquered the lands of the Araucanaian people, which allowed the nation to extend its effective borders southward as well. In 1935, as a consequence of the Chaco War that claimed 100,000 lives, Paraguay took disputed lands from Bolivia. While Paraguay triumphed territorially, both sides used the war "to clear natives off the frontier," according to one historian.[92]

Few, if any, of these conflicts were fair according to modern sensibilities, and most were tinged with racism. Warfare physically defined the new republics. They also "created a political culture of participation and lower-class involvement in the struggles of the emerging nation," according to historians of Latin America. As in the United States, these conflicts associated "citizenship with whiteness and masculinity."[93] That said, such wars were not imperialistic, since new provinces came in on a basis of legal equality. Paraguay and Chile hardly became empires, nor did the United States.

Violent, opportunistic border wars were a sad fact of life, even between republics, until international law and practice changed fundamentally much later. As Alexander Hamilton ruefully asked in *Federalist* 6: "Have republics in practice been less addicted to war than monarchies? . . . Are there not aversions, predilections, rivalships, and desires of unjust acquisitions, that affect nations as well as kings?" Hamilton hoped to deter pernicious practices that dated back to the ancient Greek republics, but the hard-nosed realist would not have been surprised to see them persist well into the twentieth century.

So why did Nicholas Trist, Ulysses S. Grant, Abraham Lincoln, and many others express such intense shame over the Treaty of Guadalupe Hidalgo, if these were common global events? They did so because outright conquest of a neighbor's property, no matter how intractable the border dispute, was as contrary to republican values as the institution of slavery. The United States aspired to better behavior. Nonetheless, some Americans justified the blatant contradictions by embellishing racial stereotypes and asserting that the biblical injunction to "be fruitful and multiply" meant that undeveloped land should go to those best prepared to put it to use.[94] If Mexicans could not use their resources well—because they were racially "inferior"—then Americans were entitled to them.

Latin Americans sometimes embraced similar arguments toward one another, despite the idealism expressed in their own revolutions. The European cultural movement known as romanticism dominated these decades, contributing to ethnocentrism. Romanticism glorified national features such as democracy and economic prosperity as "racial" characteristics, in contrast with the preceding Enlightenment, which had emphasized human equality and the inalienable natural rights of all peoples, regardless of their level of technological or material development.

Some Americans spied the arrogance, self-deceit, and excuse for larceny in these new arguments and roundly deplored them. Senator Thomas Corwin of Ohio called Manifest Destiny a form of sophistry designed to rationalize "the propriety of seizing upon any territory and any people that may be in the way of our fated advance."[95] John Quincy Adams, retired from the presidency and back in Congress, suffered a fatal stroke on the floor of the House of Representatives at age eighty, while delivering a final protest against the "unrighteous war" with Mexico.

Opponents also criticized the war as an instrument of slavery. It was a ploy by "slave-holders, smugglers, Indian killers, foul-mouthed tobacco spitting men swearing upon sacred fourth of July principles to carry spread eagle supremacy from the Atlantic to the Pacific."[96] The lands in question were mostly south of the Mason-Dixon line. Mexico had abolished slavery, and the South was eager to extend it into previously "free" territories. The Mexican-American War precipitated the collapse of whatever national consensus existed on the benefits of expansion into foreign lands. Once applauded, territorial growth was now openly equated with dangerous dueling over the peculiar institution.

David Wilmot, a freshman Democrat from Pennsylvania, fired the opening salvo when he tried to amend an 1846 war appropriations bill. The Wilmot Proviso would have prohibited slavery in any territory gained from Mexico. It passed the House several times but never cleared the Senate. Echoing popular sentiment in the South, the *Charleston Mercury* denounced the proviso as the "first step to a dissolution" of the nation.[97] Indeed, each reintroduction of the amendment further inflamed debate.

Combined with California's application for admission to the Union, the Treaty of Guadalupe Hidalgo forced Congress to take up Wilmot's challenge once again. Henry Clay of Kentucky was still on the scene, though now much older. Along with Daniel Webster of Massachusetts and Stephen A. Douglas of Illinois, he fashioned the Compromise of 1850, a collection of five bills to deal with the former lands of Mexico. For the South, the legislation offered a stronger Fugitive Slave Act and the sop of "popular sovereignty."

Popular sovereignty meant that new states would be allowed to make up their minds about slavery as they formed. It did not prohibit the institution in advance, as the Northwest Ordinance and Missouri Compromise had done. Although no one actually expected New Mexico or Utah to legalize slavery, the *principle* of state sovereignty was a sine qua non of anxious Southerners' bargain with federalism. The compromise gave Northerners the admission of California as a free state (without an accompanying slave state to sustain sectional balance) and the prohibition of slave trading within the District of Columbia. No longer would men, women, and children be manacled in the shadow of the White House. But they could be openly hunted in the North, as Harriet Beecher Stowe soon dramatized in her incendiary novel, *Uncle Tom's Cabin*.

The compromise held only a few years. The North had the bulk of new territory. Dixie was not about to watch it carved into a greater and greater number of rivals that, if admitted to the Union, might gang up one day to eliminate slavery in the Old South. Impatient to facilitate a transcontinental railroad through unorganized territory, Senator Stephen Douglas pressed a further modification through Congress in 1854. The Kansas-Nebraska Act retroactively applied popular sovereignty to the old territories of the Louisiana Purchase. It thereby overturned the prohibition on slavery above parallel 36°30' north. Upon forming, states could now adopt slavery as an exercise of their rightful powers vis-à-vis the general government.

The benign-sounding principle of popular sovereignty split the country like a melon. The founders' most dire fears came to pass, and the sectional chasm opened. The near-fatal beating of Massachusetts senator Charles Sumner on the floor of the U.S. Congress in 1856, and John Brown's massacre of settlers at Potawatomie two days later, showed that physical violence had now replaced arbitration and debate. When Abraham Lincoln won the presidency in 1860 without a single electoral vote from the Deep South, secession commenced. By repeatedly aggravating the perpetual disagreement about *extending* slavery, the nation's foreign acquisitions inadvertently brought about hundreds of thousands of Civil War deaths. They would have killed the Union as well, had the umperial president not stepped in.

The conflict was sometimes called Lincoln's War, with justification. President Abraham Lincoln embraced a nationalist interpretation of the Constitution upon which there was not then universal agreement—nor had there ever been. Lincoln argued that the Union was "older than any of the States; and, in fact, it created them as States." He pointed out that not one of the former colonies had had a constitution prior to its membership in the United States, with the lone exception of Texas. The United States was thus a single country, under one government. It had the power and responsibility to quell internal insurrections, such as George Washington had done during the Whiskey Rebellion and Andrew Jackson had threatened during the Nullification Crisis. Speaking for the Southern point of view, John C. Calhoun had argued the opposite: "I go on the ground that [the] Constitution was made by the States; that it is a federal union of the States, in which the several States still retain their sovereignty." Hamilton and Jefferson might as well have been alive, sparring under Washington's disparaging eye.[98]

Historian Daniel Farber argues that Lincoln's interpretation was the more correct, based on the fundamental prerogatives given the central government in 1789: to tax citizens, make war, regulate trade, conduct foreign policy, and so on. These were "far more sweeping powers than those enjoyed by the European Union today, and indeed, far more sweeping powers than have ever been enjoyed by any league of sovereign nations."[99] Lincoln's understanding was certainly in line with that of Alexander Hamilton, who had sweated out the summer in Philadelphia while Jefferson enjoyed the cooling breezes of the French countryside.

But questions of legality are often determined as much by victory as by logic. Southerners merely wished to be left alone, Confederate president Jefferson Davis claimed. Northerners were not prepared to do so, believing they were called to defend democracy itself. Lincoln told Congress as much on the Fourth of July, 1861. "Our popular government has often been called an experiment," he observed. "Two points in it, our people have already settled— the successful *establishing*, and the successful *administering* of it. One still remains—its successful maintenance against a formidable internal attempt to overthrow it. . . . This issue embraces more than the fate of these United States. It presents to the whole family of man, the question, whether a constitutional republic, or democracy . . . can or cannot, maintain its territorial integrity, against its own domestic foes."[100] In other words, could democracy pass the Westphalian test of sovereignty and defend itself both within and without? Or would it fail, and thereby prove a bankrupt form of government? And so, when the Confederacy bombarded and captured Fort Sumter in April 1861, the North invaded the South to put down secession once and for all.

Foreign officials questioned U.S. motives and methods. Like American critics, they were sometimes scathing toward Lincoln personally. *Punch,* the prominent British satire magazine, pictured Lincoln as a "Yankee 'Coon" up a tree, a false friend to slaves, and a bully who understood only bullying.[101] From a foreign perspective, the United States inflicted unacceptable collateral damage on civilian populations, fought for an ambiguous cause, and made allies with despots (such as the Russian czar). Lincoln had said the war was not about slavery, so they believed him.

Consequently, many Europeans openly sympathized with the Confederacy. Its permanent establishment would also conveniently halve the power of the increasingly formidable United States. As the Russian ambassador opined to Saint Petersburg, "the English Government, at the bottom of its heart, desires the separation of North America into two republics, which will watch each other jealously and counterbalance one the other. Then England, on terms of peace and commerce with both, would have nothing to fear from either; for she would dominate them, restraining them by their rival ambitions."[102]

Britain and France declared neutrality, recognizing a state of belligerency between two *foreign* nations. European businessmen made healthy profits supplying both sides. This lifeline from Europe provided cannons, bullets, gray uniform cloth, rifles, food, and all the other materiel necessary for the mostly pastoral Confederacy to endure four long years against the industrialized North.[103] Liverpool shipyards secretly built the CSS *Florida* and *Alabama,* which captured, burned, or sank more than a hundred Union merchant ships.

Their own experiences with sovereignty and empire made it difficult for foreigners to understand why Lincoln cared as much as he did about stopping the Confederacy. How did state autonomy intersect with federal power? Sir George Cornewall Lewis, the thoughtful British secretary of war and a member of the Liberal Party, expressed a common puzzlement when he mused to Prime Minister Palmerston: "The South fight for independence; but what do the North fight for, except to gratify passion or pride?"[104] Furthermore, outsiders saw Union defeat as merely a matter of time. The Confederacy alone was bigger than Britain, France, Spain, and Germany *combined.* No one believed for a minute that the United States could retain an area larger than all of Western Europe against its will.

Only the Russian czar demonstrated active friendship toward the Union. *Punch* expressed an irony not lost on Europeans. In a full-page cartoon in

1863, Lincoln clasped hands with Alexander II and said, giving the czar a cunning look:

> Imperial son of Nicholas the Great,
> We 'air in the same fix, I calculate,
> You with your Poles, with Southern rebels I,
> Who spurn my rule and my revenge defy.[105]

Lower on the social ladder, the mood was different. The British working class staunchly supported the Union as the world's foremost republic. Middle-class and genteel reformers also flocked to the cause after Lincoln's Emancipation Proclamation, including John Stuart Mill and Harriet Martineau. Philosopher and newspaper correspondent Karl Marx argued in *Die Presse* that the fight turned not on the "Northern lust for sovereignty" but on the elemental contradiction between slavery and freedom.[106]

Lincoln's War largely resolved the conflict over authority between the states and the federal government, even though the question reared its head again during the civil rights era of the 1950s and 1960s, and does so occasionally even today. The general government established its right to quash internecine conflict between the states, just as the authors of the Constitution intended.

Yet the North did not establish an empire over the Confederacy. Reconstruction restored democratic government, giving Southerners full representation and mitigating their anger. Disgruntled politicians ceased flirting with disunion whenever tempers ran high, as they had since the Hartford Convention of 1814. To heal the terrible breach caused by the massive bloodshed, white Southerners relinquished their defense of chattel slavery and white Northerners dropped their demands for full implementation of black citizenship rights. Over time, both sides downplayed the horrors of slavery as a cause of the war, with Southerners especially emphasizing states' rights.[107]

And, indeed, states' rights were at issue, meaning not only what rights states had vis-à-vis the U.S. federal government or any outside umpire, but also what rights they had vis-à-vis their own citizens. Could states enslave minority populations at will? Could a national government burn the homes and factories of civilians during a domestic conflict? Europeans faced similar questions, which they found difficult to answer in a consistent fashion. If states enjoyed absolute sovereignty, did they also have responsibilities? If they reneged on those responsibilities, whether to their own citizens or neighboring countries, did they relinquish their privileges as well?

England grappled with this quandary during the Jacobin Terror of the 1790s. Did France's revolutionary government have an unmolested right to slaughter the wealthy and decapitate the king? (According to Westphalian tradition, the short answer was *yes,* until the conflict crossed an international border.) France, Russia, Prussia, and Austria confronted a related but slightly different problem in the 1860s, when the Ottoman Empire proved incompetent to stop the internal massacre of one ethnic group by another. Should Ottoman sovereignty preclude foreign intervention in a domestic crisis that the Turks refused to resolve? (The humanitarian answer was *no,* but occupying forces were required to leave as quickly as possible.)

In the United States, the great antebellum question was whether or not the states, especially those created de novo out of federal territory, had an inviolable right to tyrannize a portion of their population. If they did not have such a right, should a higher authority intervene in defense of humanitarian principle? From the start of his campaign for president, Abraham Lincoln argued against "the 'gur-reat pur-rinciple' that 'if one man would enslave another, no third man should object,' fantastically called 'Popular Sovereignty.'" European liberals expressed a similar attitude, sympathetic to action on behalf of peoples oppressed by local governments. Protracted civil wars like the American one also seemed to beg for intervention—despite the Westphalian proscription against meddling in internal matters. "Let us do something, as we are Christian men," the *London Morning Herald* commented about the bloodletting in Virginia.[108]

Technological change played a role in this. Recently laid telegraph cables brought news instantaneously about foreign bloodshed in the States and elsewhere. As newspapers proliferated and literacy spread, middle-class opinion increasingly shaped British and French foreign policy. Humanitarian intervention emerged as a new phenomenon. Liberal Victorians challenged the limits of Westphalian-style sovereignty and voiced demands for the exercise of outside authority when local governments failed in their duty. The closest thing to an umpire or judicial force was then the Concert of Europe, an ad hoc coalition of great powers that met periodically and which, in fact, approved at least one intervention to quell foreign bloodshed. Ultimately, of course, Americans brought the war in the United States to an end themselves, when the Union conclusively defeated the Confederacy. The British and French governments had considered attempting to mediate, but Lincoln resisted their intervention. Nonetheless, the American struggle took place in a larger world that had consequences for domestic conflicts.[109]

The reverse was also true. The U.S. Civil War helped reshape the external world, speeding the worldwide trends toward access, arbitration, and transparency. Slavery had imposed draconian limits on the social opportunities of African Americans. Abolition established at least the *legal* right of all U.S. citizens to equal access to the political process and economic marketplace. It was the most stunning example of the worldwide movement toward "free labor" after 1800 that gradually abolished slavery across the Americas and serfdom in Eastern Europe. Volitional wage labor replaced coerced servitude.

The war also prompted the world's first international arbitration. In 1871, the United States and Britain were locked in dispute over claims that England had damaged the United States by allowing private dockyards to sell warships to the Confederacy in violation of neutrality laws. Honoring cultural ties that were older than their hostilities, the two countries took the unprecedented step of submitting their problem to a tribunal of five judges: one representing each disputant, and three others appointed by the impartial nations of Brazil, Italy, and Switzerland. The tribunal ordered Great Britain to pay an indemnity of $15.5 million dollars in gold. It faithfully did, showing that a great power could act with honor and accept an adverse verdict.[110]

Lastly, the Civil War furthered the trend toward transparency. President Lincoln became the world's first leader to open secret diplomatic correspondence for public view. Lincoln released his 1861 correspondence in order to assuage public discontent. Citizens could read about skirmishes between the United States and foreign governments, and evaluate policy for themselves. The practice persisted and spread. In 1910, France began publishing its own diplomatic records, followed by the United Kingdom in 1926, and Japan in 1936. By the end of the twentieth century, eleven countries practiced openness with regard to diplomatic correspondence.

As indicated by the death sentence meted out to William Mumford in New Orleans for his assault on the flag, Northerners deeply resented attacks on their national emblem. "We were born and bred under the stars and stripes," wrote a Pittsburgh editorialist after the fall of Fort Sumter. The South might have reasonable concerns, he conceded, but when it becomes "an enemy to the American system of government . . . and fires upon the flag . . . our influence goes for that flag, no matter whether a Republican or a Democrat holds it." The *Chicago Journal* made similar charges. The Confederacy had "trampled under foot that flag which has been the glorious and consecrated symbol of American Liberty."[111]

Prior to the American Revolution, flags were used primarily by fishing vessels and military units, or as the pennants of royal families. The American and French cataclysms changed this, turning national flags into a worldwide fad. Associated with revolutionary, egalitarian philosophies, nationalism and its flags spread relentlessly, from Europe to South America to Asia, Africa, and the Pacific.[112] Their colors and designs symbolized national goals and underscored identity. Flags also marked possession, meaning triumph over competitors who hoped to rule the same lands.

At the start of this period, the U.S. Congress had mandated that each time a state joined the Union, its star must be added to the American flag on the Fourth of July following admission, to demonstrate the equality between new and old members. Congress was motivated by pure nationalism, a volatile and increasingly prevalent phenomenon between 1815 and 1865. It was often not pretty, but it was hardly a program of empire.

5

Territorial Expansion versus Saltwater Imperialism

Or, How America Entered the Fray for Colonies, 1865–1920

Europeans called this the Belle Époque, or Beautiful Era. American satirist Mark Twain dubbed it the Gilded Age, meaning that glittery gold hid a baser metal. Scholars typically call it the Progressive Era. While all these terms are reasonable, this book employs Belle Époque as being the most suggestive of the optimistic, perfectionist, and "beautiful" assumptions of the general period, especially before World War One.[1]

The late nineteenth and early twentieth centuries witnessed dazzling economic growth in industrializing countries around the world, accompanied by unprecedented immigration, technological innovation, working-class strife, and social reform. To many, it seemed progress was unstoppable. Nickelodeons introduced movies, Henry Ford put millions behind the wheel, radio reached across the Atlantic, and new banks helped ordinary workers purchase homes on credit. Corporations became more complex, governments more powerful. The Industrial Revolution had arrived, coupled to the locomotive of nationalism. The political process became simultaneously more accessible and more remote as the scale of public life grew. Party machines organized voters and encouraged immigrants to "vote early and often." Senators stood for election and women got the vote. Progressives from New York to New Zealand thought they saw the light of a new era in international relations, and they did. But it was further away than they realized, and catastrophic war at the end of this era led to disillusionment.

The Belle Époque straddled a cusp in global politics. On rare occasions, it is possible to discern a fundamental discontinuity in history: a moment at which the human story takes a decisive, irrevocable turn, such as when humans invented gunpowder or the birth control pill. This was one of them. At the end of the nineteenth century most nations still sought power through territorial growth at another's expense. One hundred years later they measured power by the ability to compete in a cooperative world economy. The goals of security and prosperity remained, but the global community radically redefined the appropriate methods for obtaining them.[2] New international norms took hold. The United States sometimes embraced these norms earlier than others, sometimes not. Countries and peoples subtly copied one another and the United States was no exception. Other times, however, America gave history a decisive shove.

Political scientists call such basic transformations "regime change": when behavior considered ordinary in one era is forbidden as deviant in the next. Regimes change when participants' expectations converge on a new set of principles or practices that define what is legal, moral, or just plain tolerable.

From the seventeenth century through the nineteenth, most Europeans considered colonial expansion a proper response to the need to maintain a balance of power. European imperialism reached its zenith before self-determination became a tenet of world politics, and before Europe itself had fully adopted the pattern of one nation, one state.[3] Ruling over subject peoples from different ethnic backgrounds was routine for imperial nations across the globe. Colonial expansion seemed perfectly legitimate, and a reluctance to pursue such policies was unorthodox. Indeed, U.S. ambivalence about exercising power in foreign arenas made America seem the least "normal" of the major nations.[4] Europeans viewed its puny military with wry amusement.

During the twentieth century, however, balance-of-power politics fell into disrepute. The spreading ideal of national self-determination rendered imperialism improper. Particularly after World War II, racial theories that legitimated social inequality gave way to condemnations of racism and imperialism as both immoral and contrary to basic human rights. A statistical analysis of 132 breakaway nations from 1500 to 1987 shows that decolonization proceeded most swiftly in the colonies of those nations where popular sovereignty had the oldest and deepest roots, specifically, Britain, France, and the United States, as compared with Spain and Portugal.[5] Although imperialism enjoyed a rebirth in the Belle Époque, after this final surge it went into permanent decline. Decolonization redistributed power around the globe and branded the twentieth century.

This disjuncture was not easy or predetermined. The path did not proceed in a straight line, and sometimes it appeared that imperialism would actually become more rather than less entrenched. Almost four hundred years after 1492, altogether new territories were occupied. France seized Indochina in 1864, Germany claimed shares of Africa and New Guinea in 1884, and Italy carved off pieces of Ethiopia in 1889. Japan wrested territory from China in 1895, and the United States took the Philippines, Puerto Rico, and Guam from Spain in 1898. The number of colonial dependencies worldwide peaked at more than 150 in the year 1921. Nazi Germany and imperial Japan began their own determined campaigns of conquest in the 1930s, with catastrophic consequences.[6]

Flux in foreign relations ran parallel to regime change in the internal structure of most governments. As late as 1900, republicanism was still largely confined to the two continents of the Western Hemisphere. Princes, chiefs, kings, or emperors reigned over every European, Asian, and African country with the sole exception of France, which commenced its Third Republic in 1871, following two interludes of royal government. But what we might call the Republican Revolution, akin to the Industrial Revolution, was poised to sweep the world. China declared itself a republic in 1912 after more than two thousand years of dynastic rule. In 1920, the Republic of Turkey replaced the caliphate of the Ottoman Empire.

Even where monarchies persisted, they became less absolute. From Japan to Persia, dynasties capitulated to popular pressure, allowing legislatures to curb aristocratic prerogatives. Sovereignty came to rest in the people, rather than in royal families. As a consequence, by the time of the Belle Époque, most monarchs accepted some degree of popular representation. England stood in the forefront, having gradually reformed a system in which wealthy men had inherited seats in Parliament, purchased them for a few thousand pounds, or wheedled them from patrons in control of "rotten boroughs." The Reform Bill of 1832 increased the franchise to roughly 10 percent of the population. Further legislation widened the electorate to include most adult males by 1885. In respect to voting, much of the Old World gradually reorganized itself into a pattern of universal suffrage first set in the New World.[7]

Once again, these developments were not inevitable, nor were they uniformly benign. Assumptions about the optimal form of government changed only gradually, because of the inherent dangers in republicanism that foreigners could observe from their perches on either side of the Atlantic and Pacific. Democracy still had the reputation of being a brittle material for ships of state. America's disastrous Civil War seemed a textbook case. Likening the American experiment to "tulip mania" or the infamous South Seas panic, Sir John Ramsden smugly observed in 1861 that the world was "witnessing the bursting of the great republican bubble which had been so often held up to us as the model on which to recast our own English Constitution."[8]

Ramsden's prediction in the House of Commons proved both snide and incorrect. Republicanism continued to spread. Popular sovereignty was undeniably unstable, however, and violence trailed it. Equipped with mass-produced weapons, more people died in nationalistic wars during the twentieth century than in any preceding era. As Winston Churchill later quipped, democracy was "the worst form of Government except all the others that have been tried."[9]

Whether republics or monarchies, the number of formal nation-states climbed steadily. In 1870, Europeans recognized thirty-four states in the world similar to their own, meaning polities in control of well-defined, defensible borders. As of 1900, the club had grown to fifty-four. By 1920, seventy-five foreign countries were acknowledged as fully sovereign.[10] Since they did not enjoy a separate international status, dominions of Great Britain like Canada and Australia did not yet count, nor did any other colonies, such as Japanese-ruled Taiwan. But all were poised at the edge of a new norm—a regime in which full national independence based on a sense of distinctive identity became a paramount goal around the globe.

Some nations achieved autonomy and international recognition during the Belle Époque by merging with neighboring groups and creating larger, economically integrated units. The nation-states of Italy and Germany formed by corralling microstates that shared a language, much as the United States coalesced thirteen microstates that shared an ideology. The flamboyant, militarily savvy Giuseppe Garibaldi helped unify by force of arms seven kingdoms and duchies on the Italian Peninsula. An admirer of Lincoln who considered offering his services in the American Civil War, Garibaldi preferred republican government. But republicanism was still anathema in most of Europe, so Garibaldi submerged his dream in a new, consolidated "Kingdom of Italy" engineered by the astute aristocrat Count Camillo di Cavour.

To the north, Chancellor Otto von Bismarck, a steely nobleman with a dry sense of humor and an unsentimental outlook, similarly blended force with persuasion to unify thirty-nine German-speaking sovereignties into a single nation in 1871 under Kaiser Wilhelm I. The building materials of a defensible Germany were "blood and iron," in von Bismarck's memorable phrase. A vestigial principality like Liechtenstein, once typical of Central European microstates, became the exception rather than the norm.

Nationalism did not always lead to unification, however. Sometimes it had the opposite result, fracturing big, multiethnic empires into smaller, disconnected states. Tagged "Balkanization" because this tendency was especially common among the Balkan countries of southeastern Europe, the multiplication version of nationalism often had negative consequences for wealth and self-defense. Tiny nations like Bosnia or Macedonia might establish their borders on the world map for one or two decades, then lose autonomy to a more powerful neighbor like Austria, Russia, or Turkey for three or four. Petite units were not typically robust. Small-scale production and neighbors' discriminatory tariffs tended to keep prices high and prevent products from circulating widely. Economic growth was stunted.

When not undermined by sectional discord, larger nation-states thus had frightening advantages over smaller ones in a world that still offered no guarantees whatsoever to the weak. Yet nationalism sprang from unpredictable affinities, not rational calculations about optimal size. In some locales, nationalism might have a centrifugal effect, in others, a centripetal one.

The populace largely supported these reconfigurations, which seemed to elevate the people over the aristocracy—and sometimes over foreigners who were "less civilized," in the parlance of the day. Indeed, nationalism and the new imperialism flourished simultaneously, like twin titans destined to clash. Growing pride in one's country, reinforced by patriotic, mass education and a booming penny press in national languages, could easily tip over into chauvinism and racism. Junior members of the family of card-carrying nations often sought subordinate colonies as a way to assert their new status, catch up with older states, and take the offensive against possible predators. Germany, Italy, Japan, and the United States all joined the competition. It was not clear when or if peoples under colonial rule would turn this trend around and create their own sovereign states. Considering the fresh momentum, an observer at the start of the twentieth century might have surmised that empire would be the dominant form of government a century later, even though precisely the reverse occurred. In the end, nationalism trumped imperialism.

The United States finally hopped onto the runaway imperialist bandwagon in 1898. It was the last world power to jump, but jump it did. A primary reason was simply that it could. Nations were largely free to do whatever they could get away with, and empire beckoned as the wave of the future. Only strength constrained choices. The globe was still in what philosophers call a state of nature, meaning an era before the rule of law. There was no United Nations, nor were there any broad international treaties. There were but two organizations with global authority: the International Telegraph Union, founded cooperatively in 1865 to relay cable messages, and the Universal Postal Union, created in 1874 to expedite mail. Only the lowly postage stamp, British journalist W. T. Stead observed in 1901, enjoyed the status of "a citizen of the universe, free from all customs houses, and protected . . . in all lands, irrespective of nationality."[11] Otherwise, powerful states vied openly for colonies and adopted whatever policies they were strong enough to defend, with little fear of international consequences.

For the United States, the plasticity of the Belle Époque presented three basic choices again and again between 1867 and 1920. First, America could continue extending indefinitely the territory under its largely egalitarian system, as it had done until sectional discord made expansion too dangerous. Or, despite its long-standing critique of imperialism, the United States could follow the lead of other powerful nations and acquire overseas subordinates. Or, lastly, it could advocate an altogether new international system—an "open door"—that might make the globe more prosperous and peaceful, but that would require ongoing participation in entangling alliances to sustain a better world order.

As it turned out, Americans made all three choices, in an overlapping but largely sequential fashion. This chapter explores the first two, showing how Americans gradually eschewed territorial expansion but then acquired colonies. The next chapter explores the third, initially less clear path that beckoned around the same time. Eventually that route led to the modern world.

These three political choices seem so disparate in retrospect, and aimed at such divergent destinations, that it is easy to believe they were obvious at the time. Yet the roads crisscrossed and tangled. For a time, the United States stumbled along all three, trying to keep up with or get ahead of its competitors. Between 1867 and 1919, it annexed Alaska, created a colony in the Philippines, and championed a League of Nations to promote openness and arbitration worldwide. By the end of this experimental period, the United States had mostly ceased expanding terrestrially and begun dismantling its new saltwater empire. It had transitioned almost completely to the third way: international engagement premised on a guarantee of self-determination to every established nation, regardless of its power to defend itself. This choice, which evolved organically, helped push the entire world community in a new direction.

But forward motion slowed again around 1920, when the costs began to look too great and the benefits too meager from policies that appeared to benefit other countries more than they did the United States. The raison d'être of government was to protect the self-interests of the people over whom it exercised authority and from whom it derived legitimacy, and no one else. This was the contract theory of government, after all. For the United States, with its abundant commercial prosperity, nearly unlimited natural resources, and secure borders on two vast oceans, isolationism beckoned.

Indeed, America had the comfort of making discretionary rather than necessary choices. Its integration with world markets was comparatively minimal (foreign trade stood at 8 percent of gross national product just before World War I, compared with Britain's 26 percent), and almost all sales went to dependable European consumers. Relying primarily on its own internal markets and natural resources, the nation quadrupled its GNP in the last quarter of the nineteenth century. By 1920 the United States was the world's wealthiest nation, with no foreign debt and a trade balance in the black. The country had survived its worst trauma and disproved the begrudgers who claimed that a republic would never cohere or prosper.[12] It had beaten Europe at its own game. As one boastful enthusiast crowed, America had sent "coals to Newcastle, cotton to Manchester, cutlery to Sheffield, potatoes to Ireland, champagne to France, [and] watches to Switzerland."[13]

During the Belle Époque, the United States could intervene in or withdraw from international affairs with fewer negative consequences than probably any other nation on earth. Outside intervention sprang more from an odd combination of humanitarian and competitive instincts than from strategic threats or economic necessity. Reunited and prosperous, America had few truly vital interests at stake outside its national borders. This luxury proved time-limited.

Charles Sumner, head of the U.S. Senate Foreign Relations Committee, was rarely a man of few words. Other senators groused that he tended to lecture, but Sumner rationalized that "laggards" never take kindly to "the cracking of the whip."[14] After the Civil War, he hectored Congress and President Andrew Johnson unceasingly, pushing for black suffrage and an unflinching implementation of Reconstruction. A man of probity and propriety, he championed bills that expressed American sympathy with Crete against the oppression of Turkey, denounced the "Coolie trade" in China, and expelled a fellow senator for repeated intoxication in Congress.

But the leonine, six-foot-four senator from Massachusetts outdid himself on April 9, 1867. For three hours Sumner expounded on the history of Russian America (Russia's territory in North America) since the time of Peter the Great, urging passage of a treaty to further extend the borders of the United States. The eminent senator even proposed a name in the language of its aboriginal people: Alaska, meaning Great Land. Afterward, Sumner turned the speech into a 240-page pamphlet that, one pundit quipped, "exhausted the *subject,* as well as his *readers.*"[15] It also cinched the deal that gave the United States its last acquisition in North America, representing roughly 17 percent of its national territory today.[16] Expansion ended with a flourish.

The treaty had been signed hurriedly the week before, under circumstances nearly identical to those six decades earlier when Bonaparte proffered Louisiana. Alaska was difficult to exploit, govern, or protect. More important, its European owner needed cash. Situated thousands of trackless miles from the capitol city of Saint Petersburg, across Siberia and the Bering Strait, Russian America was a blot on paper and the most distant part of the czar's empire. Fur trappers had nearly exhausted the sea otter population, whose pelts supported the colony. Bankruptcy threatened. "Any maritime power with which we might be at war could take them from us," Russia's minister to the United States had observed to His Majesty, adding: "It is on our Asiatic possessions . . . that we must concentrate our energy."[17] A California senator had raised the prospect of the purchase first, and the Russian minister wanted Americans to continue to think it was their idea. But the decision rested with Czar Alexander II. Convinced that keeping Alaska was no longer worth the trouble, Alexander initiated its sale.

There was good reason to choose America as the beneficiary. Russia and the United States had been on good terms since the Civil War. In contrast, the czar had recently fought England in Crimea, where Britain and France slapped down his efforts to seize land from the Ottoman Empire. Alexander II had no interest in enlarging Britain's empire. Indeed, the United States might become a useful counterweight to the United Kingdom, hemming the Pacific coast of Canada on both its northern and southern borders. The czar authorized his minister, Baron Eduard de Stoeckl, to sell Russian America for $5 million in gold.[18]

The sale was easier to contemplate than conclude. Contrary to stereotypes of nineteenth-century Americans as rapacious land-grabbers, popular appetite for expansion was mercurial. It was also ebbing. Before the Civil War, private adventurers known as filibusterers had sought to annex territory from Baja California to Cuba. The popular press sometimes egged them on, but filibusterers found it hard to sway their countrymen. Even Texans had had to wait a decade to achieve annexation. After the Civil War, Secretary of State William Seward initiated several deals to obtain new lands for the United States. Over the hill by nineteenth-century standards, Seward had barely survived an assassin's knife the same night that President Lincoln was murdered. The sixty-six-year-old still bore facial scars from the attack. But Seward was a tough old campaigner, determined to rebuild and grow the nation. Even so, he found that Congress would grant him at most one new territory: a place with miniscule population requiring minimal investment.

William Seward and Baron de Stoeckl negotiated privately for two weeks while the cagey Russian lured his American counterpart into bidding the price up to $7.2 million. Stoeckl, who was married to a native of Springfield, Massachusetts, suggested sounding out U.S. politicians to elicit their support for the sale. But Seward better understood his easily spooked audience. He urged the Russian emissary to maintain strict secrecy. "Let us first see if we can agree. It will be time then to consult Congress," the secretary of state cautioned.[19] Late on the evening of Friday, March 29, Seward was playing whist with his son when the Russian minister showed up unexpectedly at their home, asking to see him.

Baron de Stoeckl told the U.S. secretary of state that the czar had approved the negotiated price. They needed only to get it on paper. Seward summoned Charles Sumner to his home near midnight. Peeved at Seward's sneakiness, and ill disposed toward the administration over Reconstruction, Sumner refused to indicate whether or not he would support the purchase. When President Johnson submitted the hastily scribbled document to the Senate after sunrise the next morning, the imperious Sumner diverted it to committee.

The Senate Foreign Relations Committee debated for a week. It reluctantly came to support the sale, though two members suggested that Seward himself be required to move to the God-forsaken wasteland.[20] There were three factors in the deal's favor: expansion no longer raised the troublesome question of extending slavery, an "exceptionally friendly" foreign government desired it, and, in Senator Sumner's words, the sale created the "opportunity of dismissing another European sovereign from our continent" (meaning there would be fewer monarchs breathing down the neck of Americans). Ten days later, Sumner ushered the treaty through the Senate by a vote of thirty-seven to two. He later admitted to his British friend and member of Parliament John Bright: "The Russia treaty tried me severely; abstractedly I am against further accessions of territory, unless by free choice of the inhabitants. But this question was perplexed by considerations of politics and comity [friendship with Russia] and the engagements already entered into by the government."[21]

The House of Representatives was far less cooperative, however, and pitched a fit once newspapers began deriding "Seward's Ice Box" and criticizing the secretive, nontransparent negotiations as a "dark deed done in the night." President Andrew Johnson was already unpopular, most people considered Russian America a worthless hunk of ice, and the country had a $2.6 billion debt left over from the Civil War (a 4,000 percent increase in the debt within five years). The Senate might approve the purchase, but the House had little motivation to produce the necessary funds.

New York newspapers were a microcosm of the suspicious public. The *World* called the treaty "one of the very neatest operations of Russian diplomacy," and the *Herald* suggested that Seward had plied U.S. senators with "California wines and Kentucky bourbon." The *Tribune* pointed out, "We already have more territory than we want." Alaska would only saddle America with the exact problems Russia wished to unload. London newspapers tended to agree: "Russia has got rid of a territory which . . . could only be a needless extra expense." America was poised to purchase an uninhabitable piece of real estate "not worth five shillings."[22]

The *New York Times,* then identified with the Republican Party, was one of the few papers to urge congressional acquiescence. It conceded that Alaska had little inherent value but predicted that one day the Pacific coast might "be as thickly studded with ports and cities as the Atlantic is now." Obtaining access all the way to the Bering Sea could only improve commercial opportunities with Asia.[23]

The House of Representatives nonetheless balked for another year at the considerable expense and Seward's failure to consult Congress. The bill to fund the purchase finally passed, 113 to 43, in July 1868, fifteen months after Seward and Stoeckl's midnight meeting, and only after the influential Speaker of the House, Thaddeus Stevens, threw his weight behind it. The treaty probably would not have succeeded had it concerned any nation other than Russia, which was viewed with gratitude for its support during the nation's supreme crisis. Compared with the purchase of Louisiana—approved and funded expeditiously—its passage was a near thing indeed.[24]

Alaska was Seward's last victory and America's only acquisition for four decades, with the exception of the Midway Islands, an uninhabited atoll boasting 2.4 square miles in the dead center of the Pacific Ocean. Nothing else went as Seward planned. He had hoped to strengthen the Monroe Doctrine, especially since France and Spain had launched new colonial beachheads in the Western Hemisphere while the Union and Confederacy were busy slugging one another in Virginia. He also dreamed of expansion. Shortly after the Alaska Treaty, Seward penned a poem in which he rhapsodized, "Abroad our empire shall no limits know."[25] But the secretary of state could not have been more wrong. Instead he faced a string of reverses. Expansion was coming to an end. Americans simply did not want more land.

Charles Sumner spoke for the majority when he warned that Alaska should not be taken as "a precedent for a system of indiscriminate and costly annexion [*sic*]." These were not empty words. To Seward's intense disappointment, Congress soon nixed an attempt to buy the Virgin Islands, which the Danish parliament was keen to sell for $7.5 million in 1867 and the islands' inhabitants approved in a popular vote. Senator Sumner's *Memoir* called the proposal a "wild enterprise" on behalf of a worthless archipelago known only for "hurricanes, earthquakes, and drought." (The United States later paid $25 million to buy the islands for strategic reasons during World War I.)[26]

The Senate also ignored a petition by citizens of Victoria in 1869 to annex British Columbia to the United States. Cut off from the rest of Canada by the 12,000-foot peaks of the Rocky Mountains, some British Columbians believed that local autonomy "could be more fully exercised as a state of the Union than as a province of the newly formed [1867] Dominium of Canada."[27] Additionally, they had a large debt they could not repay. Proponents of annexation petitioned London for approval. Neither government officials nor the British public expressed opposition to yielding a territory so unprofitable and distant from London. Parliamentary radicals like John Bright suggested that all of Canada might be better off joining the Union.[28]

The U.S. government gave the British Columbians no encouragement, however, even though the acquisition would have made Alaska contiguous with the rest of the United States. Lacking American support, local proponents lost a vigorous domestic debate, especially after a new royal governor stepped in and turned the tide of opinion. British Columbia merged in 1871 with the new Canadian Confederation, which assumed the westerners' debts and pledged to build a railway across the Rockies. Coincidentally, both Canada and Mexico underwent internal consolidation in the 1860s. Their new competency helped to fix borders north and south. Ideological and practical considerations dovetailed for American policymakers. By 1869, the United States was dragging its feet rather than racing to expand. Flagging was finally slowing to a stop in North America.

It was over the Dominican Republic that the question of future directions became most vexed, and the final rejection of Manifest Destiny most plain. Previously allied in the founding of the Republican Party, Seward and Sumner clashed in a way that saddened the Massachusetts senator for the rest of his life. Sumner found himself in disagreement as well with yet another abolitionist and old friend, Frederick Douglass. The Dominican Republic held particular symbolism for Americans like Douglass, formerly an escaped slave. Its population was mostly descended from Africans and it shared the island of Hispaniola with Haiti, the world's first black republic. It had taken five decades and the Civil War for the United States to recognize Haiti, founded in 1804 by rebellious slaves and free people of color.[29]

Hispaniola was nineteenth-century foreign relations in miniature. The great powers had long vied over the strategically located island, the second largest in the Caribbean. On the eastern end of Hispaniola, the nation of the Dominican Republic guarded the Windward Passage between the island and neighboring Cuba, through which nearly all east-west traffic sailed from Europe to Central America. As one U.S. naval captain later described it, the Windward Passage was the "cork" of the Caribbean bottle.[30] Hispaniola was also the very isle upon which Christopher Columbus had wrecked his flagship, the *Santa Maria,* on Christmas morning 1492. It retained symbolic appeal for Spain. Meanwhile, neither of the new republics on the important island had a stable government, and one continuously threatened the other.

Before the Napoleonic Wars, France and Spain had divided sugar-producing Hispaniola between themselves. In 1804, France lost its half when Haiti achieved independence. In 1821, the Spanish-speaking inhabitants on the opposite side of the island finally broke from Spain, which had previously defended them from a short-lived takeover by Haitian general Toussaint L'Ouverture (a hero to his own people but a menace to Dominicans). Six weeks after the Dominican Republic declared autonomy in 1821, Haiti again invaded its Spanish-speaking neighbor and this time stayed for twenty-two years (1821–1844). Dominicans were not reconciled to Haitian rule, however, and fought a successful war of independence. But they continued to fear the Haitian threat. For the next few decades, confronted with few good choices, Dominicans toyed with annexation either to Spain or the United States to protect their freedom from Haiti, even if it meant relinquishing nationhood. When they celebrated "Independence Day," they celebrated the break from their Francophone neighbor, not Iberia.[31]

In 1861, the president of the tiny republic finally asked Spain to recolonize, which it did for four years, until the local people again rebelled. In 1869, amid renewed turmoil, President Buenaventura Báez signed a treaty to join with the United States, under American sovereignty. In exchange, Washington would assume the republic's mounting $1.5 million debt and grant its people full U.S. citizenship.[32]

Like the Alaska negotiations, the proposed treaty attracted controversy immediately. Considering the Dominican Republic's vulnerable position, there were economic, strategic, and humanitarian reasons to contemplate annexation and even stronger reasons not to do so. It might turn into a quagmire, opponents feared. Some in the United States argued that intervention was imperialism. Others argued that not intervening would be callous. The

United States was damned if it did and damned if it didn't, depending on one's point of view.

President Ulysses S. Grant, hero of Vicksburg and savior of the Union, submitted the treaty to the Senate, where his own party and Charles Sumner proved the greatest obstacles. Historians have tended to agree with Senator Sumner's opinion that annexation would have been a form of colonialism, a slight to neighboring Haiti, and an expression of cynicism toward black self-government. Secretary of State Seward and President Grant certainly made no secret of their hopes for Samaná Bay as a future navy base, and Grant praised the fertile island's agricultural potential. But pursuit of material advantage is not proof of imperialism. No nation wanted territory that placed it at a disadvantage. In fact, every preceding acquisition had been paved with assertions about why a new territory was worth annexing. But the most important reason for scholars to reevaluate the notion that the proposal constituted a form of colonialism is that Dominicans would have entered the Union as equals.

The position of Frederick Douglass suggests that annexation would have been another iteration of American nationalism, not imperialism. In fact, with the support of the National Convention of Colored Men, Douglass argued vigorously for the full incorporation of the black republic on the same basis as the autonomous Republic of Texas before it.

At President Grant's special request, Douglass traveled to the Dominican Republic on an eight-week, congressional fact-finding mission in the winter of 1871. Before going, Douglass had sided with Charles Sumner, whom he admired as "the most clear sighted, brave and uncompromising friend of my race who ever stood upon the floor of the Senate."[33] But after his return, Frederick Douglass stood with Grant and Seward. Nations that wished to avoid imperialist takeovers were safest in large coalitions.

"Small and weak nations are plainly out of joint with our times," Douglass told one crowd. In essays for the *New National Era,* a black newspaper, Douglass implied that leaving the Dominican Republic "alone to work out her own destiny" was a form of racism when suggested by those who had not shied from incorporating California or Alaska. "Small states united are better than small states divided," he added, echoing the *Federalist Papers.* The Dominican Republic would enter the union not as an "inferior or vassal, but as an equal—first as a territory, then as a state."[34] If a free people wished to join the Union, they should be welcomed rather than rejected. "The idea that annexation meant degradation to a colored nation was altogether fanciful; there was no . . . dishonor to Santo Domingo in making her a State of the American Union," Douglass proclaimed in one of a hundred speeches he gave around the country.[35]

Some historians have been at pains to explain Douglass's support for a seemingly imperialistic foreign policy, suggesting he had become a party hack. But there is little reason to doubt that Douglass genuinely believed the argument he was making—or to reject its accuracy. Annexation on a basis of equality with other states might have spared future generations of Dominicans from turmoil and poverty. President Grant believed the same, even though he is often characterized as duped by craftier politicians or big business. When Douglass asked the president what he thought of Sumner's vehement accusations of gross exploitation, Ulysses S. Grant answered bluntly and with feeling, "I think he is mad."[36] Douglass rued the bitter enmity that the Dominican Republic provoked between Grant and Sumner. As the former slave observed, "Variance between great men finds no healing influence in the atmosphere of Washington."[37]

The Senate divided neatly, twenty-eight to twenty-eight, on the annexation question, which meant the proposed treaty failed for lack of the required two-thirds majority. Color played a dramatic but ambiguous role.[38] Scholars occasionally picture American foreign relations as unrelievedly racist across time.[39] But antiracism figures just as importantly in the trajectory of American history, or we could not explain any number of turning points, including the 1860s or 1960s. In the case of Santo Domingo, neither orientation triumphed. There were racists and antiracists in both camps. For example, some racists vehemently opposed annexation because they did not want more black citizens. Some antiracists also opposed annexation, but because it would extinguish one of the few stand-alone black republics.

Supporters touched on issues of race as well. Editors of *The New York Times,* for example, argued that annexation would guarantee the "security of the negro race in their efforts to maintain separate and independent Governments of their own."[40] Santo Domingo would be self-governed to the same degree as Kansas. Indeed, in 1899, a foreign journalist described the United States as "a continually increasing number of independent and sovereign States living together in federal union."[41] President Grant openly criticized racial prejudice as "senseless," and Seward later wrote, "The intermingling of races always was, and always will be, the chief element of civilization."[42]

In any case, annexation failed, and it may be good that it did. Dominicans remained sorely divided over the idea of joining the United States. President Báez had repressed local opposition, and America might well have found itself fighting another war of secession in due time, as Charles Sumner prophesied when he claimed that annexation would commit the United States to "a dance of blood."[43] Nevertheless, Grant and Douglass's optimistic vision did not differ greatly from that of earlier idealists who thought an empire of liberty might shelter any number of semiautonomous republics.

Between 1867 and 1898, most attempts to expand the territory of the United States failed. Expansionism wound down and Congress declined dozens of proposals that lacked the support of the public or the legislature.[44] Increasingly, expansion became identified with "imperialism," a pejorative term that had recently been coined by British liberals.[45] The long-held dream of admitting a willing Cuba or Canada, entertained by presidents since Jefferson and envisioned by poets like Walt Whitman, never came about.

The nation made its final permanent acquisition of any size, a group of islands far more distant than Santo Domingo, amid keen domestic opposition during the tumult of the 1898 Spanish-American War.[46] King Kamehameha III of Hawaii had twice before (in 1849 and 1854) considered joining his lands with America to prevent European takeover, much as the Maori chiefs of New Zealand voted to link their lands with Great Britain in the 1840 Treaty of Waitangi. But the United States consistently rebuffed the idea until the 1890s, by which point Kamehameha's successor, Queen Liliuokalani, had reversed the royal position and now opposed joining the union. In a local power struggle backed by private force, American planters in Hawaii overthrew the queen in 1893 and submitted a treaty of annexation to Washington. President Grover Cleveland, a Democrat, refused to consider it, and the proposal languished for five years.

The next president, William McKinley, approved the treaty, however, and Republicans in Congress engineered a joint resolution to evade the two-thirds-vote requirement this time and ensure passage. In annexing the islands, they rode roughshod over the sovereignty of the last Hawaiian monarch, much as President Polk had taken advantage of Mexico in 1846. But Hawaii did enter the Union on a basis of parity, as Kamehameha had envisioned when he signed the proposed 1854 treaty to join "the American Union as a State, enjoying the same degree of sovereignty as other States."[47] It and Alaska were the final two regions to do so. Borders were firming up worldwide. U.S.

territorial expansionism, most of it conducted through competitive negotiations with European empires, had at last run its course.

In 1898, the United States surprised the world and itself by overtaking territory and peoples that it had little if any intention of ever admitting as equals. In the Philippines, it acquired subjects rather than citizens, briefly embracing European-style imperialism. A war that flamed up "on behalf of the victims of Spanish oppression," as Englishman W. T. Stead observed at the time, turned into something very different. "The American Republic," he wrote, "which for more than a hundred years had made as its proudest boast its haughty indifference to the temptation of territorial conquest, suddenly . . . concluded a war . . . [with] annexations so sweeping as to invest the United States with all that was left of the heritage of Imperial Spain."[48] America also established several informal protectorates in the Caribbean. But what was more surprising yet, and unprecedented in all of human history, was that the United States soon gave up its principal colony and protectorates voluntarily. It backed into imperialism and then turned around and backed out.

The empire of 1898 was not planned. A humanitarian crisis led to foreign intervention, intervention led to war, war to occupation, and occupation to colonization. The first three steps were a dance pattern that became all too familiar in the twentieth and twenty-first centuries, but the final step was never taken again. Colonization of the Philippines was the exception to the rule of American policy. With the eerie prescience that nature seemed to bestow upon members of the Adams family, John Quincy had much earlier foreseen the temptations and dangers of these steps. At a time when Europeans were awakening to the first modern humanitarian crisis in their midst (the Greek war of independence), Adams warned in an 1821 speech that America's safest course was not to get involved with other peoples' problems:

> Wherever the standard of freedom and independence has been or shall be unfurled, there will her heart, her benedictions, her prayers be. But she goes not abroad in search of monsters to destroy. She is the well-wisher to the freedom and independence of all. She is the champion and vindicator only of her own. . . . She well knows that by once enlisting under other

banners than her own, were they even the banners of foreign independence, she would involve herself beyond the power of extrication, in all the
wars of interest and intrigue, of individual avarice, envy, and ambition,
which assume the colors and usurp the standard of freedom. The fundamental maxims of her policy would insensibly change from *liberty* to
force. . . . She might become the dictatress of the world. She would no
longer be the ruler of her own spirit.[49]

Historians debate *why* the United States acquired an empire in 1898 but
not the fact that it did. The crisis began over Cuba and then spread unexpectedly to the 7,000-island Philippine Archipelago. Revolution had simmered in
both countries for most of the century. They were Spain's oldest possessions.
Columbus discovered Cuba on his first voyage and Hernán Cortés used it to
launch the conquest of Mexico in 1519. Mexico, in turn, became the stepping-
stone to the Philippines, which became the access point for East Asian spices,
porcelain, and silk. These three Spanish possessions—Cuba, Mexico, and the
Philippine Islands—were the key transit stops in Spain's world-encircling
empire, until Mexico dropped out in 1821. Cuba and the Philippines had
missed out on the nationalism unleashed by the Napoleonic Wars, but yet
another shake-up in the monarchy renewed the opportunity. Continental
Spaniards dethroned Queen Isabella in 1868 when she resisted the trend away
from absolutism. Revolts immediately broke out in the remaining Hispanic
colonies.

    Cubans fought a bloody, failed war for independence that cost 200,000
lives between 1868 and 1878. Internal disagreements over whether or not to
abolish slavery helped undermine the cause. The United States maintained
neutrality to avoid conflict with the Spanish Empire, but following the U.S.
Civil War also found it difficult to support rebels who were at best ambivalent on the morality of slavery.[50] In the Philippines, local reformers also took
heart at liberal trends, but there, too, colonial authorities cracked down effectively on suspected dissidents in 1872 and executed a priest who dared to
pen a "Manifesto of Filipinos."

    In both colonies, rebellion was quelled but not quenched. Like American
revolutionaries a century earlier, Cubans and Filipinos remained acutely
conscious of their overlords' condescension. "When the dictionary is exhausted of Cuban resources, of the [stereotyped] question of tangos, blacks,
little black women, and mulattoes," observed an educated Filipino traveler

in Madrid, scornful jokes "for evoking laughter are directed, it seems, to the Philippines."[51]

Rebellion broke out again in the 1890s. A secret nationalist society, the Katipunan, had gained thousands of members in the Philippines by 1895, provoking another violent Spanish response in 1896. But it was Cuba, situated only ninety miles across the Florida Straits from the United States, that excited American concern. In 1895, Cuban revolutionaries took over most of the island by force, frightening civilians, challenging Spanish authorities, and precipitating a refugee crisis. Spain retaliated with 150,000 fresh troops under General Valeriano Weyler. Known as El Carnicero ("The Butcher"), Weyler had put down the previous revolution two decades earlier. He was primed to make Cuba a hell on earth.

Weyler cut the rebels' rural supply line by burning villages, razing crops, and forcing peasants into so-called reconcentration camps. Resisters faced summary execution. Smallpox, dysentery, and cholera raced through the crowded, unhygienic barbed-wire enclosures, killing as many as 200,000 civilians, from decrepit old men to infants on the breast. Both rebel insurgents and imperial soldiers destroyed food supplies to harass their enemy. Famine decimated the island population. Victims were interred in mass graves. When body collectors and grave diggers fell ill, dogs and birds scavenged the dead left out in the open.[52]

American newspapers closely followed the nearby tragedy. Cuban rebels headquartered in New York and eager for U.S. intervention saw to it that reporters splashed every atrocity across the front pages. Their cause, no longer tarnished by slavery (abolished by Spain in the prior decade), elicited wide sympathy. Editors and publishers competed to provide the fullest coverage to a public mesmerized at all class levels. Cigar makers' unions and the American labor organization AFL-CIO agitated for U.S. intervention on behalf of the islanders. Union and Confederate veterans called on the president to redeem the nation's "manhood" and rise up against "impotent Spain." Protestant clergy organized public meetings, including a demonstration of six thousand people at a Chicago music hall, to urge the U.S. government to break relations with the Spanish "cutthroat."[53] Only America's political elite resisted the lure of intervention—with such notable exceptions as the romantic, aggressive Theodore Roosevelt and a coterie of younger leaders who shared the dream of taking a larger role on the world stage. To them, domestic and international conditions demanded an American response that served both honor and ambition.

Historians who argue that 1898 was a "natural culmination" of America's long-standing imperialist ambitions tend to emphasize capitalists' desire for foreign markets.[54] The evidence for this conclusion is not only thin but also largely immaterial, because all businesses seek customers. An interest in penetrating new markets proves only the desire to thrive, and can be seen in all companies, all nations, all eras. The evidence for corporate support of the war also happens to be scant. Congress, newspapers, and the public frequently commented on the fact that businessmen opposed intervention in Cuba as too disruptive of trade (an attitude that would not have surprised the eighteenth-century physiocrats). Populist senator William Allen of Nebraska gave a blistering speech in April 1898 excoriating those "who would have permitted the 266 men who went down with the *Maine* to lie in the mud of Havana Harbor [where the ship had infamously sunk] and rot without entering a word of complaint rather than bring on a conflict of arms, because to do so would be to injure the commercial relations and unsettle business."[55]

As on all issues, of course, some businessmen expressed a contrarian point of view. U.S. investors in Cuba wanted order restored, whether under Spanish, Cuban, or American rule. But they were neither leading industrialists nor the majority. The disinterested among the economic elite made clear their opposition to intervention in 1898, including John D. Rockefeller, Andrew Carnegie, Mark Hanna, and others. As one Boston financier lectured Senator Henry Cabot Lodge, then one of the most eager advocates of a more expansive role for the United States: "You were sent to Washington to represent one of the largest business states in the country. The business interests of the state require peace and quiet, not war. If we attempt to regulate the affairs of the whole world we will be in hot water from now until the end of time." The *Commercial Advertiser* warned that fighting would be "pure waste and folly." And when the United States finally intervened, *Harper's Weekly* editors despaired: "If ever a war promised nothing but [economic] loss to the country that began it, it is this which the United States has begun against Spain."[56]

Historian Ernest May argues convincingly that the impetus for intervention came from below and for noneconomic reasons: "It seemed as if the mass of the people from coast to coast were in the clutch of feverish emotion." Newspaper editorials and cartoons denounced McKinley and the wealthy for accepting "peace-at-any-price," and valuing profits over the lives of innocent civilians. Members of the elite who believed themselves immune to popular passions looked on in horror. John Bassett Moore, America's leading jurist, scorned what he recalled as the public "clamor for intervention" that took hold in 1898. Thomas Reed, the Republican speaker of the House, compared public opinion with a destructive and implacable Kansas tornado.[57]

Nor were average Americans the only ones moved to pity, anger, or action. The Cuban collapse was world news and prompted transatlantic cooperation. The *Times* of London cautioned as early as 1896 that "absolute starvation will overtake a large proportion of the population before many months are passed." When a British relief ship attempted to deliver corn to feed the hungry in 1898, Spanish customs officials demanded a fee and blocked delivery until the U.S. consul in Havana lodged an official complaint.[58]

Ernest May calls Cuba "America's Armenia." The comparison is apt. The United States government faced a problem similar to one then confronting Europeans. In the late nineteenth century, literate publics increasingly demanded that governments solve humanitarian crises in foreign countries, as proliferating journals in the world's capitals competed strenuously to deliver compelling news from around the globe. One unforeseen consequence was that French and British leaders found themselves pressed to intervene in conflicts where they had little desire to run such risks. Knowledge of mayhem created a burgeoning expectation that Christian countries had a responsibility to "do something." Prime Ministers Benjamin Disraeli and William Ewart Gladstone ignored town hall petitions and coffeehouse babble as best they could, but they had a harder time ignoring Queen Victoria, who also read the daily papers and informed her ministers, "I cannot rest quiet without urging the prevention of further atrocities."[59]

The most prominent international cases involved the declining Ottoman Empire, which ignored Syrian interethnic massacres in 1860, crudely suppressed Bulgarian revolutionaries in 1876, and began slaughtering Armenians in 1894. Telegraphs and newspapers sped information to readers and governments worldwide, straining Westphalian norms about the illegality of intervention in domestic affairs. Private citizens in both Europe and America raised funds for these foreign causes and sometimes even enlisted to fight in them. One of the first international nongovernmental organizations, the Red Cross, got involved, and France, Britain, and Russia eventually dispatched soldiers and ships to the Middle East.

Politicians—human, too—bent with the wind. As the elderly William Gladstone retorted upon hearing of the 1894 massacre of ten thousand Armenian civilians, "Do not let me be told that one nation has no authority over another. Every nation, and if need be every human, has authority on behalf of humanity and of justice." Long uncomfortable with imperialism, Gladstone certainly did not advocate extending the empire.[60] Instead, humanitarian intervention was a new phenomenon distinct from either nationalism or imperialism. It drew on inchoate notions of collective responsibility. As mass media made distant events ever more visible, international relief campaigns emerged on the presumption that individual human rights should transcend borders. The Cuban Revolution of 1895 was merely the moment at which the American people first embraced a trend that had begun in Europe, at the level of the people. Governments and business, which typically favored neutrality over intervention as being less disruptive of the status quo, found themselves pushed in new and unwelcome directions.

William Randolph Hearst, the publisher whose San Francisco and New York newspapers led the chorus against Spain, drew an explicit parallel between the "Turkish savages in Armenia" and Cuba's fiendish General Weyler. The innovative media mogul hired a dashing war correspondent, Richard Harding Davis, and the famed illustrator Frederick Remington, and packed the duo off to Havana on his yacht. "It may not be our duty to interfere in Turkey," Hearst's *San Francisco Examiner* editorialized, "but we certainly cannot permit the creation of another Armenia in this hemisphere. . . . Cuba is our Armenia, and it is at our doors." If the European great powers had some duty to prevent malfeasance in their own vicinity, the *Examiner* implied, then the United States had the same responsibility in its neighborhood. The editors of the *Literary Digest,* a public opinion magazine that reprinted news from around the world, claimed: "Intervention is the plain duty of the United States on the simple grounds of humanity."[61]

Republican president William McKinley initially followed the precedent set by his immediate predecessor, Democrat Grover Cleveland. That is, he tried to stave off the problem by encouraging the colonial government in Cuba to be more responsive to the desires of its subjects. When McKinley took the oath of office in 1897, the decorated Civil War veteran and former governor of Ohio announced: "We have cherished the policy of non-interference with affairs of foreign governments wisely inaugurated by [George] Washington, keeping ourselves free from entanglement, either as allies or foes, content to leave undisturbed with them the settlement of their own domestic concerns." The United States should shun unilateral humanitarian rescues, McKinley implied in his inaugural address. Instead, it should embrace arbitration as the only "true method" for resolving disputes.[62]

McKinley had a particular penchant for arbitration. As governor, and against the wishes of his own party, he had pushed a bill through the Ohio legislature to recognize trade unions and create a state board for negotiating labor disputes. On one occasion, he personally conducted an eight-hour arbitration between the American Railway Union and the iron industry. But the decorated veteran was also willing to act coercively, as umpire, when the situation could not otherwise be resolved. After talks failed to prevent strike-related riots by the United Mine Workers in 1894, McKinley called out the National Guard. Conflict fizzled whenever a brigade met a division, the former infantryman observed laconically.[63]

Three years later, McKinley instructed the U.S. minister to Spain to press American concerns, hoping to achieve peace through diplomacy in this dispute as well. The effects were significant but failed to satisfy Cuban rebels. Spain recalled General Weyler, granted full citizenship rights to Cuban Creoles, and promised limited autonomy for the island. Relations between the United States and Spain improved so much that McKinley sent a naval cruiser, the USS *Maine,* to Havana, partly to demonstrate goodwill—much as Russia had sent warships to New York at the height of the Confederate rebellion. Although William Randolph Hearst's *New York World* soon thereafter leaked a scandalous private letter from Spain's minister in Washington in which he called McKinley a weak, "would-be politician," the White House patiently weathered what one newspaper headline flamboyantly damned as the "Worst Insult to the United States in Its History."[64] All that changed a week later, however, at 9:40 P.M. on February 15, 1898.

With most sailors below decks for the night, five tons of gunpowder in the hold of the USS *Maine* exploded without warning, obliterating the bow of the vessel anchored in Havana harbor. The iron-hulled battleship sank in seconds, killing 266 American sailors. The captain and chief officers were among the 80 or so who survived, since their quarters were in the stern. Those not drowned or killed outright crawled to the listing, topmost deck, which still cleared the water when the remnants of the ruined vessel settled on the floor of the shallow bay. Nearby civilians and Spanish sailors pulled them off the wreck in the dark.

The U.S. Navy launched an inquiry under the scrutiny of a horrified public. Four weeks later it concluded that an underwater mine had detonated the ship's armory. Some explosives experts remained unconvinced, but almost a century elapsed before naval engineers revised their analysis and concluded that the explosion began *inside* the vessel rather than outside, possibly from spontaneous combustion. The 1898 inquiry did not point the finger at Spain, which denied mining the harbor, but the American public did. "Remember the *Maine,* to hell with Spain!" became their battle cry. An enterprising glass company issued commemorative candy dishes in the shape of the battleship, with "Remember the *Maine*" encircling the translucent hull. Sales were vigorous.[65]

Events moved toward a violent confrontation, despite McKinley's best efforts at pacification. As political scientist David Brady shows, representatives in the Fifty-Fifth Congress were more likely to vote according to party than at any other time in the nation's history, complicating McKinley's choices. The Democrats were in the minority, so they could not pass any bills with their numbers alone. But they could embarrass and harass their opponents. The *Congressional Record* makes plain that the president and the Republican Party were practically dragged into taking stronger and stronger stands.[66]

Even before the destruction of the *Maine,* Republicans in the House of Representatives fended off three attempts by Democrats to pass bills acknowledging the Cuban revolutionaries as legal belligerents, not merely rebels. Each vote was completely partisan: not one representative crossed the aisle to vote with the other side. When it seemed to Republicans in Congress that they could not hold the tide back any longer, they pressed for a resolution that declared Cuba *ought* to be independent but did not recognize the rebel government as the new, legitimate authority. (Diplomatic recognition had long been a presidential prerogative, not a congressional one.) Anxious, conflicted, and upset—with tears in his eyes—McKinley confessed to one of his closest friends, "Congress is trying to drive us into war with Spain."[67]

Republicans pivoted toward intervention only after one of their own, Redfield Proctor of Vermont, traveled to Cuba himself and confirmed that every beastly report was true. Americans had witnessed hunger but never mass famine, not even during the Civil War, in which many Congressmen had personally served, including Union veteran Redfield Proctor. "Little children [in the camps] are still walking about with arms and chest terribly emaciated, eyes swollen, and abdomen bloated to three times the natural size," he told Congress. "It must be seen with one's own eyes."[68]

Senator Proctor had also visited a hospital in Cuba run by Clara Barton, the volunteer nurse of Civil War fame who became the nation's first prominent advocate of foreign humanitarian aid. Barton had founded the American branch of the International Red Cross in 1881 and organized relief expeditions to Ottoman Armenia in 1896. When Proctor toured the medical center that the seventy-seven-year-old Barton was then operating, the senator found patients who tore at his heart. Emaciated mothers and infants, he told Congress, had only "the scantiest covering of rags—and such rags!—sick children, naked as they came into the world."[69]

After nearly a year of partisan wrangling and the destruction of the *Maine,* Congress finally approved armed intervention in an unusually and overwhelmingly bipartisan vote (311 to 6) around 2:00 in the morning on April 19, 1898—though not before the Republicans quashed one last attempt by Democrats to sneak recognition of the self-appointed rebel government into the bill. (Only 1 Republican out of 169 broke ranks to vote with the Democrats on recognition.) The bipartisan intervention bill did not declare war, but it came powerfully close. Congress demanded that Spain withdraw its troops and set Cuba free. The bill also authorized and encouraged President McKinley to use force if necessary to make this happen. When the president called up volunteers and announced a naval blockade, Queen Maria Christina of Spain declared war on the United States—a reasonable response, given that blockade is a hostile act.

Independent moviemakers responded with the world's first commercial combat film, depicting troops atop a Havana fort replacing the Spanish flag with the American. Thousands flocked to vaudeville houses to participate from afar in what seemed the heroic rescue of starving Cubans. Weeks before American soldiers even landed in the Caribbean, *Tearing Down the Spanish Flag* was shot on a Manhattan rooftop. A subsequent film optimistically depicted the future defeat of the Spanish navy. *The Battle of Santiago Bay* was filmed in a bathtub.[70]

Historian George Herring describes President McKinley as "a master of the art of leading by indirection," and some biographers argue that McKinley was determined to resolve the problem off Florida, come what may. But historian Piero Gleijeses observes that McKinley resisted the collision with Spain for a remarkably long time. Democrats like Senator Alexander Clay of Georgia would have concurred. Senator Clay credited the Democratic Party for forcing "the Republicans to bring on the war."[71] Congressional records suggest that the president can hardly be called aggressive, at least with regard to Cuba. Today, were circumstances the same, an American president would be judged irresponsible to "allow" the well-publicized deaths of 200,000 civilians in a short period of time, and only ninety miles away. Yet humanitarian intervention was controversial, without precedent, and at odds with tradition. It took a Progressive Era assembly, susceptible to reformist zeal on both sides of the aisle, to propel McKinley into these uncharted waters. In the same week that Congress voted for intervention in Cuba, it considered bills to eliminate the sale of alcohol in the District of Columbia, strengthen anticigarette laws, enforce the Sabbath, and increase the age of sexual consent to prohibit the taking of child brides. Public outrage, partisan pressure, and a changing international definition of state duty pushed the United States toward humanitarian intervention.[72]

Once the decision was made, however, McKinley and his party implemented it in their own way. If forced to fight, the Republicans were determined to exercise whatever authority they thought necessary to control the outcome. Initially eager for intervention, Democrats soon found the terms of engagement decidedly distasteful.

The war itself lasted a mere four months. Only 345 Americans died in battle in Cuba, scarcely more than on the *Maine*. Under an amendment to the war bill championed by Democratic senator Henry Teller, Congress forbade acquisition of the island in order to make clear America's disinterestedness—and lack of imperial ambition. The Teller Amendment announced that the United States would intervene long enough to bring peace to the island, and then turn governance over to its own people. No one used the term "umpire," but congressional intent was certainly umperial rather than imperial. Spain needed to be thrown out of the game. The consequence: Cuba became independent after more than four hundred years.

But the transition to full Westphalian sovereignty would be more gradual than either the Democrats or the Cuban rebels anticipated. In 1901, as American solders prepared to withdraw, the Republican-dominated Senate devised the so-called Platt Amendment. With American troops still quartered in Havana, the Senate insisted that newly autonomous Cuba incorporate several provisions into its constitution. These included the right of the United States to intervene whenever necessary to uphold Cuban independence, and Cuba's responsibility to accept only those foreign loans it could afford to repay from customs receipts. (Lacking national income taxes, most countries financed government operations out of duties that customs agents collected in seaports.)

The Platt Amendment thus obligated Congress to defend another nation's shores and committed Washington to even greater financial supervision of Cuba than it exerted over the states. This made the island a protectorate and revolutionized the role of the United States. Short-term humanitarian intervention became long-term responsibility. Platt's provisions not only infringed on Cuba's Westphalian autonomy but also foreshadowed financial and security obligations that the United States would later take on worldwide.

Sponsored by Republican Orville Platt of Connecticut, the controversial amendment passed on a strictly partisan vote. Not one Democrat voted for it. Not one Republican voted against it. With the numbers he needed, Senator Platt made no attempt to answer Democrats' vehement objections that the United States was violating its pledge to Cuban autonomy "as plainly as men can do it," establishing a dreadful "suzerainty" over the island, placing both nations in "extreme peril," and giving the smugly imperialistic British "a sweet morsel" to roll under their tongues. To all this Democratic chatter Platt blandly replied, "I believe that it will settle what may be called the Cuban question satisfactorily to the people of Cuba and satisfactorily to our own people. I trust there will be no serious opposition to it." Apparently, outnumbered Democrats were not what the senator meant by serious opposition.[73]

Although it is clear that the Platt Amendment set a new national precedent, what has been less well studied is the broader international context. Events elsewhere shed light on why Republican policymakers opted on the fly for the particular expedients they did, trying to control explosive events for which the public would ultimately hold their party responsible. The Platt Amendment mimicked European practices that arose during the late nineteenth century to handle foreign debt crises that tended to destabilize weaker nations and provoke conflict.

The budding Industrial Revolution had transformed economic relationships worldwide. Beginning in England, cash wages and industrial profits produced domestic savings at almost all class levels. For the first time, shopkeepers, tradesmen, and better-paid day laborers lodged small "nest eggs" with banks, which lent those funds at home and abroad to generate income and pay interest to their depositors. Combined with the mounting profits that manufacturers invested with banks, these savings allowed and encouraged foreign direct investment to an extent never seen before. Money markets gradually became more accessible and integrated, just like markets for physical commodities.

The strings between nations perceptibly tightened. Some loans went to investors who repaid them with interest, such as the American and Chilean railroad entrepreneurs financed with British capital. (Chile's nineteenth-century repayment record approached perfection.) Some loans went bad, however. On occasion, governments or companies defaulted and took sanctuary behind the walls of Westphalian sovereignty to avoid collection. But investors wanted their nest eggs back, whether small or large. Lacking any international law or umpire to resolve this new situation, creditor nations sometimes resorted to physical violence, still the primary means by which nations resolved conflicts when diplomacy failed.[74]

The most notorious example involved Egypt, then an Ottoman province. There, in the early 1860s, the khedive (viceroy) undertook substantial foreign loans to modernize his domain and build the Suez Canal. With the United States embroiled in its sectional conflict, Sa'id Pasha opportunistically hoped to corner the world's cotton market and repay Egypt's new development loans with the profits. Considered "white gold," cotton was the primary raw material of the textile industry, itself the foundation of the Industrial Revolution. By the time Atlanta fell to William Tecumseh Sherman in 1864, the Egyptian khedive had converted 40 percent of all fertile land along the lower Nile to cotton cultivation. The Egyptian debt climbed from 7 million to 100 million British pounds.

Unfortunately for the khedive, however, a cotton glut emerged after the U.S. Civil War when the Southern states resumed production. Combined with the viceroy's personal overspending, the crash of the cotton market forced Egypt into bankruptcy by 1875. The Ottoman province was forced to sell its shares in the Suez Canal, which were snapped up by Britain, and a European consortium took over the Egyptian customs house in 1876 to ensure payment. When junior army officers led by Ahmed Urabi questioned the debt and attempted to reestablish local financial control, antiforeign riots broke out, hundreds were killed, and the Royal Navy bombarded the port of Alexandria. Britain occupied the country shortly thereafter, and in 1882 Egypt became a de facto colony. Previously under the indirect authority of the Turks, the province came under the more direct control of the British.[75]

People around the world, including Americans, noted the avalanche of unintended consequences. Democratic senator Benjamin Tillman warned prior to U.S. intervention in Cuba that landing the Marines in Havana might produce similar results. If a new rebel government repudiated Spain's old debts, the United States would be faced with "the necessity of entering upon the island and enforcing the obligation just as Egypt has been seized by England to collect the interest on the bonds which her citizens hold as the result of loaning money to the Khedive. Then we will have a nice situation."[76]

Senator Tillman was not the only one worried about America's mission spiraling out of control. European governments had long recognized dangers as well as opportunities in the collapse of weak or overextended states. Governments in default might be colonized by a competitor, or overthrown by an internal junta that rejected responsibility for previous financial obligations. Loans might never be repaid. The great powers could find themselves in a shooting war to establish colonial control or jostling to get first in line for debt repayment. Consequently, the strong sometimes propped up the weak for self-interested reasons, to avoid a melee. They required paternalistic supervision of customs receipts to ensure that income was not dissipated in bribes or overspending but instead went to pay creditors, who would then not have to resort to arms, with all the attendant risks.

Outside supervision was one hallmark of the Unequal Treaties that European states imposed on the Chinese and Ottoman Empires during the nineteenth century. The benefit to declining powers like the Qing Dynasty and the Turks was that, unlike Egypt, they staved off formal European occupation, though at the cost of the humiliating treaties. The Chinese and Ottomans bowed to extraterritoriality, standardized tariffs, and the exchange of ambassadors with nations they had long thought beneath them. They also allowed foreigners to collect their customs receipts in order to pay down external debts.

These Eurasian treaties were part of a global pattern in which European governments increasingly pressured other states to accept new norms of international relations. Rooted in the Peace of Westphalia, the norms had enabled Europeans to reduce armed conflict among themselves, and to some extent with their debtors. During the Belle Époque, Europeans saw crumbling China as the "Sick Man of Asia" and the Turkish caliphate as the "Sick Man of Europe." If not micromanaged, Europeans believed, these ancient empires would collapse, be devoured by colonialist competitors, and wreak havoc on global finance.[77]

The Unequal Treaties were transitional, though no one knew how long their function would be "necessary"—at least from the perspective of creditors. Historian Richard Horowitz argues that the treaties bought time and allowed weak states to retain nominal independence even though militarily overmatched. They integrated outliers in an international system that held out the hope of eventual legal equality on the same basis as European countries vis-à-vis one another.[78]

In 1895, Japan became the first Asian country to renegotiate an Unequal Treaty, followed by Turkey after World War I. But as late as 1921, when China demanded greater control over its own customs house, the *New York Herald* summed up the opinion of world bankers: "It has been assumed that should China become free of her present control her annual custom income would fall from $70,000,000 annually collected to $20,000,000 or less, where it stood before it was taken over and handled by the present organization."[79]

The Platt Amendment originated, therefore, in the context of European supervision of states on the brink of financial failure, when there was as yet no International Monetary Fund to rescue them from default. During the 1860s this problem spread to the Western Hemisphere, where European governments began to use force to collect money. In 1861, France, Spain, and Britain blockaded and invaded Mexico to collect debts repudiated by President Benito Juárez, leading to an attempt to overturn republicanism and reestablish monarchy in Mexico. Then embroiled in the Civil War, the American government could do nothing, even though the assault tickled old fears about European meddling. Later, in 1894, a French naval squadron arrived and positioned itself off the Dominican Republic to obtain payment of yet other claims. There, private American banks were already on the scene, having demanded as a precondition of their own loans that the republic allow outside supervision of its customs house. In a stronger position on this occasion, the U.S. government sent a naval ship of its own to show its displeasure with European intervention, and the French complaint was settled peaceably.

When Venezuela went bankrupt in 1902, however, shortly after passage of the Platt Amendment, President Theodore Roosevelt watched in frustration as the navies of Germany, Britain, and Italy pounded the coastline of the delinquent South American republic. (Venezuela also had debts with Belgium, France, Mexico, the Netherlands, Spain, Sweden, Norway, and the United States.) The foreign minister of Argentina, Luis Drago, tried to rally international opinion against such attacks by denouncing the use of force to collect international debts. One might say Drago asserted the principle that those possessed of powerful navies should not be allowed to break knees. Yet the author of the so-called Drago Doctrine was ahead of his time. None of the great powers accepted his plea to delegitimize such actions. In the aftermath, President Roosevelt unilaterally declared a new "corollary" to the Monroe Doctrine in his 1904 annual message to Congress: the right and responsibility of the United States to intervene in the internal affairs of Latin American republics when necessary to ensure order and prevent European strong-arming.[80]

Roosevelt began his message by praising the Platt Amendment, with whose "aid" Cuba had shown exceptional fiscal dependability. Roosevelt also lauded the reliability that "so many of the [other] republics in both Americas are constantly and brilliantly showing." Indeed, any nation that "keeps order and pays its obligations" need not fear American intervention, Roosevelt promised. But "chronic wrong-doing, or an impotence which results in a general loosening of the ties of civilized society may in America, *as elsewhere*, ultimately require intervention" (italics added). Preservation of the Monroe Doctrine, that stubborn American insistence that Europeans not intervene in the Western Hemisphere, compelled the United States "however reluctantly . . . to the exercise of an international police power," Roosevelt said. If the United States did not ensure that Latin Americans met their financial obligations, Europeans would take up the cudgel of debt collection, and might even attempt recolonization. Defaulters "invited foreign aggression to the entire body of American nations."[81]

The next month, in January 1905, the president used the new "Roosevelt Corollary" to justify a treaty with the Dominican Republic that took charge of its customs house in order to settle foreign obligations and guarantee its sovereignty vis-à-vis Europe. Democrats in Congress successfully blocked this particular treaty for three years, but Roosevelt had started a ball rolling whose momentum carried it through both Democratic and Republican administrations. From 1905 to 1933, the United States repeatedly intervened in the Caribbean to compel debt repayment and halt domestic disturbances—including the bloody lynching of a Haitian president.[82] America assumed a role that was part umpire, part policeman, and part banker: an expensive obligation that gradually became as obnoxious to its own citizens as it was to aggrieved Latin Americans. Meanwhile U.S. investors reaped rewards, of course, along with wealthy local elites hoping to benefit from economic development. By 1929, U.S. banks and businessmen were putting 46 percent of their dollars for foreign financial investment into Latin America and the Caribbean, although the figure declined steadily afterward for the rest of the twentieth century.[83]

Where feasible, efforts were made to enhance local capabilities to obviate intervention. In the 1920s, countries from China to Chile hired a Princeton professor of economics, Edwin Kemmerer, to advise them on how to stabilize their own financial systems. Their goal was to attract foreign loans on the best possible terms and repay them without provoking outside micromanagement.[84] The United States itself had previously felt the sting of subservience when it came to foreign financiers, especially vis-à-vis England. In the late nineteenth century, twelve American states restricted foreign ownership of land, hoping for a day "when the United States shall cease to be an exploiting ground for European bankers and money lenders."[85]

For a time, however, American policy in the Caribbean in the early twentieth century echoed the great powers' policy toward China and Turkey—imposing protection and financial supervision on states that could not be allowed to fail. Yet the United States was remarkably proactive in ending its short-lived protectorates, compared with European guarantors. In 1933, President Franklin D. Roosevelt introduced a "Good Neighbor Policy" of nonintervention, and in 1934 the U.S. Congress voluntarily repealed the offensive but pragmatic Platt Amendment as an untenable slight to the sovereignty of Cuba.[86] In contrast, British troops occupied Egypt for a period more than twice as long and were ejected only by force during the Suez Canal Crisis of 1956. In China, British directors presided over maritime customs collection for nearly a century, from 1854 until the Communist Revolution of 1949.

Some historians charge that the United States in 1898 "robbed the Cubans of their independence" rather than freeing them from colonialism. This is an overstatement that makes for guilt-assuaging hyperbole but cartoonish history. The Platt Amendment may well have been entirely unnecessary, and it certainly placed conditions on Cuban autonomy that would have been terribly obnoxious to Americans had France done the same after 1776. But far from being "enslaved forever" by the Platt Amendment, as one Cuban patriot dramatically claimed, the island became independent for the first time since Columbus landed in 1492.[87]

Like China and the Ottoman Empire, Cuba made a series of compromises to enhance its sovereignty in an imperfect, contentious, and rapidly changing world. Revolutionaries first pleaded for direct U.S. military assistance to oust Spain, then conceded to supervision on paper (the Platt Amendment) in order to eject their American liberators. Cubans then pressed for even better terms, which the U.S. Congress granted in 1934. The trend was to move steadily away from imperialism and toward national autonomy. Ultimately, changing mores had made even protectorates seem like unacceptable "halfway houses" on the road to independence. Countries demanded full Westphalian sovereignty, meaning the right to manage their own affairs, whether poorly or well.

If the Spanish-American War of 1898 had stopped at the Antilles, its largely humanitarian motives and effects would be more apparent. Even the imposition of temporary protectorates might seem comparatively benign, considering the possible alternatives of European military intervention or domestic collapse. But the 1898 war also became the occasion of America's only attempt to ingest foreign colonies.

Shortly after Congress appropriated funds to liberate Cuba and fight Spain, Assistant Secretary of the Navy Theodore Roosevelt sent word to Admiral George Dewey to attack the Spanish navy in the Philippines. Dewey's six new battleships rapidly demolished Spain's mossy squadron in Manila Bay. Not having considered the full implications of a worldwide assault on Spanish colonialism, Congress had failed to anticipate the farther-flung consequences.

A study of forty-one major newspapers and the *Congressional Record* prior to the war shows no public interest whatsoever in acquiring the Philippine Archipelago. President McKinley himself said that Admiral Dewey's victory cable forced him to consult a globe: "I could not have told where those darned islands were within 2,000 miles!"[88] Congress had foresworn Cuba by passing the Teller Amendment, which left "the government and control of the Island to its people."[89] But Congress made no such promise with respect to other Spanish colonies, which figured little in the popular imagination. When Admiral Dewey's fleet sailed to the Philippines from Hong Kong, they brought the exiled leader of the Filipino insurrection with them. Dewey turned captured guns over to Emilio Aguinaldo, who was eager to clinch independence.

Yet Spain's swift capitulation, and Europe's frenzied pursuit of colonies in the Far East at the time, unexpectedly raised the question of whether or not the United States should hang on to the territory. McKinley concluded it was his Christian duty to "uplift and civilize" the former Spanish colony, and prevent either another foreign takeover or "internal anarchy and mis-rule."[90] Aguinaldo found himself betrayed in the peace treaty that ended the Spanish-American War in August 1898, whereby the United States took the Philippines, Guam, and Puerto Rico in exchange for a payment of $20 million to Spain.

The United States' relationship to colonialism was decidedly odd, however. When first proposed, the treaty elicited howls of protest across the nation. An Anti-Imperialist League arose immediately, in November 1898. It claimed representatives from America's most prominent families (including the grandson of John Quincy Adams), famous veterans (Thomas Wentworth Higginson), renowned writers (Mark Twain), top industrialists (Andrew Carnegie), foremost philosophers (William James), respected labor leaders (Samuel Gompers), and revered university presidents (David Starr Jordan of Stanford and Charles Eliot of Harvard). William Jennings Bryan, who supported intervention in Cuba on humanitarian grounds, later ran his 1900 presidential campaign as a referendum against imperialism in the Philippines. Voters' campaign pins read "No imperialism for U.S."[91]

Senator William Mason of Illinois made arguments typical of the treaty opposition. The Marquis de Lafayette, Simón Bolívar, Giuseppe Garibaldi, and Tadeusz Kościusko had all taken courage from American republicanism, he pointed out. "For over one hundred years every lover of liberty has pointed to this sentence . . . 'All just powers of government are derived from the consent of the governed.' . . . [And] we will not amend that sentence now," Mason thundered. The Midwestern senator scorned different standards of justice for different races. He warned: "Go to your children, who are in the first year of the high school, and they will tell you the rule, that in all history every square foot of ground taken by force from an alien nation has to be kept by force."

Mason's colleague from Missouri, Senator George Vest, introduced a petition from the Cigar Makers' Union "remonstrating against any extension of the sovereignty of the United States over the Philippine Islands . . . or other foreign territory, without the free consent of the people thereof." Vest conceded that the federal government had the authority to acquire new territory but said, "I do deny that territory can be acquired to be held as colonies, peopled by millions of subjects, not citizens, with no hope or prospect of its ever becoming a State of the Union."[92]

Senator Augustus Bacon of Georgia went further. A segregationist who cautioned against incorporating Filipinos because they were "an altogether alien and different race," Bacon nonetheless pleaded at even greater length for the "right of self-government." Annexation of any people without their consent, even if the "yoke" of government could be made light, was "enslavement," the former Confederate soldier protested four times in four successive sentences. Racism did not obviate Bacon's sincere adherence to Thomas Jefferson's postulate that "all men are created equal." Modern psychiatrists would call this phenomenon cognitive dissonance, yet such inconsistencies were as old as the republic, and perhaps as old as civilization. They created unbearable tensions that moved the human story forward. Thus even a segregationist could and did protest that, in "the march of free institutions," annexation of the Philippines set "the dial of the clock of the world . . . back an hundred years."[93]

Outside Congress, anti-imperialists were more numerous and bipartisan. Few if any other issues united such a disparate, motley collection of Democrats and Republicans, progressives and conservatives, party stalwarts and independents, businessmen and labor-union chiefs.[94] The Anti-Imperialist League attracted 30,000 members in one year and claimed half a million contributors. They drew upon every argument at hand: racist and anti-racist, moral and practical, self-interested and disinterested, economic and political.

Even annexationists had little good to say about imperialism. One senses they hesitated to defend it directly because foreign colonies so deeply violated long-standing practice and rhetoric. Republican senator Orville Platt was a case in point. Speaking against a competing bill that proclaimed, "The colonial system of European nations can not be established under our present Constitution," the senator avoided discussing colonialism altogether. Instead, the author of the Platt Amendment waved the bloody flag and changed topics. Only the power of the federal government was in question, Platt insisted, and the Civil War had produced an answer "written on the mourning weeds of the widows who lost husbands, of the mothers who lost children, of the children who lost fathers." In 1898 it was time "to assert all the power that belongs to the nation as a nation." Federal union was meant to be more than a "rope of sand."[95]

Platt did not mention imperialism per se even once in a speech that rivaled the verbosity of Charles Sumner. Instead, he engaged in blatant obfuscation: "Who proposes to have any colonies? . . . No one. But that we have a right to govern 'the territory' of the United States as we please I think is a right not limited by anything in the Constitution."[96] Yet imperialism glimmered in Platt's logic just as it did in the speeches of others who favored the treaty, even though they were not prepared to give annexation the name it deserved in the nineteenth-century context: empire. By this point, the founders' archaic use of "empire," meaning a general government binding a coalition of equal sovereign states, had gone out of currency. Platt instead argued that it was time for the United States to act like a great nation. As he and his followers knew, this was how great nations acted during the late nineteenth century, every single one of them. They sought permanent subordinates in the form of colonies. But Platt was not bold enough to be explicit.

Nor, apparently, were any of the individuals whom historians most prominently associate with the new American imperialism. None of the so-called giants of American imperialism—Frederick Jackson Turner, Brooks Adams, Josiah Strong, or Alfred Thayer Mahan—praised colonialism outright. They worried that the United States might falter in the "struggle of the fittest," that economic growth could not be sustained without foreign markets, and that American men had lost their martial virtues with the closing of the frontier. But there is little evidence that they actually embraced colonialism as the alternative.

Even Alfred Thayer Mahan, the retired sea captain who achieved international fame with his 1890 book, *The Influence of Sea Power upon History,* and who is widely considered the most intellectually influential expansionist, questioned the wisdom of annexing the Philippine Archipelago beyond a spit of sand on which to build a naval base.[97] A later secretary of the navy confirmed that, for officers, "The United States Navy was the only True Church, Neptune was its God, and Mahan was his prophet."[98] Yet Mahan recognized that coercive takeovers of another nation's territory created hostility and that colonies were useful only when bound to the "mother-country" by ties of affection. "Such colonies the United States has not and is not likely to have,"

Mahan observed in 1890. Although he fretted that U.S. ships during wartime were "like land birds, unable to fly far from their own shores," he did not advocate outright imperialism. Rather, Mahan urged finding "resting-places for . . . coal and repair."[99]

Heeding this advice, the U.S. Navy tried for ten years after 1898 to negotiate base treaties with Peru, Costa Rica, Ecuador, Colombia, and Brazil, but failed miserably because Latin Americans consistently declined the requests, exercising their own sovereignty. Even Cuba ceded only one base under the Platt Amendment and successfully resisted all of the navy's later attempts to enlarge it.[100] Mahan is often cited as a pillar of U.S. imperialism, but it is notable that neither he nor other proponents made this type of argument explicitly. Lacking any coherent rationalization in terms of national ideology, colonialism never gained more than momentary traction.

After months of debate, the treaty with Spain passed the Senate in February 1899 by only one vote to spare beyond the two-thirds required. While most Republicans stood behind McKinley, who pressed them to cooperate, the roll-call pattern was murkier than in either the enthusiastic bipartisan vote for humanitarian intervention or the strictly partisan vote for the Platt Amendment. Most Democrats opposed and most Republicans supported the treaty to annex the Philippines, but there were defections in both directions. Afterward, the disgusted Republican speaker of the House, Thomas Reed, resigned his powerful seat in Congress. A controversial, witty man, Reed once flippantly remarked about two of his House colleagues, "They never open their mouths without subtracting from the sum of human knowledge." But in his opposition to imperialism, Reed was dead serious. "I have tried, perhaps not always successfully, to make the acts of my public life accord with my conscience and I cannot now do this thing."[101]

From the distance of a century later, the 1898 experiment with colonialism looks more like an adolescent identity crisis expressed in Euro-American cross-dressing than a determined campaign. As one American naval officer wrote in 1900, "We have left behind our swaddling clothes." An American jurist employed a similar metaphor in 1906, saying, "We are a world power and we must put world-power clothes on to meet the situation."[102] Yet even those most eager for the United States to be recognized as important were divided on what big-boy pants might look like. Most rejected colonial khaki.

Support for imperialism was fractured, ambivalent, and ultimately transitory. Anti-imperialists had the momentum of U.S. history behind them, including a critique of empire that stretched back to Tom Paine. Although they had failed to kill the treaty with Spain, their setback was temporary. Majority opinion soon reverted to type.[103] As historian Frank Ninkovich notes, American imperialism was "a rather frail addition to a family already full of robust and mature European siblings," and it died in childhood.[104]

McKinley's disastrous decision to annex the Philippines immediately proved naysayers correct in their claim that policies contrary to American ideals could be achieved only with inimical methods. Emilio Aguinaldo and other nationalists promptly opposed recolonization of the Philippines. It took the U.S. Army three years (1899–1902) to suppress the revolt. Roughly 4,000 American soldiers gave their lives to establish U.S. control, and 16,000 Filipino troops died trying to prevent it. Hundreds of thousands of Philippine civilians perished as a result of malnutrition and epidemic diseases made worse by war. Ironically, but not surprisingly, the conflict helped galvanize Filipinos' sense of communal identity despite their linguistic diversity and their dispersal across hundreds of islands. Their growing sense of a "right" to independence, even if they could not yet achieve it militarily, was part of a worldwide trend.[105]

Racist depictions of Filipinos became a convenient justification for policies that contradicted the tradition that all men are created equal. Indeed, it was an equally long-standing tradition that Americans (like other peoples) often excused actions at odds with their nobler cultural and religious values by resorting to stereotypes of their victims as deserving of poor treatment because of their supposed inferiority. In this case, using racial epithets like "goo-goos" to designate Filipinos became common. Dehumanizing the enemy has sometimes played a real role in America's wars, whether against Indians in the nineteenth century or Vietnamese in the twentieth. In the Philippines, inadequately trained and poorly supervised American soldiers harassed noncombatants and occasionally used torture in their interrogations. They waged a war in the archipelago that matched the campaigns on the Great Plains in brutality and reprehensibility. Their abuses contradicted Army policy as dictated from Washington, D.C., and even divisional headquarters in Manila, but this was little consolation to those targeted. Congress held public hearings on a conflict that became a scandal to rival Spain's wars in Cuba.[106]

Once the rebellion was finally suppressed, however, the United States behaved differently from other imperialist powers in notable ways. These differences in no way excuse the tragic misadventure, but they do reveal the fleeting and transitional character of American imperialism. The McKinley administration had already established a commission to report on conditions in the islands, and it issued a statement acknowledging as wrong "any use of the Philippine people or islands as an object or means of exploitation." The Schurman Commission (named for President Jacob Schurman of Cornell University, who was its chair) weighed the question of independence but concluded that the multiethnic islands were not yet adequately prepared to "preserve it among the nations even if it were granted."[107]

Racism certainly influenced the commission, which dismissed some Philippine ethnic groups as "weaklings of low stature, with black skin . . . and large clumsy feet" while praising others as "tall and well developed, with high foreheads" and "light skin." Yet despite racist thinking, the Schurman Commission recognized that America's own values required it to make self-determination the aim of policy. Here again, that powerful maxim, "All men are created equal," exercised its corrosive power on imperialism. Citing Thomas Jefferson's precedent in the Louisiana Purchase, which established the formula for governing unorganized territories, the commission recommended even "larger liberties of self-government [for Filipinos] than Jefferson approved of for the inhabitants of Louisiana." The end goal: "complete self-government."[108]

Indeed, the United States soon passed a series of idiosyncratic laws with regard to the Philippines that strictly limited the ability of anyone to profit from the colony, a policy quite at odds with European practice. As two business historians note, "Uniquely among colonial powers, the U.S. government restricted its own citizens from investing in its new possession."[109] In 1901, President Theodore Roosevelt told Congress that he envisioned for the Philippines "self-government after the fashion of really free nations," and in 1902 the Philippine Organic Act prohibited any sizable U.S. investment in agriculture, banking, or mining.[110] American corporations could not purchase more than 2,500 acres of land (instead of the 25,000-acre limit they desired) and U.S. banks were banned from the islands.

In 1916, Congress went further and passed the Philippine Autonomy Act, which established a legislature, extended the vote to all literate adult males, and announced plans to grant independence as soon as possible. In 1934, Congress passed the Philippine Independence Act, which committed the United States to a ten-year countdown. Japan's occupation of the archipelago during the Second World War forced a two-year delay, but on July 4, 1946, a joyous Philippine Independence Day parade wound through the streets of Manila.

Filipinos waited four decades for autonomy. It was a long time in a human lifespan but a short time for Clio, the Muse of history. Spain held the Philippines for more than three centuries—until forced out by U.S. naval bombardment. After the United States, the next government to acquiesce in the decolonization of its foreign possessions was Britain. But Britain generally resisted timetables for colonial independence both in Asia and Africa. It countenanced Indian autonomy in 1947—almost the ninetieth year of the Raj—but only after Mahatma Gandhi had drawn international disapprobation down upon the British and a socialist prime minister had taken up residence at 10 Downing Street. From a purely comparative point of view, the dismantling of U.S. imperialism was incredibly swift and peaceful. With Philippine permission, the United States continued to lease two naval bases, but when President Corazon Aquino asked U.S. troops to leave in the 1990s, they did.

American motivations were complex. Economic, racial, and tactical considerations shaped the outcome in the Philippines as much as political ideology. Unsurprisingly, the United States did not free the Philippines merely out of the goodness of its heart. Teddy Roosevelt acknowledged in 1907 that the Philippines were "a heel of Achilles." The islands' proximity to expansionist Japan placed the United States in harm's way. And once the thrill of beating colonial Spain had faded, the public came to view imperialism "as an unremunerative and indeed expensive duty," Roosevelt observed. Woodrow Wilson shared these sentiments. In his 1912 campaign for the presidency, he declared, "The Philippines are at present our frontier but I hope we presently are to deprive ourselves of that frontier." In his first annual address to Congress, Wilson commented that the Philippine Islands "are ours, indeed, but not ours to do what we please with. Such territories, once regarded as mere possessions, are no longer to be selfishly exploited; they are part of the domain of public conscience. . . . We must hold steadily in view their ultimate independence."[111] Franklin Delano Roosevelt, the second President Roosevelt, was blunter: "Let's get rid of the Philippines."[112]

Economic factors were particularly compelling in the 1930s. Grappling with the Great Depression, Roosevelt was sensitive to arguments that Filipino immigrants and agricultural goods, freely admitted, hurt unemployed domestic workers and American farmers suffering from price deflation. The federal budget was also under tremendous strain. After subtracting costs from profits, annexation resulted in a deficit of more than $100 million, not including the horrific price of retaking the archipelago from the Japanese in World War II. Imperialism was simply not remunerative. Some Filipino elites covertly opposed decolonization for similar economic reasons, though they paid lip service to nationalism. Their motives were as complex as American ones, and equally affected by self-interest. Filipinos benefitted from access to American markets and free military protection. Michael Quezon, leader of the dominant political party, once joked: "Damn the Americans, why don't they tyrannize us more?"[113]

Historian Paul Kramer argues that xenophobia, racism, and economic self-interest were the primary reasons for severing the colonial tie. By the early 1930s, anti-immigrant organizations, labor unions, and American farmers blamed "inferior" Filipinos for their troubles. Kramer acknowledges that elites in Washington also worried about the archipelago's vulnerability to Japanese attack, but he asserts that nativism—not geopolitical concerns or July Fourth principles—played the key role in convincing Americans to endorse separation. Kramer argues that Philippine independence should not be seen "as an exceptionally early moment in the history of 'decolonization.'" Americans were more anxious to liberate U.S. territory from Filipino immigration than Philippine territory from U.S. occupation.[114]

Evidence for racism is not surprising, given that racism had yet to attract worldwide disapproval. Racist beliefs slowly but distinctly lost credibility over the course of the twentieth century, yet the trend (like the trend away from imperialism itself) did not enter a decisive phase until after World War II. Nor were economic anxieties unusual in the midst of the Great Depression. Yet the vehemence and prevalence of ideological arguments against imperialism, beginning in 1898 and echoed later by Theodore Roosevelt and Woodrow Wilson, suggest that the chief factor underlying American decolonization was, in fact, a fundamental distaste for colonialism. Just as historians occasionally highlight economic and even racist reasons for nineteenth-century abolitionism, the broad consensus is that, at root, an abhorrence of chattel slavery led to the Thirteenth Amendment. Similarly, Americans opposed imperialism chiefly because they viewed it as a violation of the principles of 1776. Those beliefs provide the most cogent explanation for the early independence of the Philippines in comparison with colonies elsewhere.

Although the United States became the first great power to reject empire, it was merely at the cutting edge of a larger and growing international critique, however. Colonialism was out of sync with the trend toward democracy, symbolized by Progressive Era reforms like the vote for women, which spread around the globe during the Belle Époque. Republicanism, nationalism, and popular sovereignty gained momentum worldwide, undermining the legitimacy of imperialism. Indeed, President Woodrow Wilson set out to end the colonial rivalries he held responsible for World War I. Historian Erez Manela argues that, to Wilson, U.S. authority in the Philippines was the prototype for the later League of Nations' mandate system: "Wilson declared that America was a 'trustee' of its overseas possessions." Even before the 1920s, the language of self-determination had become the principal challenge to imperialism.[115]

In the context of world history, America's about-face in the Philippines was a repudiation of the imperial road it had briefly explored. A competing path beckoned more strongly, and it led through an open door.

6

The Open Door and the First International Rules

Or, How the United States Chose Another Way, 1900–1920

The Belle Époque and the war that followed culminated in the creation of the first worldwide, intergovernmental organization to promote peace. Its immediate inspiration is normally attributed to the "Fourteen Points," President Woodrow Wilson's 1918 statement of America's aims in entering World War I. Wilson's first point appealed for *transparency:* "open covenants of peace, openly arrived at . . . in the public view." The second and third points demanded economic *access:* "absolute freedom of the seas," the removal of "economic barriers," and "equality of trade conditions among all the nations consenting to the peace." Wilson's fourteenth and final point called for a new organization to resolve future conflicts by means of what this book loosely calls *arbitration:* nonviolent, orderly debate based on "specific covenants for the purpose of affording mutual guarantees of political independence and territorial integrity to great and small states alike."[1]

Wilson's proposals had far-reaching effect. They were embodied not only in the League of Nations but also in its successor, the United Nations. Indeed, the very idea that all nations have some inherent right to self-determination, and that world organization is required to ensure it and maintain peace, is traditionally called Wilsonianism.

Scholars have spent a century analyzing Wilson's motivations and effects. Some are complimentary. They suggest that Wilsonianism was America's most important gift to the twentieth century and that it remade international society.[2] The opposite viewpoint dominates, however. One Dutch historian argues that Wilson's proposals were "splendid, grandiose, and vague"—and "totally out of touch with reality."[3] Europeans simply did not know what to make of the president's lovely but utterly impractical ideals. Henry Kissinger, former U.S. secretary of state, concurs that Wilson's ideas were "quintessentially American." Indeed, he writes, "European leaders had no categories of thought to encompass such views. . . . Wilson's doctrines of self-determination and collective security put European diplomats on thoroughly unfamiliar terrain."[4] One Paris-based journalist avers that Wilson's views were "formed in ignorance of the actual ethnic, religious, historical, and territorial complexities. . . . He possessed a very American determination not to be confused by reality or bound by the past." Sigmund Freud, the modern founder of psychology, found Wilson pathologically deluded about "the facts of the real outer world," meaning Europe. To yet other critics, Wilson was naive, provincial, and messianic. He was hubristic and disingenuous. He opened Pandora's Box by applying principles to Europe that pertained only in America, and from it escaped the gadfly of self-determination and the monsters of fascism and Nazism. One recent popularization of this thesis calls Wilson the "worst president in American history," whose blunders "led to Hitler, Lenin, Stalin, and WWII."[5]

There are many strands in the critique of Wilson. Some can be traced to animus resulting from the impression of self-righteousness the president sometimes gave. Henry Labouchère's famous remark about the priggish, idealistic British prime minister William Gladstone could well have applied to Wilson, the son of a Virginia pastor: "I don't object to Gladstone always having the ace of trumps up his sleeve, but merely to his belief that the Almighty put it there."[6] One element of the critique of Wilson, however, ought to be laid to rest. Wilsonianism was not peculiarly American, nor was Wilson the inventor or lone advocate of the proposals that became associated with his name. Robert Pastor observes that Wilson and his trusted advisor Edward House "sat down for two hours one morning and condensed their thoughts into a fourteen-point peace plan."[7] The delivery took two hours because the plan had gestated two centuries.

World War I wrought devastation so total that it tends to obscure important continuities before and after 1914. Britain forfeited twice as many troops in the First World War as in the second. France lost half of all its male citizens between the ages of fifteen and thirty. Belgium's verdant fields were turned to mud and gore, and the monarchs of Germany, Russia, and the Ottoman Empire abdicated. After the armistice, every combatant nation of Europe, whether victorious or defeated, found itself hog-tied in ropes of debt.

These searing events detract attention from other developments that gave the peace negotiations the particular and very unusual shape they took. Shrieking shells during the war obliterated memory of numerous quiet conversations on both sides of the Atlantic in which plans for a "United Nations of the World," a "United States of Europe," and a "League to Enforce Peace" were first hatched. Scholars typically give President Wilson too much credit, or too much blame, for the ideas contained in his famous Fourteen Points, including self-determination and the League of Nations. The seeds were actually planted much earlier, by other people, in many places. They merely bloomed under Wilson's green thumb.

Well before World War I, those who gave much thought to such lofty dreams as world peace favored three prescriptions for its achievement: access, arbitration, and transparency. These ideas had champions in a number of nations, particularly France, Britain, and the United States, though they claimed adherents from South America to Scandinavia. Their pedigree was ancient. The Hanseatic League of city-states, founded around 1239, incorporated a provision for "peaceful umpirage" sanctioned by force. King George Podiebrad of Hungary tried to organize a permanent union of independent and equal European states in 1462.[8] William Penn, the English Quaker who founded Pennsylvania, wrote a *Plan for the Permanent Peace of Europe* in 1694 that envisioned an elected International Tribunal of ninety representatives from the states of Europe, in numbers proportionate to population. This body would discuss and settle important problems resistant to bilateral diplomacy and circulate open, transparent records of its meetings to all sovereigns.

Charles-Irénée Castel, abbé de Saint-Pierre, a French diplomat and early visionary of the Enlightenment, wrote a similar work titled *Project for Settling Perpetual Peace in Europe* in 1713. He proposed a League of Sovereign States with a permanent Congress of Representatives. Its senate would arbitrate disputes among the crowned heads of Europe. No country would be allowed, or would need, a peacetime army of more than 6,000 soldiers. Swiss jurist Emer de Vattel also endorsed arbitration in 1758 as "a very reasonable mode, and one that is perfectly conformable to the law of nature, for the decision of every dispute which does not directly interest the safety [basic security] of the nation."[9]

Jeremy Bentham, the English freethinker who coined the term "international," proposed similar reforms beginning in 1786—including arms reductions, free commerce, colonial emancipation across the board, and the creation of a Permanent Court of Judicature to resolve conflicts between nations. Secrecy in diplomacy would be eliminated. Navies would exist only to curb piracy. Bentham conceded that some might call such proposals for institutionalizing peace "visionary and ridiculous," but argued that it was time to make them practicable. "Let it not be objected that the age is not ripe for such a proposal," he wrote; "the more it wants of being ripe, the sooner we should begin to do what can be done to ripen it."[10]

In 1795, German philosopher Immanuel Kant famously proposed a permanent "federation of free states" to create the conditions for a "perpetual peace" among all nations. All standing armies would be totally abolished. No nation would be allowed to plunder another. Every people would be granted equal rights and respect. No longer would more powerful nations treat those less powerful "as lands without owners," counting the inhabitants "as nothing." Kant called his scheme a "league of nations." He envisioned its members as republics, though at the time there was only one wobbling republic in all of Europe.

Like the American Anti-Federalists, however, Kant was wary of implying that such a league would itself become a government or exercise coercive power over its members. "That would be contradictory," he noted, since obedience would imply "the relation of a superior . . . to an inferior." Kant's proposal shied from resolving from the contradiction. He excoriated European sovereigns for their pride "in being subject to no external juridical restraint," while paradoxically conceding that state autonomy must be rigorously guarded. International law would prevail in his system, Kant believed, but nowhere did he say how it might be enforced other than by supreme "reason."[11]

To Kant and other European philosophes before the nineteenth century, the right of self-determination and the equality of nations were obvious truths. Yet these ideas were castles in the air, sketched by architects of the future at their solitary desks, acting autonomously. There was only one place where concrete, legislative arrangements had been implemented for free trade, government transparency, and the adjudication of "Controversies between two or more States."[12] To fascinated European reformers, the United States remained a marvel: that its elected chief executives actually retired after a prescribed period, that it had created a (mostly) durable peace among competitive states, and that its constitution facilitated open commerce across borders. "The government of the United States has no model in ancient or modern times," observed François Barbe-Marbois, the French diplomat who arranged the sale of Louisiana.[13]

But after the Napoleonic Wars, and as constitutional legislatures gained prominence and power, reformers in Europe and the Americas organized multiple, overlapping peace societies to promote measures for a new global order. Many of these private societies aimed at calming rivalries in Europe, the starting point for most international conflicts. Some called for the formation of a "United States of Europe." Other organizations had a global emphasis, resulting in proposals for a "Federation of the World."[14]

Beginning in 1848, these diverse groups met episodically in so-called Universal Peace Congresses held in cities across Europe. Victor Hugo, the pride and terror of nineteenth-century France, gave the thundering inaugural address at the second such meeting, in Paris in 1849, to an audience of 1,500 delegates. "A day will come when you, France—you, Russia—you, Italy—you, England—you, Germany—all of you, nations of the Continent, will, without losing your distinctive qualities and your glorious individuality, be blended into a superior unity, and constitute a European fraternity, just as Normandy, Brittany, Burgundy, Lorraine have been blended into France." The author of *Les Miserables* and *The Hunchback of Notre Dame* prophesied: "A day will come when bullets and bombshells will be replaced by votes, by the universal suffrage of nations, by the venerable arbitration of a great sovereign senate, which will be to Europe what the Parliament is to England." The time would come, he said, when "the United States of America and the United States of Europe shall be seen . . . extending the hand of fellowship across the ocean." Hugo's visions were so novel as to read like fiction.[15]

Delegations from seven countries attended the very first Universal Peace Congress, in Brussels in 1848. British peace activists were the most vociferous and best-represented members of the movement at the first meeting, but that soon changed. Word spread, transmitted via steamships and by the transoceanic cables that linked Britain to North America in 1866, North America to South America in 1890, and Asia to the Americas in 1903. Peace organizations sprang up almost everywhere. The nineteenth century closed with more than 425 identifiable peace societies of varying sizes, most calling for disarmament, free trade, arbitration, and new international mechanisms to achieve these goals. "By numerical classification," Arthur Beales observes, "Denmark had 94, Sweden 79, Germany 72, Great Britain 46, Norway 38, Switzerland 26, France 16, the United States 15, Italy 13, Austria 9, Holland 9, Hungary 2, Belgium, Portugal, and Russia 1 each." Between them, Japan and Australia boasted another 3.[16]

Peace societies did not preach merely to the converted. Urged on by the Scottish migrant and American industrialist Andrew Carnegie, organizers in Britain and the United States petitioned Parliament and the U.S. Congress in 1887 to sign an Anglo-American Arbitration Treaty. The precedent set by Jay's Treaty of 1794 led many to believe that Britain and the United States had the best chance of blazing a new path. The famous Alabama case confirmed that impression, when London and Washington agreed to submit claims stemming from the American Civil War to international scrutiny. The two countries had also used arbitration to resolve conflicts with Brazil, Chile, Colombia, Costa Rica, Ecuador, Haiti, Mexico, Paraguay, Peru, and a variety of European powers in the second half of the nineteenth century.

But the United States and Britain had opted for arbitration with each other more frequently than with any other nation. They submitted various disputes for adjudication, including even environmental conflicts like the killing of Alaskan fur seals by Canadian hunters. (The United States lost the Bering Strait wildlife arbitration when a Paris tribunal handed down a verdict in favor of Canadian trappers, and America, like the United Kingdom earlier, paid up.)[17] Unsurprisingly, French pacifists were not content to take second place to the English, and they soon presented a similar petition for a permanent treaty with the United States to the French National Assembly. The American Congress responded in June 1888 by voting to allocate $80,000 to negotiating permanent treaties of arbitration with both Britain and France.[18]

The path to peace was not smooth, however. The U.S. Senate eventually rejected the Anglo-American Arbitration Treaty for nationalistic reasons, still fearing the might of the British lion and any impingement on Washington's freedom of action. Chile and Argentina seized the initiative instead, and they signed an agreement on the model of the rejected Anglo-American treaty. The Asociación Americana La Paz, founded in Buenos Aires in 1899, further fanned the sentiment of goodwill, while persistent disagreement over borders provided incentive for further measures. In 1902, the two republics agreed not only to arbitrate nearly all differences and reduce armaments, but also to anoint a permanent and trusted outside arbiter, Great Britain, which had ruled on a boundary dispute between them just the year before and averted physical violence along the world's third-longest border.[19]

Even poetry reflected the yearning for a better way and the belief that it was possible. Lord Tennyson, poet laureate of England during Queen Victoria's reign, immortalized these ideas in "Locksley Hall." First published in 1842, the poem looked "into the future far as human eye can see," beyond nations "snarling at each other's heels." Even before midcentury, Tennyson envisioned a time when "the war-drum throbbed no longer, and the battle-flags were furled / In the Parliament of man, the Federation of the world."[20]

Wilsonianism, therefore, preceded the birth of Woodrow Wilson by decades if not centuries. The president cannot even claim the distinction of being the first world leader to champion the cause. That belongs to Czar Nicholas of Russia, who ironically later earned the nickname "Bloody Nicholas" for the violent events of his reign.

In 1898 Nicholas II startled the normally imperturbable diplomatic corps. On a quiet August morning in the rococo Russian capitol of Saint Petersburg, he issued a call for universal world peace through his foreign minister, Count Muraviev. A suave tactician with lively eyes and an enormous moustache, Muraviev used the occasion of a routine, weekly reception for foreign emissaries to spring the unusual proposal. When his unsuspecting guests were assembled, the count pulled out copies of a letter he had prepared on the czar's behalf to give each of the dignitaries.[21]

Europe was pursuing a reckless arms race, the communiqué observed. It read, "The Imperial Government thinks that the present moment would be very favorable for seeking, by means of international discussion, the most effectual means of insuring . . . a real and durable peace, and above all, of putting an end to the progressive development of the present armaments." Sixteen years before the guns went off in August 1914, His Majesty the czar stated that more needed to be done to avoid a world war whose horrors should "make every thinking man shudder in advance." He believed a conference focused on disarmament might avert financial, political, and moral collapse, and facilitate the triumph of "the great idea of universal peace."[22]

The invitation contained turns of phrase fashionable elsewhere for decades. But the summons came from the unlikeliest person on the globe, which made it all the more arresting and showed how far talk had traveled.

The "Emperor and Autocrat of All the Russias" expressed the very ideas that Woodrow Wilson was later charged with foisting on a clueless Europe.

Nicholas II had previously evinced little interest in experiments with democracy or reform—despite being cousin to the kings of Britain, Denmark, and Germany, and married to a granddaughter of Queen Victoria. (The incestuous absurdity of the European monarchical system is illustrated by the fact that Wilhelm and Nicholas were each other's first, second, and third cousins.) As Nicholas II had told one delegation at the start of his reign four years earlier, any popular expectation of a voice in government was unfounded. "I want everyone to know that I will devote all my strength to maintain, for the good of the whole nation, the principle of absolute autocracy, as firmly and as strongly as did my late lamented father."[23]

Nicholas II ruled an empire that bristled with guns. Yet the new czar, only thirty years old, had also inherited Romanov aspirations, dating back to the Holy Alliance of the 1820s, for a universal Christian peace. Some newspaper reports claimed that his father had impressed Nicholas from childhood onward with the "horrors of war."[24] The czar was further affected by Ivan Bloch, an influential Russian who foresaw that modern weaponry would cause physical destruction that far outweighed any benefits a nation could possibly accrue from fighting. The proposal could hardly harm Russia's interests, and it might advance them. Wars were costly, chancy affairs, as the Russian Army had found in Crimea. Military budgets sluiced funds away from worthier expenditures. The state was already the world's largest, and it had no need of further territory (or it would not have sold Alaska). For all these and perhaps other reasons on which Russian sources shed minimal light, Nicholas proposed a meeting to remake international relations.

Bloody Nicholas would never be mistaken for the Prince of Peace, but the rather opaque young monarch, casting about for his role in life, turned world history around. He made the first practical gesture toward world organization by a modern ruler, two decades before Wilson's Fourteen Points. Proposals for peaceful arbitration were afoot well before World War I.

Contemporaries could hardly believe that such an enlightened notion would find shelf space in the brain of a Romanov, but the Russian bureaucracy was infamously even more close-minded. The suggestion appeared to come genuinely from the czar. Bertha von Suttner, president of the Austrian Peace Society, wrote that, contrary to anything she might ever have dreamed, the invitation was no summons "from socialistic or peace circles," but rather like a beautiful fairy tale of peace writ by "one of the highest war lords."[25]

It was a tale that she had actually helped inspire ten years before. In addition to the works of Ivan Bloch, the czar had read Bertha von Suttner's popular antiwar novel, *Lay Down Your Arms.*[26] Like Harriet Beecher Stowe, author of *Uncle Tom's Cabin,* Suttner used literary sentimentalism—one of the few tools available to an intellectual woman in her day—to stir outrage at injustice. Published in 1889, *Lay Down Your Arms* captured the imagination of the world. The book went into twelve languages and hundreds of editions. Publisher William T. Stead made it available in England for a penny a copy.[27] *Lay Down Your Arms* launched Suttner into the leadership of the international peace movement and later helped her win the first Nobel Peace Prize awarded a woman, in 1905. She not only dramatized the ruin of war but also spread word of an alternative: international arbitration.

Suttner's heartfelt melodrama ended with an appeal from Hodgson Pratt, British founder of the International Arbitration and Peace Association, to replace a system of "force and wrong" for a new "state of law and justice." All that was required was for states to "bind themselves to defer their differences . . . [to] an authorized tribunal instead of a resort to wholesale murder."[28] Bertha von Suttner, an impoverished countess who had married for love, made international cooperation appear not only necessary but possible.[29]

Some in the diplomatic corps in Saint Petersburg thought Nicholas II hopelessly naive and romantic (others, devious and sneaky), but an invitation from the czar was not to be ignored. Kaiser Wilhelm II of Germany confided to his foreign minister that he considered the czar's action "immature, sudden and stupid," but he nonetheless dashed off a compliment to cousin Nicky. The kaiser also thought he intuited a design to place empires younger than Russia's at a disadvantage. As Wilhelm II lectured his minister, "Anyone who refuses the invitation will be said to want to break the peace and that at a moment when Russia cannot go further, while others—especially Germany—can now begin and make up for lost time." Edward VII, Prince of Wales, privately scorned the invitation as "the greatest nonsense and rubbish" he had ever heard. He predicted that France would "never consent to it—nor *We.*" U.S. president William McKinley had the most positive reaction of a head of state. As he said when presented with the invitation, "Why, of course we will accept it."[30]

Peace societies were beside themselves to mobilize public support for the event, and they flooded England alone with 300,000 pamphlets in twelve months. William Stead, who interviewed Nicholas for the Associated Press, called on Americans and Britons to support the czar. Although "plentifully plied with cold douches of skepticism, ridicule and scorn . . . Nicholas II means business," Stead claimed. The czar himself was nonplussed at the reactions of other leaders, who carpingly demanded, the Romanov observed, "what he proposed to do, as if the future of the world was his business and his alone."[31]

Ultimately, the invitation was accepted by twenty-six nations, whose official representatives gathered for two months in the Dutch capital during the spring of 1899. For the first time in all human history, governments from around the world convened to engineer a better system for international relations. The congress differed from the negotiations at Westphalia two centuries earlier (and Versailles two decades later) because it convened in peacetime. It also embraced more than just Europe. Mexico and the United States attended from the Americas; China, Japan, Persia, and Thailand from Asia. The czar also invited Europe's three most famous spokespersons for peace, Bertha von Suttner of Vienna, Ivan Bloch of Saint Petersburg, and William Stead of England. In a taste of things to come at Versailles in 1919, unofficial delegates also flocked to The Hague, including Finns, Poles, Armenians, and other stateless peoples pressing for their own nations.[32]

Historian Klaus Schlichtmann suggests that the greatest significance of the conference was the participation of the extra-European, non-white nations. The Hague Conference set a precedent for the "universal participation of states based on the principle of equality." It also furthered the goal of settling disputes through due process of law rather than war. In effect, it stood in daring opposition to such pessimistic descriptions of European diplomacy as that penned not long before by Japanese writer Fukuzawa Yukichi, influenced by Otto von Bismarck. "To put it plainly, there are two Ways: to kill or be killed," Fukuzawa wrote.[33]

The Hague Peace Conference did not prevent the senseless, murderous world war that Ivan Bloch had predicted and Nicholas wished to avoid. Germany's appetite for more territory, Austria's insistence upon honor, and the pan-European system of defensive military alliances fed the conflagration that erupted in August 1914. At the conference itself, Russia's detailed proposals for disarmament were rendered mute at the outset when Germany's representative announced that his country had no interest in diminishing either its army or arms. "The German people are not crushed beneath the weight of expenditures. . . . Quite the contrary; public and private wealth is increasing," Colonel von Schwarzhoff declared. "As for compulsory military service, which is intimately associated with these questions, the German does not regard it as a heavy burden, but as a sacred and patriotic duty."[34]

Nor were Germans the only ones to balk. Had Schwarzhoff not cut the legs out from under the Russian motion, American delegate Alfred Thayer Mahan was fully prepared to counter any proposals that might pare his beloved navy. Nonetheless, the 1899 Hague Peace Conference did—just barely—create the Permanent Court of Arbitration, the first world organization to adjudicate conflict.[35]

The Russian delegation presented a preliminary proposal for a court to which nations would be obliged to submit disputes before resorting to force. The United States and Britain advanced drafts of their own. The British version won favor among the delegates, but the German delegation opposed any plan built on such noble "illusions" as eliminating war. Germany was not willing to approve a permanent institution, only "occasional arbitrations."[36] When it seemed the meeting might end in complete failure, the secretary of the U.S. delegation, Frederic Holls, and one of the German representatives traveled to Berlin to prevail upon the Foreign Ministry there.

For its own secretive reasons, the Ministry relented and the Permanent Court of Arbitration was born. At Germany's insistence, however, nations were under no obligation to submit their problems to the court. Participation was strictly voluntarily and limited to the twenty-six signatory nations, including Mexico and the United States. Nonetheless, the court was charged with adjudicating conflict when offers of mediation by "strangers to the dispute" failed. The parties in disagreement would choose arbitrators from a preapproved list of competent jurists, one of whom was former U.S. president Benjamin Harrison, appointed by William McKinley. The arbitrators themselves would select what they called a neutral "umpire."[37]

The Permanent Court of Arbitration attracted no cases its first three years. Even so, its jurisdiction grew. The 1901 Pan-American Conference in Mexico City, called by President McKinley, petitioned to join the Hague system. The other American nations deputized Mexico and the United States to negotiate with the European and Asian signatories to admit them, which was done. Some Latin Americans went even further. Fulfilling the assumption of the

1823 Monroe Doctrine that Western Hemisphere republics had more in common with one another and were more pacific than those of the East, nine countries signed an additional agreement to make arbitration among themselves compulsory rather than merely voluntary before resorting to arms.[38]

The first world leader to submit a case to the Hague court was Theodore Roosevelt. In 1902, a member of the French Chamber of Deputies told the new president: "You are a danger or a hope for the world, according as you advance toward conquest or arbitration, toward violence or justice. It is believed that you are inclined to the side of violence; prove the contrary."

"How?" Roosevelt replied, according to a letter that Baron d'Estournelles afterward sent Bertha von Suttner.

"By giving life to the Hague Court," the French deputy replied.[39]

Roosevelt responded the next day, referring to The Hague an old, rather inconsequential case involving American financial claims against Mexico. A tribunal soon ruled in favor of the United States. That same year the president submitted a more dangerous question concerning the physical violence that had already taken place in Venezuela, when that country refused to satisfy European debt claims. Prior to the assault that had prompted Roosevelt's articulation of his famous corollary to the Monroe Doctrine, Britain, Germany, and Italy had asked Venezuela to participate in an arbitration concerning the money it owed. When Venezuela refused, the three European countries had shelled and blockaded the Venezuelan coast.

Roosevelt now persuaded all parties to submit the problem to The Hague, and the blockading powers sailed away from Venezuelan waters, content to have their day in court. The final judgment was controversial. The court required Venezuela to set aside thirty percent of its customs revenue from two ports for the repayment of foreign debts, but also allowed Britain, Germany, and Italy to step first in line at the Venezuelan countinghouse. Other creditors were not pleased. But the Permanent Court of Arbitration had nonetheless parsed (and solved) a military and financial issue of the highest importance to the world's most powerful countries, averting further physical violence. When a Second Hague Peace Conference convened in 1907, President Roosevelt championed the previously rejected Drago Doctrine, prohibiting any future collection of debts by force. Europeans now accepted the new restriction, though with the proviso that delinquent nations must at least agree to arbitration, or risk military consequences.[40]

Following the lead of Nicholas II, McKinley's and Roosevelt's support for the Permanent Court of Arbitration helped to place the world on the path toward the League of Nations. Their nation's most important innovation early in this period, however, was the Open Door Policy.

The year after the Czar submitted his peace plan to the world, the United States made its first concerted effort to change the behavior of the great powers. In 1899, Secretary of State John Hay announced the American expectation that other countries would not claim exclusive trade privileges in China and that the globe's oldest nation would not fall prey to imperialism. The first demand echoed British practice, but the second constituted a new departure. It also broke fundamentally with the isolationism of the nation's founders.

McKinley's and Hay's motivations are not entirely clear. Up to 1899, the Chinese people had taken far more interest in the United States than Americans had in China. The California Gold Rush, transcontinental railroad construction, and booming commerce attracted hundreds of thousands of Chinese, just as they did migrants from Ireland, Italy, Germany, and elsewhere. Reciprocal interest in China was scant. In 1906, there were slightly more than 1,000 American missionaries in China, compared with more than 81,000 foreign-born Chinese in America. Promoters like Brooks Adams, Albert Beveridge, Josiah Strong, and Alfred Thayer Mahan extolled the potential riches of the fabled China market, but only 2 percent of American foreign trade went to the mostly impoverished customers of that nation. In fact, China maintained a trade surplus with the United States, outselling Yankees two-to-one.[41]

Stingy in funding its consulates, the U.S. government did little to promote or protect American companies in China. Germany, Britain, Japan, and other countries controlled 97 percent of outside investment in China. In 1899, only three American vessels shipped goods into Manchuria, compared with 185 British ones. Nor did American entrepreneurs appear eager to reverse these statistics. As one disappointed Chinese businessman said in describing his attempt to entice U.S. investors, "They invariably said that their money could be just as easily, and just as profitably, invested in their own country, and with better security than was obtainable in China." By the turn of the century, China was practically America's least important trade partner, measured in exports and imports. Yankee merchants sold more goods in Africa.[42]

Several historians have suggested that President McKinley and Secretary of State John Hay devised the Open Door Policy to enhance American profits and extend the American empire by penetrating Asian markets. Given the economic facts on the ground, this is unlikely. Indeed, such an interpretation seems as insubstantial as the myth of the China market itself.[43]

Charges of American imperialism have gained force partly from misconceptions about British policy, which the American government copied. In the modern era, when England first began to lose large portions of its formal empire, historians John Gallagher and Ronald Robinson articulated their extraordinarily influential thesis of "informal empire." Essentially, they argued that *all* of England's interactions with less-developed countries had been imperialistic. Even anti-imperialism was imperialism, because treaties of "free trade and friendship" were simply another means to dominance. Open markets were as imperialistic as closed ones because they allowed cheaper British products to beat out local manufactures. "The attractive force of British trade itself" was enough to do the job, apparently.[44]

Foreign direct investment, Gallagher and Robinson further assumed, was yet another form of imperialist control. Loans went to countries outside the Empire because formal control by England was not necessary. Britain was cleverer than most imperialist powers because its "distinctive feature" was a willingness to forgo formal dominance when informal control produced supremacy just as effectively. Tariff-lowering treaties with most-favored-nation clauses were Trojan horses stuffed with British capitalists. Even the United States narrowly avoided recolonization only by raising its tariffs against the rapacious British, they suggested. Six years after their articulation of "informal empire," William Appleman Williams imported Gallagher and Robinson's concept wholesale for his 1959 *Tragedy of American Diplomacy*. America, too, he said, was an informal, "Open Door Empire."[45]

Yet bitter debates in both Britain and the United States in the nineteenth century—and even today—belie the assertion that free trade and open doors were equivalent to protectionism and imperialism. Neither workers nor manufacturers could agree which technique best promoted domestic well-being: raising or lowering trade barriers. In 1903, Colonial Secretary Joseph Chamberlain posed with two identical loaves of bread in order to refute the accusation that tariffs against foreign wheat would drive up the price of food for British workers. A "protectionist loaf" would be just as big and tasty as a "Free Loaf," he said. Liberal satirists promptly lampooned the conservative leader, who seemed poised to turn the clock back to the days of the old Corn Laws. To find Chamberlain's loaf on a table, they claimed, workers would have to peer through Chamberlain's "patent Imperial Protection double magnifying spectacles."[46]

The critical fact here is that Britain had lowered its tariff barriers unilaterally, and kept them low even when other countries raised theirs. In the late nineteenth century, as historian Frank Trentmann notes, "Free Trade in Britain meant that there were no tariffs at all that discriminated against foreign imports in order to assist any branch of industry and agriculture."[47] The low tariffs and most-favored-nation clauses that Britain wrote into treaties such as those it imposed on China were applied even more stringently to its own domestic economy. Free trade (meaning importation without taxation) increased vulnerability to outside producers but enhanced everyone's opportunities for prosperity—or so British reformers thought.

Free trade also seemed to promote world peace. Indeed, since the days of the French physiocrats, this had been one of the most vehemently expressed arguments in its favor. "We stand to-day at the parting of the ways," the British prime minister told a crowd of 10,000 gathered in London in 1904 to give witness to their faith in free trade and open doors. "One road—a broad and easy one—leads to Protection, to conscription, to the reducing of free institutions to a mere name," the spokesman for the Liberal Party preached. "And the other road leads to the consolidation of liberty at home, and to treaties of arbitration and amity, with their natural sequences in the arrest and ultimate reduction of armaments."[48]

Americans had debated the advantages and disadvantages of tariffs and free trade ever since the days of Hamilton and Jefferson. William McKinley started out as a fierce protectionist. As a congressman, he sponsored the McKinley Tariff of 1890, one of the highest in the nation's history. It raised taxes on imports by 50 percent, with the intent of protecting U.S. industry and the wages of American workers.

As president, however, McKinley revised his thinking and came closer to the view of British Free Traders. "A mutual exchange of commodities is manifestly essential to the continued and healthful growth of our export trade. We must not repose in fancied security that we can forever sell everything and buy little or nothing," McKinley explained. "If such a thing were possible, it would not be best for us or for those with whom we deal."[49]

McKinley's about-face on tariffs explains his motives behind the Open Door Policy better than "informal empire" does. The president wanted to ensure equal access to Chinese markets. He genuinely thought this would strengthen Qing-dynasty China, which was then rotting "by inches," in Theodore Roosevelt's unforgettable phrase.[50] With respect to free trade, McKinley copied the British government, which had initiated the Open Door Policy in the 1840s and promulgated most-favored-nation treaties that guaranteed equal trade rights to all foreign signatories, rather than privileging itself uniquely.[51]

The Sino-Japanese War of 1895 threatened to upset these arrangements, however. In that year, Japan attacked China to obtain additional territory and special port privileges, known as concessions. Russia and Germany pressed the Qing government for additional privileges in turn, initiating what was quickly dubbed the "Scramble for Concessions." Japan, Germany, France, and Russia all grabbed bits of China for their special use, though it was not immediately clear how far they would go in restricting other foreigners' access. Sensing that America's opportunities were narrowing, even McKinley raised the question with Hay, "May we not want a slice, if it is to be divided?"[52] As doors seemed on the verge of swinging shut, the British ambassador petitioned the United States in May 1898 to join in urging other powers to maintain the policy of equal commercial access.

For reasons they did not fully articulate, McKinley and Hay—who had chosen expansion in Hawaii and colonialism in the Philippines—elected at this moment to steer an anti-imperialist course. They would not go so far as to cooperate formally with the British, however, whom many American still regarded with mistrust. So they instead repeated Adams's and Monroe's unilateral behavior in 1823. Only a few months after Britain suggested joint action, McKinley's administration decided to go it alone. In September 1899, and again in July 1900, Hay issued two "Open Door Notes." He later came to be viewed as the sole author of the Open Door Policy, which he certainly was not, since it was originally a British invention.[53]

The notes did, however, significantly amplify the meaning of English policy, especially the second note, which Hay wrote in response to a fresh crisis in China. In the spring of 1900, a spontaneous uprising known as the Boxer Rebellion took a fateful turn. Led by Chinese martial artists united around the slogan "Support the Qing, destroy the foreign," the "Boxers" vented their fury on Chinese Christians and anything or anyone else identified with the West: missionaries, railroad tracks, clocks, lamps, and so on. Using wall posters, verses, and special displays, organizers whipped up peasants' hatred of the "foreign devils" who seem poised to engulf the country. One bit of their racist doggerel toward Westerners read: "Their men are all immoral; / Their women truly vile. / For the Devils it's mother-son sex, / That serves as the breeding style."[54]

In June the Boxers laid siege to walled foreign compounds in several cities, trapping inhabitants and cutting off their food and water. Some who were caught outside were beheaded, others were beaten to death. Two of the foreigners trapped in a compound in Tientsin were future U.S. president Herbert Hoover and his wife, who pitched in to organize dwindling supplies and prevent hoarding. (Lou Henry Hoover had a bicycle tire shot out from underneath her.) Chinese Christians and foreign volunteers threw up additional fortifications composed of furniture, sandbags, mattresses, and loose timber, and stood guard through the tense, frightening weeks. More than 200 foreign missionaries and children were killed, along with tens of thousands of converts across the nation.[55]

When the Chinese dowager empress sided with the Boxers and refused to rescue their trapped victims, other nations responded in force. Made up of different national contingents under a single British commander, the world's first unified peacekeeping force crushed the Boxer Rebellion. Hostages were freed and the violence gradually petered out. Japan fielded half the contingent of roughly 20,000 soldiers, with Russia, Britain, the United States, France, Germany, and Australia providing the balance. A new prototype for international policing, the multinational army was ragged in its discipline, however. Individual troops hardly behaved in model ways, looting cities abandoned by the Chinese government.[56]

McKinley and Hay worried that even worse unintended consequences might materialize. The presence of so many foreign soldiers on Chinese soil could easily facilitate a fresh wave of port "concessions" and possible outright partition of the enormous nation into colonies, akin to the division of Africa the preceding decade. Russia's troops had occupied Manchuria and appeared to be settling in. Germany, France, Italy, and Japan seemed poised to demand fresh shares of the spoils.[57] Going beyond the British position for the first time, Hay wrote a "Second Open Door Note" to the foreign powers on July 3, 1900, while troops were still battling outside the besieged legations.

The second communiqué asked the Europeans and Japanese to guarantee China's self-rule and territorial integrity. Imperialism should not be extended, Hay asserted, echoing the sentiment of the Teller Amendment two years earlier, which had also forbidden colonization in the wake of a police action. Hay's note mentioned no enforcement provisions, since international mechanisms for collective security did not yet exist and the United States did not have any intention of playing umpire in Asia. Other countries balked at formal acceptance of Hay's request but acquiesced in practice—mostly because of the widely perceived difficulties in trying to rule turbulent China. Gradually, the Open Door principle became a feature of multiple international agreements negotiated by American presidents in ensuing years.

In the context of American history, the notes were remarkable for echoing the "noncolonization" principle of the 1823 Monroe Doctrine (and the Teller Amendment, of course), applied beyond the Western Hemisphere for the first time. Hay's notes placed the United States on record in favor of self-determination, regardless of a nation's ability to defend itself. Despite some initial vacillation, and a contradictory policy in the Philippines, Hay and McKinley attempted to devise a viable alternative to imperialism.[58] Without planning, without consulting Congress, they gently nudged the country onto a new path in the first year of the twentieth century.

It was Woodrow Wilson who widened the path into a highway. The erect, self-confident president of Princeton University entered politics in 1910, when recruited by Democratic Party bosses to run for governor of New Jersey. Reflecting the extreme political flux of the era, he won the presidency only two years later in a tight, four-way race against William Taft, Theodore Roosevelt, and Eugene Debs, representing the Republican, Progressive, and Socialist parties, respectively. All of the candidates embraced certain Progressive Era goals, and especially what Robert Wiebe calls the search for order.[59] Although their specific proposals varied, each supported government activism to improve urban living conditions, lessen class conflict, protect the environment, regulate business, and promote arbitration at home and abroad. They were not men to sit on their hands.

When war broke out in Europe in August 1914, American political leaders were stunned and horrified. Wilson immediately invoked the nation's tradition of neutrality and nonintervention outside the Western Hemisphere. He announced that citizens must be "neutral in fact as well as in name during these days that are to try men's souls." The great dividing line of the Atlantic would shield America, as it had since the days of Washington and Monroe. The European fight was "a war with which we have nothing to do," Wilson promised, "whose causes cannot touch us." The American public shared the president's pacifist sentiment, as shown in the popularity of such new silent movies as *Be Neutral* (1914), *War Is Hell* (1915), and *The Terrors of War* (1917).[60]

The Permanent Court of Arbitration had failed, of course, to stop the war, not least because Austria was under no requirement to submit its claim against Serbia for the assassination of Archduke Franz Ferdinand. "It is quite the vogue now to refer with ridicule to the two Hague conferences and the efforts made to avert the catastrophe," commented one of the U.S. arbitrators assigned to the court, but "the failure of the militarists [to safeguard national interest] has certainly been as decisive and infinitely more appalling."[61] Peace activists and many political leaders believed that the conflict merely proved the need for even tighter international cooperation.

In the first six months of the war, more than 2,000 books in English alone were released on "the problem of preventing a repetition of a similar calamity in the future and of establishing permanent peace," in the words of one bibliographer. Titles like *America and the New World State* (1915), *War and World Government* (1915), *Towards International Government* (1915), *League to Enforce Peace* (1915), *A Substitute for War* (1915), and many others provided testimony to the growing determination to create a better world system.[62]

The slaughter in Western Europe gave force and urgency to ideas that had percolated for more than a hundred years: to create, as one contemporary organizer put it, "some form of agreement between nations, a League of nations, by forming a World-Congress, World-Court, and World-Government."[63] The Hague Conferences in 1899 and 1907 had already given such ideas a higher, more respectable profile. Six years before Serbian nationalist Gavrilo Princip gunned down Franz Ferdinand and his beloved Sophie in Sarajevo, an ad hoc group in the hills of Berkeley, California, overlooking San Francisco Bay, had put forward a prospectus for what they called "The United Nations." The arms race burdened common people the world over, the group's monthly newsletter read in November 1908, while "great armies and navies are kept in readiness to destroy, to devastate, to kill." There had to be a better way to "enforce peace and prevent war ever occurring again."[64]

Four years later and three thousand miles away, in New York, another group also proposed a "United Nations of the World." They advertised their prescription for world unity right on their letterhead: the Permanent Hague Court as the "judiciary department," the parliaments of the world joined in one body as the "legislative department," and a chief executive with the title "The Peacemaker." In July 1912, the chair of the U.S. House Committee on Foreign Affairs, Democrat William Sulzer of New York, introduced a bill into Congress to invite "all the members of the national legislative bodies of the various nations of the world" to a meeting in Washington, D.C., in 1915 to discuss "universal peace." According to the supporters of the bill, 362 out of 487 member of Congress had already pledged their vote.[65]

Even before World War I broke out, advocates for world organization were arguing in favor of stricter, more coercive means to tamp down antisocial behavior among nations. Lucia Ames Mead, a New England author whose 1903 *Primer of the Peace Movement* was widely excerpted in magazines and pamphlets, commented: "Time was, and not more than two or three centuries ago, when every man carried his own weapon and avenged his own wrong. To-day, in thoroughly civilized communities, he who avenges his own wrong is a criminal. The State has established a disinterested method of settling disputes. . . . Force is employed, but not to settle the dispute. The policeman brings the contestants to a court. . . . [When] brought, they usually venture little or no resistance." An international police force, controlled by a "World Legislature" under the authority of the Hague Court, would do the same. Mead emphasized Western Hemisphere precedents. Chile and Argentina had already taken "the lead" and begun disarming proportionately. The Hague Court had been empowered "to settle disputes between nations . . . [just] as the United States Supreme Court settles disputes between our states."[66] Unstated but implied was the idea that the Old World could learn from North and South America about managing conflict.

Former president Theodore Roosevelt was more explicit. The First Hague Conference had "framed a Magna Carta for the nations," Roosevelt told the Nobel Peace Prize Committee in Norway after winning the prize for mediating the 1905 Russo-Japanese War. Further work was necessary to achieve its ideals. "I cannot help thinking that the Constitution of the United States, notably in the establishment of the Supreme Court and in the methods adopted for securing peace and good relations among and between different

States, offers certain valuable analogies to what should be striven for in order to secure . . . a species of world federation."[67]

President Wilson was conversant with the rising clamor. In December 1915, during the second year of the war, he received a letter from George Shibley, president of the League for World Peace based in Washington, D.C., an organization whose motto was "To promote the Federation of the Americas, the Federation of Europe, and the Federation of the World." Shibley urged Wilson to heed recent statements by Germany, France, and England. German chancellor Theobald von Bethmann Hollweg had publicly stated on December 9 that the war could be terminated only by a plan for peace that "will give the certitude that war will not return." One month earlier, British prime minister Herbert Asquith had told a London audience, "We shall not falter until we have secured for the smaller states of Europe their charter of independence." Shortly before, French president Aristide Briand had said "permanent peace" must be the outcome of the war.

Shibley optimistically interpreted these public comments as a demand for a "United States of Europe on the basis of equal rights—equal rights to home rule and upon the high seas and in the international court." Shibley flattered Wilson for his reputation of strict neutrality. The president was "doubtless the one who can best take the needed next step," he said. Wilson replied, "I have noted with the greatest interest the statement by Chancellor von Bethmann-Hollweg, and . . . [I] am following the development of sentiments in Europe . . . with the utmost sincere desire to be of service." This was not just a routine exchange of personal notes. The *New York Times* published Shibley's and Wilson's correspondence.[68]

Wilson was not the only world leader being pressed to consider a league once the cannons stopped booming. Although French censors banned peace publications, Parisian organizers of the League of the Rights of Man nonetheless began devising a "minimum program" for a durable postwar order. These minimums included "national self-determination [for states large and small], increased recourse to the system of Hague Conferences, [and] a League of Nations functioning by means of pacific settlement and buttressed by 'adequate sanctions.' " In Germany, prominent activists had started planning an "international union of states" even earlier, shortly after war commenced. By November 1914, three organizations had devised plans for a "peace free from recriminations" and based on a new international body. Chancellor Hollweg expressed his sympathy with such ideas, but told the

German author of a popular book titled *Bund der Völker (League of Nations)* that he was constrained by "constitutional militarism."[69]

Nongovernmental, transnational women's groups promoted similar ideas. In April 1915, the first International Congress of Women met at The Hague. Neutral in the war, the Netherlands welcomed delegates from most countries of Europe with the exception of France, which forbade its delegates from attending. Dodging German submarines and British mines, an American group headed by Jane Addams, Emily Balch, and Alice Hamilton docked at Rotterdam in time to see the blooming of the tulips in "great stretches of solid color." The Hague Peace Palace, built by Andrew Carnegie, was too small to accommodate the 1,100 voting delegates, so they met in a great hall at the national zoo.[70]

The women agreed on two primary points: the nonviolent settlement of international disputes and the franchise for women in democratic countries worldwide. Additionally, they determined that "no territory should be transferred without the consent of the men and women in it, and . . . the right of conquest should not be recognized." Printed in German, French, and English, the multinational platform demanded a new "Society of Nations" to guarantee the rights of all, including "weaker countries and primitive peoples." Rosika Schwimmer of Austro-Hungary convinced the delegates to send teams of women to all European capitals, whether neutral or belligerent.[71]

Given their decades of activism, it is not surprising that Britons plunged just as quickly into postwar planning as continental Europeans. James Bryce, former British ambassador to the United States, sponsored one of the most influential schemes for a league of nations. Lord Bryce and his colleagues commenced discussions at the end of 1914. From the very start, they contemplated national self-determination, arms reductions, and a league of nations. Historian Martin Dubin argues that scholars "seem not to understand how . . . early and pervasive an influence" the Bryce Group exerted. Its plan for a league equipped with coercive power attracted attention on both sides of the Atlantic. It may have stimulated formation of the U.S. League to Enforce Peace that began six months later, in June 1915.[72]

Around this same time, the British foreign secretary, Lord Grey, took the first government-level steps by relaying messages to Woodrow Wilson through his close friend, Edward House. President Wilson called House, who had been raised in Texas amid the turmoil of the Civil War, "my second personality." Nicknamed "Colonel" in the chivalric affectation typical of the post-

Confederate south, House traveled to Europe three times at Wilson's behest: once before World War I to urge the deescalation of tension between Germany and Britain, and twice during the conflict. On the last day of January 1915, House sailed from New York to London aboard RMS *Lusitania,* which employed the ruse of an American flag to avoid being torpedoed as it approached the coast of Ireland. (Its passengers were less lucky a few months later.)

Once "Colonel" House was in London, Grey immediately expressed to the envoy his belief that peace could be obtained only if "the United States should cooperate at the end of the war in a general organization designed to guarantee peace." Grey was "fairly insistent" upon this, House told Wilson. A few weeks later, in April, the British foreign secretary again wrote House a note in which he expressed the hope that "Germany would enter after this war some League of Nations." When spring turned to summer and summer to fall, Lord Grey asked House one more time if he thought the American president might propose "a League of Nations binding themselves to side against any Power which broke a treaty . . . or which refused, in case of dispute, to adopt some other method of settlement than that of war?"[73]

In his book *Diplomacy,* Henry Kissinger characterizes the British foreign secretary's last query as a neat ploy of realpolitik designed to ensnare America. "Grey knew his man," Kissinger says, smirking at Grey's cleverness and Wilson's naïveté.[74] But there is little reason to doubt the sincerity of the question, which Bryce and others had already raised. Grey certainly hoped and tried (as any Englishman would) to lure the United States onto the side of Britain. The following year, in 1916, Grey signed the House-Grey Memorandum that offered America the role of peacemaker in the Great War—and enforcer, if Germany refused mediation. Even so, government-level conversations about a league of nations commenced in Britain before they did in the United States. While very preliminary, these explorations were not merely for show or to impress the American president. As biographer John Milton Cooper notes, Wilson first publicly mentioned the idea of a league in February 1915, which was two months after the Bryce Group began its deliberations—and after House's first meeting with Lord Grey. It would have been hard for a British diplomat to anticipate a plan that Wilson had not yet described, and which had been first articulated in England.[75]

Nor did Europeans passively await instructions from America when it came to implementation of a league. After Wilson finally announced his support for a league of nations in his Fourteen Points speech of 1918, the British cabinet devised its own formal proposal in the "Phillimore Report," which David Lloyd George brought to the Paris Peace Conference at Versailles. This report, written by a committee under the retired judge Lord Phillimore, examined contemporary schemes, the Hague Peace Conferences, and "various proposals for a League of Nations" from the sixteenth and seventeenth centuries.[76] Meanwhile, a private British "League of Nations Society" that formed in May 1915 did its utmost to rally public enthusiasm. A French League of Nations Society started an eponymous magazine in November 1917, *La Société des Nations*.[77]

In the United States, former Republican president William Taft assumed leadership of a private group called the League to Enforce Peace. For good luck, and to symbolize the continuity they saw between the federal structure of the United States and a possible counterpart in Europe, organizers timed the June 17, 1915, inaugural conference with the anniversary of the Battle of Bunker Hill. Three hundred delegates met in the same Philadelphia hall where revolutionaries had signed the Declaration of Independence and the American Constitution. They abstained from judgment on the war then in progress, but expressed their conviction that afterward it would "be desirable for the United States to join a league of nations" binding the members to compulsory arbitration. Signatory powers would levy economic and military sanctions if one of their number commenced a war without first submitting the dispute for arbitration. The U.S. Chamber of Commerce, with 400,000 members nationwide, held a referendum on the ad hoc organization's proposition that the United States should take the initiative in forming such a league of nations, to which 96 percent of respondents voted yes.[78]

The U.S. League to Enforce Peace held its second national meeting a year later, in May 1916. League president William Taft presided. This time, Taft's former rival Woodrow Wilson gave the welcoming address at the elegant, colonnaded Belasco Theatre in Washington, D.C., where the Democratic president and his family enjoyed watching plays and the ballet.[79] Echoing Victor Hugo seven decades earlier and McKinley's Second Open Door Note, President Wilson reiterated principles then being expressed in different languages across the globe, including tongues spoken in such colonies as India and Indochina. "We believe," the president told the gathering, "that every people has a right to choose the sovereignty under which they live," and "that small states of the world shall enjoy the same respect for their sovereignty and for their territorial integrity." According to scholars, Wilson was influenced at least partly by the widespread "anti-imperialist revulsion" that followed the American war in the Philippines.[80]

Luminaries from nearly every walk of life attended the ballyhooed two-day conference. Following speeches by U.S. secretary of war Newton Baker, AFL-CIO president Samuel Gompers, Chamber of Commerce director Edward Filene, former president Taft, and a dozen others, a consensus emerged favoring an international organization. Conferees agreed, however, that "to avoid the contingency that joining such a league would draw the United States into wars with which otherwise the country would have nothing to do, . . . [it] must be overwhelmingly strong and must include at the start all the great powers."[81]

The League to Enforce Peace was far from pacifistic. On its stationery, the word "enforce" was printed in "blood red letters." Taft emphasized that the Allied nations must whip Germany in the World War and hit "her on the head" to produce "a psychological change in the minds of her people and bring about a normal view." Otherwise, it would be useless to include it in "any permanent association of nations." Months before the armistice, twelve states in the United States passed resolutions applauding the principles of the League to Enforce Peace.[82]

The war with which America had "nothing to do" ultimately proved impossible to avoid. The Hague Peace Conferences had legitimized the principle that no country should take umbrage if neutral mediators offered their services, so Wilson and House tried repeatedly to offer their good offices. But the combatants were not ready to negotiate, and their efforts proved unavailing.

Meanwhile, as during the Napoleonic Wars, the American government insisted on its right to engage in neutral trade with countries at war. The United States and Japan became principal suppliers of the belligerents, and merchants were inevitably exposed to harm. German submarines and British underwater mines sent more than a dozen U.S. ships to the bottom of the Atlantic and the North Sea. American civilians taking foolish chances in a war zone went down with the *Lusitania* in May 1916. On that occasion, Wilson sent Germany an ultimatum, demanding cessation of its "sink on sight" policy. The kaiser suspended his policy, but U.S. secretary of state William Jennings Bryan nonetheless resigned in protest over Wilson's interference in a matter that did not touch on American sovereignty per se, since the *Lusitania* was a British ship.

The extension of credit and loans to both sides (with a far greater amount going to the Allies than to the Central Powers), further embroiled Wilson's administration. When Germany, in desperation, ordered submarines to resume attacks on ships evading its blockade of Britain, Wilson found himself backed into a corner. The next U.S. vessels that went down brought America into the war on the side of the Allied Powers.

The president had not been eager to commit. He steadfastly avoided engagement for two and half years, despite wholesale slaughter in the trenches of Western Europe. ("Yanks—late to every war!" an Eton-accented character later groused in the British animated film *Chicken Run*.) In his speech to Congress requesting a declaration of hostilities, Woodrow Wilson asserted that German naval power had finally made it impossible for the United States to hide behind the Atlantic. The tipping point had been reached. Even hospital ships, guaranteed safe passage to relieve the people of Belgium, had been sunk.

These were not mere accidents, Wilson argued, but part of a long-term pattern of aggression. The secretive practices of autocratic governments made it possible for them to plot wars without the restraining input of their own people. Armed with modern weaponry, there was little to foil their plans of conquest. Only transparent, self-governed nations could forge a "league of honor, a partnership of opinion," to halt this ancient behavior. Crossing the boldface line that James Monroe and John Quincy Adams had drawn down the Atlantic in 1823, Wilson argued that the United States must help make the world "safe for democracy," the least aggressive political system yet devised. The United States owed this to itself, he implied, not just to Europeans. Although its citizens had not actively aspired to such a role, they were perhaps fated for it: "The day has come when America is privileged to spend her blood and her might for the principles that gave her birth." And spend she did. More than 100,000 American soldiers eventually gave their lives, some killed by a worldwide flu pandemic spread by U.S. troop convoys.[83]

It took some time for Wilson to flesh out his unusual war goals. In January 1918 the president presented his Fourteen Points to Congress, though he had preceded them the year before with a call for "peace without victory." Wilson's famous Fourteen Points program urged "open" diplomacy and an end to "secret covenants." Echoing voices in the world around him, he recommended a permanent "association of nations" to guarantee a future peace. On the premise that self-determination was a basic human right, Wilson also advocated home rule for groups then subsumed under the defeated Ottoman,

Austro-Hungarian, and German Empires. Colonized people in Egypt, India, China, and Korea were primed for the message and instantly saw the meaning for themselves. Vladimir Lenin and the Bolsheviks in Russia soon upped the ante, demanding an end to all secret treaties and "capitalist imperialism" worldwide. Although Wilson's demands were revolutionary, they were far from alien or new. Self-consciously or not, the president built on the anticolonialism of the Monroe Doctrine and Open Door, and the penchant for arbitration expressed in the U.S. Constitution, the Jay Treaty, the Hague Peace Conferences, and by numerous reformers during preceding centuries.

At Versailles, the victors of the war agreed that even peoples deemed incapable of immediate home rule would be placed on a timetable toward full independence—first among them, Arabs. Although the Mandate System, as it was known, did not achieve many practical changes in governance, it did speed the evolution of new norms by requiring governments to at least pretend to care about self-determination. (Again, pretense is an important clue to shifting values. As the old saying goes, hypocrisy is the compliment that vice pays to virtue.) Historian Susan Pederson observes that the Mandate System forced the imperial powers "to engage in a protracted, wearisome, and public debate about how undemocratic rule over alien populations (accepted before the Wilsonian era as an entirely normal state of affairs) could be justified." Such debates ate at the intellectual fortifications of imperialism like waves upon a dike. Each partial granting of autonomy, such as Britain's treaties with its Iraqi mandate in 1922 and 1930, raised the question, Why not more?[84]

Historian Deepak Lal criticizes Wilson for letting the "genie out of the bottle" and propagating a kind of "democratic imperialism" that consisted of trying to make the rest of the world resemble the United States.[85] But the president articulated no proposals that had not already been made elsewhere. Had these ideas been Wilson's alone, or even his primarily, they could not have taken hold as immediately as they did. The prospect of America siding with stateless peoples worldwide thrilled many because they had already thought about it long and hard. "By the time of the armistice," historian Erez Manela observes, "many in the colonial world expected Wilson to lead a transformation of international affairs and mold an international society in which the right to self-determination would be recognized and the equality of nations guaranteed."[86] The American president's chief contribution to the effort was to further legitimize the goal of self-determination by embracing it explicitly at the end of a catastrophic war, when European governments were ready to try something new.

Like Nicholas II two decades earlier, Wilson used his stature to write a prescription in the sky. Imperialism became less tolerable as a result. Some provinces and former colonies had nation-state boundaries handed to them at Versailles, while others eventually claimed independence for themselves, as the United States had done in 1776. Crowds thronged to see the American president in Paris and London, and more than 200,000 wildly cheering Bostonians greeted Wilson on his return from the peace talks, treaty in hand.[87]

Wilson set precedent for later American leaders by explicitly acting like a man apart—a kind of umpire among the warring nations—seeking solutions not aimed at territorially enriching the victors. In a move that must have seemed odd to Europeans, he refused to join the war as an Allied Power. Instead, he insisted on the ambiguous term "Associated" to indicate that America was merely cooperating with Britain, France, and Russia—not one of them. Wilson tried to act as if America was in the world but not of the world: on a side, but not taking sides. Of course, Wilson's posture of semineutrality departed from European conventions with regard to alliances. Some continental leaders understandably took offense. French premier Georges Clemenceau famously commented, "Mr. Wilson bores me with his Fourteen Points; why, God Almighty has only ten!"[88]

Wilson's greatest departure from American conventions was his willingness to suspend the Monroe Doctrine and step into continental affairs. McKinley and Roosevelt before him had enormously expanded the American role in Latin America and Asia, but on an ad hoc basis and from afar. Wilson was the first U.S. president to travel to Europe while in office and the first to attend an international conference intended to rewrite world maps. Monroe had promised in 1823 that the United States would refrain from intervention in Europe, just as the doctrine demanded that Europeans refrain from meddling in the Western Hemisphere. But in 1917 Europe was desperate, and Wilson became convinced that German militarism was dangerous, an assessment later shared by German historians.[89] There were few words more stirring to those who knew the history of 1776 than those spoken by the aide-de-camp to General John Pershing when American troops finally arrived in Paris, not far from where a generation of Frenchmen lay dying: "Lafayette, we are here."

Ironically, however, America ultimately rejected participation in the League of Nations that Wilson did so much to promote. In a complicated tale of partisanship, Wilson failed to convince the Senate to ratify the Versailles Treaty. Instead, he incurred the enmity of Henry Cabot Lodge, Republican chair of the Senate Foreign Relations Committee. The two created a spectacle of American partisanship and fickleness. They could agree on the League in principle, but not with each other.[90]

Before the United States entered World War I, Lodge, a Massachusetts senator, actually supported the League to Enforce Peace. At the same conference at which Wilson gave the league's inaugural address in 1916, Lodge also spoke, asserting that, "from the day of the Jay Treaty of 1794," the United States "had led the world in the matter of arbitration." But voluntary arbitration had reached its limit, he said. The nations of the world needed to unite in enforcing due process. Together they would not eliminate *all* wars, but they might "stop some wars and thus diminish their number." Lodge emphasized to his audience, "I do not believe that when [George] Washington warned us against entangling alliances he meant for one moment that we should not join with the other civilized nations of the world if a method could be found to diminish war and encourage peace."[91]

But Lodge whistled a very different tune when Wilson returned from Paris in 1919 with the Treaty of Versailles. Lodge did his utmost to delay and then derail the treaty as written, which he sneered "might get by at Princeton but certainly not at Harvard." Both he and Wilson had PhDs—from different universities, obviously—and each was deeply convinced of his own rightness. Wilson could be personally inflexible, especially after he had a stroke in 1919, but Lodge betrayed from the outset a patrician New England snobbishness toward the self-made Virginian. A great-grandson of George Cabot, president of the Hartford Convention of 1814, Lodge felt entitled to deference for his well-informed opinions with respect to foreign relations. Wilson had made the critical mistake of keeping the Republican leader on the sidelines during the Paris negotiations.

Although the vitriol between them appears to have begun with Lodge, the president came to despise the New Englander as well. Neither wanted to be associated with any measure desired by the other. "I never expected to hate anyone in politics with the hatred I feel towards Wilson," Lodge confided to his close friend Theodore Roosevelt. Lodge also wished to minimize American responsibility for future European problems, even though these were the very ones that tended to spill over into global war. He was convinced that the United States must not become an umpire. As he lectured the Senate in 1919,

"The less we undertake to play the role of umpire and thrust ourselves into European conflicts the better for the United States and the World."[92]

So the Republican senator appended fourteen proposed "reservations" to the Treaty of Versailles, though he knew that under no "set of circumstances in this world could he [Wilson] be induced to accept a treaty with Lodge reservations appended to it."[93] The reservations were aimed mostly at strengthening American autonomy within the League of Nations and were not themselves inherently objectionable. Some, in fact, were good ideas: for example, that the League would not be able to compel American troops to serve abroad without congressional authorization. None of the reservations was a deal breaker so far as other signatory nations were concerned, but to Wilson they were anathema. Although Lodge professed provisional support for the League of Nations, the effect of his actions, as he anticipated, was to kill the treaty. Democrats loyal to Wilson voted against the treaty with its reservations, and Republicans voted against the treaty as originally written. Yet another group voted against *both* versions as incompatible with American tradition. William Borah of Idaho led this pack of so-called Irreconcilables. He spoke for them all when he proclaimed on the Senate floor that no caveat was strong enough to meet the test of George Washington's great rule, "no entangling alliances."[94]

For his part, Wilson left the presidency a man broken in health. The structure of international relations must change radically, he continued to believe, "if civilization is to escape the typhoon." The alternatives were unimaginable. "I do not hesitate to say that the war we have just been through, though it was shot with terror of every kind, is not to be compared with the war we would have to face next time."[95]

Although disappointing to many worldwide, America's failure to join the League of Nations did not cast the pall over the public that it did over the former president. This was not surprising, given the nation's long-standing allergy to involvement in European disputes. It would take a punishing depression, a brutal attack on American territory, and another world war to persuade its reluctant citizens that the deadly consequences of isolationism were worse than the risks of international engagement. After a bruising flirtation with world reorganization, the Belle Époque was over.

7

War against War

*Or, How the Democracies Stumbled and
the World Caught Fire, 1920–1939*

The bombers spotted the USS *Virginia* anchored peacefully in the swell off
Cape Hatteras, North Carolina, on the morning of September 23, 1923. Target in sight, they went into a dive and dropped their charges from 3,000
feet. One 1,100-pound explosive screamed past the *Virginia* and slammed
harmlessly into the water, but the second scored a direct hit. The masts,
bridge, smokestacks, and upper story of the gray American warship disappeared in a massive fireball. As the smoke cleared, the ruined hull listed and
sank beneath the waves.

The USS *Indiana* and *South Dakota* came under attack two months later,
this time by twenty men armed with acetylene torches at the Brooklyn Navy
Yard. First they cut away the sterns of the ships, then the bows. Cranes
hoisted the charred and twisted steel onto freight cars destined for a Philadelphia scrap yard. Elsewhere, in newspapers around the country, a discreet ad
appeared: twenty-one new and used battleships for sale. The following spring,
twenty-five miles off the coast of Sydney, Australia, demolition experts laced
the flagship of the Royal Australian Navy with dynamite, opened the port-
holes, and detonated their charges. The veteran battleship HMAS *Australia*
sank to its watery grave in twenty minutes, under the mesmerized gaze of her
former crew. In Japan, sailors and civilians craned their necks to see the tur-
ret of the dismantled *Fuji* suspended over a dock. Sentimentalists pleaded for
preservation of the historic warship *Mikasa,* also scheduled for the iron heap.
At a formal gathering in Norfolk, Virginia, the United States Navy announced it had commissioned its last battleship "for years to come."[1]

Peacemaking in the 1920s took a dramatic turn away from restraint of aggressors and toward self-restraint. Americans heaved a sigh of relief that they had not joined the League of Nations and obligated themselves to come to anyone's defense other than their own. They resolved never again to send their boys "over there," as in the lilting lyrics of George M. Cohan's patriotic song. They would rather sink their own battleships than send them on patrol. The defeat of the Treaty of Versailles seemed as inevitable in retrospect as its passage had once seemed assured. Woodrow Wilson retired to a brick mansion that friends helped him purchase on a tree-lined street near Washington's elegant DuPont Circle. Senator Henry Cabot Lodge emerged as the savior of American independence.

Neither Republicans nor Democrats had given up on peacemaking, however. Nor had other peoples who signed the Treaty of Versailles, joined the League of Nations, and pledged themselves on paper to a new world order of access, arbitration, and transparency. Despite their political isolationism, American citizens continued to press for open markets, peaceful settlement of disputes, and diplomatic frankness during the affluent Roaring Twenties. Growing commercial ties pointed to the possibility of a more cooperative world, giving courage to intrepid investors. Private groups like the British Boy Scouts and American Rotary Club were organized along transparent, do-it-yourself lines. They proliferated far from their origins with a goal of promoting "good citizenship" and international friendliness around the world. They even promised rehabilitation for ostracized Germany, initially banned from the League of Nations.[2]

Teachers played their part in trying to educate a new, globally aware generation. From Maine to California, they disseminated tracts about the Paris Pact published by the National Student Forum, a nongovernmental effort supported by the Carnegie Endowment for International Peace. A national committee of more than 300 school superintendents, principals, and eager-beaver civic leaders advised local working groups in each state. By the close of the 1930 school year, 2,635 high schools had taught 200,000 students about the Treaty of Versailles. A few plucky pupils had traveled to Europe on summer junkets to observe the League at work, and more than 5,000 children had written to pen pals on other continents. In Los Angeles, the city school district disseminated a handbook on forming World Friendship Clubs, to help teachers retool the elementary curriculum. It offered wise quotations to festoon classroom blackboards, including the words of George Washington:

"My first wish is to see the whole world at peace and the inhabitants of it as one band of brothers." Students were encouraged to view the modern Olympic Games as "fostering sane international relations" through friendly competition and offering an alternative to the "dark fetish" of unsportsmanlike nationalism. The Maine State Department of Education told its teachers, "A tolerant attitude on the part of the rising generation may be properly cultivated through a careful study of the political and economic problems of our own and other nations." The American Legion added its voice to the chorus, exhorting teachers "to inculcate in their pupils the appreciation, not only of our own national virtues, but also of those of other nations and races, and an understanding of and sympathy for their glories and ideals."[3]

High-level officials expressed a more cautious but similar optimism that military force was outdated and peace might be at hand. In 1921, Henry Cabot Lodge and Irreconcilables such as Senator William Borah of Idaho led the campaign that resulted in the authorized destruction of the USS *Virginia,* HMAS *Australia,* and Japanese imperial ship *Fuji.* They secured Senate ratification of the Washington Naval Treaty, by which Britain, Japan, and the United States sank or scrapped much of their fleets. Presidents Warren Harding and Calvin Coolidge slowed the pace of American military intervention in the Caribbean and Central America, and Herbert Hoover inched toward a "Good Neighbor" pledge of nonintervention in the internal affairs of other American republics. By the end of the decade, the "irreconcilable" Borah had become the primary advocate for the adoption of the 1928 Kellogg-Briand Pact, outlawing aggressive wars forever. American goals remained much the same as they were in 1918, but policymakers rejected military means of achieving them, turning to ever more unorthodox expedients. The United States might applaud collective security, but it refused to be an enforcer or umpire.

Then, with little warning, the Great Depression disabled the American and world economies at the opening of the 1930s. Democracy began breaking down in Europe, Asia, and Latin America. The hopes for peace tarnished rapidly. Fascists and militarists came to power in popular elections. They promised a return to prosperity and greatness through conquest. In tension with the objective of self-determination encouraged by the Treaty of Versailles, "empire" experienced a renaissance. Benito Mussolini, the Italian founder of the Fascist movement, wrote approvingly in 1932, "For Fascism, the growth of empire . . . is an essential manifestation of vitality, and its opposite a sign of decadence. Peoples which are rising, or rising again after a period of decadence, are always imperialist." Anyone who stood in the way would meet with "severe measures."[4] Adolf Hitler similarly appealed to national chauvinism and the ambition to rule over subject peoples. He promised "Aryan" triumph over "inferior human material" such as Jews, Slavs, and "colored" nations. "The mass of the people do not consist of professors or diplomats," he indoctrinated his followers. "What they wish to see is victory for the stronger and destruction of the weaker."[5] Unsurprisingly, new conflicts arose with the popularization of such explicitly aggressive doctrines.

Meanwhile, U.S. interest in solving foreign problems shrank further. The worse the economy became and the more that thunderheads of war threatened, the more resolved Americans became to stay aloof. Nor were Americans the only ones to explore every possibility for avoiding the looming conflict. Britain and Australia also opted for appeasement and isolation. In 1933, the students in Oxford University's debating society voted 275 to 153 in favor of the motion, "This House will in no circumstances fight for its King and Country." The famous author of *Winnie the Pooh* wrote in a political tract the next year that, though his own nation had been willing in the previous war to kill millions to defend "its reputation," there was no honor or prestige in war. Honor was a bankrupt concept in politics, A. A. Milne argued. "It is as meaningless for a nation to talk about its honour as it would be for a cholera germ to talk about its honour; or a bath-mat; or the Multiplication Table."[6]

Like many Americans, Britons embraced the convenient interpretation that arms manufacturers created war scares for their own immoral profit. The wisest response was to ignore these merchants of death. The Depression made it easy to scapegoat corporations, and public tribunals such as America's Nye Committee and Britain's Royal Commission on the Private Manufacture of Arms obliged.[7] Ocean barriers (and the English Channel) also provided a comforting sense of distance from foreign disasters. In 1939, Britain's prime minister expressed sympathy for the plight of Czechoslovakia, created fifteen years earlier by the Versailles Treaty and then being devoured by Adolf Hitler, but Chamberlain renounced responsibility for "a quarrel in a far-away country between people of whom we know nothing."[8]

In Australia, renewed tensions between Germany and its neighbors prompted one popular writer to observe, "Europe's history has been blood-soaked for two thousand years; . . . [It] is the world's cock pit and bear pit, the bloodiest and dirtiest continent in the world."[9] Europeans fought over scraps of territory smaller than an Australian sheep station in the outback. It seemed Europe had learned nothing from the Great War, in which Australia lost more men than the United States from a population one-twentieth the size. In grassroots statements as well as government policies, the United States, Britain, Australia, and other war-weary countries made it clear that, this time, war would have to come to them. They would not go to it.

And so war came, beginning in Asia, not long after the democracies attempted to outlaw it altogether.

When the Monroe Doctrine was penned in 1823, U.S. citizens little conceived of strategic threats emanating from anywhere other than the far side of the Atlantic. The Pacific Ocean had long lived up to the Portuguese name given it by Ferdinand Magellan: Mar Pacifico, or Peaceful Sea. Americans had acquired an interest in the Pacific Rim following the conquest of California, the annexation of Oregon, and the purchase of Alaska. The Pacific washed what became America's longest coastline. This engagement deepened with the acquisition of the Hawaiian and Philippine Islands in 1898. From William McKinley to Warren G. Harding, American presidents paid increasing attention to the affairs of Japan, and to the European powers as they impinged on territorial security and access to foreign markets across the Pacific.

Diplomats found that most issues in the region were susceptible to compromise. As demonstrated by the placid responses to the Open Door Notes, Theodore Roosevelt's successful mediation of the 1905 Russo-Japanese War, and even the Gentleman's Agreement of 1907 (when Roosevelt averted a breach with Japan over insulting anti-Asian laws passed by "infernal fools in California"), international disputes typically stopped short of physical blows.[10] World wars started in Europe, not in Asia or the Americas.

Yet cause for concern remained. China, for one, was terribly unstable in the 1920s. After the three-century Qing Dynasty collapsed in 1912, China's new republican government exercised little control, and warlords dominated the impoverished countryside. Japan looked better, especially if judged by its modern navy and army, but its burgeoning population still suffered from periodic food shortages and political violence. Latching onto European models after 1895, Japan had steadily colonized weaker countries in the region, including Korea, whose six-century-long Chosun Dynasty fell in 1910.

Russia, meanwhile, was embroiled in civil war from its Asian borders to Saint Petersburg. Of the European nations, only Britain retained a significant navy after the submarine predation of World War I, and the League of Nations was untried as a force for peace.

Every government wanted greater security, but they had few means to achieve it short of expanding their navies and fortifying their shores. This presented prohibitive costs, however, especially as economies struggled to achieve normalcy following the World War. Americans had tired of naval expenditures, and the war had bled Britain anemic. In the Far East, especially, capital was scarce and markets in disarray. In other words, money was tight. It seemed there had to be some better way of achieving security.[11]

Almost simultaneously, members of the American, British, and Japanese governments signaled an interest in naval disarmament. The idea suddenly seemed everywhere. In December 1920, Japan suggested a "naval building holiday" if the United States would reciprocate by suspending the armament program it had begun in 1916 in response to German and British assaults on neutral merchantmen. Senator William Borah of Idaho responded to the Japanese idea by proposing a joint resolution that called for consultation among Britain, Japan, and the United States, on the premise that America "is now and has ever been in favor of a practical program of disarmament."[12]

The following June, the Senate voted unanimously in favor of Borah's motion. In the House, only 4 out of 336 representatives had the temerity to oppose it. That same month, Prime Minister Lloyd George told a meeting of the Imperial Dominions that his government welcomed any proposal for arms limitations that America cared to make—a sentiment British diplomats had repeatedly communicated sotto voce. Two weeks later, Secretary of State Charles Evans Hughes invited France, Italy, Japan, and the United Kingdom to a conference in Washington to discuss naval disarmament. The British House of Commons greeted the news with lusty cheers. "The world has been looking to the United States for such a lead," Prime Minister Lloyd George told them. The conservative, patrician Hughes also made the unusual choice of inviting the smaller colonial powers and one nation with little influence and almost no navy at all—namely, China—to discuss general principles regarding the Far East.[13]

The Daughters of the American Revolution opened their Washington hall for the august occasion. The nation's capital had periodically hosted Pan-American conferences, but this was the first global conference ever called by the United States, in the United States. Delegates took their seats at green baize tables arranged in a horseshoe, surrounded by a curious audience composed of members of Congress, the diplomatic corps, journalists, and such notables as Vice President Calvin Coolidge, William Jennings Bryan, and Alice Longworth, the beautiful and unconventional daughter of the deceased Theodore Roosevelt. President Harding gave a short welcoming address, stating that his nation's one hundred million citizens wanted "less of armaments and none of war." To the wonder of the sedate European delegates, who were unused to boisterous, American-style audience participation in diplomatic proceedings, the onlookers responded with ringing applause. Following a discussion of procedural questions, the conference elected Charles Evans Hughes chairman, at the suggestion of British foreign secretary Arthur Balfour. Shortly before the noon lunch break, the elegant Secretary Hughes rose to thank the delegates and make some prefatory remarks.[14]

What followed had no precedent in the history of the world. There is only one way to end an arms race, Hughes stated firmly, unveiling his surprise, "and that is to end it now." The secretary proposed that all new shipbuilding stop immediately and that the world's three largest navies proportionately destroy their vessels, to reduce aggression and misunderstandings. Hughes was suggesting that the three best-armed nations should willingly diminish their power. The United States would scrap the greatest amount: fifteen battleships, or approximately 850,000 tons. The British, Hughes said, turning to Lord Balfour and his colleagues, would need to dismantle almost 600,000 tons. The Japanese would have to dispatch fifteen big ships, equivalent to 450,000 tons. The only other countries with blue-water navies were Italy and France, whose fleets were negligible. Lord Lee, the nonplussed first lord of the British Admiralty, apparently turned pink and told his American counterpart that he would "have to think now and not talk for a number of days."[15]

Despite the unexpected character of Hughes's proposals, they actually met many of the goals then held by Japanese and British leaders eager to obtain greater security with less expenditure. Hughes proposed a tonnage ratio of 5:5:3 for the American, British, and Japanese navies, in consideration of the fact that the first two possessed territory in both the Atlantic and Pacific. The French and Italian navies would sustain a ratio of 1.75 compared with the others. The Japanese initially balked, preferring a ratio of 10:10:7, which would have allowed them a navy 70 percent as large as the American and

British fleets, instead of only 60 percent. Japanese concerns were calmed, however, by British and American promises not to add any new fortifications to their possessions in the Far East, including the Philippines and Singapore, which would give the Japanese an edge in the region and increase their security from attack.

The French and Italians complained about the inferior position with which they would exit the conference, until the American assistant secretary of the navy quietly pointed out that their navies were already smaller than projected under the treaty. They would not have to destroy any ships and could build more. The Italians raised no further objections, as they would have parity with France, their traditional rival. In exchange for accepting the lowest ratio, however, the French government convinced other delegates to take submarines off the bargaining table. This raised the hackles of the British, since the elimination of the German navy after 1919 meant that French submarine "defenses" could be targeted only at the British Isles. The conference consequently established limits only on capital ships and aircraft carriers, since Britain refused to give up its antisubmarine destroyers if the French insisted on keeping their submarines. The British had originally hoped to ban underwater warfare altogether.[16]

The dickering at the conference reveals the extent to which even recent allies still harbored ancient suspicions. The specter of Napoleon Bonaparte hovered just as distinctly behind the delegates' armchairs as the ghost of Archduke Franz Ferdinand.[17] But European wrangling did not diminish the accomplishment of an unprecedented reduction in arms, nor the remarkable fact that competitive nations were willing to make themselves more vulnerable to one another, even though they recognized that others might rearm when treaties expired or conditions changed. Indeed, every country reserved the right of self-defense. The treaty was premised solely upon the "good faith," and the "will and honor," of those who signed it, in the words of Henry Cabot Lodge, whom President Warren Harding had strategically named to the American delegation to ensure Senate support. The United States also insisted that there be absolutely no enforcement provisions, as it had no desire to undertake such moral, military, or financial hazards.[18]

There was one item, however, on which all parties agreed readily. In a so-called Nine-Power pact that also included the delegations from Belgium, China, Portugal, and the Netherlands (which did not have significant navies), conferees voted unanimously to "respect the sovereignty, the independence and the territorial and administrative integrity of China," and to maintain the principle there of "equal opportunity" for foreign trading nations. With the Nine-Power Treaty, the five naval powers and four observers pledged they would do their utmost to help the world's most populous nation "develop and maintain for herself an effective and stable government." The door would remain open. With the clear intent of preventing any further erosion of China's position, the signatory powers formally agreed with the Anglo-American policy to which they had previously given only passive assent. The conference also resolved to raise China's tariffs, close foreign post offices there, withdraw all unauthorized foreign troops, and explore the cessation of extraterritoriality to confirm the Asian nation's Westphalian sovereignty.[19]

Henry Cabot Lodge commented, "No doubt we shall hear it said that the region to which this agreement applies is one most unlikely to give birth to serious disputes, and therefore an agreement of this character is of little consequence." But nations "longing for conquests" had been known to fight over less. It was time to make "the great experiment." The Pacific Rim was a reasonable place to start. A few years later, the United States would become the first foreign creditor to relinquish full tariff control to the Republic of China.[20]

American delegates at the Washington Naval Conference hoped to substitute new international norms for military enforcement of treaty commitments. One of the delegates was the intellectually brilliant Elihu Root, a scion of the Republican Party whose experience and outlook represented a bipartisan meeting point on foreign policy. Former secretary of war under McKinley, Root had advocated military preparedness and opposed neutrality at the start of World War I. Yet as secretary of state under Roosevelt, he also had a hand in several international arbitrations, earning him the Nobel Peace Prize in 1912. Root believed in what a later generation would call soft power: global cultural change. Commenting at the Naval Conference on the use of submarines against civilian ships in the Great War, Root observed that peoples fighting for their lives had traditionally felt compelled and entitled to use every weapon at hand. But the United States hoped that "stigmatizing . . . violation[s] of the fundamental rules of humanity" would lead countries to alter their future behavior voluntarily.[21]

Root used the word "stigmatize" twice. The Washington Naval Treaty would reshape international expectations and "stigmatize . . . the doing to death of women and children and noncombatants." If it worked, no nation would "dare to do" in the future what was done to the *Lusitania*. This was not merely foolish optimism, Root argued. "Cynics are always nearsighted, and oft and usual the decisive facts lie beyond their range of vision." In time, world public opinion would exert sanctions on renegades as terrible "as any criminal statute of Congress or of Parliament." The people might sometimes be confused or misled, but faced with a clear breach of norms, their judgment was not only "the greatest power known to human history," but also "the power that is the hope of the world."[22]

Like most leaders of both parties, cautious Elihu Root had an idealistic side. Later widely quoted for saying "Men do not fail; they give up trying," Root expressed a common American emphasis on choice as determinative of fate. Well aware of the scope of human malfeasance, the former corporate lawyer believed that the most stable form of compliance was voluntary compliance. In the long run, states could not be forced to act peaceably. Ultimately, they would have to *want* not to fight. David Starr Jordan of Stanford University had argued much the same on the eve of the 1918 armistice. It would "require a vast deal of education and some hard knocks" to make Germans tractable, he wrote, but peacemakers had to "work through public opinion," which was a surer long-term guarantee than outright coercion. The spread of republican government after the war made public views more salient than ever before.[23]

Although William Borah helped start the ball rolling, the support of the Irreconcilables in Congress was not assured. In an ironic role reversal, Senator Henry Cabot Lodge found himself pleading for the idealistic treaty in a two-week Senate debate. Fortunately for his case, editorial and public support was overwhelming. *Literary Digest* polled 803 newspapers around the nation, finding 703 in favor, only 66 opposed, and 14 uncommitted. The Senate finally passed the measure 92 to 2, with the reservation that the treaty implied "no commitment to armed force, no alliance, no obligation to join in any defense."[24]

The Washington Naval Conference eliminated sixty-six battleships in all, "a greater triumph than that of any admiral in history," the scholar William Braisted observes. The United States scrapped twenty-six dreadnoughts, Britain and its Dominions destroyed twenty-four, and Japan eliminated sixteen. It was a painful sacrifice for sailors who adored their ships, but in the words of Australian prime minister Stanley Bruce, regret was "tempered with the hope that the world will see [in] the magnitude of our offering, and the manner in which we make it, a measure of our practical belief in the principles enunciated at the Washington Conference, which constitute the only hope of a permanent international peace." A young and ebullient Winston Churchill, whose mother was born in Brooklyn, told the U.S. ambassador in London that mere words could not express "his rejoicing as an Englishman of his pride in his American ancestry."[25] Yet for all the treaty's ambition, it was less audacious than the next measure for international peace to which Americans and others turned in the hope that world opinion, sped by newspapers, telephones, and radio, would eventually be stronger than force.

In February 1923, even before the *Australia, Fuji,* and *Virginia* met their fate, the ubiquitous William Borah called for a universal treaty to make war "a public crime under the law of nations." Borah was flamboyant and prominent, so his words on the Senate floor were remembered. As the laconic but occasionally witty President Calvin Coolidge commented, "Senator Borah is always in session." Fellow Republican Herbert Hoover similarly observed that the square-chinned "Lion of Idaho" had "a positive genius for newspaper publicity."[26] But Borah's idea of using law to trump war had a lineal descent easily traced from the arbitration plans of the nineteenth century through the Hague Conference to the League of Nations. The Outlawry movement, as it was known, was popular in America but not peculiar to America. Edward Filene, retail mogul, Rotarian, and head of the U.S. Chamber of Commerce, captured national sentiment perfectly in 1916: "If the average American could become convinced as to what is the next practical and possible step forward in the substitution of law for war, there would be no question about his support."[27]

Yet it was a bold French statesman with a giant mustache and arresting eyes who took the next step, following paths forged by the philosophes, Victor Hugo, and other compatriots. A former union organizer, Aristide Briand had successfully championed the separation of church and state in France in 1905, advocated formation of a league of nations during the Great War, and led the French delegation to the 1921 Washington Naval Conference. When he became foreign minister in 1925, Briand did more than any international leader to find a way through the thorny brambles of European relations. In 1925 he helped negotiate the Pact of Locarno, by which Germany renounced any further use of force in Europe and gained full membership in the League of Nations. At the Swiss alpine resort of Locarno, Briand and German foreign minister Gustav Stresemann met and embraced, and seemed to place Europe's most devastating war firmly behind them. (The Nobel committee jointly awarded them the Peace Prize in 1926.) That same year, the French prime minister, Édouard Herriot, suggested it was time to form a "United States of Europe" in cooperation with the League of Nations. Briand ran with this idea also. In 1929, he invited the proliferating countries of Europe (twenty-six after the Treaty of Versailles) to a conference to explore federal union. But the prophetic idea died a stillbirth the next year, when none of the attending delegates could bring himself to sacrifice any degree of national sovereignty to a united Europe, including the French foreign minister himself.[28]

Aristide Briand left his personal mark and name to posterity, however, on the movement to ban war. In 1927 Briand proposed a bilateral Franco-American treaty to outlaw wars of aggression between the homelands of Washington and Lafayette. U.S. secretary of state Frank Kellogg initially had little enthusiasm for a measure to prevent such an unlikely event, but Progressives, such as Senator Borah and the famed Jane Addams, took up the idea as one of their many crusades. A leading Progressive and founder of the social work profession, Addams gathered 30,000 signatures in support of the treaty. She and a delegation from the Women's International League for Peace and Freedom presented them to Coolidge personally in December 1927. Borah met with Secretary Kellogg, and urged him to broaden the pact into a multilateral agreement. The French and American ministers both warmed to the suggestion, and Briand graciously yielded precedence to his American counterpart in what became popularly known as the Kellogg-Briand Pact, though it was also sometimes called the Briand-Kellogg Pact, which was technically more correct since the Frenchman had conceived of it.

The treaty prohibited the use of war as "an instrument of national policy" except in self-defense. For Borah and many others, it complemented not only their pacifist goals but also their staunch opposition to modern versions of empire. Military interventionism, they believed, led too easily to imperialism, as shown in the Philippines. They shunned commitments that hampered American freedom of action, endangered American soldiers, and sullied American ideals. Progressive isolationism grew out of the fierce debates over imperialism and empire that began in 1898 and lasted until Philippine independence.[29]

The American Senate ratified the Kellogg-Briand Pact almost unanimously, again with the stipulation that it carried no enforcement obligation. Realists could vote for the measure since it cost nothing. Idealists and isolationists like Borah could support the toothless treaty since they already believed, Christopher McKnight Nichols observes, that it would be "contradictory to answer illegal force with force." Aristide Briand was one of those idealists. At a dinner in Geneva, guests received a menu card with a cartoon that showed the world's statesmen trying to kill Mars, the Roman god of war. The figure of Briand stood to one side, trying to persuade the superannuated deity to commit suicide instead.[30]

In accordance with the new practice of treaty transparency, the Kellogg-Briand agreement was duly registered with the League of Nations on September 4, 1928. It was ratified by almost all nations then in existence, including Germany, Italy, and Japan. Another world war and 60 million deaths later, it inspired the covenant of the United Nations and served as a legal basis for the prosecution of war criminals at Nuremburg and Tokyo. But when Briand died in 1932, his pact was still sometimes dismissed as an "international kiss" of the continental sort, left hanging in the air.[31]

Some scholars assert that the United States exercised "leadership without responsibility" in the 1920s by trying to construct a utopian "world without politics."[32] It is arguable whether the United States' refusal to provide enforcement was negligent, considering that the nation had not formally accepted any ongoing commitment outside the Western Hemisphere. Wisely or not, it made—and therefore broke—no promises. But Americans were certainly not the only ones dreaming big. Unfortunately, there were others whose grandiose dreams were far more dystopian.

The United States was less intertwined with Europe in the 1920s than Woodrow Wilson proposed, but considerably more than ever before, especially on a financial level. This had numerous unforeseen, and perhaps unforeseeable consequences. In 1929, countries tied together by trade and loans stumbled badly, pulling one another down. Once again, war loomed on the horizon. Americans who thought themselves well insulated from world struggles suddenly found they were not.

Although industrial economies had boomed during the 1920s, several factors threatened economic stability. One weakness was overproduction or, to look at the matter from another angle, underconsumption. This chicken-and-egg conundrum surfaced first in agriculture. Before the Great War, increasing mechanization had allowed farmers to turn over more and more land. Then, between 1914 and 1918, Argentina, Australia, Canada, and the United States broke and planted millions of virgin acres to compensate for Europe's inability to feed itself. When European production recovered in the twenties and record harvests poured into grain silos, farmers found themselves awash in surpluses. Prices plummeted in a buyer's market. Intra-European trade also diminished as a consequence of new protectionist tariffs established to shut out competitors. While some parts of the globe still suffered from malnutrition amid this agricultural bonanza, many subsistence regions of Africa and Asia that might have wanted to import food had no cash. By 1929, with demand stagnant, the cost of a bushel of wheat was at its lowest point in four hundred years, and well below what it had cost farmers to grow it. Such agricultural plenty meant cheaper food for wage earners in industrializing cities during the 1920s, but rural life was dismal.[33]

War debts also weakened the international economy, as countries tried to regain their equilibrium. Although Woodrow Wilson had advocated a "peace without victory," he was a minority of one among the great powers at the negotiations in France. The Versailles Treaty infamously pinned a stinging "war guilt" clause on Germany and unilaterally saddled the exhausted belligerent with a colossal bill for reparations. Despite repeated rescheduling of payments, the German government struggled to meet the $33 billion debt to its former enemies. The victors had daunting obligations as well. France, Britain, and Russia each owed close to $4 billion that they had borrowed to fight the war. Italy and Belgium owed $3 billion and $1 billion, respectively, while smaller European states had combined debts of another billion. Europeans owed some of these monies to one another. France, for example, owed half its debt to Britain. America was the primary creditor, however. Europeans owed more than $7 billion to the U.S. Treasury, which was as financially unforgiving toward its debtors as the Allies were toward their former enemy.[34]

Europeans could meet their loan obligations in two ways: earn the money or borrow it. The former proved challenging. The agricultural depression reduced income for most countries. Manufacturing compensated somewhat, but earnings were compromised there as well. The United States erected new tariffs in the 1920s that made it difficult for Europeans to earn dollars in the affluent American marketplace. Republicans and Democrats had disagreed about free trade for decades, with Republicans mostly favoring high tariffs to protect U.S. manufacturing. Republican control of the White House and Congress from 1919 to 1931 meant escalating tariffs. In 1921, the Republican chairman of the House Ways and Means Committee, Joseph Fordney of Michigan, pushed an Emergency Tariff Bill through Congress, raising the low tariff rates that had prevailed under Wilson's Democratic administration.[35] The Fordney-McCumber Act the next year increased tariffs to nearly 40 percent. The Smoot-Hawley Tariff of 1930 tacked on another 20–100 percent, depending on the item. This not only disadvantaged Europeans, who were walled out of the U.S. market, but also American farmers, who exported a high percentage of their production. When other nations retaliated by raising their barriers, farmers suffered far more than manufacturers, who relied heavily on domestic customers.

Faced with little choice, foreign nations opted for a circular pattern of high finance. Germany borrowed money from private American banks to pay England and France. England and France used German reparations to pay the United States. The United States used English and French payments to loan new money to Germany, and so on. This financial merry-go-round kept turning only so long as American banks provided the grease and did not demand any substantial retirement of the debt.

Logical long-term solutions, like cancelling war debts or lowering tariffs, were far from obvious to Americans. The United States had been a debtor nation for all of its history before 1914. From the establishment of the federal government forward, it had an excellent repayment record. Americans were unused to the role of creditor and felt little obligation to rescue Europeans or anyone else from their imprudent adventures. The British had been bankers to the globe since the start of the Industrial Revolution, however. Sensing the fragility of the international economy, they suggested in the twenties and early thirties that the U.S. Treasury release the Allies from some of their obligations, in return for a proportionate cancellation of German reparations. But this had little appeal, even though the war had been a common cause. President Calvin Coolidge expressed his own view as well as much popular sentiment when he replied tersely, "They hired the money, didn't they?"[36]

The world economy perched at the edge of a precipice. Overproduction and international debts weakened the ground, and the collapse of the American stock market triggered an avalanche. In preceding centuries the financial distress of one nation or even one region was unlikely to have a strong effect on others. The gigantic American marketplace had assumed such importance, however, and the world had become so much more integrated, that the failure of securities in the U.S. economy sent shock waves around the planet.

In the 1920s, the U.S. stock market had boomed in response to the demand for new inventions like cars and refrigerators. The middle class began investing their excess income in speculative stocks and bonds. With as little as 3 percent down, investors could buy securities on credit, with the intention of reselling them and reaping a healthy profit once the stocks appreciated in price. But in October 1929, financial experts began warning of a worldwide economic slowdown. Securities were overvalued, they believed. Spooked stockholders began selling shares, and values started sliding dangerously downward. On October 24, Black Thursday, they plummeted. Investors found that the stocks they had bought so cheaply on credit had fallen far below their original asking price. Frightened in turn, bankers began calling in the shaky loans they had made to speculators. This triggered more sales as investors tried to get their money out of the market quickly, depressing prices further.

The downward spiral sucked banks under. Thanks to their historic distrust of big business *and* big government, Americans had no system of large, interstate private banks. Most were solitary institutions with a single storefront.[37] These banks had few reserves beyond whatever was in the vault or could be called in as loans past due. The stock market panic prompted a run, and small private banks were quickly depleted of cash. Since most did not have branches, there was no ready mechanism for moving money expeditiously from one institution to another to meet fluctuating customer demand. Nor did the federal government intervene to loan banks the money they needed temporarily or to insure investors' deposits.

Once banks went bankrupt, depositors found their savings stripped. The close of one immigrant banking institution in New York City wiped out the assets of 400,000 people in one blow, costing $286 million. With no money in their accounts, more debtors defaulted, including 1,300 cities and three state governments. More banks closed. In one year alone, 2,294 institutions went under. Economists estimate that the Great Depression cost the United States $3 trillion (based on values in the year 2000). Unemployment nationwide climbed to 25 percent. In Chicago, a manufacturing center, 40 percent of the labor force was out of work.[38]

Although countries dependent on American cash and trade felt the shock waves immediately, some sections of the globe were sheltered. Closed economies with minimal involvement in international markets were least disturbed by the crisis. One of those was the Union of Soviet Socialist Republics (USSR), the first Communist country, founded in 1917 by Vladimir Lenin and other members of the Bolshevik party. With its back to the world community, the Soviet Union increased its relative share of global economic output in the 1930s. America's portion fell by a third, while Russia's almost doubled. Some saw this as evidence of communism's superiority in cushioning citizens from the ups and downs of laissez-faire economics. What they did not see was the extent of famine and political repression in the USSR's new command economy. Also relatively unaffected were subsistence communities. Nations with few exports or imports did not have much trade to lose, but they remained as poor as ever.[39] During a major downturn, integration with the world economy proved patently costly in the short run. Less apparent were the long-term costs of remaining aloof while more open economies industrialized and integrated over a period of decades.

Not surprisingly, Germany felt the American contraction first. Not only did cash cease flowing but desperate U.S. banks also began calling in old loans. Customers made runs on banking houses in Austria and Germany, fearful that their local institutions would soon be cashed out. German reparations to England and France stopped, preventing those countries from repaying the United States. President Herbert Hoover called a one-year moratorium on all international debts, but this only postponed the final reckoning.[40] The Republican-led Congress responded with the Smoot-Hawley Tariff, despite a petition by more than 1,000 U.S. economists who warned it would spell disaster. In 1930 Hoover signed the bill into law, and within two years more than twenty countries had retaliated with similar beggar-thy-neighbor import taxes. In the early 1930s, all European nations defaulted permanently on their debts, with the exception of Finland. The U.S. Congress again retaliated. Senator Hiram Johnson, a former Irreconcilable, sponsored a law in 1934 prohibiting any further loans to nations in default to the U.S. Treasury—a measure that later complicated efforts to help countries resist foreign aggression. Secretary of State Cordell Hull became a leading proponent of free trade during the Democratic Roosevelt administration, but mercantilism nonetheless resurfaced worldwide.[41]

The last country to abandon universal free trade was the one that had done the most to bring it about. This was Great Britain, not the United States. After 1815, America combined protectionist tariffs with "reciprocity" to build up domestic industries. Reciprocity meant bilateral agreements to reduce tariffs on particular goods in exchange for reductions by the other party. Under James Monroe and John Quincy Adams, the United States abandoned the Hamiltonian vision of minimal, nonrestrictive tariffs used primarily to cover federal operating expenses. Historian George Herring observes, "Congress in 1815 enacted reciprocity legislation that legalized the program of discrimination Jefferson and Madison had advocated since 1789."[42] Trade favors would be carefully negotiated and jealously prized.

In fact, after 1815 Britain and the United States switched places. England dropped the Navigation Acts after the Napoleonic Wars, passed the Corn Laws, opened the empire's doors to foreign merchants, and championed most-favored-nations agreements in lieu of either protectionism or reciprocity. Until the Great Depression, free trade decisively replaced mercantilism. British historian Frank Trentmann likens free trade to a civic religion that "derived its power from popular enthusiasm, from passion and morals, and from its connection with national identity and social emancipation. . . . It appealed to the ethics of fairness and international understanding."[43] When it came to trade, Britons were the most idealistic people on the planet from 1822 to 1932. But in that last year, rocketing unemployment, the collapse of prices for domestic agriculture, and the new U.S. tariffs finally brought the "free trade nation" to its knees. Britain reestablished mercantilist "imperial preferences" to shield itself and the Dominions from external competitors during the Great Depression. A Free Trader in his youth, Winston Churchill gradually came to support the resumption of tariffs, although it was Neville Chamberlain, supported by John Maynard Keynes, who transformed an emerging "Buy British" campaign into the first general tariff. In 1932, Parliament essentially reestablished the Corn Laws and other such acts, and began taxing foreign food and manufactures.[44]

Export-oriented Third World countries whose foreign earnings crashed with the Depression also took measures to defend themselves. Brazil, the fifth largest nation in the world, defaulted on its loans in 1938. Others took extreme measures as well. Trying to repay debts to Europe and the United States, foreign investors around the globe dumped their holdings in the American stock market to raise cash, further depressing the Dow Jones Industrial Average. World trade shrank by two-thirds, dropping from $36 billion in 1929 to $12 billion in 1932.[45]

With foreign markets closing, the global agricultural depression deepened. The price of West African cash crops dropped nearly 70 percent. Latin Americans, significant exporters of raw materials since 1492, experienced profound suffering as prices for their sugar, coffee, rubber, nitrates, wheat, and beef hit rock bottom. The Brazilian government burned coffee beans to stay the fall in prices. Families in Kansas and Oklahoma burned corn to stay warm. Urban workers began losing their jobs. One quarter of the American population was out of work. In Germany, a third of workers lost their jobs.[46]

The Great Depression abruptly reversed the trend of the preceding fifty years toward access, arbitration, and transparency. The intricate economic causes and effects of the Great Depression go beyond the scope of this account, but its consequences were writ large on world history. Dictatorships flourished and democracy faltered. Countries with weaker, less stable systems fell first. Military coups overturned constitutional governments in Argentina, Brazil, Chile, El Salvador, Guatemala, Honduras, and Peru within one year of the 1929 crash.[47] Latin American militaries decisively rejected political liberalism, mimicking powerful new trends first evident in Italy and Portugal, where economic and political chaos had already toppled democracy. In the mid-1920s, Italy and Portugal embraced the related systems of Fascism and corporatism.

A constitutional monarchy, Italy had introduced universal manhood suffrage in 1912 and proportional representation in 1919. Proportional representation was one of the two major electoral systems that emerged in the early twentieth century as republicanism swept the globe. In societies with proportional representation, parties competed for a share of the vote. A party that won 10 percent of the total returns garnered 10 percent of seats in the parliament, for example. Parties tended to proliferate, since any percentage of the vote brought at least some members into government. Because parties rarely won an absolute majority, competitors had to form multiparty coalitions to pass legislation once the assemblies convened. Such coalition governments were notoriously unstable, however, since they often depended on agreements among ideological groups that otherwise vehemently opposed one another.

The other major electoral system, constituent representation, was found in only a few countries, including the United States and Great Britain. Voters elected candidates to represent geographical areas, rather than parties, and in a given race the candidate with the greatest number of votes won. This system tended to produce two or three major parties, since smaller factions frequently ended up with no share in government at all. Socialist parties, for example, might consistently win 10 percent of the vote and never seat anyone. Because governments with constituent representation were more homogenous, they tended to be more stable than those with proportional representation—though arguably less fair to minority points of view.

In Italy, proportional representation proved disastrous to democracy. Having a plethora of contending parties prevented the nation from achieving stable government. Five successive governments between 1918 and 1922 found themselves locked in parliamentary stalemates. Then, in 1922, a splinter group seized power. Led by the skilled propagandist Benito Mussolini, the Fascists appealed to both workers and industrialists. They promised to run the country efficiently by restructuring the divisive electoral system. They advocated "strength through unity," by which they meant repressing the opposition, censoring the press, and using state power to forcibly coordinate the interests of corporations, trade unions, farmers, and property owners.

Mussolini enjoyed wide popular support. He recognized the opportunity presented by modern communications to engage in mass persuasion, and spoke directly to the people over the radio. Styling himself "Il Duce" (the Leader), Mussolini exuded a macho charisma with his broad shoulders, heavy jaw, and shaved head. The dictator encouraged a cult of personality that appealed to many Italians eager to assert their nationalism. Mussolini also banned strikes, eliminated free speech, and raised tariff barriers. He achieved minimal economic gains in exchange for curtailing democracy and free trade (in effect, closing off political and economic access), but his Fascist government did, famously, make the trains run on time. Mussolini also turned to imperial conquest with his promise to establish a new Roman Empire.

Portugal, which became a republic in 1910 after three hundred years of rule by the House of Bragança, also suffered from political factionalism that frustrated economic growth and national unity. In 1926 the neophyte republican government was overthrown in a bloodless military coup. The leader of the coup appointed a respected professor of economics to run the country. António de Oliveira Salazar devised a new constitution that declared Portugal a "unitary, corporatist republic." He called it the Estado Novo, or New State. With the support of the army, Salazar assembled a cadre of bureaucrats and intellectuals to steer the country. Political parties were banned, opponents were imprisoned, and strict censorship was enforced. Salazar decoupled democracy from capitalism, restricting public access to the political process while retaining private ownership and enterprise. Brazil, the world's most populous Portuguese-speaking nation, soon copied Portugal's authoritarian model. President Getúlio Vargas declared an Estado Novo in 1937.

Corporatists and Fascists tended to blend together. Sometimes they were nearly indistinguishable. Both viewed liberalism and electoral democracy with contempt and reviled Marxists as public enemy number one. They had no compunctions about subordinating individual rights to the needs of the state, and rejected transparency as an obligation of government.

But there was an important distinction that made the second group more threatening than the first, with important consequences for foreign relations. Corporatists did not directly challenge emerging international norms like arbitration and self-determination. Fascists, in contrast, strongly advocated territorial conquest. Carrying imperialism to its most horrific conclusions, they believed in a natural social hierarchy that gave them the right to rule, enslave, and even murder those they considered racially inferior. Fascists glorified national traditions to the point of violent bigotry. Once in power, they rewarded women for reproducing as many ethnically pure children as possible to advance the military glory of "the Fatherland." Notably, Fascist Italy later entered World War II on the side of Nazi Germany. Corporatist Portugal remained neutral and quietly favored Britain. Corporatist Brazil sent troops to fight alongside the Allies in Europe and cultivated a special relationship with the United States. Neither Brazil nor Portugal was aggressive—and neither endured foreign occupation after the war.

Initially, in the context of the Great Depression, the Italian and Portuguese systems both generated much admiration. Their apparent success made it difficult for weak democratic governments to maintain legitimacy. Fascist groups sprang up in Spain, Portugal, Poland, Austria, Greece, Hungary, Romania, Norway, Finland, and Britain, as well as in Mexico and Argentina.[48] Fascism was particularly popular in France. Like its near neighbors, Italy and Portugal, France was notoriously unstable. Between 1929 and 1934, a new coalition government formed every three to four months. Socialist factions excoriated one another for bourgeois tendencies while Communists criticized Socialists for counterrevolutionary ones. Royalists, Catholic extremists, Fascists, and anti-Semitic parties collaborated to undermine republican government. The Fascists had become the fastest-growing political party by 1936. Liberals and leftists finally set aside their differences long enough to form a defensive alliance, the Popular Front, that same year, but its candidate, Léon Blum, was nearly beaten to death by thugs seeking the restoration of monarchy. When he took office as both the first Socialist and the first Jewish prime minister, the anti-Semitic right wing adopted the slogan—sadly realized a few years later—"Better Hitler than Blum."[49]

In Germany, political and economic instability had the most tragic and far-reaching consequences of all, and they eventually transformed America's relationship to the world. Germany became a republic following the abdication of Kaiser Wilhelm in 1919. Delegates met in the small town of Weimar, where they devised a constitution based on proportional representation. They created the office of president and invested it with the authority to dissolve the Reichstag and call new elections whenever the chancellor failed to sustain a coalition that could pass legislation. The Weimar assembly also gave the president power to suspend basic freedoms in a national emergency. Fearful of bolshevism after the Russian Revolution, delegates had communism in mind when they made this provision. As it turned out, they had more to fear from the totalitarian right than a totalitarian left.

Proportional representation fostered multiple parties, the largest of which was the moderate-left Social Democratic Party. In 1919, the Social Democrats won 38 percent of the vote. This was the high-water mark of their fortunes, however, since they refused to compromise either with liberals or Communists, their natural allies, in order to form coalition governments. As a consequence, German governments were typically coalitions of the center and moderate right. Without the cooperation of the Social Democrats, these coalitions generally lasted only a few months. The Social Democrats thus played the part of spoilers, keeping other parties from implementing alternative agendas while failing to achieve their own. Right-wing parties constantly assailed liberal democracy as unworkable—which it indeed seemed to be.[50]

German society meanwhile continued to revere the Prussian military values that had unified the nation in 1871. Even Socialists considered the army high command a bulwark of stability in the fragile republic. When the chief of the army attempted a coup in 1920, the liberal government quickly forgave the treasonous act, unwilling to criticize the military. The failure of the liberal government to stand up for itself merely underscored the Weimar Republic's weaknesses. Economic events proved its final undoing. The worldwide agricultural depression deeply affected German farmers in the late 1920s. When the American stock market crisis hit in 1929, urban unemployment soared. By the winter of 1933, six million Germans were unemployed.[51] President Paul von Hindenburg, the senior general in World War I, dissolved the Reichstag and called a new election.

The plebiscite brought sudden fame to the Nazi Party. Under ideologue Adolf Hitler, this faction had campaigned ceaselessly for the preceding seven years, with minimal electoral success. The Nazis criticized democratic liberalism as an alien ideology associated with Jews, who represented 1 percent of the German population, and whom the Nazis incongruously accused of spreading totalitarian communism as well. Hitler advised his associates to hold their noses when they entered the democratic Reichstag, but he also understood that the German people were not yet ready to end their experiment with popular sovereignty. So he followed a constitutional path while holding to his clear, overarching goals. Germans were a superior race on which Jews were parasites, Hitler claimed. To fulfill their destiny, Germans not only needed to rid themselves of Jews, who sapped their lifeblood, but also to acquire *lebensraum,* "living space," in Eastern Europe. The Slavs who occupied those areas were mere *untermenschen,* or "lower men," who in Hitler's plans were best used for brute labor. Germany also ought to avenge itself on France, which had humiliated it in World War I.

To achieve these goals, Hitler advocated a Third German Empire, the Third Reich, following in the footsteps of Charlemagne's Holy Roman Empire and the second German Empire, which had lasted from 1871 to 1918. The trends toward arbitration of conflicts, open markets, and transparency in government were completely contrary to all his plans, and he intended to reverse them. Empire would be the way of the future.

The Nazis made headway first among rural Germans suffering from the agricultural depression. In 1928 the party won around 800,000 votes, or roughly 3 percent of the vote. In 1930, once the Great Depression hit urban areas, the Nazis claimed 6.5 million votes, making them the nation's second-largest party.[52] The voters pinned Germany's economic woes on punitive war reparations, the failures of democracy, and the American stock market. Germans had long blamed Woodrow Wilson for failing to make "peace without victory" come true—in effect, for not being a forceful enough umpire to overrule French and English claims at Versailles. The German Embassy in Washington had even declined to lower its flag when the former president died in 1924. Justified or not, the Nazis' indictment resonated with a dispirited populace hungry for easy answers to trenchant problems. And average Germans had no idea that Hitler planned to lead them into another war with France and Great Britain.[53]

The Nazi Party's unexpected electoral success made Hitler chancellor. Then, at the nadir of the Depression, he called for new elections, in the hope of forging a coalition that would give him the two-thirds majority needed to rewrite the German constitution and disestablish democratic principles. On the night of February 27, 1933, fire mysteriously broke out in the chambers of the Reichstag. At Hitler's urging, President Hindenburg invoked an emergency decree suspending individual liberties and human rights. The Nazis used this decree as a cover for their violent intimidation of opponents. When the 1933 election was over, the Nazis had won 17 million votes, or nearly 44 percent of the total.

Another 12 percent of Germans voted for the Communist Party, yielding them 81 representatives in the German parliament. But Hitler allowed none of them to take their seats. Instead, his secret police arrested the Communists along with 20 of the 120 Social Democrats who had won. All that remained was for Hitler to convince the cowed members of other political parties to go along with him. They did. By a vote of 441 to 94, the Reichstag voted Hitler emergency powers for four years. When these results were announced, the Nazi leader turned to the benches of the Socialists and announced, "And now I have no further need of you."[54] Within a month, the Nazis had purged the civil service of Jews and established the first concentration camp for their political opponents, at Dachau. By the summer of 1933, roughly 30,000 German citizens had been imprisoned. In August that year, following the death of Field Marshall von Hindenburg (from natural causes), Hitler merged the presidency with the chancellorship, making himself supreme ruler, or *Führer*.

The Nazis ensured their popularity by implementing effective programs to end the Depression. They guaranteed farmers' prices, gave contracts to small businesses for public works, reduced domestic taxes, and created government jobs by clearing slums and building the autobahn, Germany's first system of highways. The government negotiated bilateral trade agreements in which it purchased imports with so-called compensation marks, a restricted currency that could be spent only on German goods. This created a de facto barter system that further decreased international liquidity but ensured steady sales for the Third Reich and its partners.[55] Foreign markets became more firmly closed. These and other measures drove German unemployment down by two million the first year. By 1934, Hitler had convinced the German people that he was a benevolent dictator, despite his unusually vitriolic racial views. Other Europeans were not as certain, however, especially when Hitler instituted universal conscription, expanded the armed forces, and remilitarized the Rhineland—all in violation of the Locarno Pact and the Treaty of Versailles.

Italy and Germany were not the only nations veering away from democracy and bent on improving their position at almost any cost. Democracy was equally fragile in Japan, which first adopted universal manhood suffrage in 1925. In the rough seas of the Depression, the government there also adopted an increasingly aggressive posture.

Since the Meiji Restoration, Japan had driven itself to achieve full parity with the West. Within fifty years it had thrown off the Unequal Treaties, placed constitutional limits on the monarchy, built an industrial base, defeated Russia, colonized Korea, and won port concessions from China in Manchuria. It was a picture postcard of self-improvement. At Versailles, Japan was one of the five victors that dictated the peace. But to some Japanese this was not enough. They found continuing evidence of an attitude of superiority among Westerners. Japan failed to win approval for a Racial Equality clause it had hoped to append to the Treaty of Versailles, for example, largely because of the staunch opposition of Australia, which sought to defend the White Australia Policy on which its autonomous government had been founded in 1901. (President Wilson backed Australia on the motion.) A 1924 U.S. Immigration Act that excluded Asians also bespoke unrepentant prejudice, as did new Canadian restrictions on Asian immigration in 1928. (Japanese critics of these policies conveniently ignored the fact that Japan did not have to cope with the problem of foreigners flooding its cities, to which it may also have reacted xenophobically.)[56]

Some Japanese nationalists argued that the Washington Naval Treaty reflected the same racist attitude. Although France and Italy received an even lower quota than Japan, these critics complained that their nation had walked away from the conference with an inferior number of warships compared with "the West." Militarists eager to grow the Japanese Empire also considered foreign opposition to Japanese territorial expansion into China sheer hypocrisy. "The Western Powers had taught the Japanese the game of poker,"

Foreign Minister Yosuke Matsuoka later commented. But "after acquiring most of the chips they pronounced the game immoral and took up contract bridge."[57]

As in the case of Germany, certain Japanese complaints had a ring of truth. Only three years after Japan set upon its imperialist course to catch up with the west, the territorially rich United States began expressing its wish that colonialism not be further extended. Although Japan agreed to the Open Door and helped establish the League of Nations, self-determination for other Asian peoples necessarily impeded the expansion of land-poor Japan. The timing of its imperialist quest ran against the rising tide of nationalism.

Despite an outward appearance of stability, Japanese society was rocked by turmoil over these issues even before the Great Depression. Numerous business and government figures were assassinated, including two prime ministers. The legislature possessed limited powers, and right-wing organizations criticized any degree of democracy as un-Japanese. Foreign trade barriers narrowed Japan's economic options. Not only had Communist, Fascist, and corporatist governments abandoned free trade, so had Britain and the United States. Drawn to German geopolitical thinking, militarists argued that Japan had best get busy acquiring its own sphere, to ensure, as one internal report put it, "the permanent subordination of all other peoples and nations of Asia to Japan."[58] The army and navy answered only to the emperor, who stood aloof and allowed contending parties to pursue their different strategies. Militarists used "army terrorism," in the words of historian Akira Iriye, to intimidate the civilian government.[59]

Factions within the army that hoped to end debate made their move in September 1931. Without permission from any governing body, army plotters blew up a section of the South Manchurian Railway that was under Japanese control. They accused Chinese saboteurs of the crime and attacked the Chinese city of Mukden. Japanese troops advanced from their bases in colonial Korea and within a few months occupied all of Manchuria. To provide a cover for outright imperialism, they placed the former Qing emperor, deposed in 1912 at the age of six, on the throne of a puppet state in Manchuria, calling it Manchukuo. The Japanese claimed to be protecting Emperor Pu Yi as a "humanitarian" act, but an internal document made the real intent plain: "Manchuria and Mongolia will be made an essential part of the existence of the empire."[60] After 1932, all of China north of the Great Wall came under Japanese control. Arguably, World War II began at this moment.

The leader of China, Chiang Kai-shek, appealed to the League of Nations. Japan's invasion violated numerous treaties, including the Treaty of Versailles, the Nine-Power Treaty, and the Kellogg-Briand Pact. But the league had little will and few mechanisms to resist aggression. Cinema newsreels showed Chinese women and children being bombed from the air, yet no other country wished to sacrifice its lives and wealth to defend them. Indeed, there was little precedent for doing so and no law to compel it. Throughout history, nations had fended for themselves when attacked, or gone under. Japanese aggression was the first test of the League of Nations and of numerous treaties signed in the 1920s. It was also a test of American nonentanglement.

The Chinese had every incentive to drag in the rest of the world, despite decades spent castigating foreign devils and European imperialists. But the league merely appointed a commission, headed by the Earl of Lytton, to investigate China's accusations. In February 1932, the British cabinet secretly considered urging the league to level economic sanctions until Japan withdrew from Manchuria, but decided that sanctions would be ineffective without participation by the United States, which was not a league member. Even if America could be induced to cooperate, the cabinet concluded, other nonmembers would probably initiate an opportunistic trade. Public opinion would be apathetic, and there would be isolationists in both Britain and the United States "who disapproved of the policy altogether or were lukewarm." Countries that evaded the blockade would suffer little international disapprobation. As the British assessment concluded, "The moral deterrent to their evasion would be weak; the inducement of profit, strong."[61] Following the Lytton's Commission's on-site investigation of the Manchurian Crisis, the League of Nations formally censured Japan a year after the invasion, but without invoking sanctions. Japan was the only member of the league to vote against the motion, and it subsequently withdrew from the organization in disdain, never to return.

The United Kingdom had good reason to doubt American resolve. Even before the British cabinet's internal debate, President Herbert Hoover had informed U.S. secretary of state Henry Stimson that sanctions were not worth the damage they would do to the American economy, which benefitted significantly from trade with Japan. Also, if sanctions were applied and failed, the United States might be tempted to use further force, which Hoover did not want. In January 1932, Secretary Stimson declared what came to be

known as the Stimson Doctrine. The United States refused to recognize any
change in international borders brought about by means contrary to the Versailles Treaty. Since Manchukuo declared "independence" as the result of the
Japanese invasion, the U.S. would not recognize the new country. This feeble
consequence impressed militarists not at all. It only fostered resentment of
the United States for seeming to deny the Japanese empire's new status and
prowess. Like the original Open Door Notes, the Stimson Doctrine sought
nothing beyond voluntary compliance. It was all principle and no practice.
The Chinese described Stimson's policy as having the "head of a dragon and
the tail of a rat."[62]

Japanese militarists tapped anti-imperialist and anti-Communist arguments in their justification for expansion into China, claiming they wished
only to rescue Asia for Asians and free it from foreign interference. Their arguments intertwined with those of advocates for Indian independence at the
same time, including Mahatma Gandhi and his numerous admirers around
the world. Militarists even echoed the Monroe Doctrine. Japan claimed it
was merely trying to protect nations within its sphere of influence. This
blurred the character of the Japanese offensive in Manchuria for observers on
the other side of the Pacific. In the United States, a number of African American writers argued that Japan was standing up for Asian manhood and that
China acted the part of "Uncle Tom." Marxist scholar W. E. B. Du Bois
commented scornfully on Stimson's objections: "The United States (which
stole a large part of Mexico, invaded Nicaragua and Santo Domingo and
raped Haiti, annexed the Philippines and Porto Rico, dominates Cuba, because of her economic interests and investments) is now explaining the
Golden Rule to Japan."[63] Other African American writers took China's part,
recognizing the similarities between Japanese militarism and European fascism, but most critics of American race relations initially sympathized with
Japan as a colored nation that dared to defy the West. The burgeoning worldwide critique of empire, hastened by Wilson's Fourteen Points, ironically
served Japanese imperialism.

Yet even though Japan's militarists pretended to benevolence, they embraced doctrines of racial superiority reminiscent of Hitler's. Their approach
to expansion was equally brutal. In 1937, the Japanese Empire widened its
war in China. The poorly organized and underarmed Nationalist government fled to the interior, abandoning China's coastal cities to their fate. In
Nanking, then the capital city of the republic, rampaging Japanese soldiers

were encouraged by their officers to behead male civilians and rape females of all ages. Roughly 300,000 Chinese were individually executed in what became known as the Rape of Nanking. American missionaries wrote home that "women are being carried off every morning, afternoon and evening," and that ordinary citizens were being hunted like "rabbits in the street."[64] Elsewhere, the imperial air force strafed urban populations, and the army forced hundreds of thousands of Korean and Chinese girls, some as young as age twelve, to serve as prostitutes, or "comfort women," for Japanese soldiers. In 1938 the Empire proclaimed an "East Asian Co-prosperity Sphere" to embrace Japan, Korea, China, and other Pacific Rim countries, though none joined voluntarily. Censorship in Japan, as in Germany and Italy, prevented the press from reporting alternative or international points of view. Japanese citizens mostly accepted reports that their government sought peace in Asia, and that the perfidious Chinese had conspired to prevent it.[65] When Nazi Germany and Fascist Italy withdrew from the League of Nations shortly after Japan, the three formed their own triple alliance, known as the Axis.

The Axis wars of conquest were initially local. Japan invaded China in 1931, Italy attacked Ethiopia in 1935, and Germany absorbed all of Austria and portions of Czechoslovakia in 1938. European powers treated these events as reprehensible but mostly unavoidable, especially whenever Hitler declared, "This is the last territorial claim which I have to make." The formal rights of weak nations were of recent vintage and still existed only on paper. The Western democracies had no desire to enter new wars and were prepared to tolerate a fair amount of aggression before committing lives or resources to a fight. None was prepared to defend China militarily.

In Great Britain, Prime Minister Neville Chamberlain explained to Parliament that "from time to time the frontiers [of the new states] would have to be adjusted" to keep the general peace. No umpire, empire, or international organization could intervene. States needed to defend themselves. Russia advocated forcibly stopping Germany's expansion, but the leaders of France and Britain were nearly as anti-communist as Hitler was and they rejected Stalin's repeated overtures. Mussolini scornfully dismissed the complaisant Western powers as decadent. "These men," the dictator commented to his son-in-law, "are not made of the same stuff as Francis Drake and the other magnificent adventurers who created the Empire. They are after all the tired sons of a long line of rich men."[66]

In his stirring appeal to the League of Nations in 1936, Emperor Haile Selassie of Ethiopia tried in vain to remind member nations of the commitments they had made to one another. An attack on any was supposed to be repelled as an attack on all. Otherwise, what was the meaning of collective security? Italy had violated not only the Covenant of the league but also bilateral treaties that absolutely prohibited the resort to force under any pretext as a substitute for arbitration. The rules of the international order after World War I were explicit on this point. Yet Benito Mussolini found that he could destroy another government and annex its territory without the League of Nations' moving a muscle. "God and history will remember your judgment," the dignified young monarch warned.[67]

Eventually, Axis attacks became too widespread to ignore. When Hitler invaded and annexed the remaining portion of independent Czechoslovakia in March 1939, Britain and France decided they must draw a line somewhere, or appear so weak as to ensure further aggression. Appeasement had failed. Two weeks after the fall of Czechoslovakia, British prime minister Chamberlain announced in Parliament that His Majesty's government would come to Poland's defense should it be attacked. The Soviet Union took no comfort from the Western powers' belated ultimatum, however, since up to that point the European powers had mostly tolerated the anti-Communist Nazis. U.S. senator Harry Truman of Missouri gave voice to a common sentiment, and to the Soviets a frightening one, when he welcomed German attacks on Russia: "If we see that Germany is winning we ought to help Russia, and if Russia is winning we ought to help Germany, and that way let them kill as many as possible." It did not much console them that Truman added he did not want to see Hitler ultimately "victorious under any circumstances."[68]

Soviet dictator Joseph Stalin had no intention of playing anyone's fool. When France and Britain failed to convince Polish officials to allow Russian troops to cross their territory if Hitler attacked, Stalin turned his back on the West and shocked the democracies by approving a Treaty of Non-Aggression with Hitler. Signed by the foreign ministers of the two nations in August 1939, the Molotov-Ribbentrop Pact contained further, secret protocols planning the division of Eastern Europe between them, including Poland. In allowing Germany yet more *lebensraum,* Stalin's Machiavellian treaty bore similarities to the Munich Agreement of 1938, when Britain and France accepted the first partition of Czechoslovakia. On that occasion, Poland, Hungary, and Germany all helped themselves to a slice of their neighbor. Now Poland was on the chopping block. Through the Molotov-Ribbentrop Pact, the Soviet empire stood to gain a deep buffer against Hitler and recoup pieces of its territory that the Bolsheviks had traded away for peace with Germany in 1918. The pact also deflected Hitler westward.

By this time, the League of Nations was all but defunct. The world had almost entirely reverted to a state of nature, with virtually no rules of play or enforceable limits on the behavior of sovereign states. Imperialism in its most rapacious form stood to gain the upper hand. Only Britain and France, and whatever physical force they could muster, stood as a bulwark against unending conquests by the new dominant powers of Europe. Asia was on its own. Ultimately, the German, Italian, and Japanese governments bore total responsibility for the conflagration that followed, regardless of whatever historic grievances they nursed—none of which justified wholesale murder. It was they who scorned access, arbitration, and transparency, and decided that imperial expansion over subject peoples was worth any price.

World War II in Europe started little more than a week later, on September 1, 1939, when Germany unveiled its new technologies of conquest. Planes and tanks rapidly overshot the static defenses of the archaic Polish army, some of its units still mounted on horses. German forces surrounded Warsaw on September 9. The Soviets invaded from the east eight days later. The double occupation of Poland was intentionally cruel. The Soviets secretly executed 26,000 prisoners of war from the Polish army. More than one million civilians were exiled to Siberia or Central Asia. The Nazis meanwhile waged war on the entire population, giving full scope to their racial theories. "The Poles' dirtiness is unimaginable," Hitler told his propaganda chief. "Their capacity for intelligent judgment is absolutely nil." With the Führer's approval, the Gestapo immediately shot or imprisoned 15,000 intellectuals. They seized male and female orphans for a stud program designed to breed better workers, executed the mentally disabled, and herded Jews into walled ghettos. Before the war's end, the Nazis would murder three million Jewish Poles and three million Catholic Poles, or nearly a fifth of the population. On German maps, Poland once again ceased to exist as a nation-state, just as it had in 1795.[69]

The French and British declared war against Germany on September 3 but made no serious attempt to save Poland, despite their putative guarantee. The so-called Phony War ensued. The United Kingdom imposed an economic blockade, but the resources of Austria, Czechoslovakia, and Poland easily made up for Germany's lost imports and exports. The French reinforced their northern border along the supposedly impregnable Maginot Line, a string of border fortresses, and the British Expeditionary Force landed in France to aid in defense. While the Germans consolidated their occupation of Poland, the Soviets invaded Finland, though the Finns courageously fought them off. The League of Nations expelled the Soviet Union, and a Polish government-in-exile found welcome in London. Little further happened, until the Phony War abruptly ended.

On April 9, 1940, Germany began an assault that swept across Norway, Denmark, Holland, Belgium, Luxembourg, and France. In a matter of weeks, the Nazis subjugated and occupied six countries, including a world power, France, which they would hold for five years. British, French, and Belgian defenders were pushed west onto the beaches at Dunkirk, a small town in France facing the English Channel. Hundreds of thousands of soldiers queued in serpentine lines while the Royal Air Force struggled to defend them from the Luftwaffe's gunners. Despite strafing that left blood in the water and sand, 338,000 men were rescued over the course of ten days by what Prime Minister Winston Churchill called his Mosquito Fleet: legions of small civilian boats that rushed to aid the Royal Navy. France formally surrendered on June 22, 1940, in the same railway car in the Compiègne Forest in which Germany had signed the armistice in 1918. The proud, ancient nation was partitioned into two states: "Free" France, under nominal French control with headquarters in Vichy, and occupied France, under German administration in Paris. Hitler toured the Champs-Élysées and the Paris Opéra. To Churchill he extended an olive branch, saying all he wanted from Britain was that "she should acknowledge Germany's position on the Continent." Even Neville Chamberlain, then terminally ill, scorned the offer and declared, "We are a solid and united nation, which would rather go down to ruin than admit the domination of the Nazis."[70]

The United Kingdom became the sole country opposing the engorged Third Reich, with the support of its distant Commonwealth. Almost every other nation of Western and Central Europe was either occupied or—in the case of Iceland, Ireland, Spain, Portugal, Switzerland, and Turkey—neutral, in the hope that Germany would not see any advantage in attacking it. The English Channel offered slim protection in the age of airpower, and Britons hunkered down in preparation for aerial bombardment and amphibious invasion.

Appointed prime minister in May, Winston Churchill used stirring oratory and his commanding voice to beseech Britons not to give up. "We shall not flag or fail. We shall go on to the end," he insisted. "We shall fight on the beaches, we shall fight on the landing grounds, we shall fight in the fields and in the streets, we shall fight in the hills. We shall never surrender." Broadcasting words spoken in the House of Commons to people all over the globe, many under German, Italian, or Japanese domination, the prime minister vowed that even if Britain's home islands were subjugated and starving, the empire would fight on from its Dominions overseas until "the New World, with all its power and might, steps forward to the rescue and liberation of the old."[71]

Shell-shocked Britons took courage from the prime minister's conviction. But the single most crucial member of his radio audience, as Churchill well knew, was the U.S. president, Franklin D. Roosevelt. Twelve days later, Churchill again laid bare the choice that Hitler's actions posed for both the New World and the Old. "If we can stand up to him, all Europe may be free and the life of the world may move forward into broad, sunlit uplands. But if we fail, then the whole world, including the United States, including all that we have known and cared for, will sink into the abyss of a new Dark Age made more sinister, and perhaps more protracted, by the lights of perverted science. Let us therefore brace ourselves to our duties, and so bear ourselves that, if the British Empire and its Commonwealth last for a thousand years, men will say: 'This was their finest hour.'"[72]

A month later, the Nazis started bombing cities in England, Wales, Scotland, and Northern Ireland. In September and October, German planes pounded London on fifty-seven consecutive nights, using the dome of Saint Paul's Cathedral as a navigational landmark. The Royal Air Force (RAF) fought back, dueling in the air with the Luftwaffe. Although significantly outnumbered, the RAF was aided by radar, a technology invented only a few years earlier, which allowed ground crews to spot enemy planes as they crossed into British airspace. RAF pilots shot down enough Germans to deter an immediate land invasion. They also retaliated by attacking German population centers in earnest beginning in December 1940, six months after the onset of the Battle of Britain.[73]

The United Kingdom's future still hung by a thread, but the RAF showed that it was possible, and necessary, to defy Hitler. Although it was the Führer's first reverse, he remained cocksure. In late 1940, the Germans cut back on scientific efforts to develop better radar, confident that the fight was nearly over. Had Franklin Roosevelt—FDR—not been listening to Churchill's broadcasts, they might well have been right.

8

Up to the Neck and in to the Death

Or, How America Became an Ally, 1939–1945

Americans looked sympathetically over their oceanic barricades at the agony of Africa, China, and Europe. Newsreels, newspapers, and letters home from travelers stirred pity at the misfortune of innocents on the far sides of the Atlantic and Pacific. Modern mass communications left nothing to the imagination. Shocked citizens sitting in ornate movie palaces absorbed the images of women and children being gunned down or bombed from the sky. Many viewers had had schoolteachers who encouraged sympathy with foreign peoples, millions of whom were now perishing. Yet for most of a decade, Americans had steeled themselves to resist all blandishments to fight another war to make the world safe, for democracy or anything else.

Only blood spilled on American soil could have lured them into a conflict they had steadfastly avoided. Faced with violent attacks on Hawaii, Alaska, and the Philippines in 1941—and an existential assault on democracy worldwide—the United States finally accepted, in cooperation with Great Britain and Russia, the need to respond. And when the Second World War ended in 1945, the Allied nations banded together at last to replace the state of nature with a unanimous code of law.

Between the first attacks on Northern China in 1931 and the collapse of Poland in 1939, the American people and Congress positioned themselves behind increasingly strict neutrality laws. Following the 1934 hearings in Congress that blamed World War I on arms manufacturers, the Neutrality Acts of 1935, 1936, and 1937 reflected the belief that Americans could seal themselves off from the world's conflicts. With each reiteration, the acts became more stringent. By 1937, they required the president to acknowledge hostilities anywhere they broke out and immediately embargo munitions to all belligerents there, regardless of how, why, or when they had entered into conflict. The laws also prohibited private loans to any belligerent and forbade U.S. citizens from traveling on the vessels of nations at war.

Isolationists sought to close every loophole through which the nation had earlier been pulled into World War I, even if it meant sacrificing neutral trading rights and seeing Europe go up in flames. Like Thomas Jefferson and James Madison, they were determined to restrict the economic activities of American citizens during wartime—not to sanction aggressors, in this case, but to protect U.S. neutrality.

According to randomized opinion polls, newly prominent in the 1930s, 84 percent of the American public agreed with these congressional restrictions. In 1936, 60 percent also believed, according to a Gallup Poll, that even "if there is another general war in Europe, the U.S. can stay out." Indeed, citizens felt the United States *should* stay out. "With almost monotonous regularity the polls . . . showed 94–95 per cent declaring themselves against U.S. participation," another surveyor observed at the time.[1]

Although President Roosevelt disagreed with the Neutrality Acts, he signed them. But he made his own opinions clear in an October 1937 address in Chicago, when he denounced "the present reign of terror and international lawlessness [that] began a few years ago." No one should imagine that America would escape, he warned, or "that this Western Hemisphere will not be attacked." Yet even the president's mild call for a vague "quarantine" of rogue nations elicited swift condemnation from congressional opponents and much of the press. They were unwilling to hazard the manifest dangers of enforcing the treaties to which Roosevelt referred in his speech: "the Covenant of the League of Nations, the Briand-Kellogg Pact and the Nine Power Treaty."[2]

The first cracks in the wall of isolationist sentiment appeared after Hitler's invasion of Poland. Six months earlier, in April, the Senate Foreign Relations Committee had rejected Roosevelt's request that Congress modify the Neutrality Acts to allow belligerents to purchase war supplies from the United States on a cash-and-carry basis. Poland's rapid collapse, and the failure of the Anglo-French guarantee, gave Roosevelt a second opportunity to make his case for selling planes and other munitions to Britain and France.

At a special session of Congress in late September, Roosevelt reminded legislators: "Since 1931 the use of force instead of the council table has constantly increased in disputes between nations—except in the Western Hemisphere where in all those years there has been only one war [the Chaco border war], now happily terminated." If Congress allowed Europeans to arm and defend themselves against dictatorial conquest, the growing violence might be confined to the far side of the Atlantic, he said. As written, the Neutrality Acts practically assured the defeat of countries that had not used the interwar years to arm themselves, as the aggressors had done. The Neutrality Acts were not neutral, Roosevelt argued. They privileged the strong and well prepared over the weak and unprepared. The United States should be "guided by one single hard-headed thought—keeping America out of this war," Roosevelt insisted. It could not do that by pursuing the Jeffersonian policy of economic self-denial. That had not even worked in 1812.[3]

Roosevelt chose not to wax sentimental over the suffering of Europe, the continent to which Americans were most closely tied by culture and history. To Congress he emphasized the economic and security interests of the United States, careful not to sound unduly humanitarian. Isolationists often took the opposite tack, conceding that, as Representative William Blackney of Michigan said, "Every sensitive American is heartsick as he watches the lamps of the Old World—the lamps of peace, of liberty, of security, of justice—flicker and go out one by one." But, Blackney pointed out, emphasizing the isolationists' stern credo, "It is America's problem to see that the lamps of our own country shall not go out."[4]

The majority of Americans agreed that the United States had no responsibility to anyone other than its own people. But by October 1939, the month after Poland's defeat, an overwhelming 84 percent wanted to see Germany stopped. External events had begun to convince a worried populace that taking care of the nation required giving at least minimal assistance to distant democracies resisting invasion. After the fall of Poland, public opinion in favor of loosening the Neutrality Acts jumped from 43 percent to 60 percent. From that moment onward, the citizenry showed remarkable constancy. Support for lifting the embargo was strong "no matter when the question is asked or how it is worded," a polling analyst observed in 1940. "Congressional debates, newspaper comment, radio broadcasts, the activities of pressure groups, apparently had little effect upon the attitudes of the American public."[5] Events had changed minds.

Congressional sentiment also began to shift. After a six-week debate, the legislature passed a new neutrality statute that lifted the embargo on war materiel, so long as belligerents paid for goods in cash and carried them away on their own ships. Three months after the fall of France, in September 1940, Congress passed the first peacetime conscription bill in American history, inducting one million men between the ages of twenty-one and thirty-six. The American army was so poorly equipped for a mass influx of soldiers that, for target practice, recruits aimed wooden sticks at trucks with the word "tank" painted on the side.[6]

Although a majority of Americans told pollsters in November 1940 that they would prefer all-out war to Britain's defeat, a significant minority still strongly believed that the United States should remain neutral no matter what. During the months that the Nazis occupied Western Europe and Japan deepened its hold on China, a group of prominent citizens formed the America First Committee (AFC). They included Democrats like Burton Wheeler of Montana, Progressives associated with the Republican Party like Hiram Johnson of California and Robert La Follette, Jr., of Wisconsin, and businessmen such as advertising genius Bruce Barton and Robert Wood, head of Sears Roebuck. They believed the dangers of intervention far outweighed those of standing on the sidelines.

The most charismatic participant making the case for neutrality was Charles Lindbergh. From his commanding position as an aviation pioneer, Lindbergh argued that the Luftwaffe was unstoppable, Britain would soon surrender just like France, and the United States should stay out and rely on its ocean defenses and growing armaments. Britain had 5,000 planes and Germany had 25,000, he pointed out. A student group at Yale University bluntly stated its conviction that the United States should mind its own business at all costs: "We demand that Congress refrain from war, even if England is on the verge of defeat." One of the Yale organizers (who was also a son of the vice president of Quaker Oats Company) later commented that the thrust of his college education had been to teach him that "the U.S. had gained nothing and lost a great deal through participation in World War I."[7] He didn't want to see the United States make that mistake again.

Many others who opposed intervention did so in the belief that war would bankrupt the nation, not yet recovered from the Depression, and lead to the suppression of civil rights. They argued that Hitler had not yet revealed any ill intentions with regard to the Americas and that the conflict, in the words of the America First Committee, was yet "another chapter in the series of conflicts between European states that has been going on in war and peace for hundreds of years." The proponents of nonintervention were politically diverse and included the eminent historian Charles Beard, socialist leader Norman Thomas, and a wealthy young Bostonian named John F. Kennedy, who sent a check for one hundred dollars along with the compliment, "What you are doing is vital." Troubled by deviation from George Washington's golden rule, they and many others paid close heed to America First. By December 7, 1941, AFC had 450 chapters and more than 250,000 members.[8] Their plan: build trade within the Americas, prepare a hemispheric defense, and wall out the world. Rarely had the Monroe Doctrine seemed more relevant.

In later years, historians and other commentators tended to dismiss non-interventionists as cranks, anti-Semites, and naïfs. Their belief that the United States could fight Hitler alone if necessary—after he had conquered and gained control over all the resources of Europe, the Middle East, and North Africa—seems preposterous indeed. But anti-interventionists were correct that involvement in another world war would profoundly reshape the nation, with unforeseeable consequences. America First not only raised salient questions about global intervention but also added to the vitality of American democracy at a time when political openness was under attack worldwide.[9]

Eventually, events overtook arguments. Isolationists underestimated Der Führer. The aggressive powers simply kept coming, and with each ratcheting up of the conflict, the United States waded a little further into the mess. Hitler's relentless assault westward led Roosevelt to seek deeper and deeper defenses. Unlike World War I, where soldiers fought in trenches for months on end, new technologies had created "a mobile war, in the air, on the land, at sea," as Churchill emphasized to the U.S. president.[10] Three months after modification of the Neutrality Act, Roosevelt gave fifty overage destroyers to Britain in exchange for ninety-nine-year leases on eight British territories in the West Indies and Newfoundland, on the oceanic approaches to the United States. Britons appreciated the gesture, but Americans got the better long-term deal.[11]

Shortly thereafter, Britain occupied Iceland to prevent a feared German takeover of the last independent country in the North Atlantic other than England itself. Churchill soon found he needed to employ his dwindling resources elsewhere, however. By then, July 1941, American ships were convoying supplies across the North Atlantic under the Lend-Lease Act. The United

Kingdom managed to convince Iceland to accept American troops instead of British ones, and Roosevelt dispatched 4,000 soldiers to the neutral country midway between Europe and North America, just under the Arctic Circle. The United States could not risk Germany's occupying and using it for an "eventual attack against the Western Hemisphere," the president pointed out to Congress.[12]

The terms that Iceland demanded for the protection it acknowledged needing were considerable, and they set a precedent for later "friendly" basing agreements worldwide. As Iceland's prime minister wrote Roosevelt, not only would the United States have to guarantee the sovereignty of Iceland and help it "in every way in their power," but it must also "undertake defense of the country without expense to Iceland and promise compensation for all damage occasioned to the inhabitants by their military activities." It must supply whatever "necessities" Iceland required, and withdraw "immediately" after the war.[13] The ancient Viking nation thus reaped virtually every economic benefit and few liabilities associated with being part of a defensive coalition during a time of radical, unpredictable peril.

Throughout this period, Winston Churchill assiduously cultivated the trust of Franklin Roosevelt, well aware that isolationists in the United States preferred building a Fortress America to fortifying the British Empire. Neville Chamberlain's earlier appeasement policy had created serious doubts about the capacity and will of England to resist Germany. These doubts played into Roosevelt's ongoing calculations about how far to go in supporting Great Britain. The American industrial plant could produce only so many guns, planes, ships, and tanks in short order. If the United States supplied England and the ancient nation capitulated, the Nazis would capture any weapons that America had sold the British. Those weapons could then be turned on the United States or other countries in the Americas. But if Britain avoided defeat, the United States would have a strong buffer on the reassuringly far side of the Atlantic.

Churchill's reputation as a "bulldog" thus became especially critical. Desperate for American aid, the prime minister pointed out that the oceans would offer precious little protection should the British fleet fall into Hitler's hands, as had occurred in France. The president's advisors cautioned that this was an excellent reason not to supply Britain, to the detriment of American preparedness. "I might guess wrong," Roosevelt admitted to a close associate as he weighed the options. One irate isolationist charged that Roosevelt was "shooting craps with destiny."[14]

Nonetheless, Roosevelt placed his bet on Churchill and rolled the dice. After winning an unprecedented third term as president in November 1940, the president had submitted a lend-lease bill to Congress. The United Kingdom was not asking the United States to fight its war, Roosevelt reminded Congress, but if the Nazi menace were to be turned from the shores of the Americas, Britain had to be supplied. In a December "Fireside Chat," Roosevelt reminded the American public that only the week before, Herr Hitler had declared Germany to be in eternal opposition to democracy. "I can beat any power in the world," the Führer boasted. The United States must act in time, the president urged. "Until the day shall come when there is clear intention on the part of the aggressor nations to abandon all thought of dominating and conquering the world," Roosevelt warned, the United States must become an "arsenal for democracy." If the United States refused to help, he said, and Great Britain went down, "All of us, in all the Americas, would be living at the point of a gun."[15] Congress passed the bill in March 1941.

Three months later, the United States had yet another supplicant. Hitler turned eastward once his plan to invade Britain stalled. On June 22, 1941, the Nazis attacked the Soviet Union, violating the Molotov-Ribbentrop Non-Aggression Pact. Hitler also sent troops to the Mediterranean to shore up Mussolini's army, which had invaded Greece, Egypt, and Libya. But Germany's southern maneuvers were a newspaper sidebar. *Lebensraum* in the great Slavic heartland was the centerpiece of Hitler's vision, and he calculated that the fall of the Soviet Union would also frighten the United Kingdom into surrendering. Churchill immediately sought an alliance with Communist Russia, and Roosevelt persuaded Congress to open America's arsenal to the Soviet Union as well.

Hitler's armies swept rapidly over the Polish and Baltic territories that Stalin had seized the year before. The Russian air force was destroyed within days and the Nazis penetrated 1,000 miles into the Soviet Union. Saint Petersburg (Leningrad) was under siege by September, Moscow by December. In occupied territories the Germans implemented the same policies now routine in Poland. They screened the population for racial characteristics, executed "undesirables," and issued ration cards and work permits according to racial classifications. Villages were razed nearly at random and prisoners sent west to labor in Germany. The population of Ukraine fell by nine million in three years.[16]

Neither of the two nations spilling their lifeblood to stop Hitler was a perfect ally in American eyes. Had Roosevelt the temperament of a German Social Democrat, he might have scorned a coalition with either of them. Britain was still the land of George III, to those with a long memory. The America First Committee denounced England as "snob-ridden, caste-ruled, and imperialistic." Even the president worried about the prime minister's "reactionary imperialist attitudes."[17] Indeed, Churchill later commented to Roosevelt, "I have not become His Majesty's First Minister in order to preside over the liquidation of the British Empire."[18]

Soviet Russia, on the other hand, epitomized everything that Americans historically deplored: political systems that were closed, violent, and secretive. Nonetheless, Churchill could have been speaking for both himself and Roosevelt when he quipped, after Hitler's surprise attack on Russia in 1941, "If Hitler invaded Hell, I should at least make a favorable mention of the Devil in the House of Commons." What he actually told the Commons was that all previous rivalry "fades away before the spectacle that is now unfolding." Churchill did not doubt that Stalin would dominate whatever territory he could at war's end, but half of Europe free was better than none.[19] Ever the pragmatist, Roosevelt surely agreed.

Despite their differences on imperialism, core values otherwise united Britain and America. Their joint commitment to capitalism and democracy gave them a shared vocabulary. Even though unacknowledged, their policies had also shadowed each other since at least the 1823 Monroe/Canning/Polignac Doctrine. Language and culture, too, proved meaningful. Roosevelt and Churchill first met in an official capacity for a three-and-a-half-day session aboard a warship off the coast of Newfoundland in August 1941. At the so-called Atlantic Conference, they found themselves singing in an ecumenical Sunday service the hymns they had learned at home as children, including "Onward, Christian Soldiers." Everyone knew the words. Even the Jewish Felix Frankfurter, one of Roosevelt's closest aides, commented that the symbolism of that Christian service "gave meaning to the conflict between civilization and arrogant, brute challenge; and gave promise more powerful and binding than any formal treaty could, that civilization has brains and resources that tyranny will not be able to overcome."[20] Churchill commented in his memoirs, "Every word seemed to stir the heart. It was a great hour to live." Yet, he also pointed out, "Nearly half those who sang were soon to die." The very ship on which they sat was hit and sunk by the German navy four months later.[21]

After the service, Churchill gave Roosevelt, in his wheelchair, a tour of the doomed HMS *Prince of Wales,* then the fleet's newest battleship. Both enthusiastic sailors, the garrulous leaders found they enjoyed each other's company. The visit continued over caviar and vodka, followed by roasted grouse and champagne. They had arrived with multiple agendas, but one goal was simply to test each other's mettle. Churchill was rumored to be a drunk, Roosevelt was known to be a cripple. Both took great pains to impress the other. The prime minister mused to American Averill Harriman before the event, "I wonder if he will like me?"—and demanded during the event, "Does he like me?" Churchill later admitted, "No lover ever studied every whim of his mistress as I did those of President Roosevelt." The word "need" hardly begins to describe the urgency felt by the British, facing occupied Europe twenty-one miles across the channel and still anticipating a German invasion.[22]

President Roosevelt, in turn, wanted to show that the United States was a reliable partner, despite the siren call of isolationism. Congress was just then debating whether to extend peacetime conscription or to allow the newly trained U.S. Army to demobilize. It renewed the draft by a single vote on August 12, the last day of the Atlantic Conference, and only at the special urging of General George C. Marshall, whom Congress saw as less sympathetic toward England than Roosevelt. "Coming when it did," wrote one official, the close congressional vote "impressed the British Chiefs of Staff, as nothing else could have done, with the difficulties and hazards of their colleagues' position."[23] Roosevelt had also arrived at the Atlantic rendezvous with hundreds of gift boxes for the embattled British sailors on the ship, each containing three pieces of fruit, half a pound of cheese, a carton of cigarettes, and a signed note from the president. Aboard the *Prince of Wales,* Roosevelt insisted on walking the length of the heaving deck in front of the assembled crew to attend church service—his longest public procession since contracting polio in 1921.[24] America, too, would not give up.

But the primary accomplishment of the conference was the Atlantic Charter, a statement of eight principles that expressed the most enlightened hopes of the preceding two hundred years—and established the direction of international relations for the rest of the century. The Atlantic Charter emphasized even more strongly than Wilson's Fourteen Points the right of all peoples "to choose the form of government under which they will live" and to be consulted on territorial changes. Displaying the pacifist ideals they hoped to promulgate, and the extent to which they had both turned their backs on expansionism, the United States and Britain jointly declared they sought no territory for themselves in the war. Instead, they wished "to see sovereign rights and self-government restored to those who have been forcibly deprived of them." They pledged themselves to facilitate for "all States, great or small, victor or vanquished . . . *access,* on equal terms, to the trade and raw materials of the world" (italics added). Above all, they stated boldly, they "believed all of the nations of the world, for realistic as well as spiritual reasons, must come to the abandonment of the use of force."[25]

Any statement of principle is a guide to behavior rather than a description of it. Leaders and citizens of both nations were well aware that any observer could find numerous examples where Britain and the United States fell short. Indeed, aboard ship, Roosevelt explicitly challenged Britain's system of imperial preference, whereby England and the Dominions gave one another special economic consideration. "Those Empire trade agreements," the president tartly alleged, "are a case in point. It's because of them that the peoples of India and Africa, of all the colonial Near East and Far East, are still as backward as they are."[26] Churchill was too polite to point out that, ahem, African Americans in the United States still could not vote in "backward" Southern states—and that Britain had only reinstituted Imperial Preferences in response to new U.S. tariff policies.

Yet despite these inconsistencies, the Atlantic Charter raised the hopes and strengthened the courage not only of those subjugated by Hitler but also of others struggling for a political voice, from South Africa to South Carolina. It did not create these goals, but it made them more attainable. Nelson Mandela, then a young organizer of the African National Congress, recounted that the Atlantic Charter gave him and his colleagues a powerful new tool. "We hoped that the government and ordinary South Africans would see that the principles they were fighting for in Europe were the same ones we were advocating at home," Mandela later wrote in *Long Walk to Freedom.*[27]

Soon to be embodied in the United Nations, the Atlantic Charter raised global consciousness about what might be possible and what could no longer be endured. The phrase "human rights" came into vogue to describe the so-called fundamental freedoms that differentiated the Allies from their rivals.

The Allies' goals, so opposite from those articulated by Hitler and Mussolini and implemented by the Japanese, betokened not a perfect world but a better one. They were based partly on what Roosevelt called the "Four Freedoms": freedom from fear, freedom from want, freedom of religion, and freedom of speech. Such freedoms were not fully realized anywhere, but only the democracies were committed to them. Churchill explained this distinction in the characteristically poetic phrasing that later won him the Nobel Prize for Literature (not for peace, as might have been expected): "The Atlantic Charter is not a law—it is a star." Peoples under British rule in India and Africa soon hung their wishes upon it.[28]

The other purpose of the Atlantic Conference, at least from the British point of view, was to discuss American cooperation in containing Japan. Events in Western Europe between 1939 and 1941 were so riveting that they often overshadowed those in East Asia. Yet Japan posed a dire threat to Hong Kong, Singapore, India, Australia, New Zealand, and other parts of the British Commonwealth. It had already seized colonies belonging to France and the Netherlands. Churchill hoped Roosevelt would join him in warning the emperor.[29]

Isolationists could be expected to object to strong measures against Japan, and it was also the case that America's interests in the East diverged from those of the United Kingdom. Although the United States had opposed Japanese expansion in China in 1931, its trade with Japan was then profitable and growing. In contrast, trade with China was minimal, especially compared with British trade there. Japan was a good customer for the United States. Logic demanded placating it. Japan also did not appear likely to cross the trip wire of the Monroe Doctrine. The Pacific Ocean was more than twice the width of the Atlantic. Unlike Germany, Japan presented no obvious security threat to the Americas. The Philippines were vulnerable, of course, but the U.S. Congress had already voted to grant them independence. They would soon be free to defend themselves. By the laws of physical self-preservation and economic self-interest, the United States should have been willing to confront Hitler, appease Japan, and turn a blind eye to the fate of the old Middle Kingdom.

As it turned out, it chose to act in nearly opposite ways. Indeed, what made American foreign policy baffling, irritating, and sometimes inspiring was its ideological character. For onlookers, self-interest was easier to read. From the Open Door Note of 1900, to the Fourteen Points of 1918, to the

Washington Naval Treaty of 1922, to the Kellogg-Briand Pact of 1928, to the Atlantic Charter of 1941, eight U.S. presidents from both parties had championed the principle of national self-determination for all peoples and for China in particular. During Roosevelt's era, Congress also showed a willingness to forgo easy and obvious profits by passing four neutrality acts, when American merchants might have collected a tidy sum from the neutral trade that the "dirty thirties" offered in Asia, Africa, and Europe. Additionally, the United States demonstrated a continuing sense of responsibility for its money pit in the Philippines, where Americans had invested substantially in mass education, public works, and self-government with the hope that the island nation would grow strong enough to resist recolonization in the future.[30] Like his predecessors, Roosevelt resolutely maintained that China was for the Chinese, and the Philippines for Filipinos.

But Hitler's depredations and the Axis alliance gave Japan an unprecedented opportunity to consolidate its hold across Asia and Oceania. German occupation of France and the Netherlands, combined with the weakening of Britain, meant that all of Europe's colonial possessions in the Far East were ripe for the taking. Japanese troops first crossed the southern border of China into French Indochina (Cambodia, Laos, and Vietnam) in September 1940, a year before the Atlantic Conference. The colonial representatives of the Vichy government capitulated, and Japan positioned itself to attack the Dutch East Indies (Indonesia) next.

The Roosevelt administration decided on the only nonviolent course open to it, which was to refuse to sell Japan the goods necessary to carry out its wars. Of course, this was the same tactic America had already employed against belligerents in Europe under the neutrality acts. It stood some chance of working. Japan depended heavily on the United States for strategic materials, including airplane fuel, copper, brass, and premium-grade steel and iron. Petroleum was particularly critical. Japan imported 80 percent of its fuel supplies from the oil fields of California, Oklahoma, and Texas. After July 1940, the United States developed an increasingly strict embargo list in the hope of forcing the imperial government of Japan to back down. The militarists had absolutely no intention of doing so, however. If they could not purchase oil from the United States, they would confiscate it from the East Indies. Cheap rice they would take from Indochina.[31] In July 1941, when Japan completed its military occupation of Indochina, Roosevelt froze all Japanese assets in the United States. Britain applied the same sanctions, and the Dutch government in exile (holed up in London, having fled the Nazi occupation) followed suit two days later. Churchill sailed away from the August rendezvous in the North Atlantic confident in Americans' seriousness.[32]

But economic sanctions had little effect when conquest remained an alternative. Knowing the weakness of the Europeans and the strength of noninterventionist sentiment in the United States, the Japanese concluded that surprise attacks against the Americans, British, and Dutch would deter Western critics, who would balk at the high price of a showdown with Japan, considering the fight against Hitler. The United States had shown no inclination to use force to preserve peace, and the Europeans were otherwise engaged. The Nazis and Fascists appeared on the verge of triumph. "Nothing ventured, nothing gained," Japan's foreign minister, Matsuoka Yosuke, concluded. "We should take decisive action." Prime Minister Tojo Hideki agreed: "Sometimes people have to shut their eyes and take the plunge."[33]

On the morning of December 7, 1941, without warning and while carrying on peace talks with the U.S. State Department, Japan bombed Hawaii, the Philippines, Guam, Wake Island, Hong Kong, and British Malaya. The next day, it invaded independent Thailand and attacked Midway Island. This was the start of a coordinated, vast, and initially successful campaign by Japan to occupy the Pacific islands and all of Asia. Within little more than a month, Japan controlled much of Oceania and Southern Asia—short of India, Australia, and New Zealand—and had begun the conquest of British Burma (Myanmar). Japanese submarines infiltrated the waters off Alaska and came within sight of the California coast. Six months later, a Japanese invasion force snatched two of the Aleutian Islands belonging to the United States.

The U.S. Army Air Corps in the Philippines was nearly obliterated on the first day of the surprise attack, but it was the assault on Hawaii that most deeply shocked the American public. More than 2,400 Americans were killed in the dawn raid on the U.S. Navy base at Pearl Harbor, where Japanese fighter pilots sank or severely damaged eighteen vessels, including eight U.S. battleships. After the planes dropped their charges, one circled back and strafed an American flag flying near the base hospital until it was torn to shreds. Only seven nurses and a handful of doctors were on hand, and they worked frantically to save the thousands of wounded and dying. When the numbers overwhelmed the staff, private citizens loaded injured sailors in their own cars and drove them to a nearby civilian hospital. Fearing the arrival of Japanese parachutists, or an invasion force akin to that which had assaulted Nanking, the American nurses told one another they "would fight to the death and never be captured alive."[34]

The Senate unanimously approved President Roosevelt's request for recognition of a state of war with Japan (88 to 0). In the House, only 1 of the 389 representatives present voted against the resolution. When Mussolini and Hitler declared war on the United States on December 11 in support of their Asian ally, President Roosevelt appealed to Congress once again: "The long-known and the long-expected has thus taken place. The forces endeavoring to enslave the entire world now are moving toward this hemisphere. Never before has there been a greater challenge to life, liberty and civilization." Congress then declared war on Italy and Germany, again opposed only by Jeanette Rankin, a founder of the Women's International League for Peace and Freedom. Roosevelt reminded the American people in one of his "Fire Side" radio talks that Japan's actions capped "a decade of international immorality" that had begun with the unprovoked assault on Manchuria in 1931.[35] World War II had been ten years in the making.

For the British and the Chinese, the bombing of Pearl Harbor was a godsend. The word "joy" sprang readily to the tongue. The wife of a Chinese officer observed that, in their "joy over Pearl Harbor," Guomindang officials "went about congratulating one another as if a great victory had been won. . . . At last, at last, America was at war with Japan!" President Chiang Kai-shek burst into an old opera tune and played *Ave Maria* all day. China had finally become strategically important. American money and equipment would flow in, he believed.[36] In England, Winston Churchill made a phone call to the American President and then "went to bed and slept the sleep of the saved and thankful." He later wrote in his memoir, "No American will think it wrong of me if I proclaim that to have the United States at our side was to me the greatest joy. I could not foretell the course of events . . . but now at this very moment I knew the United States was in the war, up to the neck and in to the death. . . . We should not be wiped out. Our history would not come to an end."[37]

Chiang Kai-shek and Churchill recognized what Americans were just beginning to admit, that if the world was to remain inhabitable, their participation in external affairs was no longer optional. Organically, over the course of time, the United States had become indispensable to maintaining order against the evils of chaos on a crowded, militarized globe. Not only did the

United States possess more natural and human resources than any other nation in the world, but its shielded location in the Americas also gave it peculiar advantages. The Western Hemisphere republics had behaved precisely as James Monroe and John Quincy Adams predicted they would. Despite their rivalries, republicanism gave them a bond and they rarely warred on one another. This meant the American republics could husband their wealth rather than spend it on armed conflict. And although the seas were not impassable, such wide oceanic barriers enhanced the safety of every nation in the hemisphere from outside mischief. Thus, they enjoyed without effort a security that countries like Belgium and Poland would never experience.

The United States's geopolitical position was even further improved by its large size. The nation might get dented around the edges, but it was inherently one of the most secure on a dangerous planet. On December 8, 1941— even in August 1945—it remained relatively unscathed. All of these advantages made it the most logical default power in a supreme crisis.

Geopolitical good fortune was not the whole explanation, however. The sine qua non that made the United States the most natural and capable enforcer of world peace by 1941 was its set of core values. The United States had many faults and inconsistencies, but it had championed arbitration and national self-determination more persistently than any other nation up to that point in history. While recognized as far from perfect, and often vehemently criticized for good reasons, it had nonetheless earned a unique respect. In part because the United States was so transparent, other nations could see what they were getting in an ally or protector.

This quality also alerted others to America's defects, which, because of its system, it could do little to hide. One of the most troubling—at least from the perspective of those who wanted protection—was its fickleness. After Pearl Harbor, Churchill observed that "silly" people, of whom there were many, believed that "this numerous but remote, wealthy, and talkative people" would never be united enough to "come to grips" with the hard issues. "They would never stand blood-letting," such skeptics insisted.[38]

Indeed, the same advantages that made the United States the most desirable umpire gave it the least motivation to accept the job. It would *always* have a lesser stake in Afro-Eurasian security than Afro-Eurasians. Fickleness was understandable given the discretionary character of American choices. The United States enjoyed an enviable self-sufficiency even within the peaceful Western Hemisphere as a result of its continental dimensions, favorable topography, extensive mineral resources, and relatively well-educated work-force. It could indulge in isolationism with fewer negative consequences than any other country on earth. But in 1941, the American people finally chose not to.

The global war lasted another four years. In a series of conferences, the "Big Three" settled on a policy known as "Germany First." That is, they agreed Hitler was the linchpin of the Axis. His defeat was essential to the defeat of the other two aggressors, who had advanced opportunistically. In 1943, the Allies also agreed on a policy of "unconditional surrender." The United States and Britain needed to reassure their suspicious Soviet partner that they would make no separate peace with the Nazis at the expense of Communists. The need to build trust made transparency in war aims essential. Uncondi-tional surrender would also ensure that Germans could never again claim that, undefeated on the battlefield, they had been tricked into an armistice.

Lastly, the Big Three eventually agreed to establish a new organization to replace the League of Nations. The principal difference would be a Security Council of five permanent members and six elected members that had the power to sanction future aggressors. The permanent members would have an absolute veto over any action of the Security Council. President Roosevelt presented the germ of this notion to Joseph Stalin at the Tehran Conference of 1943. Any postwar league should be supplemented, the president believed, by what he at first called the "Four Policemen." These great powers would "have the power to deal immediately with any threat to the peace and any sudden emergency." Stalin indicated cautious assent.[39] Roosevelt suggested America, Britain, China, and the Soviet Union for the task. France was added later, and the four proposed permanent members of the Security Council became five.

Among the American public, support for participation in an international security body had grown steadily. The Second World War taught Americans that it was better to deal with global crises sooner rather than later. Polls showed that sentiment in favor of "joining a League of Nations after this war is over" had shot up from 35 percent before Pearl Harbor to 90 percent in October 1944. A poll in 1943 also found that more than 75 percent of Ameri-cans from both parties and all socioeconomic groups favored "an interna-tional police force after the war" in which the United States would participate.[40] Congress concurred in a resolution sponsored by Representative William Fulbright of Arkansas, calling for U.S. participation in "the creation of appropriate international machinery with power adequate to maintain a just and lasting peace, among the nations of the world." Seventy-five percent of Americans told Gallup pollsters they agreed with Congress.[41]

Politicians and the public had begun to break with the past, yet in ways still consistent with tradition. Since the nation's founding, the majority of Americans had accepted the necessity of policing among states during an extreme crisis, such as the Whiskey Rebellion and the Civil War. When the nation's existence seemed imperiled, the federal government adopted the role for which it had been created: to stand astride warring contenders and umpire their rivalry. After 1941, however, the *states* in question were foreign rather than domestic.

The Great Depression had also left its mark. The Allies were painfully aware of the extent to which economic autarky had fed political violence. Hostile, exclusive trading blocs had vindicated the physiocrats' theory that open doors fostered peace while closed ones fomented war. The world needed a new trading order based on maximum feasible access. Banks also could not be allowed to fail en masse, either domestically or internationally. Economic collapse was everybody's problem. Material security had become every bit as important as the sanctity of borders. To accomplish all these objectives, the Allies laid the foundations for the World Bank, the World Trade Organization, and the International Monetary Fund at the Bretton Woods Conference of 1944.

The United States also pioneered foreign aid on a bilateral basis. In 1940, President Roosevelt had appointed Nelson Rockefeller, then a dashing young wunderkind (later, vicepresident under Richard Nixon), to convince North and South Americans during the war that their interests were mutual rather than conflictual. Applying lessons from the New Deal, Rockefeller devised America's first experiments in foreign economic development, doling out innovation grants to individuals and governments from Mexico to Tierra del Fuego. Rockefeller likened the United States to a "rich family in a poor town" (something his kinfolk would know about). Poorer countries "don't want charity, but they would like to be helped to stand on their feet," Rockefeller argued. "Today our welfare and security depend on the welfare and security of other peoples."[42] In an initial draft of his 1943 State of the Union address, President Roosevelt asserted that aid for economic development must eventually reach even the African "Hottentots." If helped to a better standard of living, he said, they and other marginalized peoples "would have greater capacity to participate more greatly in the trade of the world and by that . . . assure greater markets for producing for the manufacturing nations of the world, including the people of the United States of America."[43]

The Allies' various strategies gradually worked. With the exception of Argentina and Chile, the Americas swung to the side of the Allies in the war. (Heeding their own economic interests, and under no compunction to follow the United States, the two southernmost American republics did not declare war against Japan and Germany until the conflict was almost over.) In Europe, the Soviet Union took the brunt of the damage and deserved the lion's share of credit. Even on D-Day, when Allied troops finally arrived on the beaches of Normandy, they found themselves facing only 10 German divisions, compared with the 185 divisions fighting Russia in the east. Nazi Germany surrendered unconditionally to Allied forces on May 7, 1945.

The war in the Pacific ended three months later when the United States dropped two atomic weapons—developed collaboratively by American and British scientists working with refugee physicists from Denmark, Germany, and Italy. War planners had estimated that as many as 268,000 American soldiers would be killed or injured in the planned land invasion of the Japanese home islands. Assistant Secretary of War John C. McCloy commented in a meeting between President Harry Truman and the Joint Chiefs of Staff, "We ought to have our heads examined if we don't explore some other method by which we can terminate this war than just by another conventional attack and landing."[44] During the July meeting of the Big Three at Potsdam, the Allies issued an ultimatum to Japan: surrender immediately or face "prompt and utter destruction."

Eleven days later, a U.S. B-29 bomber released the first weapon over Hiroshima. When the Japanese war cabinet still refused surrender, the American Air Force dropped a second bomb on Nagasaki three days afterward. Approximately 170,000 Japanese died in the two blasts. The following day, Emperor Hirohito finally countermanded his still-divided war cabinet and notified the Allies of Japan's willingness to surrender. British historian J. A. S. Grenville observes, "President Truman was probably therefore right in believing that only the atomic bombs could shock Japan into *immediate* surrender." Iris Chang notes that the blasts finally halted the horrific eight-year ordeal of Nanking and other occupied Chinese cities.[45] On August 15, 1945,

Emperor Hirohito announced Japan's defeat over the radio. It was the first time his people had ever heard the human voice of their supposedly divine ruler.

The most glaring difference between World War II and other conflicts was the unprecedented targeting of civilians. Beginning with the Japanese raids on China and the German blitz against Poland and England, and continuing with retaliatory Allied bombings that incinerated entire cities, all the belligerents killed millions of innocent noncombatants. There was no justification for this barbaric practice except that, as war became more "total," participants believed they had little choice but to attack the civilian populations that produced the planes, tanks, and other goods necessary for battle. But the scope of violence also went beyond this, especially within the countries occupied by the Third Reich. The Nazis believed that some peoples should be exterminated simply because of their supposed inferiority, based on their religion, race, sexual preference, political beliefs, or physical characteristics. The Nazis targeted Jews in particular, but they also coldly murdered Slavs, homosexuals, the mentally disabled, Gypsies, and communists.

During the war the Allies were aware of Hitler's vicious ideologies, but not the scope of his genocide. After the liberation of Poland and Germany, the death camps came into full view for the first time. They overwhelmed even the most battle hardened. U.S. General George Patton turned away at one of the camps for fear of vomiting. General Dwight Eisenhower forced himself to tour the facilities in order to thwart any future attempts to dismiss the allegations of genocide as propaganda. "I assure you that whatever has been printed on them to date has been an understatement," he told General George C. Marshall, chairman of the Joint Chiefs of Staff and his superior officer. "The things I saw beggar description."[46]

Revealed at the war's end, these practices revolted people around the world. They profoundly delegitimized conquest, expansionism, and racism. Once dismissed by many as a quixotic ideal, self-determination was consequently enshrined in the new Covenant of the United Nations. Regardless of size or ethnicity, all nations were guaranteed the right to self-governance, backed by the threat of collective force if others tried to take it from them. This concept spurred decolonization around the world during the next two decades, eventually making empires as obsolete as horse-drawn buggies. Nation-states became the new norm.

Axis atrocities also fueled a global movement to recognize and protect individual rights. Paradoxically, therefore, Allied victory served to both enhance and diminish the sovereign rights of nation-states. In previous conflicts, sovereign immunity, like diplomatic immunity, meant that rulers did not have to account for their actions to any supranational authority. They could do whatever they wanted to their own citizens within their own borders, and the battlefield code of honor allowed for surrender under a white flag after they had brutalized the inhabitants of other countries. But recent international agreements unexpectedly made it feasible to hold individual officials accountable. In 1864, continental European nations had agreed to a set of common laws for the humane treatment of civilians and prisoners of war. Collectively known as the Geneva Conventions, these regulations were designed to protect noncombatants. The United States ratified them in 1882 at the urging of nurse Clara Barton.[47] Along with the 1928 Kellogg-Briand Pact, the conventions provided a new legal framework for the prosecution of Axis officials. By holding individuals responsible for government actions, the Allied powers turned Briand's "international kiss" into a stinging slap.

An international military tribunal conducted the first trials at Nuremberg, Germany, in 1945. Twenty-two Nazis leaders were prosecuted. Nineteen men were found guilty, by a panel of judges from Britain, France, Russia, and the United States, on the charge of war crimes (violations of the Geneva Conventions) and crimes against peace and humanity (Kellogg-Briand). Of them, seven were sentenced to prison, twelve to hang. In Tokyo the next year, twenty-five Japanese leaders faced similar charges. Seven were sentenced to death and eighteen to imprisonment. Later trials brought lower-echelon war criminals to the stand. The Allied powers collectively enforced the rulings of the tribunals, executing or imprisoning the convicted as prescribed.

The trials exposed not only crimes against Jews and other civilians, but also the inhumane treatment of prisoners of war by the German and Japanese militaries. Although Germany had housed most POWs under the terms of the Geneva code, they had made separate accommodation for captured Russians, whom they penned in open-air, barbed-wire enclosures, even during winter. The vast majority of American, British, French, and other European prisoners survived the war. Among the Russian POWs, however, more than half died of exposure, starvation, or execution. Some died from excruciating medical experiments carried out on live victims.

The Japanese made fewer ethnic distinctions among prisoners, but also made no effort to honor the Geneva Conventions, which they had not signed and which Japanese militarists dismissed as part of the claptrap of European imperialism. Although civilian leaders initially communicated that they would honor the conventions, this quickly fell by the wayside.[48] Instead, thousands of prisoners were worked to death as slave laborers or died of exposure and starvation. As in Germany, some became the victims of medical experiments, including vivisection. The wounded were sometimes used for bayonet practice, to harden soldiers to human suffering, or publicly humiliated in order to dampen "pro-Anglo-American feeling" among the Japanese populace. Women of all nationalities, including Dutch colonists in Indonesia, were routinely raped, with the knowledge and compliance of superior officers. Approximately 40 percent of all military and civilian prisoners in Japanese custody died, including women and children, compared with 5 percent of Japanese soldiers in Allied custody. To put these figures another way and focus on the experience of Americans, only one in twenty-five American POWs died in Nazi captivity, while one in three died when captured by the Japanese.[49]

As one consequence of the war crimes tribunals, most countries of Western Europe passed laws allowing individuals to exercise the right of conscientious objection to military service. Previously, only a few states had made provisions for conscientious objection, including Great Britain, the United States, the Netherlands, and the Scandinavian countries. Most (including Germany, France, and Russia) either imprisoned or executed men who refused to fight. With these changes in the law, war crimes defendants in the future could no longer claim they were "just following orders" and had no choice in their actions. They could choose not to serve in the military. Just as important, they could refuse to follow an illegal order, and in fact had an obligation to do so.

The Allies examined their own consciences as well. Considering the extraordinary, purposeful brutality of the Axis powers, there was little comparison with the policies of the Allies. Nonetheless, the Allies had also committed acts that violated their own ethical norms. Retaliatory bombing raids by Britain and the United States had reduced civilian centers in both Germany and Japan to smoking graveyards of rubble. The atomic bombings of

Hiroshima and Nagasaki left behind radiation that afflicted survivors for years afterward. The Soviets' execution of Polish prisoners of war violated the Geneva Conventions just as surely as German and Japanese policies.

The United States and Canada had also interned most of their civilians of Japanese descent, although not all. In the United States, Japanese American men who passed a security review were allowed to volunteer for military service, 4,000 students were given leave to attend college, and approximately 30,000 Japanese American civilians were allowed to relocate away from the West Coast, which was considered militarily vulnerable. Nonetheless, more than 100,000 civilians with nowhere else to move were incarcerated in remote, sparsely furnished camps for the duration of the war. Canada acted even more harshly. Japanese American families were kept together, but the Canadian government sent nearly 22,000 Japanese Canadians to separate facilities for males and females. Canada also refused to allow many to return home until 1949, four years after the war ended. Unlike in the Axis countries, however, civilians were not murdered, and all received food and housing adequate for survival. Yet the internment of citizens without due process grossly violated their civil rights. Many lost their homes, possessions, and livelihoods. Suffering pangs of remorse years later, the Canadian and American governments eventually issued formal apologies and monetary compensation.[50]

Germany also made amends. In Berlin in 1958, individuals who had been part of the German resistance to Nazism founded a nongovernmental organization called Aktion Sühnezeichen (Action Reconciliation). In a reversal of events at the end of the First World War, they crafted their own war-guilt clause, stating, "We Germans started the Second World War and for this reason alone, more than others, became guilty of causing immeasurable suffering to humankind. Germans have in sinful revolt against the will of God exterminated millions of Jews. Those of us who survived . . . did not do enough to prevent it."[51] Volunteers with Action Reconciliation hoped to help Poland, Russia, and Israel. At first, however, none of those countries was willing to accept such assistance, lacking the compassion to forgive the Germans, or the courage to trust them. So volunteers instead built synagogues, churches, recreational centers, and water reservoirs in Dutch, Greek, Norwegian, and French villages that the Nazis had razed. In 1961, one of the first groups of German volunteers helped rebuild the cathedral of Coventry, a town the Luftwaffe had hammered nearly into oblivion. British volunteers returned the gesture two years later, helping to restore a hospital destroyed in the Allied fire bombing of Dresden. Eventually, following lengthy negotiations, Israel, Russia, and Poland allowed individual Germans to volunteer in those countries.[52]

Germany took action at the governmental level as well. In 1953 it began giving economic aid to Israel. Germany made reparations to other nations and individual victims as well, ultimately paying out the equivalent of more than $60 billion. Then, in the late 1960s, Chancellor Willy Brandt took steps to reconcile with Poland by guaranteeing that Germany would never challenge the territorial compromises made at the end of the war. The Allies had compensated Poland in 1945 for losses on its eastern border with Russia with new lands on its western border with Germany. Many Germans resisted the idea of permanently conceding this territorial loss, but Brandt courageously signed agreements to that effect. On his first state visit to Poland in 1970, the German chancellor unexpectedly knelt in atonement at the memorial to the Warsaw Ghetto Uprising of 1943. Brandt's willingness to humble himself astonished and moved both Poles and Germans. His act remains a symbol of repentance to this day.

The reverberations of World War II continued to negatively affect Japan's relations with China and Korea, however, primarily because Japan failed to make similar amends. Into the 1990s, Japanese textbooks still praised Japan's "benevolent" rule over Korea and northern China during the 1930s and 1940s, and the government refused to apologize publicly or to make any financial gestures for its aggression. Iris Chang observes that Japan has "doled out less than 1 percent of the amount that Germany has paid in war reparations to its victims."[53]

Despite an unwillingness to suffer a loss of face, or to bend publicly like Willy Brandt, Japan was nonetheless part of a new global consensus that arose from the horrors of World War II. For the first time in human history, nations routinely expected one another to exhibit a conscience (sincere or not). The United Nations General Assembly formalized this trend with a "Universal Declaration of Human Rights" in 1948. This document declared a new "common standard of achievement for all peoples and all nations" that proclaimed the right of all individuals to equality under the law, protection from arbitrary arrest, and freedom of speech and religion. Nations that did not abide by these guarantees were judged as not measuring up. Public opinion finally started to fill the shoes cobbled by Woodrow Wilson, William

Borah, Elihu Root, David Starr Jordan, and progressive anti-imperialists around the world.

Although most of the nations that voted for the UN declaration were republics, many were not yet especially democratic. And no democracy on earth fulfilled all of its promises at all times—comprised as they were of flawed human beings. But the Universal Declaration of Human Rights expressed a new ethos and a fundamental reorientation of global politics. At the urging of Eleanor Roosevelt, the president's widow, the UN General Assembly passed the 1948 motion without one dissenting vote. Only South Africa, Saudi Arabia, the Soviet Union, and five states under Russian control abstained. Tellingly, even they were unwilling to take an outright stand against the new code. World opinion had changed too profoundly.

The weaknesses of democratic government helped lead to World War II. After the war, though, democracy's future was brighter than ever. The United Kingdom and United States had shown that democracies could function under the most calamitous circumstances, and could defend not only themselves but also the globe. They displayed the moral capacity to achieve the first "peace without victory," refusing to take vengeance on the German, Italian, and Japanese people following surrender. After 1945, most peoples became convinced, like Churchill, that democracy was the worst of all systems except for the others that had been tried. In following decades, colonial subjects and victims of domestic oppression would use the UN "common standard" to demand access to the political process, arbitration of their grievances, and transparency in law. Democratic nations would be held to the expectations they had created, as well as to the broadened dictates of their own consciences. Decolonization and desegregation followed.

Yet the war also created the basis for a new international division. Both the Soviet Union and the United States had stumbled into World War II. Fearing disaster, each had been determined to stay out. Ironically, they were stronger than ever at the war's end. Russia's new prowess was based not only on its spectacular, costly victory over Hitler, but also on the de facto control it soon exerted over the Eastern European nations it had liberated. It also formally annexed Latvia, Lithuania, and Estonia, and obtained additional territory from Japan and Poland. By 1945, the Soviets had more land and greater material resources than at any point since 1917. They fielded the world's largest standing army.[54]

The United States strengthened itself primarily from within, rebuilding its economy and industrial plant in response to the crisis. Alone of the Allies, it had enjoyed the blessing of fighting the war far from its own shores. Men had died, but homes, towns, and factories had gone unharmed. It also exited the war with an array of foreign bases that had been built to carry on the fight, such as in Iceland, though Roosevelt fully expected to bring his troops home. The American army would shrink once again, he assumed. As the president told Stalin in 1943, "England and the Soviet Union would have to handle the land armies in the event of any future threat to the peace." At the Yalta Conference in 1945, the last Allied meeting Roosevelt attended before his sudden death from a brain hemorrhage, he reiterated that U.S. troops would not be able to remain in Europe more than two additional years.[55]

Yet international events once again reshaped expectations and constrained choices. American troops would not go home as planned.

In the wartime film *Casablanca,* the owner of Rick's American Café (played by Humphrey Bogart) tells his French friend, a Vichy collaborator, "I stick my neck out for nobody." To this the jaded official sagaciously replies, "A wise foreign policy." The unanticipated increases in Soviet and American power—and the innate tension between Communist totalitarianism and the global trend towards economic integration and national self-determination—trapped the two wartime allies in a treacherous rivalry. One would become an empire, the other an umpire. With the development of atomic weaponry, both became superpowers. When Hollywood portrayed "American" Rick as deciding to hazard his neck after all for the sake of the world, audiences found themselves applauding his courage.

9

The Buck Stops Here

Or, How the United States Assumed the Burden
of Preemptive Intervention, 1945–1947

The simultaneous translator thought quickly. Had the red-faced Soviet leader called the Filipino delegate a "stooge," a "lackey," or a "jerk"? *Kholui* had several colloquial meanings. The translator swiftly decided on "jerk," though a later consultation of the Russian dictionary revealed a *kholui* to be "a servile, fawning creature, happy in subservience." Premier Khrushchev had certainly meant "lackey" *(stavlenik)* when he took the podium to interrupt Lorenzo Sumulong.[1]

A distinguished, handsome member of his country's UN delegation and a senator back home, the immaculately attired Sumulong had just expressed support for the Russian motion demanding immediate emancipation of all colonial peoples. Son of Juan Sumulong, one of the negotiators of Philippine independence in the 1930s, Lorenzo Sumulong strongly supported the movement toward decolonization then spinning around the globe. No country should be allowed to subjugate another. But, he added in words calculated to sting the motion's author, the new ruling should also apply to "the inalienable right to independence of the peoples of Eastern Europe and elsewhere who . . . have been swallowed up by the Soviet Union."[2]

Jumping to his feet, Khrushchev demanded a point of order. UN president Frederick Boland allowed the Russian to approach the podium, where Khrushchev threw out his arm, gesturing for the Philippine senator to step aside. The head of the Soviet Communist Party then denounced Sumulong. "This jerk—this stooge of American imperialism," other delegates heard over their headsets, "he is obviously touching on matters which are not procedural and the president is obviously not stopping him. Is that justice?"[3] Khrushchev then retook his seat but pulled off his right shoe and brandished it as Sumulong resumed his speech. When the calm Philippine delegate showed no sign of backing down, Khrushchev banged on the table with the heel of the dress shoe and then both his fists, to the delight of East European delegates. After a moment's hesitation, they and Soviet foreign minister Andrei Gromyko joined in, pounding their desktops in a boisterous chorus. President Boland of Ireland again rapped the gavel for order, and Khrushchev put his laced shoe in front of him on the desk, ready at hand.

U.S. assistant secretary of state Francis Wilcox took the podium soon thereafter to second Sumulong's plea. "Everyone here in this Assembly is fully aware of the sad fact that there are a number of states in Eastern Europe which do not have their complete independence," Wilcox stated. Khrushchev whacked the desk again, but this time it was Romanian delegate, Eduard Mezincescu, who demanded that the chair silence the offending speaker. Sedate, bespectacled Boland smacked his gavel sharply once more, though he allowed the Romanian to take the podium to rebut Wilcox. Beetle-browed and scrappy, Mezincescu upped the ante.

The president of the General Assembly nurtured a bias against Communists and in favor of the colonial powers, the Romanian charged. Of all people, the Irish should understand the desire for freedom, Mezincescu continued, in ambiguous phrasing that was either complimentary or contemptuous. Now thoroughly irritated, President Boland banged the gavel so hard that it shattered and the hammer somersaulted over his head. "Because of the scene you have just witnessed," the Irishman clipped, "I think the Assembly had better adjourn." The Assembly gave the chairman a standing ovation before filing out of the huge auditorium at the United Nations headquarters, built along the East River in New York on land donated by the Rockefeller family. In the words of the Associated Press, it was "the wildest scene in the history of the United Nations." Had Gilbert and Sullivan been watching, they might have stolen the plot line.[4]

The next day, Lorenzo Sumulong took the podium again, this time to protest Khrushchev's characterization of him as "a 'stooge' or 'jerk' or a 'lackey,' or what not." Soviet behavior ill-suited the dignity of the UN. But the irrepressible Khrushchev merely doubled over, guffawing at his desk. Once again, Gromyko and the Eastern European delegates copied Khrushchev and also started laughing at the Philippine delegate.[5] Indeed, despite their rudeness, the Communists had the last laugh. The UN General Assembly had grown by

65 percent since its founding fifteen years earlier. Bolstered by dozens of new nations from Asia and Africa, it passed the Soviet motion and formally drove a stake through the heart of colonialism. From December 14, 1960, onward, imperialism was officially dead or at least dying. Dependent peoples had an absolute "right to complete independence, and the integrity of their national territory shall be respected." Anything less was "contrary to the Charter of the United Nations." All peoples must be respected "without distinction as to race, sex, language or religion."[6]

Eighty-nine members of the ninety-nine-member General Assembly voted in favor of Resolution 1514 in 1960, including the Philippines. None voted against, although nine abstained. In favor of the motion in principle but opposed to Soviet manipulation, Britain, France, the United States, and six others joined together in mute protest. Yet divergence from the position of these great powers occasioned no reprisals toward countries that normally tended to vote with the so-called Western Bloc. Even within Western delegations, diversity was tolerated. No one was expected to laugh at boorish jokes or pound the desk in unison. An African American member of the U.S. delegation broke ranks to hail the final vote along with Asians and Africans, many representing the newest member states. "I wanted to crawl under the table when we abstained," Zelma George told a *New York Times* reporter on the scene, "but I decided to just stand and applaud instead."[7]

The human story is replete with ironies. "Do I contradict myself?" American poet Walt Whitman asked in his celebration of humanity and himself. "Very well then I contradict myself, (I am large, I contain multitudes)." But the UN vote might have confounded even Walt Whitman. Led by Soviet Russia, the last of the great powers to give up its coerced minions, the United Nations went on record in 1960 as opposing one of the oldest forms of government: empire. The inherent incompatibility of imperialism and nationalism resulted in a formal, final win for the latter.

Meanwhile, those great powers that had been first to liberate their colonies stood on the sidelines during the UN vote. In 1947, England granted independence to India, Pakistan, and Burma. In 1956 and 1957, the British Empire waved good-bye to Sudan, Malaysia, and Ghana. France also granted independence to two colonies in 1956, Tunisia and Morocco. But 1960 was the year of wonders. In the months preceding the tumultuous UN debate, France voluntarily severed colonial ties with what became seventeen new nations in Africa and Asia.[8] All of these events were accompanied by intense negotiations and often by violence. It was not an easy process. But the de facto demise of imperialism mostly preceded the de jure ruling in 1960.

Strikingly, the Soviet Union was last to comply with its own motion. The Communist empire invaded Hungary in 1956 to check its autonomy, and built the Berlin Wall in 1961 to prevent East Germans from fleeing to freedom in the West. Nations that wanted out of the Warsaw Pact could not leave it. Yet even Russia watched impassively three decades later when the Hungarian government removed its barbed-wire fences in 1989, and frenzied, joyful citizens in Berlin tore down the concrete wall, shard by shard. Regardless of variations in timing, after World War II the imperial powers mostly acquiesced in a peaceful process of decolonization. New nations proudly and sometimes defiantly declared their own independence, but the great majority never had to fight long wars of liberation like that hazarded by the United States in 1776 or Vietnam in 1946. Historical momentum was on their side.[9]

There were some bruising exceptions to this rule, and they have tended to blur our vision of the larger historical trend. Imperialism entered its final decline in the same years that the United States instituted the most important change in the history of its foreign policy: the so-called Truman Doctrine. This policy committed Americans to defend the sovereignty of foreign peoples at a time when the number of "peoples" was rapidly multiplying. Decolonization shares the same dates as the Cold War, roughly 1946 to 1991. As the fracas on the floor of the United Nations reveals, the two were interrelated. Superpower intervention hastened decolonization. Decolonization, in turn, irritated superpower relations by multiplying the number of potential allies for which Russia and America felt compelled to compete. Whenever these trends collided, mayhem (and sometimes farce) resulted. It became difficult to tell who were the real anti-imperialists: Communists or capitalists.

For nearly a century and a half, from 1776 to 1917, the United States had stood aloof from international crisis management. From 1917 to 1941, it accepted the need to intervene in extremis. During the two pivotal years between 1945 and 1947, the United States adopted responsibility for ongoing, and sometimes even preemptive crisis management.

This short period was the key turning point in American foreign relations, with consequences that reverberate to the present. The self-proclaimed Truman Doctrine made the United States the primary enforcer of the new world system. Although this disorderly "order" was collectively engineered, group enforcement of the new norms proved elusive. A split vote among the veto powers on the UN Security Council undermined cooperation almost immediately. A nuclear arms race created difficulties unanticipated by UN founders. Coordinating multiple governments was vexed in a world where intercontinental ballistic missiles made nuclear annihilation possible in a matter of minutes, yet cross-border threats required a coherent and timely response if reality was to approximate UN guarantees of "universal" self-determination and human rights.[10]

The United States consequently assumed a role akin to the one that the nation's founders had originally envisioned for the federal government: that of an umpire, to compel acquiescence. With the significant exception of the Communist world, most other countries encouraged this development, sometimes at the price of their pride. These years introduced all the controversies that complicated world history through the end of the century. They also revealed the anti-imperial intentions and results of U.S. policy at the outset of America's adventure as world umpire.

To Western Europeans, unlike Americans, decolonization was the immediate strategic headache during the late 1940s and 1950s, not Moscow and its ambitions.[11] Decolonization was the primal threat to the world they had built since 1492. One main reason for this difference in the Allies' perspective was that the United States had prepared itself to abandon colonialism well before the war broke out, whereas those Europeans who were victorious in 1945 fully intended to keep their dominions.

For Americans and Filipinos, all that remained was to organize the parades. Congress had passed the Philippine Independence Act in 1934. Less than a year after World War II ended, the new Philippine government invited America to participate in its independence festivities. President Truman intended to go, but business kept him in Washington. General Douglas MacArthur was invited to address the populace instead. Seventy-seven-year-old Emilio Aguinaldo, Filipino leader in the 1898 war against Spain, had lived to see the day. The head of logistics gave U.S. Army officer William S. Triplet three days to prepare a contingent of Filipino Scouts to lead the procession. Triplet informed his superior that all he needed was 6,000 pairs of new combat boots.

Despite his can-do attitude, however, Triplet, a seasoned veteran of both the European and Pacific theaters, accepted his assignment with trepidation. A Filipino regiment of the regular U.S. Army, the Scouts were still being re-assembled after the disruption of the war. They would become foreign rather than domestic troops on July 4, 1946. Triplet worried that when they carried the U.S. flag down Rizal Avenue, still under reconstruction following the three-year Japanese occupation and the horrific Battle of Manila, his men and their symbol of "colonial oppression would draw a barrage of decayed eggs, fruit, and small deceased animals."[12]

Triplet was aware that Philippine nationalism had grown more intense in the year between liberation from the Japanese and liberation from the United States. More than 1,000 Americans had died and 5,000 had been wounded dislodging Japanese troops from the capital city, but that sacrifice was already receding into memory. Apparently it had not been forgotten altogether, however. As the battalion and its star-spangled pennant swung around the block onto Rizal Avenue, Triplet wrote, "We were greeted by a continuous roar of applause from the dense crowd of observers. . . . I had never imagined that U.S. troops would ever again be welcomed in Manila, but there it was," the old soldier observed. "It was a good day."[13]

General MacArthur told the throng of approximately 600,000 Filipinos that they had captured the world's imagination. On the Republic of the Philippines, he said, the first Asian colony to achieve independence, "the eyes of all oppressed peoples are cast with the burning light of a new faith"—faith in the potential of Asia "to attain political liberty." The same day, the previous colonial power hosted a parallel celebration in Madrid, Spain, accompanied by a church service and a Te Deum. The event also attracted substantial attention in California, which had a large Filipino population. The night before independence, a sixteen-year-old Filipina beauty queen presided over a ball for 1,200 Filipino Americans in Los Angeles, at which she read the Independence Proclamation. On the morning of July Fourth, 7,000 proud immigrants paraded to City Hall, where the Philippine flag was hoisted. Matrons in piñon-lace dresses sang the new national anthem, and motorized floats competed for prizes. The float "Progress" won first place, followed by "Tropical Fruits." Event organizers seated five American Purple Heart–wearing veterans of the gruesome 1942 Bataan Death March on the reviewing stand. The Los Angeles Times ran five stories on the day of the historic event, celebrating the outcome (and end) of America's forty-eight-year run at imperialism. A local veteran of the 1898 war recalled it as a "mistake," but added, "Things have a way of working out, haven't they?"[14]

In their final negotiations, the United States promised the Philippines continuing military protection, and the Philippines granted land for American bases. A Filipino economist writing in the *Los Angeles Times* explained the new relationship in terms calculated to show the benefit to both peoples. When McKinley annexed the Philippines, Vicente Villamin recounted, the president had promised "no oppression, exploitation or imperialism." The United States largely kept its promises, Villamin asserted. Generous free trade after 1900 had hastened the development of small industries, created a strong market for Filipino products, and kept national debt low.

But war against Japan had depleted the treasury and destroyed factories. Previously self-supporting, the islands now faced $1 billion in reconstruction costs. The new nation needed an immediate loan of $400 million, plus a reliable market for its products once normal economic activity resumed. The Philippines faced an uphill battle to create an economy strong enough to pull eighteen million people out of poverty. Just before independence, the U.S. Congress agreed to give preference to Philippine goods for another eight years, and appropriated $520 million to reimburse both private citizens and the Philippine government for wartime damages.

Lest Americans question what was in the deal for them, Villamin pointed out that Filipino soldiers had saved American lives in the war, shortening the battle and thereby saving perhaps $10 billion in war costs. The world remained an exceedingly dangerous place, and a continued "close" relationship was advisable. Villamin did not say, though he may have realized, that a military presence in the islands was a double-edged sword for the United States. It protected the approaches to Hawaii and the West Coast at the cost of exposing Americans to conflicts far from their own shores.[15]

The U.S. experience in the Philippines was rife with mistakes, beginning with the very fact of being there. But its peaceable ending showed a way forward that others emulated. The pageantry of decolonization assumed a certain style. In July 1946, representatives of fifty nations attended the birthday fete in Manila. In March 1957, nine years later, seventy nations attended the equally festive independence ceremony for Ghana. Dignitaries from around the world came to demonstrate their approval for the proceedings. Elizabeth II could not attend, but she sent the Duchess of Kent, who graced a garden party for 5,000 guests and opened the first session of the Ghanaian Parliament with a message of rejoicing from the then thirty-year-old queen.[16]

President Dwight Eisenhower dispatched Vice President Richard Nixon to the celebration, where he met Martin Luther King, Jr., for the first time, under the bright tropical sun of Accra. President Kwame Nkrumah had invited nearly every black American of note, from King to Congressmen Adam Clayton Powell to UN Undersecretary Ralph Bunche. Men and women garbed in native kente cloth and tribal leaders with umbrella bearers mingled with visitors in Western suits. To attendees as well as onlookers, the event augured a better world being made in real time. It seemed like racial justice personified. Appropriating Churchill's words, the African American newspaper *Defender* dubbed the Ghanaian celebration "Britain's finest hour": In lifting "the yoke of colonialism from the necks of the oppressed natives of West Africa, . . . England has added a new chapter to the history of modern civilization."[17]

Ghana's liberation was a crest in the tide running against racism, which world events had increasingly delegitimized. "Every act of racial discrimination or prejudice in the U.S. hurts America as much as an espionage agent who turns over a weapon to a foreign enemy," Richard Nixon preached to his countrymen in 1954.[18] White hands shaking brown ones symbolized widening access to political power around the globe.

Not all transitions were as smooth as Ghana's, however. In India and Pakistan, no multinational fete accompanied independence. Their devolution from the British Empire in 1947 created two nations separated along religious lines. Roughly one million people died in postcolonial violence between Muslims and Hindus in the months following liberation from Britain. At its establishment, India became the world's largest democracy, but the chaos attending its birth also foretold the difficulties that many new multiethnic nations would experience. Nationalism could be as volatile as imperialism, and sometimes more so. Creating a stable government, as the American revolutionaries found in 1789, was often harder than overthrowing one.

Other aspirants to independence found European governments more recalcitrant than they had hoped, in light of the Atlantic Charter. When Indonesia declared its independence from the Netherlands in November 1945, the Dutch dispatched 140,000 troops. After four years of fighting and thousands of casualties, a tearful Queen Juliana conceded Holland's bitter defeat. Indonesia became autonomous, although the Dutch retained portions of New

Guinea (the largest island in the archipelago) until 1962. In Algeria in 1954, French interior minister François Mitterrand told revolutionaries, "The only negotiation is war." The Gallic nation opposed independent Arab rule in Algeria for eight years, at a cost of two-thirds of its currency reserves and nearly one million French and Algerian lives.[19]

Even in Ghana the celebration was years in coming. Although Britain comported itself with the greatest forbearance of all the colonial powers except the United States, Kwame Nkrumah was nonetheless imprisoned twice in a colonial jail. On the 1957 map of Africa, his new nation was a tiny square in a field still divided among Britain, France, Belgium, Spain, and Portugal. As an editorialist for the *Los Angeles Times* observed, Ghana's triumph would "haunt the dreams of European colonial powers."[20] Decolonization was a mixed, difficult, and often violent process.

One frustrated revolutionary was Ho Chi Minh, a cosmopolitan fifty-five-year-old nationalist and Communist Party leader who worked with the American army in dislodging the Japanese from Indochina. Conditions were appalling. During World War II the collaborationist Vichy government administered the French colony, but the Japanese army had used Indochina as a granary—a policy that resulted in famine and killed nearly two million people during the five-year occupation. The U.S. Office of Strategic Services (OSS) equipped Ho and his guerillas with flamethrowers and revolvers to battle Japan. One U.S. agent pronounced him an "awfully sweet guy."[21]

As the prospect of Japanese defeat became more tangible in the spring of 1945, the threat of French recolonization became equally real. When Japan formally overthrew the Vichy regime in Vietnam in March 1945, Charles de Gaulle requested help from the United States in rushing French troops to Indochina to oust Japan. But the United States had taken a consistently anti-colonial stance. In 1942 Franklin Roosevelt pressed Churchill to grant India independence, and in 1943 he stated his firm conviction that "Indochina should not be given back to the French empire after the war." In a subsequent memo to Secretary of State Cordell Hull, Roosevelt called the case of Indochina "perfectly clear." France had "milked it for one hundred years. The people of Indo-china are entitled to something better than that." Joseph Stalin agreed. In discussions at the Allies' Tehran Conference, he asserted that France should forfeit Indochina as the price for collaborating with Nazi Germany. Transporting French soldiers to Indochina would undercut those goals.[22]

French national identity was in tatters, however. Officials were determined to restore the grandeur of their nation (and its territorial claims) on the battlefield in Indochina. Germany had humiliated France in almost every conceivable way, robbing it through forced payments, labor conscription, and confiscations to serve the Third Reich. Considering "the shock inflicted on French prestige," President Charles de Gaulle believed it essential that World War II "not come to an end without our participation. Otherwise, every policy, every army, every aspect of public opinion would certainly insist upon our abdication in Indochina. On the other hand, if we took part in the battle," the president asserted, "French blood shed on the soil of Indochina would constitute an impressive claim."[23]

De Gaulle was so deeply convinced of this imperative that he exerted every means at his disposal to bend the wealthier, better-equipped Americans to his will, even before the defeat of Germany. In September 1944, a month after the liberation of Paris, he ordered French intelligence agents to suspend all cooperation with American OSS agents to indicate his displeasure at U.S. anti-imperialism.[24] When Japan overthrew the Vichy puppet government in March 1945, and while the Allies were still battling toward Berlin, de Gaulle played on American anxieties about its Communist ally.

Although the urbane president spoke in a "very quiet, affable, friendly fashion," American ambassador Jefferson Caffrey reported to Washington, de Gaulle questioned U.S. resistance to transporting French troops in North Africa and southern France to Indochina. "What are you driving at?" the Frenchman had asked Caffrey. "Do you want us to become, for example, one of the federated states under the Russian aegis? The Russians are advancing apace as you well know. When Germany falls they will be upon us." Rather than suggesting that French troops go out to meet the Soviets, however, de Gaulle indicated that the reoccupation of Indochina was his top priority and implied that it was the price of French loyalty. "If the public here comes to realize that you are against us in Indochina there will be terrific disappointment and nobody knows to what that will lead. We do not want to become Communist; we do not want to fall into the Russian orbit, but I hope that you will not push us into it."[25]

Ho Chi Minh and his associates, meanwhile, had an entirely different set of hopes and expectations. They envisioned an autonomous nation-state as a consequence of the Allied victory under U.S. leadership. The Viet Minh, the nationalist coalition fighting for Vietnamese independence, urged peasants to rescue downed American pilots whenever possible in order to cultivate good relations. They told OSS intelligence agents that the Vietnamese people "liked America best because of her generous promise to give the Philippines independence, her friendly attitude with the small and weak nationalities and her liberal help to those who fight Fascism." Borrowing freely from both Communist and liberal traditions, Vietnamese nationalists appealed to America to stand by them. On September 2, 1945, two weeks after Japan's surrender, the revolutionaries declared independence with the blessing of Vietnam's last monarch, Bao Dai. Dressed in a simple khaki uniform and wearing white rubber sandals, Ho Chi Minh told a jubilant crowd in downtown Hanoi, "All men are created equal; they are endowed by their Creator with certain unalienable Rights; among these are Life, Liberty, and the Pursuit of Happiness."[26]

Ho's speech hewed more closely to the models of 1776 and 1789 than any other anticolonial declaration of the era. It opened by quoting the American Declaration of Independence, followed by the French Declaration of the Rights of Man and the Citizen. The speech continued with a list of grievances similar to the charges Americans had levied against George III. Although Ho Chi Minh employed a rhetorical strategy he undoubtedly hoped would bring Westerners to his side, the Vietnamese leader also genuinely admired George Washington and U.S. policy in the Philippines. He knew that the United States was poised to do what no other colonial power had yet done: free a colony voluntarily. At a state dinner in Hanoi to honor visiting Chinese and French dignitaries, Ho Chi Minh placed the American representative, Frank White, at his side. When White suggested that others might resent the seating arrangement, Ho replied, "But who else could I talk to?"[27]

The goal of popular sovereignty was not imposed from outside. Indeed, the Vietnamese had already grasped and adapted this new "standard of civilization" for their own purposes. It was outsiders who tried to limit its application to Indochina. Despite American qualms and Vietnamese hopes, 20,000 British troops marched into Saigon two weeks after Ho Chi Minh's historic declaration. There they allowed French officials to raise the tricolor once again.[28]

There were powerful voices on both sides of a vigorous debate within the American government about whom to placate, the French or the Vietnamese. But at least initially, anticolonial perspectives seemed ascendant. Certainly the French thought so. An internal report for the French Foreign Ministry in

March 1945 fretted that "the colonial problem is one of the few issues on which American opinion is not divided. For different reasons, emancipation of European colonies is desired as much by Republicans as by Democrats, by conservative industrialists and radical intellectuals, by the *Chicago Tribune* as much as the *New Republic.*" French officials believed that Americans were incorrigibly eager to make a buck while liberating oppressed peoples. In a way, their perception was accurate. Yankees saw the two goals as complementary—and moral. Ending colonialism would unlock markets and prevent a return to global depression. "The open door," the internal French report complained, however, "would favor powerful Americans over European competitors." Another French report asserted in August 1945, "Every American is anti-colonial by instinct and because he owes his existence to an anti-colonial reaction."[29]

Ho Chi Minh obviously favored the U.S. point of view. He downplayed his Communist ideology and held open elections in January 1946, in which the Viet Minh won 230 of 300 seats in the National Assembly. The Vietnamese president also wrote six letters appealing to the Truman administration for formal diplomatic recognition and support. In February of 1946, he reminded President Truman that the French had "betrayed in war-time both the Allies and Vietnamese." France's attempt to reimpose colonialism violated the promises made at the UN's founding in San Francisco. The United States should prevent this occurrence, "as guardians and champions of World Justice." Ho pleaded, "What we ask has been graciously granted to the Philippines. Like the Philippines our goal is full independence and full cooperation with the United States." In other letters, Ho Chi Minh emphasized his admiration for America's "modern technical achievements" and asked to send a delegation of fifty students to undertake training in the applied sciences.[30]

Unfortunately for the Vietnamese, Harry Truman was not Franklin Roosevelt. After Roosevelt died suddenly in April 1945, the new U.S. president assured Defense Minister René Pleven of France that "no one in the United States wanted more than him personally to see France restored to all its power."[31] Unlike his predecessor, Truman had served ten years in the traditional, balky U.S. Senate. He was instinctively more conservative than Roosevelt, who had tried harder to effect substantial change in Eurasian politics. The Missourian entered office with little interest in colonial issues. Instead, Truman reiterated the customary, noninterventionist stance embodied in the Monroe Doctrine. "With the existing colonies or dependencies of any European power we have not interfered, and shall not interfere," the 1823 document read, in phrases that easily described Truman's attitude toward France.

Truman soon settled into a policy of benign neutrality toward his ally's colonial ambitions. Although he did not give France the material support that de Gaulle craved, he also never responded to Ho Chi Minh's letters. From 1945 to 1947, the U.S. president largely ignored events in Vietnam. To the extent that he was willing to deviate from the rules set by George Washington and James Monroe, it was in relation to matters he considered of supreme importance. Vietnamese independence, and decolonization generally, did not rank.

What riveted President Truman's attention, and the attention of many Europeans as well, were Soviet measures that suggested Joseph Stalin might become a menace. When Truman first met Stalin at Potsdam, Germany, he came away with a mostly positive impression and the conviction that the Allies could continue to work together. "I can deal with Stalin. He is honest—but smart as hell," Truman observed. Russians were "pig-headed," but so were Southerners. On his White House desk, Truman placed a small wooden sign from a friend back home. On one side it read, "I'm from Missouri" (nicknamed the "Show Me" state). The other side read, "The Buck Stops Here!" Although inexperienced in world affairs, the new president was practical, forceful, and open to learning. He believed that the United States had been too soft in some negotiations, but he still considered cooperation with the Russians eminently possible.[32]

Russian perspectives were very different from American views. A lifetime spent murdering his domestic opponents had made Stalin a hard, suspicious, obdurate man. At the height of Allied cooperation, on the eve of American soldiers' suicidal assault on Normandy, Stalin commented about the British and American leaders coming to his rescue: "Churchill is the kind who, if you don't watch him, will slip a kopek out of your pocket. . . . Roosevelt is not like that. He dips in his hand only for bigger coins." Vyacheslav Molotov, the Soviet minister of foreign relations, later described Roosevelt as "an imperialist who would grab anyone by the throat" and Truman as a less clever imitation. As the war ended, the USSR hoped to expand its sphere of control well beyond Russia's borders to gain leverage against capitalist nations it saw as implacable enemies. "There has been a return in Russia to the outmoded concept of security in terms of territory—the more you've got the safer you are," former foreign minister Maxim Litvinov observed ruefully to a Western reporter in 1946. Such candid statements were risky, however. "Litvinov remained among the living," Molotov later admitted, "only by chance."[33]

More important than differences in personality and perception among the Allied leaders was a fundamental disjunction between Soviet and Euro-American assumptions about how to create a stable platform for the future. The majority of governments had come to believe that the peace of the world depended on economic cooperation and access, combined with firm guarantees of self-determination for all nations. Conversely, the Soviets believed their security rested upon having a closed economic sphere and strict political control over surrounding states. Stalin explained this to the Supreme Soviet assembly in February 1946. World peace might be attainable if capitalist nations did something they would never do, he said: if they "periodically redistributed [the raw materials and markets of the world] among the various countries in accordance with their economic importance." Since this would not happen, future wars were unavoidable.[34]

Russian security concerns were extreme, but understandable. Germany had twice invaded across the lowlands of Poland, causing catastrophic damage. The USSR's Anglo-American allies now held a monopoly on the most destructive technology ever invented. Any nation in Russia's position would have wanted and insisted on the strictest security guarantees. Indeed, most Americans empathized with the Communist nation's position after its devastating sacrifices during the war. But Soviet demands far exceeded what other nations, some of them comparably damaged, believed was truly necessary to guard against aggression. Russia had the force at its disposal to cow almost all of its immediate neighbors, and it soon did. That it would seek so much control was not immediately apparent, however. The Bolsheviks' anti-imperialist oratory and egalitarian philosophy still thrilled admirers around the world.

Scholars debate about which bloc, East or West, bears the greatest blame for exciting the fears of the other and thereby stimulating the Cold War. It is an interesting and important question, but not pertinent here. Extraordinary suspicions arose on both sides. The United States' atomic supremacy undoubtedly fed Soviet anxieties. Contemporary observers noted many occasions when American provocations, rigidity, or simple diplomatic ineptness instigated or worsened Cold War tensions. The critical question is why the United States assumed the primary responsibility for countering Russia. Why did it deviate from a longstanding policy of limited, ad hoc engagement with Europe and embrace ongoing intervention?

The primary reason was simply that Russia's ambitions seemed to keep getting larger, and to be on a trajectory that might threaten the very nations that the United States had just sacrificed so much to defend. Should that happen, America would be back in the same position it was in when only Britain stood between Hitler and the Western Hemisphere. The secondary reason—as we shall see—was that the United Kingdom decisively stepped aside in 1947 and challenged the United States to take up the burden. Finally, deep in their political DNA, the majority of Americans believed that when all else failed, a general government must step in. The founders had created a structure to quell existential conflict among states of the union. Now, extraordinary events appeared to call for *some* kind of power—an umpire, arbiter, bouncer, playground supervisor, policeman, whatever—to quell conflict among the states of the world. Wisely or not, the public came to see intervention as vital to the security of *all* nations, including the United States. Requests from foreign governments strengthened this conviction.

Concerns about Soviet ambitions arose initially in relation to Eastern Europe. At the 1945 Yalta Conference, Churchill, Roosevelt, and Stalin agreed that after the war the Eastern European states would hold "free and unfettered elections as soon as possible on the basis of universal suffrage and secret ballot." This did not happen, to the distress of officials in America and Europe. Not that they were especially shocked, however, given what they knew about Soviet communism and the sacrifices the Red Army had made to expel Nazi occupiers from these buffer states. Stalin understood this, and also that his former allies would be reluctant to lose any more men, especially in places like Poland or the Baltics. In the words of Norman Naimark and Leonid Gibianskii, Russia's tactics were "finely calibrated to the task of keeping the Western powers from intervening."[35]

Yet although the Soviet dictator insisted that he sought only "friendly governments" in Eastern Europe, his policies made no friends. Examples abounded. In Poland, the Red Army waited on the other side of the Vistula River for sixty-three days during the tragic Warsaw Uprising of 1944, while the Nazis slaughtered the Home Army and mass murdered civilians. In the eastern portions of Germany, the Russians seized whatever transportable assets they could find as reparations, removing about a third of its industrial capacity. Russian soldiers were given license to rape, vengefully brutalizing as many as two million women between 1945 and 1946 in parts of Germany they controlled. In Yugoslavia, citizens seen talking with an Englishman or American were arrested. William Donovan, head of the OSS, felt alarmed enough at the multiplicity of worrisome reports emanating from Eastern Europe in May 1945 to warn that the United States needed to do more to strengthen Western European governments. If capable of self-defense, he said, they would keep Russia back from the Atlantic Rim. It was always "better to fight abroad" than have to "fall back on our hemispheric defense."[36]

Closer to the danger, British officials agreed. More habituated than Americans to Europe's brutal realities, they were prepared to abandon those countries that could not be saved. One official reported in 1945 that the British Foreign Ministry did not even bother to "collect information about atrocities against indigenous civilians in East Europe."[37] But England was also prepared to fight vigorously for those areas not yet under Soviet dominion. Visiting the United States as a private guest of Harry Truman, Winston Churchill famously observed in a March 1946 speech in Missouri that an "iron curtain" had descended from the Baltic Sea in the north to the Adriatic Sea in the south. Behind it, he warned, all the ancient capitals of Central and Eastern Europe were under totalitarian control: "Warsaw, Berlin, Prague, Vienna, Budapest, Belgrade, Bucharest and Sofia." Churchill articulated publicly what most officials were still willing to discuss only privately. Nonetheless, the war-weary populace in both Britain and the U.S. reacted hostilely to the warnings of the old imperialist. As one irate Seattle woman wrote the White House, "Does criticism of Russia negate the fact that millions of Britain's colonials are living in slavery?" Former Vice President Henry Wallace seconded her sentiment a few months later when he said that he feared English imperialism more than Soviet communism (and attacked Republicans as dodo birds, doomed to extinction). Indeed, it was not yet clear that the British Empire was waning, while the Russian was waxing.[38]

Had the Soviet threat been confined to Eastern Europe, America's role probably would not have changed as dramatically as it did. But Russia tried to squeeze territorial concessions on its southern approaches as well. This was less expected, since countries like Iran and Turkey had not been occupied by the Nazis. They did not need "liberating." In 1945, the Soviet Union refused to withdraw troops from Iran (which had provided bases for the transport of supplies) on the timetable to which all the Allies had agreed. Instead it encouraged a secessionist movement in the Iranian province of Azerbaijan, bordering Russia. A breakaway, "independent" republic there would undoubtedly have become part of the rapidly expanding Soviet complex. In 1946, Stalin also demanded military bases inside Turkish territory to guard the Bosporus and Dardanelles, the narrow waterways linking the Black Sea with the Mediterranean.

Both Iran and Turkey resisted these maneuvers. Iran submitted a complaint to the new UN Security Council asking for Russian withdrawal. Turkey insisted on its sovereign right to defend waterways passing through its own territory. Britain and the United States staunchly supported both positions, and the Middle Eastern nations eventually prevailed. But it was an uncertain process, during which Stalin kept pressing his claims.

In December 1946, after yet another failed meeting of minds with Moscow, Truman discussed his dilemma with Press Secretary Charles Ross. The Russians, he said, "confront us with an accomplished fact and then there is little we can do. They did that in the case of Poland. Now they have 500,000 men in Bulgaria and some day they are going to move down and take the Black Sea straits and that will be an accomplished fact again. . . . I don't know what we're going to do." Earlier that year, an American diplomat who had served in the USSR since the early 1930s had composed a lengthy missive on Russian paranoia and Bolshevik hostility. In his famous "Long Telegram," George Kennan predicted that Soviet success would "really depend on the degree of cohesion, firmness and vigor which the Western World can muster." In January 1947 the U.S. ambassador to the Soviet Union, Walter Bedell Smith, told the secretary of state that he believed Russia would not be content until it thoroughly dominated the Near East. "Confronted by this chill menace Turkey has little hope of independent survival unless it is assured of solid long term American and British support," Smith wrote home. Turkey meanwhile lobbied for economic and military assistance.[39]

Greece presented another headache. Communist movements were flourishing across the weakened continent, including in France and Italy. But in Greece armed guerillas had begun an actual civil war. Britain tried to put out the fire but found its dwindling resources stretched to the breaking point. Monies earmarked for defense had to be spent on food for the Greek people. Meanwhile, the Greek government lodged complaints with the United Nations about illegal arms flowing across its border from Communist-controlled

Albania, Bulgaria, and Yugoslavia. It also requested funds urgently from the United States, which had yet to offer material support, and additional money from the United Kingdom, which had been helping continuously. The British cabinet dug deeper into its purse "in order to stop the rot." But in February 1947, under extreme pressure from the chancellor of the Exchequer and failing to convince the Truman administration that it needed backup, the Foreign Office simply sent Washington an ultimatum: step up, or watch Greece go under.[40]

Britain was done. It had strained its resources "to the utmost" and would be unable to continue helping Greece after March 31, 1947. Domestic problems now far outweighed foreign ones. A Gallup poll showed that 69 percent of the British public ranked housing, fuel, and food shortages as the three most urgent issues during the stranglehold of that exceptionally frigid winter. Only 4 percent considered foreign policy a top priority. German bombs had destroyed four million English homes and thousands of factories. Britons were still on rations. Not until 1954, almost a decade *after* the war, would they be able to freely purchase butter, eggs, sugar, cheese, and meat. World War II had cost England $30 billion, one-fourth of the nation's wealth. If the United States wished to continue a "policy of effective and practical support for Greece," it would have to do so on its own dime, commencing in five weeks. The same applied to Turkey. A few months later, the United Kingdom notified Truman that "financial stringency" required drawing down its troops in occupied Italy as well.[41]

Up to this point the United States had resisted any permanent commitment. The American public expressed its clear expectation (and demand) that the nation retrench, as it had done after all previous conflicts since the War of Independence. Two hundred "Bring Back Daddy" clubs had sprung up across the country after Japan's surrender. Mothers mailed baby booties to Congress. Under domestic pressure, Truman demobilized even more quickly than advised by General George C. Marshall, discharging 35,000 troops per day at the end of 1945. The armed forces shrank from 12 million to 1.5 million. By June 1947, the U.S. Army was only the sixth largest in the world.[42]

The Truman administration appreciated its advantageous position. Britain had long taken responsibility for peace in Europe, to the extent that the Continent enjoyed peace. Since the Napoleonic Wars, the United Kingdom had "held the line" against aggression on the Continent, as they described their version of containment. In the months leading up to the British ultimatum,

U.S. State Department officials privately expressed the view that so long as the British "were going in anyway," the United States could hang back. That way, read one memo, the United Kingdom "would be blamed [by the Greeks] if all wasn't immediately perfect; by staying out US would not share opprobrium."[43]

Naturally enough, British officials recognized U.S. self-interest at work. Lord Halifax, ambassador to Washington, wrote home at the end of the war that the Americans preferred to avoid any long-term commitments "so long as His Majesty's Government continues to be willing to keep the initiative." Six months later he counseled that England's government needed "America to shoulder the burden of wider responsibility that is now hers." Yet another British analyst echoed Halifax: the United Kingdom must convince the United States "to shoulder the burden of wider responsibility—even if this means pocketing our 'ego' to some extent."[44] Prime Minister Clement Attlee, who replaced Churchill, made a similarly brave and self-abnegating argument in 1946: "We must not, for sentimental reasons based on the past, give hostages to fortune. It may be we shall have to consider the British Isles as an easterly extension of a strategic area, the centre of which is the American continent."[45] The English exercised rare leadership by encouraging new leadership.

Undersecretary of State Dean Acheson fielded the first transatlantic phone call from Whitehall about the memoranda on Greece and Turkey that he called "shockers." Within the week, President Truman and George C. Marshall, recently appointed secretary of state, called congressional leaders to the White House. The first question that representatives raised was, "How much?" Second, did the Greeks really need U.S. intervention, or would America merely be "pulling British chestnuts out of the fire?" Marshall and Acheson retorted that it was not a question of British chestnuts, but "the security of the United States." The Soviets now controlled Eastern Europe. Communist parties that looked to Russia for direction had expanded dramatically in Italy, France, Austria, and Hungary. Iran, Turkey, and Greece were all under duress. If those latter countries were compromised, Soviet domination might even overspread the Middle East and India. The bipartisan congressional delegation listened closely to Secretary Marshall, the former general, widely respected as the man whose impassioned testimony in Congress had helped narrowly avert the dissolution of the draft army in August 1941 (by one vote). Marshall had brought the nation through four years of hell to victory in 1945. Ramrod straight and deeply serious, the earnest ex–army chief of staff commanded attention.[46]

"In the last 18 months the position of the democracies throughout the world has materially deteriorated," Marshall and Acheson emphasized. "It is a question of whether . . . three-fourths of the world's territory is to be controlled by Communists." This was not a matter of "vague do-goodism . . . [but] of protecting the nation itself."[47]

To politicians who had seen democracies around the world fall apart in quick succession ten years earlier, and Nazism advance as a result, these words hit home. They agreed with the State Department that "if Communism spreads to all the critical areas where it threatens now, war will be inevitable." They wanted to avoid that outcome at almost any cost. "The choice is between acting with energy or losing by default," Marshall told the congressmen, a phrase that struck a special chord with Republican senator Arthur Vandenberg, the influential head of the Foreign Relations Committee. On the spot, the bipartisan delegation pledged support for Truman's proposals.[48]

Officials spent the next two weeks laboring over a speech to persuade Congress and the American people. The first draft emphasized the Soviet menace and British decline. Since the nation's birth, it pointed out, "British foreign policy backed by British industrial and financial and naval strength has maintained a balance of power and thus a measure of order." But "the shambles of war" had so reduced the United Kingdom that it was "no longer equal to its historic task" and "a page in history has been turned." Subsequent drafts downplayed geopolitics, never a favorite theme of Americans. References to England became minimal, lest Congress complain about rescuing "British chestnuts"—a curiously ubiquitous phrase in Congress and among the suspicious public. Instead, the administration gradually crafted a speech that emphasized the plight of Greece and appealed to humanitarian concerns as much as strategic ones. Privately, though, the administration thought, as presidential assistant Clark Clifford scribbled in the margins of one draft, "This is a grim task we are accepting. Nothing to recommend it except *alternative is grimmer. Tough!*"[49]

On Wednesday March 12, 1947, President Harry Truman gave the speech that, more than any, changed the destiny of the United States and the world in the second half of the twentieth century. Addressing a joint session of Congress, he outlined the problem. Greece had sent "an urgent appeal for financial and economic assistance." The Nazis had razed the country during their retreat, destroying ports, railroads, and more than 1,000 villages. "Eighty-five percent of the children were tubercular." In the midst of this postwar tragedy,

a "terrorist" minority was now making Greek recovery impossible and threatening to take over the nation. Britain had given all it could and the UN was
still engaged in fact-finding to determine whether Greece was under outside
pressure from Communists in Albania, Bulgaria, and Yugoslavia. (Shades of
the Lytton Commission in the 1931 Manchurian Crisis.) The very existence of
the state was threatened. "There is no other country to which democratic
Greece can turn," the president asserted. Turkey, too, needed assistance. "We
are the only country able to provide that help," Truman reiterated.[50]

The president then delivered the crucial line. "I believe that it must be the
policy of the United States to support free peoples who are resisting attempted subjugation by armed minorities or outside pressures," Truman asserted. The United States would spend the next six decades attempting to
reach this bar.[51]

President Truman requested $400 million for the first year. American civil-
ian and military personnel would follow, if requested by host countries.
Democratic nations all had inadequacies, he said, and aid should not be taken
as evidence that the United States "condones everything that the Greek government has done or will do." But one virtue of democracy was transparency:
"Its defects are always visible and . . . can be pointed out and corrected."[52]

Congress debated Truman's proposal in surprisingly thoughtful, bipartisan terms for nearly two months. Its momentousness was apparent to all. The
doctrine would bring about a fundamental reversal of the nation's traditional
policy for the foreseeable future.

Republicans and Democrats who argued against the bill raised objections
that echo to the present. Just "because British imperialism has led that country to make commitments, which she can no longer fulfill," Republican
Robert Rich of Pennsylvania charged, "President Truman asks us to take up
the burden, jettison the basis of our foreign policy . . . and contradict the
wisdom of our years." Giving aid to Greece and Turkey would convert
the United States from a "haven and refuge for the oppressed and, therefore,
the most popular country, into the most unpopular country charged with
interfering everywhere." Let churches or the UN step in instead, Rich suggested. Republican George Bender of Ohio warned, "If we go into this Greek
thing we shall be pouring in money and the blood of our sons for generations." Congressman Bender pointed out in another session that "Turkey refused to enter the war in 1943 when she was requested to do so by the Allies."
(Turkey declared war only in February 1945, largely to join the UN at its

founding.) Why should the United States help nations that did not deserve it? Democrat Chester Holifield of California denounced the president's proposal as "radical," "abrupt," and "drastic." Truman's proposal would overturn all American precedent, meanwhile "killing the United Nations in its infancy." Couldn't the British be persuaded to carry on? Was there really "no alternative to unilateral action of the United States?" One of the few members of Congress who had protested the Japanese internment, Holifield pointed out that Turkey had little claim to being democratic. The proposed assistance, he claimed, was a patent attempt to protect Euro-American investments "in the oil deposits of the Middle East."

Republican senator Hugh Butler of Nebraska dashed further cold water on the proposal. The Truman Doctrine asked Americans to accept "the entire burden for remaking the world . . . [and] adopt a permanent policy of spending hundreds of millions, perhaps billions, of dollars of American money in this crusade." The United States had limited resources, which it should spend on its own people. "I would suggest therefore," Butler said, "that the salvation of Greece is largely in the hands of the Greeks." Florida Democrat Claude Pepper, the leading Southern liberal, predicted that other nations would interpret the doctrine as evidence "of a new and expanding American imperialism." If troops were stationed abroad, the American uniform might become "the leverage by which reactionary and perhaps corrupt governments may at least psychologically intimidate the opposition to their own domestic policies." The United States risked stepping into "the imperial quicksands of the world," Pepper warned, and "cram[ming] democracy down people's throats."[53]

Bipartisan support for the Truman Doctrine was ultimately stronger than bipartisan opposition, however. Republican senator William Knowland of California acknowledged that the Truman Doctrine might lead to war with the Soviet Union or involve the United States in propping up "reactionary regimes" around the world. These were real risks. But World War II had taught "that you do not stop aggression by yielding to it." The Greco-Turkish aid program "menaces no one," Knowland said, and would "not disturb the Soviet Union in the enjoyment of any rights and privileges to which that country is entitled." The riskiest, "most dangerous and irresponsible course, would be to do nothing," the Republican leader argued.

Democratic senator Herbert O'Conor observed that "down through the years" Britain had been "the world's bulwark against disaster." It was now spent. The United Kingdom had passed the baton to America "to head off a third world war before it reaches the shooting stage." Democrat William Fulbright of Arkansas asserted that the UN was not yet in a position to solve the problems that had arisen. Russia had already used its veto ten times in less than two years. The UN Charter "was but the first tentative step toward the creation of rules of conduct for all nations" and still a flimsy shield against aggression. More than 80 percent of the world's population lived in Africa, Europe, and Asia. If those millions were lost behind "the Iron Curtain, our future would indeed be dark," Fulbright asserted. Russia's expansion "already is so great that she threatens the power to survive of all other independent nations except our own."[54]

It was Republican senator Arthur Vandenberg who did the most to forge consensus. "Politics stops at the water's edge," the chair of the Senate Foreign Relations Committee had famously pledged in 1945. Now he told Congress, "If we desert the President of the United States at [this] moment we cease to have any influence in the world forever." Vandenberg had met with the Soviets in a variety of settings since the war and still hoped that Moscow and Washington might "live and let live." He strongly believed, however, that this could only happen if the United States made it "immutably plain that we are the lineal descendents of those rugged old pioneers whose flag bore the motto 'Don't Tread on Me.' " Vandenberg did not relish the hazards to which the new course would expose the nation, he wrote one acquaintance, but, he said, "Our only choice is the lesser of evils." Vandenberg amended the final bill to allow the United Nations to terminate the American program whenever it was prepared to assume responsibility. Vandenberg described this concession as "the greatest act of voluntary allegiance," since it meant the United States would waive its veto power in the UN Security Council. The senator's actions and words convinced a Republican-controlled House and Senate to vote with Democrat Harry Truman.[55]

Indeed, what made the early Cold War unusual was the extraordinary degree of cooperation between Republicans and Democrats. Internationalists of both parties engineered the transition to an interventionist U.S. foreign policy. Ninety-three Republicans voted against the Truman Doctrine, but the majority in both parties voted in favor. "For the record," writers in the *New York Times* observed, "both Houses of Congress have now approved the President's program by larger majorities and with more decisive bipartisan support than they have given to any other major controversial measure in the whole field of American foreign policy since the outbreak of war in Europe."[56]

The Truman Doctrine enjoyed the support of another well-informed constituency besides Congress. A State Department survey of 225 newspapers from around the nation found that 150 of them printed editorials in the week following the president's address expressing mild or strong approval. The greatest number (117) urged acceptance "without partisan debate" and asserted that the nation faced a basic choice: "Assume our place as principal world power or give Moscow a blank check."[57]

The public concurred. Historians have tended to portray Harry Truman as having scared "the hell out of the American people" with his short, untelevised speech. This characterization is so omnipresent that it is featured even in the book *The Complete Idiot's Guide to the Cold War*.[58] Yet this paints the administration as more manipulative, and the public as more gullible, than evidence seems to warrant. Although Republican Arthur Vandenberg advised Truman to speak strongly, Marshall and Acheson both counseled the president to speak in the "frankest terms" but not "provocatively." Specifically, they suggested, "We should avoid accusing the Soviet Union directly." The first draft of Truman's speech contained *eight* references to communism. In the speech he actually gave before Congress, Truman used the term "communist" only *once* and never mentioned the Soviet Union by name. The president's talk was hardly more inflammatory than speeches Roosevelt gave over the four-year period prior to Pearl Harbor, in his less successful attempts to overturn stubborn public opinion. Truman was attempting to lead, not mislead.[59]

Americans were apparently ready to follow. The majority disliked communism intensely and probably endorsed their government's policy for the same reasons that the president proposed it. Gallup polls showed that 75 percent of those questioned had followed the debate on the Truman Doctrine. Identical percentages of Republicans and Democrats (56 percent) supported the bill. A few months later, Gallup asked if Russia should simply be allowed to "control Greece and any other countries she wants to," should material aid prove inadequate to stabilize the region. Nearly 70 percent of the public expressed a willingness to send troops or declare war in cooperation with the UN to prevent further Soviet expansion—even if Russia developed its own atomic bomb, as it was expected to do. Unlike British or French citizens, only 3 to 4 percent of whom ranked foreign policy problems as more important than food and fuel shortages, nearly 50 percent of Americans in

1947 described international security as the "most important problem facing this country."[60] The people had spoken.

It is hard to locate causes for their concern other than in the events themselves and in ongoing press attention to postwar trauma in Europe and Asia, where twelve million men had recently served and nearly half a million had died. The Great Depression and the New Deal also played a role, helping convince Americans that it was the duty of the federal government to intervene in times of extraordinary distress to protect and aid the people. In 1944, *The Nation* proclaimed that "only a New Deal for the world, more far-reaching and consistent than our own faltering New Deal, can prevent the coming of World War III." At the onset of the Cold War, 70 percent of British citizens and 78 percent of Americans told Gallup pollsters they believed Russia wanted to dominate the globe. In 1947, 73 percent of Americans considered another war likely. They intended to prevent it.[61]

Citizens of all stripes also showed a growing willingness to use federal power when states failed in their duties. The founders had created a general government for precisely this purpose. After 1947, this had both internal and external implications. As Gallup interviewers reminded Americans that year, "At present, state governments deal with most crimes committed in their own states." In the case of a lynching, they asked, "Do you think the United States Government should have the right to step in and deal with the crime if the state government doesn't deal with it justly?" Almost 70 percent of the public answered yes, including a majority of Southerners.[62]

Although Americans well understood the distinction between foreign and domestic states, the urgency of postwar problems—which seemed to require someone to assume the role of umpire or enforcer—made this line seem less important than in the past. In 1947, when the entire postwar world appeared to be at stake, Americans showed a new readiness to step across it. They accepted a role that seemed not only necessary but also heroic, as antiwar activist Ron Kovic described in *Born on the Fourth of July*, his memoir of the Vietnam War years.[63] Many rank-and-file Cold Warriors hoped, like Tom Paine, that America really would redeem the world. Their exalted idealism sometimes slipped into disillusionment over national inadequacies and hypocrisies, but it also sustained many through what quickly became a long, murky, and occasionally bloody struggle.

IO

A Coercive Logic

*Or, How America Spread Freedom and Wealth
and Compromised Its Ideals, 1947–1991*

The Truman Doctrine created the basic framework for American foreign relations after 1947. Events cascaded from that moment onward, from a heroic defense of Berlin, to a disastrous war in Vietnam, to the spectacular expansion of the world economy. The two overarching phenomena of the period 1947 to 1991 were the Cold War and global economic integration. They were related, yet separable: the Cold War ended, while economic cooperation grew.

America's new role affected both its international reputation and its domestic identity. It blended elements of realpolitik and idealism that would not have surprised the nation's founders, similarly confronted with what had seemed to them awkward, unpalatable alternatives. U.S. soldiers stood guard and risked their lives around the world, while their worried families carried on without them. Foreign peoples sometimes appreciated and other times resented America's oversize influence. The Cold War was *fought,* embroiling citizens in the violence that is the ultimate recourse of enforcement. Atrocities have accompanied every single war in human history. The United States bore the blame, as it should have, for atrocities on its side—especially those men and women who shouldered the guns and kept the secrets. Considering the fundamental choice made in the Truman Doctrine, it is doubtful that heavy costs could have been avoided. In the poignant words of President Jimmy Carter, the responsibility "was a challenging and, at times, tormenting experience."[1]

Many who benefitted directly from American protection did not share these burdens. Whether citizens or foreigners, they were sometimes the nation's fiercest critics. They enjoyed greater security without personally making the excruciating compromises that—to those responding to emergencies amid the smoke and shriek of conflict—survival seemed to require. Even measures taken within the letter of American and international law occasionally violated the spirit of the Atlantic Charter, the Fourteen Points, the UN Charter, and other idealistic documents underpinning the modern order. The fact was, there was really little way to look good championing a cooperative world system whenever ordinary human beings refused to cooperate, which they often did, whether for bad reasons or good. Americans woke up many days with egg on their face—or worse.

Nevertheless, the world was indeed more secure in the second half of the twentieth century than in the first, and the number of U.S. military personnel on active duty declined from its peak of twelve million in 1945 to two million, on average, between 1974 and 1991.[2]

When the Cold War finally ended, rather unexpectedly and for reasons still under debate, it left behind scars and a steelier federal government (much like the Civil War did). Russians, Europeans, and Americans could all claim some portion of the credit for the peaceful, nonnuclear conclusion. The United States' most important contribution may well have been its willingness to outwait and outspend bolshevism while fostering economic and political alternatives. These alternatives yielded material rewards for Americans and most of their allies during the period from 1947 to 1991.

Economic historians call this era a "Golden Age" and the "Age of Affluence."[3] It saw the dramatic opening of world markets, the unification of Western Europe, and the transformation of Japan into an economic powerhouse. Spectacular growth, as it turned out, happened only in a world without empires and imperialist rivalries, where tariff barriers diminished and states competed without violence. Liberalized trade facilitated the transfer of information and technology, created full employment, and stimulated a baby boom across the globe. Infant mortality fell and life spans lengthened. Between 1950 and 1973, gross domestic product per capita tripled in Germany, Spain, and Austria. GDP in France and Italy grew by 150 percent and more.[4]

Although many of the newest nation-states struggled to enter the ranks of the industrial world, some prospered. Once considered "poorly endowed," Japan was proclaimed an economic "miracle" by 1972, having grown at an annual rate of 8.2 percent in real terms. Within twenty-five years, the Land of the Rising Sun went from abject ruin to full membership in "the rich countries' club." The so-called Asian Tigers transformed themselves, too—specifically, the former colonies of Singapore, Hong Kong, South Korea, and Taiwan. China joined the trend late but made up for lost time once it liberalized its economy after 1979. Using capitalist methods, Chinese communism lifted 300 million citizens out of poverty within two decades. The U.S. economy also did well, expanding 3.9 percent per annum in the same years.[5]

The United States shaped and speeded these trends in the service of its own material interests, but also because of an ideological preference for freer trade access, international arbitration, and political transparency that dated back to the Continental Congress. One method it adopted was to support European integration, despite the competition this would create. The United States worked hard to foster the sense of international trust that the physiocrats believed went hand in hand with robust trade. For more than forty years, Americans paid 25–40 percent of the budget of the United Nations, plus 31 percent of annual UN peacekeeping costs, in addition to their own national military expenditures. The United States granted diplomatic immunity to all visiting dignitaries, welcoming onto its soil international leaders who routinely denounced America and everything it stood for.[6]

Washington did not always turn the other cheek, however. In the words of Lord Ismay, the Indian-born first secretary-general of NATO, the European goal was "to keep the Russians out, the Americans in, and the Germans down."[7] Why did other countries want the Americans "in"? To keep a lid on world problems. But those who coerce suffer consequences along with those who are coerced. After 1947, the United States sometimes played a deeply conservative and even reactionary role, opting for security over progress. This warred with national ideals, altered self-perceptions, and sharpened internal discord. The United States also spent much of its wealth on international defense. This disadvantaged domestic concerns like education and infrastructure.

To achieve the security objectives that it and other nations sought, the American government occasionally acted like a bully. But bullying, as is often the case, was a symptom of weakness. By advocating a democratic international system, it had given away much of the power it could have netted from World War II. As a result, its responsibilities outweighed its powers. Despite Khrushchev's slurs in 1960, other nations were not lackeys or stooges. Weak or strong, they had more independence, choices, and protection than at any other time in world history. They guarded and optimized their autonomy—just as the United States did. Pursuing their own interests, allied and neutral nations often chose to follow the United States, but just as routinely flouted it.[8]

For the most part, this dissension went unchecked, even when it was resented (such as when French president Charles de Gaulle publicly criticized American policy toward Vietnam, or Arab states slapped an oil embargo on the United States because of its support for Israel).[9] But when deviation seemed to have weighty implications for national or world security, the U.S. government resorted to arm-twisting. On these occasions, government officials opted for risky, illegitimate, clandestine, and sometimes heinous meddling as the surest way to influence outcomes, since the United States had no imperial authority to go along with its umperial duties. It also faced a Cold War competitor infamous for underhanded methods, and this prompted retaliation in kind. Secret interventions frequently backfired, however, because of the relative transparency of the U.S. government. Local peoples often resisted as well. Most clandestine fixes did not hold.

In addition to ad hoc interventions, the United States assumed the costs of a permanent security guarantee. For the first time in world history, every nation had a "right" to self-determination, regardless of its ability to defend it. This was easier to legislate than implement. The UN had no physical means to enforce the guarantee, and the United States stepped into the breach. In exchange for allowing American bases on their soil, nations like Japan and Germany could worry correspondingly less about outsize neighbors, like China and Russia. Tiny countries in disputed territories, such as South Korea, Kuwait, and Israel, gained invaluable leverage. Multiple nations accepted U.S. bases because they trusted Americans more than they trusted anyone else to enforce the rules of play that stabilized the world for the second half of the twentieth century.

Fortunately, where U.S. policy became more rigid during these decades, European policy became suppler. Sheltered under America's security umbrella, European countries sometimes took up the banner of idealistic political innovation when the United States dropped it. To an appreciable extent, it was

they, not the descendants of George Washington, who finally led the way out
of the Cold War. When it ended, the last empire folded.

Harry Truman had his hands full. All the patches seemed to come undone at
once. In the spring of 1947, the world appeared poised to collapse. Crop-
killing weather, food shortages bordering on famine, and unrepaired physical
damage across Europe and Asia threatened virtually all the nations so recently freed from Nazi and Japanese occupation. "The patient is sinking
while the doctors deliberate," Secretary of State George Marshall warned in a
radio address in April 1947, a month before Truman signed the congressional
appropriation of aid for Greece and Turkey.[10] Soon thereafter, Marshall proposed a $4 billion program to reconstruct all European countries, many tee-
tering on a new political precipice. As it had just weeks before in the Truman
Doctrine, the administration emphasized humanitarian concerns and the
importance of resuscitating world trade for the benefit of Americans as well
as others. Congress debated the proposal for months while continental leaders made plans for utilizing America's help. Skeptical U.S. congressmen
dubbed the idea of once again saving Europe "Operation Rat-hole."[11]

Then, in March 1948, the Soviet Union engineered a coup d'état in Czechoslovakia against the only popularly elected government in Eastern Europe.
Shortly thereafter, Congress passed the Marshall Plan by the wide margins of
69 to 17 in the Senate and 329 to 74 in the House. Although half of the tax-
phobic Americans polled said they did not wish to pay anything extra to
fund the plan, a remarkable 40 percent said they would reach into their own
pockets to bolster Europe.[12]

Three months later, the Soviet Union blockaded the western sectors of
Berlin to force its former allies to evacuate the city. The Allies had initially
divided the capital of the Third Reich like a pie for the purposes of occupation, pending a final peace treaty. Now the Soviets wanted total control of
the iconic city, located deep in those eastern regions of Germany that Russia
had vanquished at such a high cost. Independently of one another, the
United States and Britain immediately undertook aerial relief flights to help
those sectors of the city under their authority, though they soon coordinated
their efforts. Piloted by Americans, Australians, Britons, New Zealanders,
and South Africans, planes landed in West Berlin every one to five minutes

for nearly a year (June 1948 through May 1949) with millions of tons of coal, food, and other basic supplies.

Geopolitical and humanitarian motivations were tightly fused. Berliners dubbed the American pilots "Candy Bombers" because they dropped small parachutes filled with raisins and sweets for children waiting on the approach to Templehof Airport. Flier Gail Halvorsen spontaneously began the practice to raise the spirits of Berlin's shell-shocked youngsters. Grateful boys and girls called the twenty-seven-year-old American the "Roisnenbomber" and "Onkel Sam." France refused to participate in the airlift to aid Berlin. Perhaps it was easier for those who had defeated Hitler to feel compassion for everyday Germans than it was for those humiliated by him. France diverted its spare transport planes to its own battle in Indochina. French public opinion simply would not support humanitarian aid to the former enemy.[13]

The Soviet Union lifted its blockade in 1949 but repeatedly demanded that the West abandon Berlin. Subsequent presidents endorsed Truman's stand. "We will not retreat one inch from our duty," Dwight Eisenhower announced in the face of renewed Soviet pressure in 1958. Three years later, the Communist government of East Germany built a wall to prevent its citizens from escaping to the Western sectors of the former capital city. As President John F. Kennedy told the encircled residents of West Berlin in 1963, "You live in a defended island of freedom, but your life is part of the main." Sensing Germans' recurrent anxiety and doubt, the president's brother Robert Kennedy gently added, in private, that Germans "must wean themselves from the suspicion that the United States has written off its solemn obligations if a senior American official failed to visit Berlin once a month to reaffirm them."[14] The umpire stood by his call; the Soviets had played foul. The United States would protect West Berlin's right to remain in the game—and guarantee its fundamental survival. Indeed, the United States and its allies kept armed troops in the city's western sector for another thirty years.

The first Berlin crisis also set the stage for yet another amplification of the Truman Doctrine: the U.S. decision to join the North Atlantic Treaty Organization. When five European countries signed a fifty-year defense pact in March 1948, British foreign secretary Ernest Bevin asked for "an immediate pledge of military support by the United States." In light of the Soviet overthrow of Czechoslovakia's government, French minister Georges Bidault advocated even more strongly for U.S. military participation. But President

Truman initially refused. The Pentagon still planned to ship its remaining troops home. Western Europeans would have to defend themselves.[15]

The Berlin airlift prompted a reassessment. Ten months into the Soviet blockade of the city, the Senate approved American participation in NATO, the successor to the Treaty of Brussels, by a vote of eighty-two to thirteen (another landslide and bipartisan vote). The Western European self-defense pact widened in 1949 to include not only the United States but also Canada, Denmark, Iceland, Norway, Portugal, and Italy. Greece and Turkey joined soon thereafter, expanding NATO to fourteen members. Russia retaliated by forming the eight-member Warsaw Pact in 1955. Thus, despite Roosevelt and Truman's initial intentions, the United States left ground forces in Europe after all, where they remained as of this writing.

Although European governments did not relish their dependence on the United States, they preferred it to vulnerability to the Soviets. While urging American involvement, England and France husbanded their own autonomy, strategically yielding and reclaiming it, depending on circumstances. They were not willing to join someone else's empire. Foreign Secretary Bevin limited reliance to the maximum extent feasible because, he said, the United States might otherwise "tell us what we should do." The British people agreed. They reported to Gallup in 1947 that they would rather not accept help if it meant "America will want a say in running Britain's affairs."[16] In 1957, a coalition of nations led by France formed their own European Community to increase self-sufficiency. In 1963, finally confident of his nation's security vis-à-vis Germany, President Charles de Gaulle withdrew French naval ships from the NATO fleet and in 1966 asked the United States to evacuate the eleven air bases it maintained on French soil.

Not all countries had the luxury of declining American assistance, for the simple reason that it was not offered. When funds for South American development dried up after World War II, Brazilian ambassador Oswaldo Aranha advised his successor to use every means possible to secure U.S. aid. "We have no other source of help in a world drained and miserable," he wrote in 1947. "We must knock on this door until it opens like the door to the house of a friend, which it should be." Brazil eventually finagled a small loan, but Latin Americans mostly went away empty-handed as the U.S. Treasury poured billions into postwar Europe.[17] America's economic well-being was tied to Europe's revival, and the peace of the Continent was far more fragile than the mostly stable Western Hemisphere. Latin American governments might sometimes pose problems for their own people but generally not for others.

Asia called next. When North Korea invaded South Korea across the 38th parallel on June 21, 1950, the United States stepped up again. Only six months earlier, Secretary of State Dean Acheson had publicly intimated that Korea was outside the U.S. "defense perimeter." But the North Koreans crossed an exceptionally bright line, violating the explicit postwar rule that no country should be permitted to deprive another of its sovereignty. Here, too, "free peoples" seemed to be "resisting attempted subjugation by armed minorities or outside pressures." South Korea appealed to the UN Security Council, which condemned North Korea in the absence of a Russian veto. (The USSR was then boycotting the UN over its pique on another Cold War issue.) Australia, Belgium, Britain, Canada, Colombia, France, Greece, the Netherlands, New Zealand, Turkey, and Thailand all sent soldiers to repel the Communist troops streaming southward. But the United States organized the effort, paid the bills, and provided 50 percent of all ground troops. It also sustained more battlefield casualties and deaths than any other participant, including South Korea itself.[18]

The three-year war in Korea also prompted adoption of NSC-68, a position paper of the National Security Council that identified the two overarching goals of American policy as developing "a healthy international community" while "containing" the Soviet system. To do this, the United States would have to maintain superior military strength for the indefinite future while minimizing physical confrontations. It must avoid directly challenging the USSR, and "always leave open the possibility of negotiation." This was a "heavy responsibility" with burdensome financial consequences. NSC-68 staked out implementation of the Truman Doctrine for the rest of the century.[19] It also led to development of the hydrogen bomb and sped up a frightening nuclear arms race. "Mutual assured destruction" became the gun that the blocs held to each other's head for the next four decades.

Finally, Truman's fateful reorientation led to the formal adoption of clandestine methods previously eschewed by Americans. Even before the Cold War, the Truman administration had begun discussing the idea of institutionalizing intelligence operations. As OSS director William Donovan pointed out to the president in August 1945, "All major powers except the United States have had for a long time permanent worldwide intelligence services." Only the United States had "no foreign secret intelligence service." A committee charged with discussing solutions further noted, "It appears to have been contrary to national policy to engage in clandestine intelligence or to maintain a foreign espionage system." In contrast, Britain created a spy agency in 1909 to keep up with German snooping, and the Soviets expanded the czar's permanent intelligence system after 1917.[20]

Truman had decided to propose a spy agency even before articulating his transformational doctrine, but the 1947 legislation on Greece and Turkey created a demand for new tools. Truman had not just overreached the Monroe Doctrine. He had revised and broadened it. Truman eliminated Monroe's prohibition against intervention on the other side of the Atlantic and extended the geographical purview of the Roosevelt Corollary, America's promise to curtail "wrong-doing." This had the ancillary effect of weakening FDR's Good Neighbor Policy, as the United States became willing once again to intervene in the domestic affairs of other nations both worldwide and in Latin America. Police duty produced reliance on distasteful police methods. Mechanisms were devised to foil Communist activities in other countries, much as hardened undercover detectives infiltrated domestic crime networks. Six months after Congress approved aid to Greece and Turkey, it passed the National Security Act of 1947, authorizing the Central Intelligence Agency (CIA). Its first planned covert operation—insurrectionist broadcasts aimed at Eastern Europe—was called Project Umpire.[21]

Although the United States adopted realpolitik tactics by creating the CIA, it did so in a curious way. Almost comically, in retrospect, it became the first country to announce its "secret" agency and submit it for a public vote. As stealthy as the CIA was, for six decades it was the most transparent of the international spy agencies that collected intelligence and intervened in the internal affairs of other countries worldwide. Cuba, Czechoslovakia, Poland, the Soviet Union, North Vietnam, and other Communist countries also clandestinely meddled in faraway conflicts, supplying arms, agents, and expertise to nudge events in particular directions that favored one internal faction over another. But with only one exception—Russia—these were all surreptitious bullies, not empires. Interventions tended to be short-term and case specific. To some degree, newly minted UN prohibitions against overt aggression and annexation may actually have promoted unprecedented efforts to influence events on the sly.[22]

Other democracies engaged in similar practices, reflecting the extent to which many feared for their security during the Cold War. They were nearly as nontransparent as their Communist rivals. The United Kingdom did not openly acknowledge or legislatively authorize MI-6, the British Secret Intelligence Service (SIS), until 1994. Forty years after Sir Ian Fleming began scribbling the fictional exploits of an MI-6 agent with a "license to kill," James Bond finally came out of the closet. In 1994, Britain officially permitted acts outside the country that were normally illegal (like murder), if authorized by the director of SIS. Australia also began a spy agency during the early Cold War, in 1952. However, it was not until 2001 that the relatively candid democracy Down Under acknowledged its intelligence agency and submitted it for legislation. Tales of the CIA abounded throughout the Cold War partly because it was the only intelligence agency subject to legislative scrutiny or public discussion. It remains the only such agency (of which the author is aware) bound by a Freedom of Information Act.[23]

CIA transparency had continuing repercussions for popular and scholarly understandings of covert operations, or "dirty tricks." More easily researched than other nations' secret agencies, the CIA and its iconic role were often overestimated, though comparisons will remain speculative until hard data are released worldwide. Nonetheless, CIA activities were the most visible portion of a large iceberg formed from international waters. Its first major venture, the 1953 intervention in Iran, illustrates the confusing illusion of CIA omnipotence—sustained partly by a long Hollywood tradition of spy movies in which jaded American operatives lurk behind every lamppost.

The conflict in Iran began over oil. Although the United States was self-sufficient in petroleum for much of the century, exploration and drilling became important foreign investments for private American companies early on. Between 1938 and 1950, government policy toward these investments underwent a series of important changes. In 1938, Mexico nationalized its oil fields amid bitter labor strikes, seizing the assets of British and American companies that had invested considerable sums. Franklin Roosevelt had no wish to tangle with Mexico over a matter that touched on its sovereignty, especially within the context of his Good Neighbor Policy and the looming world war. Although Mexico eventually provided some compensation to the oil companies, the event provided a harsh lesson about financial vulnerability. In 1943, Venezuela seemed poised to do the same, but this time industry executives and the U.S. State Department worked closely with the local government to achieve a compromise and forestall economic losses. All parties agreed to the "fifty-fifty" principle: after operating costs, net profits would be divided equally between Venezuela and the U.S. companies. Scholar

Daniel Yergin calls the contract "a landmark event in the history of the oil industry."[24]

World War II, as we have seen, fueled nationalism and decolonization. Afterward, American oil companies found they needed to appease new patriotic impulses in the Middle East as well. The State Department applauded these moves, which resulted in revised agreements between the Saudi monarchy and the Arabian-American Oil Company. Essentially, the fifty-fifty principle was transplanted from the New World to the Old. "The Saudis knew the Venezuelans were getting 50/50," the U.S. assistant secretary of state for near eastern affairs later commented. "Why wouldn't they want it too?" The corporation began splitting the proceeds in 1950, and the American government sweetened the bitter pill for the companies by reducing their income taxes at home. Corporate profits and international amity were preserved, and Saudi revenues nearly tripled. The only losers were the U.S. Treasury (whose receipts from domestic oil corporations declined by $37 million the first year alone) and American taxpayers, who made up the difference.[25]

Not surprisingly, nearby Iran wanted the same deal. There, however, the concession holder was a British company, the Anglo-Iranian Oil Company (today's British Petroleum, or BP). Anglo-Iranian was the oldest of the foreign companies invested in the Middle East, invited there in 1900 by a Persian entrepreneur seeking riches in the foothills of the dirt-poor former empire. From the time of the first oil strike in 1909, up until 1949, the company paid Iran 16 percent of annual profits. This was a fabulous arrangement for Great Britain. The company represented the United Kingdom's largest single foreign investment. By the late 1940s, at a time of real privation in Britain, Anglo-Iranian was bringing in 100 million pounds sterling per year, as well as enormous quantities of fuel.

Unsurprisingly, the company's owners were reluctant to offer the kind of contract that Iranians now wanted. They instead offered a "supplemental agreement" in 1949 that increased profit sharing, but not to the 50 percent level that American oil companies were granting their partners. The Iranian National Front, a minor political faction drawn mostly from the urban middle class, began organizing. Its foremost spokesman was parliament member Mohammad Mosaddeq, who advocated the outright nationalization of oil production. It was a popular position in a nationalistic debate, but fraught with challenges in an industry requiring significant resources and technical expertise. British officials refused to budge. The Iranians could accept the supplemental agreement or not.[26]

When the English complained to Americans about Iranian intransigence, State Department experts encouraged the company to make a better offer. In their view, the industry needed to recognize Iran's legitimate demands and respond realistically. U.S. officials urged British officils to push the private corporation toward a more reasonable posture. Yet Anglo-Iranian Oil remained obstinate, rejecting a simple fifty-fifty split on profits until the negotiations became so convoluted and contentious that it was hard to achieve any agreement whatsoever. According to one scholar, the British "always seemed one concession short of a final settlement, especially in the early years of the controversy."[27]

Mosaddeq's controversial proposal gathered steam, but Iran's constitutional monarchy became more precarious as well. A religious group that favored nationalization, Fedayan Islam, assassinated the Iranian prime minister to forestall compromise with Britain. Widespread rejoicing and open praise of the murder by some attested to the decline of political civility in the fledgling democracy.[28] In May 1951, the Majles (Iranian parliament) passed Mosaddeq's bill nationalizing the petroleum industry without compensating Anglo-Iranian Oil, and Mosaddeq became prime minister shortly thereafter. The United Kingdom responded with a boycott of Iranian oil.

Without its obnoxious but best customer, Iran's economy faltered. The Persians had little economic leverage, for oil supplies then well exceeded world demand. Although Iran cut its price for petroleum, revenue still declined. Strikes ensued. Mosaddeq left power, regained power, and eventually moved to dismiss the Majles, which became increasingly factionalized. The parliament frequently lacked a quorum and sometimes erupted in fistfights. Nationalism, religious extremism, and Britain's unfair, paternalistic handling of Iran's understandable demands escalated the crisis. When British officials pointed out that the shutdown of the oil industry was bad for Iran's economy, the passionate Mosaddeq dismissed such considerations as unworthy of a patriot. Like the English, Iranians did not want outsiders telling them what to do. "It would be better for Iran to be rid of all foreign influence," Mosaddeq asserted, "even if disorder and communism follow."[29]

The United States tried doggedly to broker Anglo-Iranian cooperation in order to stabilize the Middle Eastern country. Both parties appealed to the United States to take their side in the controversy. America supported "the right of sovereign states to nationalize," in Secretary of State Dean Acheson's words, provided they made "just compensation." It had taken the same position in Mexico not long before—and would take the same position vis-à-vis the Suez Canal in 1956. U.S. officials privately deplored British intransigence. "Never had so few," Dean Acheson later complained, "lost so much so stupidly and so fast."[30]

The Truman administration found its power to arbitrate a solution frustrated by the prejudices and stubbornness of both disputants. International constraints further complicated matters. Iran bordered the Soviet Union. If it became much weaker, it could fall into the Communist orbit. Russia had tried to split off Azerbaijan only a few years earlier. Iran's oil fields heightened its desirability as a prize. A small coterie of British officials sympathized with Mosaddeq's patriotism and considered covert intervention unethical, at least in normal times. But even those inclined to dismiss self-serving oil company complaints worried that Iran might be lost to the Soviet sphere. Historian Roger Louis observes that, among the British, "there existed a virtual consensus within government circles that covert action was politically necessary and morally justified" because of the Communist threat.[31] The Truman administration sympathized with Iranian nationalism, but it also needed Britain's support in the Korean War. Once again, there were few good options.

Even though it was a messy situation in a faraway country, American officials kept trying to solve the problem, lest it get worse. The Truman Doctrine created a role they felt bound to fulfill. Gradually forced by escalating events to pick a side, the umpire started leaning toward the team it knew better. The English also presented their case more adroitly than the Iranians. British officials skillfully maneuvered their U.S. counterparts into becoming ever more involved. Prime Minister Mosaddeq was resourceful, but elderly and idiosyncratic. He sometimes received diplomatic visitors in his pajamas, worked from his bed, and wept openly when moved, raising red flags about his mental state. Meanwhile, powerful domestic rivals in Iran gathered strength, including the ambitious local Communist Party, the Tudeh, which looked to the Soviet Union with admiration. Relations between Iran and Britain hit an all-time low when Harry Truman retired and went home to Independence, Missouri, in 1953. The four-year crisis showed no signs of abating.[32]

The Eisenhower administration reached decisively for the intelligence tools forged by Truman. As commander of the 1945 landing in Normandy and the first chief of NATO, General Dwight D. Eisenhower had a greater appreciation than the Missouri civilian for low-intensity, low-cost methods of conflict resolution. The military man was also more willing to move preemptively to solve problems that, in his judgment, threatened to knock the West off its vertiginous tightrope duel with the Soviets. Within weeks of taking office, the Eisenhower administration approved covert participation in a plan long advocated by the British secret service, though consistently resisted by Truman. The CIA would amplify existing unrest by paying for large street demonstrations and encouraging Iranians already working against Mosaddeq.[33]

It was a simple, low-tech approach, but it worked. The Americans and British both knew that if you pushed on a weak government there was a reasonable chance it would fall. They hoped that a better government would take its place. Casualties in Iran did not approach those risked by conventional or nuclear war. Indeed, after three days of street fighting that killed 300 people, army opponents assumed power and arrested the prime minister. The shah appointed a new one. In Mary Ann Heiss's concise formulation, the embattled Mosaddeq "was toppled from his place as the head of the Iranian government by a coalition of domestic dissidents working in partnership with covert operatives within the British and U.S. governments." Roger Louis explains that Mosaddeq's expulsion of the British embassy in October 1952 forced MI-6 to hand the final dirty work to the CIA, but that "the plan to destroy the Mosaddeq government was British in inspiration, British in the covert financial assistance provided to Mosaddeq's enemies, and British in the actual attempts to replace him." Less legitimate than internal opponents, and less secretive than MI-6, the CIA took the rap.[34]

Yet choosing sides in an another country's internal affairs almost always created new problems, as the United States experienced in Guatemala the next year. There, leaning on a reformist government that was favorable toward communism resulted in a series of military dictatorships for more than thirty years, each worse than the next. Covert intervention might upend a weak regime, but it could neither create nor control an effective replacement. Puppets were not really puppets: they had minds, interests, and weapons of their own. Over the years, scholars have increasingly concluded that use of the CIA in both Iran and Guatemala was prompted almost entirely by the strategic assessment that weak governments created opportunities for either the Soviet Union or local Communists to take power, not by economic interest. But covert operations flatly contradicted the trend toward greater transparency, thus enraging both Americans and foreign nationals when they eventually learned of the operations. Intervention was cheap in the short run and expensive in the long run. It also flagrantly violated America's claim to support national self-determination and local sovereignty.[35]

CIA actions can be understood only in a context that is still being clarified. To this day, we know less about British manipulations than American actions. In accordance with its sovereign policy, the United Kingdom has released no documents on the Iranian operation. Almost everything we know about the British role comes from declassified CIA documents.[36] Iran itself is mostly inaccessible to foreign researchers, but Persian historian Fakhreddin Azimi shows that scheming royals, clerical opponents, Anglophilic elites, and opportunists in Mosaddeq's own party did much to unseat the elected prime minister, for their own reasons. "No prime minister faced as much protracted domestic and foreign opposition as Mohammad Mosaddeq, and none lasted as long," Azimi points out. British and American measures would not "have proved effective without concerted Iranian collaboration." Had the SIS and CIA waited, as the shah repeatedly advised, Mosaddeq might have fallen anyway. Domestic opponents in Iran were already conspiring toward the same end, including some inclined to assassination. Whatever they might have done would have been on their heads, as unremarkable in historical retrospect as any number of sad coups that have foiled democratic moments around the world.[37]

After Mosaddeq's arrest, Iran won a new oil agreement based on a fifty-fifty profit split. In the final outcome, Iran achieved all of its economic demands. Ironically, one unintended consequence of Britain's intransigence was that it lost its commanding position in the Persian oil industry. The Iranians no longer wanted to deal solely with British companies and so, since they still wanted Western capital and expertise, they gave the business to a consortium of foreign companies to dilute British participation. Of the profits and opportunities that went to foreign investors, British investors ended up with only 40 percent, U.S. oil companies 40 percent, the Dutch 14 percent, and the French 6 percent.[38] Americans definitely received a significant share of profits—along with Europeans—though this occurred only after a prolonged period in which the U.S. government held out against British requests for intervention.

Money isn't everything, however. The political consequences were toxic for all involved. To counter domestic opponents and keep an eye on the SIS, CIA, and Soviet spies also operating in the country, the shah created a secret police force in 1957 that became infamous for its brutality. Meanwhile, the Russian intelligence arm, the KGB, spread rumors and forged documents to make it seem that America continued to plot the local government's overthrow. The Persian monarch never fully trusted the ally that had enhanced his power.[39]

Weapons like covert intervention enjoyed a half-life akin to plutonium's. The USSR failed to gain control of Iran, but religious extremists who had heard of the CIA role in the 1953 coup eventually did. To accomplish its objectives, the United States employed traditional expedients that great powers had used since 1648. They cost America much of the moral high ground it had won in World War II. To some, including its most idealistic citizens, covert intervention made the Land of the Free little better than the Soviet Union. Extremely few, however, were willing to vote with their feet and migrate from the former to the latter. Indeed, America continued to attract people from around the globe for the freedom, security, and wealth it offered its diverse citizenry.

Although CIA activities gave the United States a black eye, it was in Vietnam that America received its worst pummeling. There, decolonization, the Cold War, and American determination to control events created a truly toxic mix. Historians have long argued over which president bears greatest responsibility for U.S. entanglement in Vietnam. Some take President Truman as their starting point, emphasizing his coddling of France and refusal to grant recognition to Ho Chi Minh. Others start the narrative with Dwight Eisenhower, who condoned Vietnam's division into two competing countries in 1956. Yet others focus on Lyndon Johnson, who allowed America to be sucked into a quagmire that they think John Kennedy might have avoided. These debates are important, but to some extent they skirt the larger reality.

There were five Vietnam presidents. Whether Republican or Democrat— whether from Massachusetts, Missouri, or California—five chief executives with widely differing life experiences felt compelled, against their own personal inclinations, to fight Communism with a capital C in Indochina. The dynamics of the Cold War imprisoned them all in its compelling and coercive logic. Americans had seen Hitler conquer all of Europe in a matter of weeks, and Stalin dominate half of Europe in a matter of months. It had cost millions of lives and billions of dollars to expel the former. The Truman Doctrine pledged Americans to hold the line against further advances. Every place that this line was drawn became a nuclear-powered test of will. The nation that steeled every nerve to sustain Western enclaves in Berlin and on the Korean Peninsula was hardly going to let go of South Vietnam, which seemed an obvious parallel (even if it was not—as few things are in history). The effort appeared worthwhile when it succeeded, as it did in Germany and South Korea, but foolish and corrupt when it did not, as in Vietnam.

The United States initially found itself pressed to take sides in a distant dispute between indigenous nationalists and a European colonial power. Prior to 1945, this seemed an easy choice between right and wrong. Roosevelt had made clear his support for Indochinese independence. Although escalating enmity between Russia and America soon complicated the matter, the Truman administration did little to privilege one side over the other before 1950. In that year, the Korean War gave France new leverage. It allowed France to make the point that, in the words of General Jean de Lattre, "if Korea and Indochina [were] part of the same war, then the United States should be willing to fund the French effort." Communists had won the civil war in China the year before and were now poised to do the same in Korea and Southeast Asia. French officials argued that their triumph in Indochina would stem the advance of communism in Asia.[40]

The Korean War also gave Paris new importance in the struggle to sustain a credible deterrent against the Soviets in Europe. NATO found its slender resources considerably strained as troops were diverted to the fight in Asia. The United States and United Kingdom proposed rearming Western Germany, admitting it to NATO, and adding German troops to the equation. Still deeply suspicious of its ancient enemy, France initially opposed the plan. Indochina led it to offer a quid pro quo. If France regained its empire, it would have less to fear from "the Boche." As Kathryn Statler shows, the French government came to view Germany as the key to extracting American cooperation. Its efforts "to coax the United States into seeing the French cause in Indochina as an allied one were deliberate and long-standing." The strategy worked. The United States assumed the financial responsibility for France's colonial war from 1950 to 1954, while France allowed the negotiations over Germany to move forward. Eventually, a rearmed West Germany joined NATO in 1955.[41]

France was unable to prevail militarily, however. The Viet Minh won a signal victory at Dien Bien Phu in 1954, capturing and imprisoning more than 11,000 regular French troops and Foreign Legionnaires.[42] International negotiations in Switzerland established three states out of the multiethnic territory previously known as French Indochina: Cambodia, Laos, and Vietnam. In Vietnam, the so-called Geneva Accords temporarily divided the nation. On the advice of his Chinese allies, Ho Chi Minh agreed to a time-limited, administrative division of Vietnam at the 17th parallel until local elections could take place, after which the nation would be reunified under an elected government. Shortly after the Geneva Conference, however, indigenous opponents of Ho Chi Minh formed a permanent government in the south and refused to hold the promised elections.

By this time, not long after the armistice in Korea, the United States had come to view Vietnam as part of its own larger strategy of containing communism. President Eisenhower cultivated and encouraged Ngo Dinh Diem, the new, anti-Communist president of South Vietnam. But Diem failed to develop a popular following and came to rely almost entirely on American resources to stay in power. To prevent South Vietnam from becoming the leading "domino" in a series of Southeast Asian states that might fall to communism, the United States committed itself to stabilizing a corrupt, increasingly despised southern government.

From 1954 to 1965, under Eisenhower and Kennedy, American support was primarily financial and advisory. But full-scale military involvement ensued when President Lyndon Johnson concluded that nothing short of bombing North Vietnam would prevent reunification of the two halves of the country under Communist leadership. As one analyst for the U.S. Department of Defense apportioned American interests in March 1965, 70 percent of the reason to send regular troops was to avoid a "humiliating defeat" that might catastrophically damage "our reputation as a guarantor." Many officials believed that the United States could not afford to back down, lest its authority—and the believability of its deterrent power—come into question in a location even more explosive, such as Berlin. A 1965 Gallup poll found that the overwhelming majority of Americans (70 percent) agreed war was necessary, as did the next president, Richard Nixon. In 1970 he told the American public that in the tense global contest against communism— where readiness to retaliate helped avoid the need to retaliate—the country could not afford to be perceived as a "pitiful, helpless giant."[43]

Tragically, the Vietnamese people endured yet another full-scale war as a result, this one far bloodier than the battle against the French. The United

States unleashed its firepower on the southern half of the divided nation, trying to quell domestic insurgents (dubbed the Viet Cong) and cut off regular troops infiltrating from the nation-state of North Vietnam. Fearing that China would invade southward if U.S. infantry troops marched into North Vietnam itself, as had occurred in North Korea, America found itself in the absurd and horrific position of fighting among a vulnerable civilian population while trying to keep it loyal to the Western bloc. The South Vietnamese government, its ostensible ally, also proved difficult to manipulate, especially once the Nixon administration worked its way to the peace table. More than 58,000 American soldiers died in what became the country's worst and longest war between 1945 and 1991. The majority of Americans eventually became convinced that intervention had been a mistake. Their European allies fully agreed.[44]

The Vietnam War ended for the United States in 1973, when America agreed to withdraw, though internal conflict continued in Indochina. The regular army of North Vietnam finally crossed the 17th parallel in 1975, overthrew the government of South Vietnam, and reunified the country. Although the elderly Ho Chi Minh had died of natural causes in 1969, his government had triumphed. The navy of the defeated Republic of Vietnam loaded 30,000 sailors and their families onto its thirty-five ships and sailed to the Philippines.[45] Refugees on foot and in small, private boats poured into surrounding countries. Approximately one million eventually immigrated to the United States. They were the luckier ones. More than four million Vietnamese out of a population of thirty-eight million had perished in the war and its aftermath. In contrast with its previous generosity toward defeated Germany and Japan, the United States refused even to extend diplomatic relations to Vietnam for twenty years after the conflict. Like the French in relation to Germany, defeated Americans found compassion, grace, and humility in short supply.[46]

War on their borders also destabilized neighboring Laos and Cambodia, both of which had fragile postcolonial governments. U.S. bombers covertly crossed into their territories in an attempt to cut off Vietnamese supply lines. These attacks made the local governments look incompetent to defend their national interests. In Cambodia, a leftist coup sent Prince Norodom Sihanouk into exile. The new regime, known as the Khmer Rouge, instituted a "reform" that killed more one million civilians who were deemed counterrevolutionary—some simply because they wore eyeglasses that made them look educated.

Mass terror came to a halt only when Communist Vietnam toppled Communist Cambodia.

The war destabilized the United States, too. By 1974, American public opinion had gone beyond disgusted. President Nixon was forced to resign over his clandestine harassment of domestic opponents who criticized the war. The Senate and House of Representatives both undertook sensational exposés of CIA interventions in Cuba, Chile, Congo, the Dominican Republic, and elsewhere. Congressional hearings aired the nation's sordid doings and the Government Printing Office made transcripts available to all buyers, foreign and domestic. Americans and many others were now ready to heap blame on the United States government for the fall of every leftist regime in the world and the existence of every right-wing one—often in perfect ignorance of local conditions and the covert maneuvers of other governments. Chilean historian Joaquín Fermandois later identified this as the myth that the "CIA did it all." Journalist Michael Lind observes that by the mid-1970s "a majority of Americans surveyed opposed sending U.S. troops to defend any ally from invasion—with the sole exception of Canada."[47]

Nixon's administration was not as out of sync with American public opinion as might be suggested by its escalation of the conflict in Indochina. In 1969, the president had optimistically pronounced what pundits immediately dubbed the Nixon Doctrine: "as far as the problems of military defense, except for the threat of a major power involving nuclear weapons, the United States is going to encourage and has the right to expect that this problem will be handled by, and responsibility for it taken by, Asian nations themselves." Nixon subsequently extended the challenge to other regions of the world. No one else picked up the burden, however, nor did Nixon ever really put it down.[48]

A few years later, the German ambassador to the United States suggested to Secretary of State Henry Kissinger that perhaps America and Russia should consider mutual troop withdrawals in central Europe. In reply, the German-born Kissinger bluntly observed that if the United States and USSR diminished their forces, the Americans would retreat thousands of miles, while the Soviets would move only a few hundred. As the record of their conversation reads: "If the German Foreign Office talks about troop withdrawals, Mr. Kissinger continued, U.S. public opinion—and the U.S. Senate—will be encouraged to call for them. Europeans should remember that when they make proposals, we may accept them. Ambassador Pauls hurriedly said that he was not [actually] proposing mutual withdrawals but simply thought that they could be discussed."[49]

As Kissinger knew, Americans were tiring of their burden, and had begun to wonder if it was really a necessary one or merely self-imposed. The war in Vietnam had weakened national identity, slashed faith in government, and prompted most Americans to question why *they*, in particular, "had" to keep intervening in causes that few understood very clearly. Some rabid patriots became rabid critics. Both postures were understandable, given the pressures, but neither was helpful. Former defense secretary Robert McNamara perhaps best summarized the common conclusion about Vietnam when he eventually admitted, "We were wrong, terribly wrong."[50]

Nonetheless, the Truman Doctrine remained the warp and woof of national policy and international expectations even after the war in Southeast Asia. Through the 1980s, whenever a true international emergency arose, eyes turned round the world to see what the United States would do. A muddled combination of volunteering and being volunteered by others drove decision making. The first Gulf War was a good example. When Iraq invaded Kuwait in August 1990 to force its tiny neighbor to relinquish sovereignty, Iraq's leader, Saddam Hussein, violated the Charter of the United Nations more explicitly than any leader had since Hitler in 1941. Hussein renamed the neighboring kingdom the "Nineteenth Province" of Iraq. The UN Security Council voted fourteen to zero the very next day to condemn the cross-border invasion and demand Iraq's withdrawal. The problem was, however, the UN had no military forces, only peacekeepers who monitored treaties *after* parties in conflict agreed to cease fighting.

Like previous British prime ministers, Margaret Thatcher made plain to President George H. W. Bush that it was incumbent upon the United States to act coercively, before Kuwait ceased to exist. Bush agreed. Within a week, he announced deployment of American troops to rescue a nation with which the United States did not even have a defense treaty. Nigerian scholar Ugboaja Ohaegbulam blandly observes that the president's "next task" was mobilizing "the UN Security Council to adopt resolutions to force Iraq from Kuwait" and building "a worldwide coalition, including members of the Arab League." Interventions that would have been unbelievable to the founders had become routine "tasks."[51]

The key Arab League member was King Fahd of Saudi Arabia, who told another senior member of his royal family that he was convinced Hussein wanted "to own all the Arab Gulf countries." When the U.S. defense secretary, Dick Cheney, asked the king if he desired American protection, Fahd Al Saud debated it briefly with his advisors and then answered Cheney simply, in English, "Yes." Dozens of nations sent men, money, and materiel to repel Iraq, but the United States carried most of the burden. Americans provided the vast majority of tanks and airplanes (the most expensive pieces of hardware), and flew 84 percent of all combat sorties. Almost half a million U.S. soldiers served in what was called Operation Desert Storm—representing more than two-thirds of all foreign troops. This was a greater percentage than even during the 1950–1953 conflict in Korea. It was as if America's global responsibility had grown rather than declined over the decades (or the military capability of its allies had atrophied).[52]

Fortunately, the Cold War eventually came to an end. This momentous development, unforeseen until almost the last minute, finally seemed to offer the opportunity of reevaluating President Truman's historic pledge. Perhaps the United States would not have to police the world forever. The umpire might retire.

One consequence of the United States' sometimes occupying the moral low ground during the tough decades from 1947 to 1991 was that this allowed the Western allies to take the high ground. They sometimes used it very well. As Czech immigrant Vojtech Mastny observed in 1985, "Bearing the brunt of the East-West military competition, the United States has been more preoccupied than its allies with the balance sheet of troops and weapons."[53] This meant that Western Europeans had greater freedom to act as doves because Americans were willing to play hawk. In 1975, the allies outpaced the United States on a new agreement with the Soviet Union, which they prodded Washington to accept. The Helsinki Accords did not bring the Cold War to an end, but they proved an essential step in that direction. They also exposed the role that the new world order allowed weaker nations to play, as public opinion forums assumed an importance as real as military prowess.

Following Stalin's death in 1953, Russia had periodically called for a pan-European conference to bring World War II "to a formal conclusion" by recognizing the territorial and political divides that became fixed after 1945.[54] These accomplished facts included the permanent division of Germany into two nations, single-party Communist regimes across Eastern Europe, and the USSR's outright incorporation of Latvia, Lithuania, and Estonia. Although Moscow had a secure military grip on the region, it hankered after legitimacy, believing that outside acknowledgment would secure Soviet control. Naturally, the USSR did not want the United States invited to the conference. Equally unsurprising, the United States and its allies had little interest in a peace accord that excluded Europe's primary defender, or that legitimized the Soviet Union's post-Yalta machinations.

The impasse began softening in 1969. Both sides became more interested in détente, or what the new West German chancellor, Willy Brandt, called *Neue Ostpolitik.* Having been hunted by the Nazis during World War II, Brandt was a stalwart champion of Germany's postwar democratization and improved relations with all the countries of Europe. His "New Eastern Policy" led to controversial treaties with the USSR and Poland that finalized Germany's loss of territory to those countries in World War II. In effect Brandt made a separate peace, to resolve the outstanding issues between West Germany and its eastern neighbors and pave the way for normal relations. At the same time, he effectively reduced Poland's long-term dependence on Russia. If Germany no longer hankered for territory east of the Oder-Neisse line, Poland had less need of a Soviet big brother to defend those contested lands. Like the French, Poles retained an understandable fear of German nationalism.

In March 1969 the Warsaw Pact issued yet another "Appeal to All European Countries" for a general conference aimed at reaching a multilateral agreement. This time, the foreign ministers of NATO communicated their willingness to entertain negotiations if the United States and Canada were included. Finland, which belonged to neither NATO nor the Warsaw Pact, was in the best position to broker a compromise, having walked a fine line between the blocs for twenty years. As one Finnish official described this, "No country, not even the United States, acts without thinking about what others will think. A small country must think even more."[55]

In April 1969, Finland boldly took the initiative to make something happen, illuminating the role that militarily unimportant nations could play in the democratic post–World War II order. (That same year Ireland sponsored the Nuclear Non-Proliferation Treaty, eventually signed by 190 countries.) The neutral Nordic nation, population four million, delivered diplomatic notes to thirty-two European states, plus the United States and Canada, inviting them to Helsinki for preparatory talks.

The Conference on Security and Co-operation in Europe (CSCE) met for two laborious years in the petite Finnish capital. In writing the so-called the Final Act, Western Europeans took the initiative to fill "Three Baskets" (a neutral term proposed by the Swiss delegation) with mutually acceptable rulings. No one articulated the conference goals in precisely these terms, but arbitration, access, and transparency defined the negotiations. Basket One of the Final Act arbitrated the political provisions long sought by the Soviet Union. It declared Europe's post–World War II borders permanent and inviolable, and, at Norway's suggestion, all parties agreed to notify one another well in advance of "major military manoeuvres" to avert potential clashes. In the words of John Maresca, deputy head of the U.S. delegation, Basket One enshrined "the geopolitical status quo in Europe." It was "the first such general and agreed pronouncement of the frontiers of states throughout Europe since the Versailles Treaty in 1919."[56]

The second set of agreements, Basket Two, contained economic provisions that lowered trade barriers and allowed the Soviet Union freer access to Western technology and goods. For decades following World War II, the Western allies, including Japan, had closely coordinated with one another to avoid exporting new types of equipment that might advance Soviet military capabilities—despite the loss of revenue this represented. As a consequence, the Soviet Union was so technologically behind that, as late as the 1980s, the entire city of Moscow was able to receive only sixteen long-distance telephone calls at a time. Signatories at Helsinki agreed to relax business transactions and make scientific research more transparent in order to facilitate international trade.[57]

European negotiators used Baskets One and Two to entice Soviet negotiators to accept Basket Three—the one that best reflected Western objectives. Among other concessions, Basket Three contained promises to allow freer political expression within the Soviet Union and to ease restrictions on citizens' travel to other countries. Austria, the Continent's foremost haven for political refugees, introduced the debate on human rights that led to Basket Three. Italy reminded conferees that, post–World War II, sovereign governments could not simply trump the rights of individuals.[58] For the first time, the Soviet Union signed an accord that specifically incorporated the 1948 Universal Declaration of Human Rights. The Communist dictatorship went on record endorsing the notion that individual rights ranked above states' rights. Had he been alive, Thomas Jefferson may have applauded.

Basket Three contained precisely the sorts of ideals long advanced by the
United States, from the Declaration of Independence to the Atlantic Charter.
Yet Presidents Richard Nixon and Gerald Ford, along with hawkish Secretary of State Henry Kissinger, showed little enthusiasm for the Helsinki negotiations. Neither the Americans nor the Russians for that matter believed
that the USSR would do anything more than pay lip service to human rights.
As Russia proclaimed in the 1968 Brezhnev Doctrine (used to justify invad-
ing Czechoslovakia to prevent liberalization), the Soviet Union and its partners had *already* built "a society free from all oppression and exploitation."[59]
A former Jewish refugee from Nazi Germany, Kissinger fervently believed
that the Western Europeans' willingness to concede the post-1945 Soviet fait
accompli was callow grandstanding. America could have gotten empty concessions on human rights years earlier "if we had been willing to go as far as
this," he complained to Helmut Sonnenfeldt, an advisor on Soviet affairs. "I
have always said that the only question is which European will sell out first,"
the dismayed secretary of state added. Some egotistical allies simply enjoyed
thumbing their noses at America, he was convinced. "They can write it [the
treaty] in Swahili for all I care. . . . The Conference can never end up with a
meaningful document."[60]

The United States was thus one of the more reluctant recruits to the so-
called Spirit of Helsinki. President Gerald Ford even considered boycotting
the meeting called in Finland to sign the Final Act. U.S. citizens across the
political spectrum also rejected what they saw as window dressing on Soviet
abuses. Ford's harshest domestic critics claimed the agreement formally
ceded Eastern Europe to the USSR in exchange for flimsy, nonbinding vows.
The Helsinki Final Act was not even a formal treaty, merely a statement of
principles. (Its Finnish sponsors might well have paraphrased Churchill: Helsinki was not a law but a star.) Once again, American fears were bipartisan.
The conservative *Wall Street Journal* ran the headline, "Jerry, Don't Go,"
while liberal AFL-CIO president George Meaney provocatively invited Ford
to attend a public dinner honoring the famous Soviet dissident Aleksandr
Solzhenitsyn. The president declined.[61]

The Ford administration was not merely reluctant to legitimate the Iron
Curtain. Secretary of State Kissinger feared that the Helsinki talks might
endanger the overriding goal of détente: to slow the nuclear arms race by re-
assuring paranoid Soviets that the United States was prepared to coexist
peacefully. This included granting the USSR its sovereign right to maintain a

totalitarian system within its own borders. Kissinger candidly acknowledged that domestic human rights in Russia were a sacrifice on the altar of nuclear de-escalation. Until Helsinki, "The necessity of shifting from confrontation toward negotiation seemed so overwhelming that goals beyond the settlement of international disputes were never raised," Kissinger pointed out. "But now progress has been made—and already taken for granted. We are engaged in intense debate on whether we should make changes in Soviet society a precondition for further progress [on easing the Cold War]. . . . This is a genuine moral dilemma."[62]

In a world of bad choices, U.S. policymakers were committed to what they saw as the unpopular but necessary one. This option also had an ancient pedigree: the Treaty of Westphalia, or, *cuius regio, eius religio*. In Richard Nixon and Soviet leader Leonid Brezhnev's landmark summit in May 1972, they avoided any mention of human rights in their joint statement on "Basic Principles" for U.S.-USSR relations. Lesser conflicts were best ignored. The Soviets had the right to determine the "religion" of their region, regardless of how God-forsaken communism might seem to Westerners. In exchange for Basket Three—something inadvisable to ask for and impossible to enforce—the conferees at Helsinki now seemed to be handing Eastern Europe to the Soviets permanently.

Nonetheless, acquiescing to Western European desires, American policymakers eventually came on board. With the Helsinki Final Act of 1975 all signatories pledged to respect human rights, including "freedom of thought, conscience, religion or belief." Kissinger even played a role in getting the USSR to agree that while post-1945 borders were inviolable, they could be changed "by peaceful means and by agreement." (This modification allowed for approval of the act by all parties, and eventually paved the way for the wholly unexpected, but voluntary reunification of Germany under democratic, capitalist government in 1990.) The Ford administration's only act of rebellion against the consensus was to issue a public statement reiterating its continuing nonrecognition of Estonia, Latvia, and Lithuania as provinces of the Soviet Union rather than independent nations. Congress expressed its position by acknowledging the sixty-fifth anniversary of "Lithuanian Independence" (post–World War I) in February 1983.[63]

It was an ironic twist. In the Helsinki negotiations, European and American leaders swapped places. At the start of the twentieth century, presidents like Woodrow Wilson and Franklin D. Roosevelt were renowned—and sometimes lampooned—for their starry-eyed leadership. At Helsinki, it was Western Europeans who lit the way with their optimism and Americans who turned a gimlet eye on the route forward. As Vojtech Mastny asserts, "Henry Kissinger, America's first foreign-born secretary of state, injected into the U.S. policy his particular brand of European realpolitik. . . . And the West Europeans appropriated to themselves something of the American predilection for high-sounding but ineffectual phrases about peace and international cooperation."[64]

It is arguable which choice was more idealistic: to save the world from nuclear annihilation or to defend human rights within the Soviet bloc. Moral ambiguity led different countries to differing emphases at any given time. Geographically insulated, North Americans were sometimes less compromising than their allies. As historians James McHugh and James Pacy observe, "The military and political prominence of the Soviets was, in some respects, a more real concern to Britain and the European members of NATO than it was to Americans and Canadians." They *needed* to get along with Russia. The Western Europeans were also more dependent than the United States on exports for their financial well-being, so economic incentives for integration of the two halves of the Continent were stronger.[65]

But in hindsight it is clear that European countries neighboring Russia also intuited earlier than the United States did that both de-escalation and liberalization were within reach by 1975. Proximity may have strengthened Europeans' willingness to compromise, or they may have found it easier to avoid a bunker mentality precisely because the United States largely took upon itself the quotidian nightmare of defense. Whatever the reason, continental leaders showed greater prescience than Washington. The least powerful European states played some of the most creative roles. Finland, Switzerland, Norway, Austria, and Italy all nudged negotiations and global expectations in new directions.[66]

Meanwhile, Leonid Brezhnev of the USSR made the same mistake as Kissinger, underestimating the power of a nonbinding pledge. Normative trends play an important part in shaping reality. Too late did the Soviet Union realize it had signed an agreement that finally gave internal dissidents an effective external forum. Periodic tongue-lashings by nongovernmental organizations like Helsinki Watch in support of Andrei Sakharov and other protesters contributed to Russian consciousness of the need for real change.

Normative shifts inspired domestic reform, as well. Upon taking office in 1977, President Jimmy Carter inquired if America itself was in compliance with the Helsinki Accords. When Secretary of State Cyrus Vance pointed out that prohibitions on citizens' travel to Cuba, North Korea, and Vietnam violated the agreement, Carter eased the bans. The new president also grappled with the painful reality of America's moral compromises in fighting the Cold War. At the outset, the former governor of Georgia established a new section within the State Department to make human rights abuses more transparent, including the behavior of its authoritarian allies. "I knew from my experience in the South that this policy would not be painless, nor could it be based on a blind adherence to consistency," he later recalled. But by placing human rights high on the list of American priorities—and monitoring violations—Carter further nudged the world in the direction of common standards. Carter also signed an agreement with Panama restoring its sovereignty over the Panama Canal Zone.[67]

Multiple players and events gradually steered the Cold War toward resolution, in a complex story beyond the scope of this account. President Ronald Reagan significantly increased U.S. defense expenditures—signaling that America had lost none of its will to oppose Russian expansionism—while holding out an olive branch to new Soviet leaders.[68] Nicknamed the "Great Communicator," the former actor and governor of California deftly combined unyielding opposition to Soviet totalitarianism with a welcoming attitude toward Russian moves in the direction of friendlier relations with both its immediate neighbors and distant rivals. Perhaps most important, a younger generation took over the Soviet Union in the mid-1980s. Communist Party chairman Mikhail Gorbachev called for *glasnost* (openness and transparency) and *perestroika* (economic liberalization to promote growth). As one top advisor urged, "We have to go all the way in democratization, glasnost, and economic reforms, not halfway." In 1989, Gorbachev repudiated the Brezhnev Doctrine. The Soviet Union would no longer intervene in the internal affairs of Eastern Europe to ensure one-party rule. Soviet spokesman Gennady Gerassimov wittily declared that the "Sinatra Doctrine" had replaced the Brezhnev Doctrine. Like the famous American crooner, Eastern Europeans were henceforth free to do it their way.

Poles elected their first non-Communist postwar government in 1989. Russian troops withdrew from Hungary, and Germans tore down the Berlin Wall. Although the Soviets hoped that Russia's new liberalism would attract voluntary allegiance to the Warsaw Pact, the alliance disbanded. In 1991, the Soviet Union cracked apart and formally ceased to exist. With the strong support of U.S. President George H. W. Bush, West and East Germany reunited as one country, despite the initial objections of fearful governments in France and Britain that still flinched at the image of a powerful Germany. Poland, Hungary, and the Czech Republic applied for membership in NATO.[69]

The end of the Cold War obliged cartographers to draw fifteen new nation-states on maps of the world. Decolonization was nearly complete. Imperialism had fallen away in stages after 1946, rather like the boosters on a moon rocket. This process had not yielded a uniformly better world, however. Many postcolonial societies were fractured by interethnic conflict and political corruption. Historian Peter Kenez points out that economic liberalization transformed Russia, in the short run, "from a reasonably egalitarian society to one where the gap between rich and poor was wider than in any country in Western Europe. . . . [T]his happened in all post-communist societies."[70] Nonetheless, the hope of self-government and national autonomy had proved more alluring than association with any empire, despite the economic benefits such an association might yield. International relations became freer as well. Representatives from 190 nations mingled more or less respectfully in the halls of the United Nations. The trends toward access, arbitration, and transparency had proved as potent in reordering world affairs as the threat of hydrogen bombs and NATO rifles.

Democratic capitalism outlasted both communism and imperialism for one other fundamental reason: economic performance. This fact deeply affected the trajectory of world history from 1947 to 1991. America attracted a following as much for its material success as its military leadership.

In 1947, at the start of this period, the United States was the richest country on the globe. It had achieved this feat over the course of two centuries by assembling states in an economic union, removing tariffs between them, facilitating cooperation through a set of common and predictable laws and practices, and using the federal umpire to compel acquiescence. The United States enjoyed the world's largest, most accessible mass market. Products were cheaper to make, sell, and buy in America than almost anywhere else. Naturally enough, this system did not work all the time (or necessarily forever). The nation and the world experienced periodic setbacks, especially when confronted with spiraling defense costs, natural disasters, industrial stagnation, and international events like the OPEC oil crisis of 1973. Free-market capitalism simply generated wealth more reliably than systems in which states operated as economic islands. By 1991, at the end of this period, regional coalitions to lower exchange barriers and facilitate integration operated on almost every continent.

American leaders first became convinced that such changes were desirable during World War II. They believed that economic collapse in the 1930s had fostered militarism. From Truman through George H. W. Bush, every presidential administration operated on the assumption that the only way to resolve persistent conflict over resources was to help the rest of the world catch up with America as quickly as possible. They embraced this daunting goal for strategic, economic, and humanitarian reasons that they saw as perfectly congruent. They preferred not to accomplish it by giving away money or making America less competitive, but they accepted that both might be necessary on occasion. Instead, they hoped to convince Europe, as the secondary engine of the world economy, to utilize the same organizational methods that had allowed America to flourish economically.

Naively or not, Americans did not consider this approach to be cultural imperialism, although others accused them of it. After all, the Singer sewing machine had also spread worldwide, but people did not all dress the same as a result. Tools could be culturally neutral, they believed. Strong allies made good allies. As President Eisenhower retorted when one advisor suggested in 1956 that Europe might be more easily managed if it remained weak, "Weakness could not cooperate, weakness could only beg."[71] The U.S. government also sought economic success for democratic Japan, seen as the potential engine of Asia.

Norwegian historian Geir Lundestad argues that, in this respect, "the United States behaved rather differently from other leading powers in history." Across the millennia, divide and rule had been the norm. "For Vienna, London, Paris, and Moscow it was entirely out of the question to promote an alternative center [of power], since this might come to weaken the position of the imperial capital."[72] Americans tended not to think in these terms, largely because the political structure they understood best was one in which states cooperated to further mutual commercial interests in a framework of friendly rivalry. Ambition did not have to be ruthless, or pursue a zero-sum strategy.

Naturally enough, Americans wanted to remain number one in the world. But they knowingly fostered a competitive framework in which that position could never be guaranteed. Their entire domestic existence as an assembly of equal states was a refutation of monopolistic "empire," except to the extent that the founders used the word to connote "umpire." Democratic federations seemed innately "good," and they hoped Europeans might develop one of their own.

Proposals for a United States of Europe had originated on the Continent itself. They were inspired by the Enlightenment, as well as by an appreciation for the advantages of interstate cooperation on the American model. After 1947, Europeans undertook new initiatives to devise better structures for cooperation. In 1951, France and Germany formed the European Coal and Steel Community in conjunction with Belgium, Netherlands, Luxemburg, and Italy. In the words of French foreign minister Robert Schuman, the organization aspired to make war "not only unthinkable but materially impossible."[73] Prewar economic incentives would be inherently more effective at forestalling conflict than wartime sanctions could be at ending conflict once national pride was at stake.

The European Economic Community (EEC), also known as the Common Market, followed in 1958. It broadened the range of goods and services on which the six nations were prepared to cooperate. Members stopped charging one another custom duties and began integrating agricultural policies. Like the Americans before them, Europeans initially tore down tariff walls among themselves while erecting them against the outside world. Agricultural policy, for example, protected continental farmers by discriminating against foreign imports.[74] Then, in 1993, the EEC reorganized itself again into the European Union. Over a period of six years, the EU removed the border checkpoints between European countries, issued a common passport and common currency, created a parliament, and began rotating the presidency among member countries. Europeans conceded free access to one another across all borders.

Ancient suspicions and modern rivalries posed stumbling blocks, but compared with the period between the Peace of Westphalia and World War II, the process proceeded rapidly. For example, when the United Kingdom applied to join the European Economic Community in 1962, France vetoed its application. President Charles de Gaulle alleged that Britain was insufficiently "European" because of its close ties with the United States. De Gaulle spitefully vetoed a second application in 1967.

British officials also did not always present their case well. When he petitioned German chancellor Willy Brandt for help, Foreign Secretary George
Brown told his counterpart, "Willy, you must get us in, so we can take the
lead."[75] The nimbler Brandt had a vision of Western European harmony that
dovetailed with *Neue Ostpolitik,* however, and refused to take umbrage at England's arrogance. He patiently pressed various members of the French government to withdraw their objections, while coaching his British counterparts in more persuasive deportment. In 1973, three years after de Gaulle
died, Britain was finally admitted to the pact along with Ireland and Sweden.
Within a decade, the European Community had expanded 50 percent beyond its six founding members, establishing a trend toward European unity
that continues to the present.

Scholars debate the extent to which the United States mattered in this process. Some emphasize European initiative, while others point to American
encouragement. It is undisputed, however, that the United States actively
promoted integration and jump-started the process when it asked Europeans
to work together to devise goals for the use of Marshall Plan funds. Congress
and the general public showed as much interest in this process as the executive
branch. In 1947, Senator William Fulbright introduced a joint resolution in
favor of a United States of Europe. The State Department pointed out that
this was a matter for Europeans to decide, but the plucky, big-eared Arkansan
persisted. "It is my belief that if all we are able to do is to recreate the prewar
crazyquilt of jealous sovereignties, neither Europe nor the Near East is a good
risk," he hectored Congress. "No one can guarantee that a federation will absolutely prevent all sparks, but at least there will be a chance that it may."[76]

Others agreed. Newspaper editorials in the *Saint Louis Post-Dispatch,
Wall Street Journal, Christian Science Monitor, Washington Post,* and various
prominent dailies called for European coordination, during the winter and
spring debates in 1947 about funding for the Truman Doctrine and Marshall Plan. Americans did not want to keep crossing the Atlantic to solve
problems that erupted in poisonous, fratricidal feuds. Eighty-one prominent
citizens signed an appeal in the *New York Times* for a "United Europe."
Sumner Welles, former undersecretary of state for Roosevelt, observed in
the *Washington Post* that "one of the most heartening developments in
Europe . . . has been the rapid increase in the popular demand for the establishment of a European federation." Yet another editorialist cautioned in the
Wall Street Journal that the "German problem" could be solved only by

transcontinental unification. Europe needed Germany's industrial might and organizational creativity, but also a guarantee that it would never again become aggressive. Europeans wanted, needed, and hated the idea of a strong Germany. This contradiction could never be resolved on a continent "divided into completely independent sovereign States, each with its economy in a watertight compartment."[77]

John Foster Dulles, who had helped draft the preamble to the UN Charter, articulated the case to the National Publishers Association. "As we studied the problem of Germany," he explained, "we became more and more convinced that there is no economic solution along purely national lines. Increased economic unity is an absolute essential to the well-being of Europe." Although it was not the prerogative of the United States to impose new institutions, "American blood, shed in two European wars [gave it] the moral right to speak," he said. Dulles suggested that the nation's "Continental friends" should use the precedents of American federalism and their own "human resourcefulness" to devise new solutions.[78]

The consensus favoring European economic unification arose from the old American faith in making currencies convertible, eliminating bilateral trade barriers, and forging a single market.[79] If Europeans adopted them, supranational institutions might regulate and supervise the system just as the general government ran interference among the states in North America. Far from creating a new empire, such a solution might actually prevent future attempts by aggressive nations to form one.

Europeans took the lead in devising their own institutions. Indeed, it is unlikely that any European today would eschew credit for the historic achievement that transformed the Continent from the most fractious one on the planet to perhaps the most harmonious of them all—save Australia and North America. The retreat of imperialism and advance of European cooperation were mutually reinforcing. Events like the Dutch defeat in Indonesia in 1949 spurred interest in economic and political integration as an alternative to colonial trade networks.[80] Intra-European rivalry had fueled imperialism. If this rivalry could be tamed, the need for colonies might logically dissipate—and it did.

But U.S. support had some important consequences for the particular way that economic unification shaped up. Perhaps the most important was U.S. insistence that Germany be allowed to reindustrialize and regain its central position on the Continent, backed by the American military commitment to

NATO. Since the United States guaranteed that Germany would be kept "down" and the Russians "out," other Europeans could allow Germany to take a leadership role without fear. Their freedom and lives would be defended. Interstate rivalries would be fought on soccer fields rather than Flanders Fields, in boardrooms rather on battleships. Markets would flourish and living conditions would improve for all.

Geir Lundestad argues, "The Europeans could undertake their integration on the premise that the United States was the overall balancer in Europe in general and the guarantor against anything going seriously wrong in West Germany in particular." Director of the Nobel Institute in Oslo, the Norwegian scholar calls America the "arbiter." He draws back at "umpire" or "judge" as terms that imply "too much objectivity." Lundestad instead suggests "pacifier," "guarantor," and "balancer" as alternative labels, plainly struggling with the best descriptor for what was an utterly new phenomenon.[81] World history simply provided no other examples of a powerful nation-state that simultaneously competed in and refereed what all participants agreed needed to be as fair a game as possible—despite the fact that the world was seldom fair.

The United States undertook a similar role toward Japan. A principal aggressor, like Germany, Japan was nonetheless the best candidate to stabilize Asia and lead it to the economic viability deemed essential for world peace. American leaders assumed that only open access to markets could ensure this viability. President Roosevelt had called the removal of commercial "barriers" the fifth of the "Four Freedoms" on behalf of which World War II was waged. Yet how could Japan be trusted to become a good citizen if it reaccumulated great resources? The British, Australians, and New Zealanders had little confidence. The Chinese had none whatsoever, though their opinion became less important to the United States when the Communist leader Mao Zedong took power in 1949, signed a pact with Russia the next year, and entered the Korean War on the side of the North. Events in China made Japan the "ultimate domino," Aaron Forsberg points out.[82] If it fell over, all hopes for Asia might be destroyed.

Seeking bipartisan support for a viable postwar strategy, President Truman brought Republican John Foster Dulles onto his team of advisors in 1950 to negotiate peace with Japan. Up to that point, none of the nations that fought Japan had signed a peace treaty with it. Its surrender was deemed sufficient. The United States was almost alone in believing that Japan should be actively rehabilitated and welcomed back into the international fold. America waived reparations for war damages, and encouraged Australia, Belgium, Britain, Burma, New Zealand, the Philippines, and Taiwan to do the same for the good of world economic recovery. This was not easy to swallow. Australia and New Zealand, for example, refused to forgo damages or countenance the economic resuscitation of Japan without security guarantees. Dulles recognized that the essential problem was "to devise some arrangement which would protect Japan from outside aggression and at the same time re-assure to the greatest extent possible Japan's former enemies that Japan would never be a threat to them."[83]

The solution was an international peace treaty underwritten by new military alliances that made the United States the guarantor of peace in Asia. On September 1, 1951, Australia, New Zealand, and the United States signed the ANZUS Pact in San Francisco. Essentially, this was the Asian equivalent of NATO, designed to keep the Chinese out, the Americans in, and the Japanese down. For the remainder of that drizzly week in California's foggy port city, delegates from more than fifty nations debated the terms on which peace should be made. On the day they decided to forgive Japan, the island nation formally renounced territorial acquisitions dating back to the Sino-Japanese War of 1895, including the lands of Korea and Formosa (Taiwan). The same day, September 8, 1951, the United States and Japan signed their first defense pact. Together, ANZUS and the U.S.-Japan Security Treaty allowed postwar rehabilitation to go forward on terms that made everyone feel safe. American troops never went home.[84]

The consensus was hard won. Britain and a number of other countries had been deeply suspicious, and they remained so to some extent. Prior to the final vote, Egypt, Belgium, Burma, New Zealand, and Russia all expressed reservations about a treaty many considered too magnanimous. U.S. leaders were not the only ones with a nonpunitive vision of the future, however. At the conference in California, the finance minister of newly decolonized Ceylon quoted the Buddha, saying, "Hatred ceases not by hatred but by love." Liberating the Asian giant from poverty would do more for peace than chaining the archipelago, Finance Minister J. R. Jayewardene argued. Forced disarmament could never be as permanent as voluntary disarmament. Mohammed Khan of Pakistan strongly seconded this sentiment. The question was not whether the treaty was ideal, but whether it was better than the alternatives. "If this is a treaty of benevolence, it is benevolent both to Japan and ourselves," the Pakistani said, urging other nations to embrace a new spirit redefining international affairs.[85]

Not everyone was happy with the process by which the treaty had been devised, however. Although the Dutch representative expressed provisional support, he also expressed annoyance about not being more fully consulted by the United States, which had conducted the treaty negotiations. Robert Schuman of France defended America, alluding to the "shadow" of conflict between the great powers that made more intimate multilateral cooperation difficult. "Peace will be achieved by steps," the Frenchman who bore the cross of a German name pointed out. "We owe a special homage to Mr. John Foster Dulles," Schuman graciously acknowledged. It was not the first time that America would field and survive complaints about high-handed umpiring.[86]

The Japanese themselves were fortunate to have a far-sighted prime minister with an extraordinary talent for navigating rough waters. Shigeru Yoshida astutely redefined Japan's economic and strategic interests, and the best strategy for achieving them. As a young diplomat in the early 1930s, Yoshida had met Woodrow Wilson's friend Colonel House, who urged that Japan not abandon diplomacy for aggression as Germany had done in World War I, lest it endanger its accomplishments. "Unfortunately," Yoshida wrote in his memoirs, "Japan for no adequate reason embarked upon a major war and caused whatever had been achieved by her up to that time to be completely destroyed." In 1944, Yoshida had been imprisoned for advocating peace. Later, as president of the Liberal Democratic Party, Yoshida steered Japan toward complete disarmament. The nation could rearm if it chose to do so after rebuilding, "But let the Americans handle our security until then," he told a young aide. "It is indeed our Heaven-bestowed good fortune that the [new] constitution bans arms. If the Americans complain, the constitution gives us a perfect justification." No nation would dare attack so long as U.S. forces were present, and Japan could focus its meager resources on rebuilding. Through Yoshida, Japan snatched victory from defeat. As he told his cabinet the year following the blast over Hiroshima, "History provides examples of winning by diplomacy after losing in war."[87]

The linchpin of Shigeru Yoshida's plan was economic access. Japan needed more than nominal forgiveness. It needed markets. Postwar ostracism initially made it impossible for the Japanese people to erase their enormous trade deficit. During America's seven-year occupation of Japan (1945–1952), the United States had donated more than $2 billion in economic aid for the import of food and raw materials. The deficit surged to more than $1 billion a year when occupation came to an end in 1953. That same year, two years after the San Francisco conference, America and Japan signed a new pact of friendship and commerce that echoed John Adams's model treaty of 1776. They accorded one another's citizens "national treatment," meaning that foreigners and locals would enjoy the same commercial rights in domestic markets. They also extended one another most-favored-nation status. It was Japan's first commercial treaty following the war, and the beginning of Japan's extraordinary flowering.

Shortly thereafter, the United States advocated Japan's admission to the General Agreement on Tariffs and Trade. Britain opposed the move that would grant its former enemy most-favored-nation status, however. Japan's rapacious commercial practices in the 1930s still haunted finance ministers around the world, as did its wartime atrocities. But the United States persisted in its campaign to rehabilitate the Asian nation, and Japan won membership in GATT in 1955. The next year, the United Nations finally admitted Japan as a full member, completing its redemption. Australia followed America as the second country to reestablish normal bilateral ties, concluding a trade agreement with Japan in 1957, four years after the United States.

The Japanese proved better bargainers than the Americans, however. Japan's agreement with the the United States allowed it to restrict foreign capital to protect its trade balance. Japan also implemented a government-directed reindustrialization policy that was more coherent than that followed by laissez-faire America. In the 1960s, Tokyo legislators further elaborated the Yoshida Doctrine, limiting defense spending to only 1 percent of GNP. The Japanese economy bloomed, growing fifty-five-fold in three decades.

While the United States provided Japan's defense, America went from a $400 million trade *surplus* with Japan in the early 1950s to a trade *deficit* of $3 billion by 1971. "Paradoxically," historian Aaron Forsberg astutely remarks, "friction was the inevitable consequence of strategic and economic cooperation." Close interaction led to chafing. Japan's exclusion of U.S. products and companies episodically provoked the ire of Congress. Dependence on American firepower, personified by thousands of men in uniform, sometimes wounded Japanese pride and inflamed nationalism. But democratic political institutions flourished along with Japan's economy, and the archipelago became the backbone of U.S. Cold War defense in Asia.[88]

Ultimately, the domestic economic accomplishments of Europe and Japan were attributable primarily to their own peoples. But the United States had helped significantly. After World War II, the developed countries set out to create a different, more benign international order. Economist Michael Spence notes that "the opportunity was probably created by the horror of the war itself, and the devastation right after." But, he points out, "opportunity is not . . . always seized."[89] Encouraged by Great Britain, Germany, France, Japan, and many other nations, the United States took the initiative at several critical turning points. "The United States was the economic giant among nations; there was no one with whom to share that responsibility," historian Richard Gardner observes. "It also, in a sense, 'policed' itself—adopting liberal aid and trade policies appropriate to a surplus nation because it quickly recognized that if it failed to do so the rest of the world would go broke."[90] Because these liberal policies served Americans' self-interest as well as their historical values, and because Americans had a cultural predisposition to believe in the periodic necessity of an umpire to impose order, the people gave their tax dollars and their lives to implement them.

In 1991, the age of empire ended. Decolonization had created nearly 150 countries, many with "little economic viability," according to Michael Spence. "From a purely economic point of view," the Nobel laureate asserts, "some of them should have been parts of larger states."[91] Indeed, the triumph of nationalism was sometimes a hollow victory, even though peoples worldwide had fought for it steadfastly. Territorial security against outside invaders was ensured, but there were no guarantees of internal success. Help was available, however, through myriad aid programs mounted by wealthier countries from the 1950s onward, following the precedent set by the Marshall Plan. When the World Trade Organization (WTO) was formed in 1995 to replace the General Agreement on Tariffs and Trade, more than 100 nations almost immediately joined the transnational body designed to implement the vision of the physiocrats: a world with minimal economic borders.

Even Communist China clamored for admission to the WTO, having abandoned economic autarky more than a decade earlier to escape its poverty. Communist Party chairman Deng Xiaoping, a veteran of the civil war that brought Mao Zedong to power, instigated the policy known as *gaige kai fang* ("reform and openness") in 1979. Former secretary of state John Hay would have been pleased to witness China actively seeking most-favored-nation status. Although a crackdown on prodemocracy demonstrators at Tiananmen Square in 1989 revealed the brutal limits of change, Chinese communism nonetheless moved much closer to the center of the international bell curve in matters of access, arbitration, and transparency. The globe's largest republic, home to one out of five humans, picked up new tools for its own purposes, on its own initiative, in its own way. Like the Japanese and other "developing" nations before them, the Chinese negotiated special protective tariffs to shield its own infant industries while obtaining substantially freer entrée to mature foreign markets. In 2011, for example, a Jeep Grand Cherokee that sold for $27,000 in the United States cost $85,000 in China—a price difference that effectively walled Detroit out of the Forbidden City. China meanwhile undercut U.S. domestic manufacturers with $49 microwaves and other ultracheap goods exported to the American market. For the Chinese, there was little to dislike about so-called U.S. dominance.[92]

American presidents met many of their international goals between 1946 and 1991. They also reaped many of the negative consequences foretold by Cassandras in Congress. The United States sometimes ended up defending governments whose domestic policies were indefensible when matched with the UN Universal Declaration of Human Rights. The nation poured the blood of its children and wealth of its families into the sands of the Cold War. Realpolitik diminished America's popularity and tarnished its reputation. Just as Senator Claude Pepper had warned, some nations interpreted America's attempt to defend the world as a new imperialism. In figuring the best approach to international crises, the government sometimes guessed wrong and did wrong. Although few foreigners (and no Amerindians) had ever seen the United States as morally innocent, Americans themselves were surprised to discover they were less so than they had assumed. National identity and unity suffered.

Yet policymakers had also surmounted some of the countervailing dangers warned of by Cassandras on the Hill. The Soviet Union had been contained. World War III did not materialize. Eastern Europeans slogged through four decades of semi-imprisonment, but Western Europeans enjoyed a new Golden Age. The atomic standoff held. Companies innovated and citizens prospered.

Values that America valiantly defended during the Cold War spread, even when the United States unintentionally subverted them, as in Vietnam and Iran. Popular sovereignty and international cooperation assumed a momentum of their own, far from Tom Paine's City of Brotherly Love.

Less confident than before in government's ability to achieve the nation's mission, most Americans nonetheless still believed their country had one. This sense of common cause, fundamental to the coherence of any people, was never clearer than on a cloudless September morning in 2001.

Conclusion: Good Calls, Bad Calls, and Rules in Flux

Or, Who Wants to Be Ump? 1991–Present

Since the heyday of the Greek city-states, republics have been defended by civilians. At the Battle of Marathon in 490 BCE, farmers who were part-time soldiers defeated the professional forces of Persia, the most powerful Eurasian empire up to that time.[1] At Lexington and Concord in 1775, farmers-cum-militiamen fired the first shots in a campaign that defeated the British Empire, the largest in all recorded history. In the air over Pennsylvania on September 11, 2001, citizens also came to the people's defense. Twenty-nine minutes into the hijacking of United Flight 93, a determined group of male and female passengers stormed the cockpit that four Islamic terrorists had commandeered. They knew that other suicide teams had already flown hijacked planes into the World Trade Center towers in Manhattan, and that their flight was on a death mission, too. "Everyone's running up to first class," flight attendant Sandra Bradshaw fearlessly told her husband on the phone. "I've got to go. Bye."

The Lebanese hijacker-pilot, Ziad Jarrah, turned the flight control column on the Boeing 757 hard left, then hard right, trying to shake off the passenger revolt. When the Americans kept coming, he angled the plane sharply upward, then dove toward the ground, trying to halt the onslaught against the flimsy cockpit door. Three minutes into the desperate struggle, once it became clear he would soon be overpowered, Jarrah shouted, "Allah is the greatest" and gunned the plane down into the rolling countryside at 580 miles per hour.[2]

Nine days later, an anguished President George W. Bush asked, "Why do they hate us?" Observers interviewed in a variety of countries supplied answers, trying to explain the tragic assault: angry over historical injustices, Muslim terrorists had lashed out. Events like the CIA-backed Iran coup of 1953 and modern U.S. support for Israeli sovereignty had bred such intense resentment that fanaticism was practically inevitable. The Muslim "street" was a ticking time bomb whose fuse had been lit by America.[3]

Yet cross-border transgressions are never inevitable. In fact, considering the frequency with which nationalities despise, stereotype, and resent one another, coming to blows is comparatively rare. Transgressions result from specific, deliberate, strategic decisions. There are multiple solutions to any given problem. Britain, for example, chose to liberate its human chattel by raising an excise tax to remunerate owners. Bloodshed was avoided. In contrast, the Confederacy in the American South opted to defend slavery by seceding, and Abraham Lincoln decided to invade. The U.S. Civil War was not predetermined. Little is inevitable in history except choice.

On 9/11, youthful members of a clandestine organization, many exiled from their own countries for their violent extremism, committed a monstrous act on their own initiative while claiming to speak for the entire Muslim world. Al-Qaeda exploited an animus far less focused than Poles might logically be expected to harbor toward Russia, or Vietnamese toward the United States, or Kurds toward Turkey, or Aboriginals toward Australia. And its leaders cleverly manipulated disparate grievances to advance a broader agenda.[4] Their goal: "To create an empire of all the world's one billion Muslims, ruled by a single leader." Their method: sapping the morale of opponents by slaughtering Muslim civilians whom they deemed insufficiently religious, and Christians and Jews considered "infidels." Their payoff, in the words of Osama bin Laden: "to enter paradise by killing you."[5]

Al-Qaeda targeted Americans not because the United States had anything to do with the collapse of the ancient caliphate in World War I, but because America was the nation with the greatest power to foil the plan of recreating it. Al-Qaeda also considered American protection contaminating. In his 1996 fatwa calling for holy war against the United States, Osama bin Laden focused on the sin committed mutually by Saudi Arabia and America in using Western troops to protect Kuwait and Mecca from Iraq just a few years before. The Saudi king had ignored objections from the mujahideen that Muslims ought to be self-sufficient in matters of defense. Instead, the Arab king joined in the "clear conspiracy between the USA and its' [sic] allies and under the cover of the iniquitous United Nations." The king had permitted "the most filthy sort of humans" to enter the Holy Land. He substituted man-made law for God's law (Sharia), an offense known to "strip a person" of Islamic status. Human rights, bin Laden charged, were an empty concept. Arbitration and explanation were irrelevant. "There is nothing between us [that] need[s] to be explained, there is only killing and neck smiting."[6]

The neck smiting on 9/11 affected U.S. citizens in more ways than one. The physical blow was both wrenching and uniting. Like the passengers aboard Flight 93, many instinctively rushed to defend the nation. Retailers across the country sold out of American flags. The *San Diego Union* printed paper copies of the flag for residents of the country's eighth-largest city to post in windows and on fences. The NBC television network changed the rainbow feathers on its peacock logo to red, white, and blue.[7] Americans overwhelmed blood banks with offers to help devastated New Yorkers. The armed forces accepted thousands of applications from men and women want-ing to serve. Major League Baseball cancelled games for a week. When the season reopened, fans sang the *Star-Spangled Banner* in tears. Perhaps never before had Americans felt so acutely the sense of being one, except on December 7, 1941.

But the terrorists nonetheless scored at least a partial victory in psycho-logical warfare. Self-doubt crept in alongside renewed patriotism. The terror-ists had hit a nerve. The Cold War was over, yet American troops were still stationed across the globe. Nor was the world fully at peace. Ethnic and reli-gious conflict roiled Southern Europe and East Africa. Some academics, most famously Chalmers Johnson, had already pointed to continued basing agreements as proof of America's hidden intent all along to create an empire. Muslim rage was "blowback." Others suggested that the United States de-served opprobrium and even attack for its conduct of foreign policy since 1945, if not since 1776. Ward Churchill, a professor of ethnic studies at the University of Colorado, became infamous for calling the office workers in-cinerated in the World Trade Center "little Eichmanns," akin to the German bureaucrats who had administered the Nazi regime.[8]

Postmodern essayist Joan Didion, whose book criticizing "the sedative fantasy of a fixable imperial America" came out, coincidentally, two weeks after the attack, was equally pointed. Dubbed "the poet laureate of disillu-sion," Didion later dismissed the pervasive feeling of tragedy after 9/11 as government manipulation of bourgeois emotion to advance the Republican administration's "preexisting agenda." Linguist Noam Chomsky, continuing three decades of pseudo-scholarly diatribes on topics outside his discipline, told Americans that attacks would continue until they recognized that their own country was the leading terrorist nation. Filmmaker Michael Moore leveled similar accusations and more in *Fahrenheit 911,* subtitled *The Temperature at Which Freedom Burns.* Moore alleged that President Bush's oil investments had led him to protect Saudis implicated in the airplane attacks on New York and the Pentagon. Moore's work might be dismissed as poor journalism if wild conspiracy theories were not so popular and widespread. *Fahrenheit 911* became the top grossing "documentary" of all time. A poll in 2006 found that 36 percent of Americans considered it "very likely" or "somewhat likely" that the U.S. government itself either executed or permitted the acts against its own citizens on 9/11.[9]

In any human endeavor requiring supreme effort, morale helps determine outcome. If citizens are uncertain about their own or their government's motivation, they will find it difficult to prevail against enemies, inertia, pessimism, and all the other forces that continuously complicate human achievement. Diagnosing America's problem as "imperialism" has been tempting but damaging. Al-Qaeda advanced the same interpretation, of course, but that is not sufficient reason to reject it. "Empire" either does or does not fit the historical evidence. It must be examined on its own terms. Physicians will attest that the first step in curing any disease is accurate diagnosis. Treatment based on an incorrect assessment may kill the patient.

Calling the United States an empire has yielded no practicable solutions because the nation and the world system in which it fits are simply not structured in that way. The nation cannot stop being something it is not. Consequently, this flawed characterization merely saps morale, especially if one presumes that being stronger and wealthier than most other nations proves imperialism, which is a phenomenon more widely reviled today than wife beating. (Imperialism is roundly rejected, while some cultures still accept corporal punishment and even the "honor" killing of women.) Within these parameters, all that the nation can do to "reform" is stop being rich and powerful. That would satisfy al-Qaeda, but any putative moral victory would be Pyrrhic indeed for America's citizen defenders. Or, the United States might reduce its defense programs. At times, it has. On the eve of 9/11, reduced funding of controversial CIA operations meant that the U.S. devoted less than 2 percent of its intelligence budget to collecting information in the field about foreign threats. Several thousand Americans paid the price on 9/11.[10]

A more realistic, evidence-based diagnosis is that the United States is the enforcer of what is, most of the time, the collective will: the maintenance of a world system with relatively open trade borders, in which arbitration and economic sanctions are the preferred method of keeping the peace and greater and greater numbers of people have at least some political rights. When sanctions and incentives fail, the United States is (generally speaking) expected to step up. It easily and too often exceeds its authority in doing so because it has none, under the present system.

Nonetheless, domestic and international expectations create real tensions. Other nations demand a response to economic and physical threats, and Americans do so as well. President Barack Obama's foreign policy after 2008 did not differ appreciably from that of George W. Bush because it was based on the same fundamental assumption. The United States must financially and militarily defend those "resisting attempted subjugation." This burdens America's army, economy, and psyche. In 2010, the percentage of U.S. GDP devoted to defense was double, triple, even quadruple that spent by its allies in Europe and the Americas.[11] In Ireland and Iceland, students went to university for free, while young Americans accumulated enormous college debts simply to qualify for work. The Truman Doctrine lives on.

It does not have to. If the American public wishes to reevaluate this national commitment, the logical questions to ask are: What would happen if the United States ceased to fulfill this role in the world? Can the role be eliminated? If not, who else might perform it? How can the United States persuade another nation, group of nations, or supranational body to undertake the responsibility, with minimal loss of global amity and stability? Can America exercise the best kind of leadership by creating new leaders?

Alternatively, the United States might choose to continue playing umpire. If no other entity is willing to do so, and the United States still is, yet other questions cry for attention. What should be the quid pro quo? To what extent, if any, should it receive exemptions from rules it expects others to follow, because of the vulnerability to which this role exposes the nation—or do such exemptions breed arrogance? What is the significance of the fact that the U.S. Congress, a democratic assembly, does not always ratify schemes of international cooperation championed by the president (from the Versailles Treaty, for example, to the Kyoto Protocol on Global Warming)? What, specifically, should the United States seek to "get" from playing umpire—financially, strategically, or psychologically? These are difficult questions, but at least they have answers.

Considering the high stakes, Americans have been understandably reluctant to let go. Yet there is nothing to stop them from assuming again the role they played up to 1947, when Britain relinquished leadership. Institutional mechanisms transcending the United States (or any state) are already in place. Czar Nicholas II's Permanent Court of Arbitration, the first such international body, still operates. As recently as January 2012, it dissected and resolved a conflict between Exxon Mobil and Venezuela.[12] (Venezuela, again—though this time without coastal bombardment!) If the gains seem worth the risks—and it is an important "if"—the United States could conceivably pass the umperial responsibility back to Britain, or to someone else. The consequences might be horrific, or they might be benign.[13] They would certainly be dramatic, should the United States draw back behind its wide oceans once more. Yet they will never materialize if the United States numbly continues to shoulder the load that no one else wants—and with which others fundamentally trust America.

In the prelude to the 2012 presidential election, iconoclastic contender Ron Paul took the position that it was time to retire the umpire. He advocated closing all American military bases in foreign countries. Even earlier, the Texas Republican had commented, "There has been a treaty with South Korea for 50 years or so, which means that no matter what happens over there, we have obligated the next generation of Americans to go over there and fight. . . . I don't think we have the moral right or the constitutional right."[14] Ron Paul's objections did not differ greatly from those posed by congressional Democrats and Republicans in 1946.

Such observations are not comfortable for most Americans, fearful of changing a foreign policy that has been effective in averting world wars. Nor have U.S. allies latched on to them. For the majority of nations, it has been both easy and advantageous to allow the United States to perform the function of referee, even when it makes the wrong call, as any umpire sometimes does. Defense spending has declined steadily for the nation's partners. The world has been happy to let Americans do much of the globe's dirtiest, most dangerous work, because they are trusted even when they are disliked. There has been no groundswell to move the UN out of New York, oust U.S. troops from NATO, reject American loans, exert collective sanctions against the U.S. economy, or do any number of things that would communicate fundamental dissatisfaction with existing arrangements.

Instead, just the opposite occurs nearly every day. In the fall of 2011, India, Indonesia, Japan, and Singapore requested reassurance that the United States was not going to pull back from Asia and leave them to face China alone. In Australia, Labor Party prime minister Julia Gillard invited President Obama to base 2,500 Marines alongside local troops at a military installation in Darwin "to expand the existing collaboration between the Australian Defence Force and the US."[15] America continues to subsidize world security.

Americans may wonder if these commitments benefit others more than the United States. This is an interesting and debatable question, and far from merely hypothetical. Regardless of the answer, the gains may still be great enough to fulfill the primary purpose of any government: making life more secure and prosperous for its own people. But overstretch threatens. Good leaders avoid responsibilities too great for them to bear responsibly. Frederick the Great of Prussia observed, "He who defends everything defends nothing."[16]

It is not the place of a historian to speculate on the future or make recommendations. Her job is to understand the past as objectively as possible, using the tools of context and proportion. In context, the United States played an instrumental role in curbing the ambition of totalitarian Russia in the second half of the twentieth century and in facilitating worldwide economic growth. Proportionately, the mistakes it made in the process were not as negative as they might have been, considering other possibilities—including nuclear annihilation—and compared with the actions and wishes of most other nation-states. People still died in wars and genocides, but far fewer in the second half of the twentieth century than in the first.

In fact, the percentage of the world population killed in war has fallen steadily in every decade since the Truman Doctrine. Despite newspaper headlines that perennially suggest the world is going to hell in a handbasket, interstate violence has declined remarkably. George Shultz, who hit the beach as a Marine during the Battle of Peleliu under Roosevelt and served as secretary of state under Reagan, later characterized the United States as a "reluctant" power. That may be true—but more important, it has been willing. William Appleman Williams viewed world history through the wrong end of the telescope. On balance, American diplomacy in the twentieth century has been far more triumphant than tragic.[17]

Although the United States has recognized and cooperated with both dictatorships and democracies in these processes, so have most countries, following

Westphalian proscriptions against judging the internal affairs of other nations. Dictatorships are supposed to be tolerated, just as Catholics and Protestants learned after 1648 to tolerate their heretical neighbors (whom God himself was presumably going to punish for all eternity). Ambassadors from countries that stoned adulterers, kidnapped dissidents, mutilated the genitalia of women, and executed writers have all received (and exchanged) the same friendly handshake at the UN. The Truman Doctrine never purported to bring Greece, Turkey, or any other nation to moral salvation, merely hold them together so that someday they might improve themselves.

Unfortunately, the end of the Cold War did not obviate the Truman Doctrine, for the elementary reason that threats to security remained. Bad things continued to happen, as they probably always will. Ironically, the job description of umpire actually expanded in the 1990s and after the year 2000. Expectations increased rather than diminished. The number of small, weak countries grew. Not only was the umpire supposed to forestall interstate aggression between them, it was now also supposed to prevent aggression by states toward their own citizens.

Borrowing from Hegel and Marx, one might say that a new dialectical process outside the control of any one state came into play. Just as nationalism challenged and overturned imperialism between 1648 and 1991, universalism progressively subverted nationalism after 1948. Universalism was the antithesis of Westphalian doctrine, which forbade any country from telling another what it could or could not do within its own borders. In the older world system, sovereignty functioned like a bubble around the state. It could not be penetrated without being annihilated. Within the Westphalian bubble, government authority was inviolable.[18]

In contrast, universalism made national boundaries permeable, at least hypothetically. The 1948 Universal Declaration of Human Rights granted moral priority to the individual over the nation-state. Governments now had a responsibility not just to exercise effective control but also to do it benevolently, or face negative international consequences. In 2005, the United Nations formalized this as the state's "duty to protect." Outsiders might pass judgment on whether or not states were in compliance. Yet any kind of external supervision inherently compromises sovereignty, just as the Federalist founders compromised the autonomy of the first thirteen states.[19] In the second half of the twentieth century, countless private and governmental organizations—from Helsinki Watch to the International Criminal Court—

nonetheless took up the responsibility of backstopping the Universal Declaration. When states failed in their duty to protect individual citizens, more powerful nations felt obligated to step in, particularly the United States. If these actors failed in turn, apology was expected and sometimes even given.

In previous world history, apology was a form of humiliation extracted only at the point of a gun. It was the bête noire of national honor. Only after World War II did nations start issuing apologies more readily, revealing radical change in international norms for proper state deportment. As we have noted, German chancellor Willy Brandt knelt at the memorial to Poland's Jews killed by Nazi forces. In 2011 the Dutch government apologized for atrocities committed during its attempt to repress Indonesian nationalism in 1947. The American and Canadian governments have both apologized for the internment of Japanese residents during World War II. In August 1988 the U.S. Congress approved $1.25 billion to compensate 120,000 persons of Japanese descent. The following month, Canada approved $238 million to repay 22,000 residents that it had treated similarly.[20]

In 1998, President Bill Clinton took this one step further, apologizing for what his nation did *not* do. "We did not act quickly enough after the killing began," Clinton told those who had survived a government-orchestrated massacre of one million people in Rwanda four years earlier. The Arkansan tempered his remorse with allusions to the similar negligence of surrounding African nations, which arguably had a greater duty to stop the carnage on their borders. Nonetheless, it was Clinton, a white American born 8,000 miles away, pleading mea culpa. Two years later, Belgian and Canadian leaders apologized as well.[21] Such pleas for forgiveness further inflated expectations about what "responsible" Western nations ought to do during world crises. Based on proximity, apologies from the Organization of African Unity and League of Arab States might have been more fitting. Nonetheless, while Westphalian standards damned outside countries for interfering in internal affairs, universalist standards damned them for not doing so fast enough.

The proliferation of nation-states following the demise of empires further complicated peace and order. Before the twentieth century, there was no such thing as a "failed state." Governing groups unable to defend themselves or exert viable internal control disappeared, unless they became part of a protectorate. No state was "entitled" to exist. It protected itself or went under. Expanding empires or nation-states gobbled up territories that were lightly or poorly administered. They then policed their own domains, requiring no outside assistance. After 1945, however, UN agreements guaranteed all international borders under the right of self-determination. Today, the "world community" ensures the existence of small states.

As a consequence, facing no predators, nation-states have nearly quadrupled in number. The newest are typically the weakest, and many are poorly organized. Those without effective internal policing or legal due process have sometimes fostered mayhem with international consequences, from piracy to terrorism. The need for outside policing has grown commensurately. Former U.S. secretary of state Condoleezza Rice observed in 2012 that the task of dealing with those "unable to defend or govern themselves" constituted one of the gravest challenges to American diplomacy.[22]

There are many examples of the difficulties of umpiring after the Cold War and in the new millennium. The disasters of Sarajevo and Srebrenica in the mid-1990s are particularly instructive. (If we had but world enough and time, to paraphrase poet Andrew Marvell, we might consider Somalia and Sudan as well.) This book concludes with the Balkans, where the twentieth century began and ended. In World War I, strife that started in southeastern Europe drew the United States into international crisis management. Although Americans hoped to diminish their responsibility for world affairs once the Cold War ended, the Balkans pulled them back.

In the busy year of 1991, the Soviet Union ceased to exist and the United States orchestrated the liberation of Kuwait from Iraqi occupation. The first event seemed to suggest that the United States no longer need act as point man for peace in Europe. The second gave Americans plenty to do elsewhere. To Europeans tired of the large American presence in the life of the Continent, change was welcome. "We do not interfere in American affairs; we trust that America will not interfere in European affairs," stated Jacques Delors, the French president of the new European Union. "This is the hour of Europe!" crowed Jacques Poos, foreign minister of Luxembourg, when continental leaders confronted their first internal security crisis that same year, determined then and for the future to resolve problems on their own.[23]

The issue was Yugoslavia. Formed at the end of World War I, Yugoslavia ("Land of the Southern Slavs") had been held together for half of its history by the remarkable World War II partisan and Communist, Josip Broz Tito. Born of a Slovenian mother and Croatian father, the (mostly) benevolent dictator embodied ethnic union. His death in 1980, and the fracture of the Soviet Union into fifteen new states in 1991, precipitated Yugoslavia's breakdown. The European Community hoped against hope that the once-stable Slavic union would hang together and thereby minimize geopolitical disruption at a volatile time. But Balkanization resurfaced when Slovenia, Croatia, and then Bosnia-Herzegovina split from Serbia, the largest and most powerful of the six republics that comprised the nation-state.

Any divorce occurs for multiple reasons, but an important factor in 1991 was the increasing belligerency of Serbia, which tried to assert primacy over other republics in the confederation. Serbia's president was Slobodan Milosevic, an authoritarian former Communist who stoked nationalist fears to build his personal power. For much of the twentieth century (aside from interethnic violence that flared up during World War II), Croats, Bosnians, and Serbs had lived together peaceably. Yugoslavs enjoyed one of the more open Communist economies and a quality of life similar to that of Western Europeans. Their internal differences were primarily religious. Croats and Slovenes mostly identified as Roman Catholics, Bosnians as Muslims, and Serbians as Eastern Orthodox Christians, reflecting the different imperial phases of Balkan history, from Roman to Turkish to Austro-Hungarian rule. This diversity was sometimes celebrated as characteristic of Yugoslavia. Generations of intermarriage and secular government seemed to render the differences innocuous. Spiritual affiliations did not manifest themselves in personal appearance or dress. Yugoslavs were religiously identifiable only by their first or last names.[24]

After the Berlin Wall came down in 1989, however, arrangements that once seemed immutable came into question. Democratization overturned one-party rule across the Soviet bloc. Without a unifying Communist ideology, ethnic and religious differences assumed greater importance. State-controlled media in the Yugoslav capitol city of Belgrade began emphasizing the past glories of Serbia, the easternmost of the constituent republics, and the least democratic. In 1989, Milosevic staged a rally that drew one million Serbians to mourn the tragic defeat of Serbia at the hands of the Turks 600 years earlier. A medieval event was thereby granted modern relevance. Local Muslims still posed a "Turkish" threat, Milosevic ominously warned. "Armed battles" could be foreseen, he told his people. Radio Television Belgrade parroted Slobodan Milosevic's inflammatory, anti-Islamic message. An English scholar resident in Belgrade at the time later commented, "It was as if all television in the USA had been taken over by the Ku Klux Klan."[25]

Most tellingly, when it came time for the chairmanship of the Yugoslavian federal presidency to pass to Croatia, Serbia (which controlled half the votes in the executive body) balked at the normal rotation. Yugoslavia was left without a recognized leader for months. German and French officials pressed Serbia to stop its obstruction, but the European Community also voted to withhold recognition from any state that attempted to secede. Although the other Yugoslav republics supported federation, Milosevic's intransigence frightened them, especially when it became clear that no outside power (neither European nor American) was going to make him behave.

In June 1991, Catholic-identified Slovenia, the richest of the six republics, broke off. Croatia, just across the Adriatic Sea from the boot of Italy, followed. Their defection made the remaining republics, mostly smaller and less affluent, more anxious than ever about staying in a federation with domineering Serbia. Milosevic protested that all he wanted was Yugoslav unity, but, in the words of the German official charged with Balkan affairs, "The unity of Yugoslavia was in fact being most strenuously undermined by those who pretended loudest to be its defenders."[26]

A member of the U.S. National Security Council later commented that President George H. W. Bush realized "Yugoslavia was being led toward the abyss by a few demagogic politicians, [but] simply knew of no way to prevent this from occurring."[27] For the first time since World War II, the United States had been asked to stay out of a continental dispute with major security implications. The European Union would mind its own backyard.

This was not all bad. For many American officials, the Balkan challenge presented a welcome opportunity to pull back. U.S. secretary of state James Baker emphasized to his staff, "We don't have a dog in this fight." President Bush was also content to ignore a region that did not demand his attention when so many others did. As Baker explained in his memoirs, they both believed that "it was time to make the Europeans step up to the plate and show that they could act as a unified power. Yugoslavia was as good a first test as any." In other words, would the European Union play ump?[28]

Within days of declaring their independence, Slovenia and Croatia were embroiled in civil war with Serbian rebels as well as with regular troops of the Yugoslav National Army. No part of Yugoslavia was religiously or ethnically homogeneous. In fact, it had been Tito's policy to scatter different groups around the country to encourage mutual tolerance. Encouraged and armed by Milosevic, minority populations of Serb Orthodox Christians in Slovenia and Croatia now opposed secession. In control of the former capitol of Yugo-slavia, Milosevic and his followers in Serbian Belgrade had the resources of the Yugoslav National Army at their disposal.

The European Community moved quickly to tamp down the violence and helped negotiate independence for Slovenia, which had a minimal Serbian population. Croatia, however, contained a significant population of Ortho-dox Serbs. Internecine war soon broke out there, too, but the greater extent of ethnic intermingling made a negotiated settlement elusive. The United Na-tions responded by leveling an arms embargo against all of the former Yugo-slavia. Unfortunately, the embargo dramatically favored Serbians, who were already well supplied with arms and in control of national munitions facto-ries. The Bosnian Muslims and Catholic Croats had nothing. *Christian Sci-ence Monitor* correspondent David Rohde observed, "The embargo simply locked into place the huge military advantage enjoyed by the Serbs, the larg-est group in the former Yugoslavia, who controlled the Yugoslav National Army and its vast stockpile of ammunition." The United States went along with the UN Security Council decision, though President Bush's undersecre-tary of defense, Paul Wolfowitz, opposed the embargo as "totally and disas-trously one-sided in its effect."[29]

Violence worsened and Serbian forces soon conquered large regions of Croatia, which they hoped to annex to a "Greater Serbia." Germany began insisting to the other European nations that they recognize Croatia. Under German pressure, other nations of the Continent, and eventually the United States, followed suit—despite concern that Croatia's secession would trigger more defections and intensify the war. Indeed, the former Yugoslav province of Bosnia-Herzegovina (roughly 40 percent Muslim, and often called just Bosnia) declared independence in March 1992. Serb paramilitaries responded with extraordinary violence against both Croatia and Bosnia-Herzegovina, in a campaign of what they called "ethnic cleansing." They sought to justify annexing pieces of both republics by wiping out all vestiges of Muslim and Catholic habitation and claiming that only fellow Serbs resided in the con-tested territory. "It meant," Richard Holbrooke of the International Rescue Committee later wrote, "the killing, rape, and forced removal of people from their homes on the basis of their ethnic [and religious] background." Serbian commanders believed rape especially effective at destroying civilian morale and prompting flight, particularly when perpetrated on Muslim children and teenagers, mostly girls.[30]

For the next three years, from 1992 to mid-1995, Serbian guerillas in Croatia and Bosnia waged war against civilians, with the complicity and material support of Slobodan Milosevic in Belgrade. The United Nations negotiated three cease-fires and sent almost 40,000 blue-helmeted Peacekeepers to enforce them, with the greatest number of troops coming from Britain and France. The Serbs kept up their murderous attacks, however, and Milosevic claimed he could not control the paramilitaries outside Serbia's own borders. The United Nations and the European Community resisted using violence to make Serbian paramilitaries back down, believing that NATO bombs would further inflame Serbian nationalism and undermine the peace initiative. Prime Minister John Major of the United Kingdom and French president François Mitterrand opposed lifting the arms embargo as well. Doing so, British foreign secretary Douglas Hurd asserted, would only "level the killing field" and expose lightly armed European Peacekeepers to retaliation. "Don't add war to war," Mitterrand insisted. Europe would neither arm the Bosnians and Croats nor defend them. "Diplomacy is the only solution," they insisted for almost four years.[31]

From afar, the U.S. government, now under Bill Clinton, urged the exact opposite: arm the local people to protect themselves and bring in NATO air support. But French and British officials dismissed the advice. The United States was too aggressive, they asserted, nor did it have vulnerable peacekeepers on the ground. Indeed, Washington was reluctant to send more U.S. soldiers abroad when they had so recently returned home from Kuwait. Still hoping for a much bruited "peace dividend" at the end of the Cold War, the weary American public had little stomach for further intervention, especially where it clearly was not wanted by the European Union and was presumably not needed. President Clinton admitted to the allies that there was no absolute guarantee that bombing attacks would work anyway. UN Peacekeepers might indeed suffer retaliation. In a position to make the final decision, Britain and France ruled out the use of air power. When Serbian planes began violating UN-declared no-fly zones, NATO bombers retaliated only briefly, with what the press called "pinpricks."[32]

Two towns in Bosnia came to symbolize the limits of nonviolent persuasion. Sarajevo was the capital of Bosnia-Herzegovina. In April 1992, Serbian forces placed artillery in the hills overlooking the pretty European capital of half a million residents. They then cut off all electricity and water to the town, imposed a land blockade to prevent food from reaching residents, and began strafing the city, to force the government to capitulate. The ill-equipped Bosnians refused to leave, even after Serbian shells leveled the parliament building. For four years, Serbian troops waged a siege against the civilian center, reducing the modern town to rubble, preventing 70 percent of UN food aid from getting through, and killing tens of thousands. The Serbian blockade was so effective that even UN Peacekeepers could not get supplies.

Finally, in May 1995, NATO issued an ultimatum to the Serbs. Stop bombing Sarajevo or face retaliation. When the Serbs ignored the demand, NATO planes struck—and the Serbs took 350 UN Peacekeepers hostage as "human shields." CNN televised images around the world of UN Peacekeepers tied to trees and handcuffed to telephone poles, and French soldiers waving white flags of surrender. Horrified, the UN negotiated the release of the hostages and restricted NATO's use of force even further. The planes were grounded.[33]

The most infamous atrocity of the war took place little more than a month later. The small mountain town of Srebrenica lay north of Sarajevo, only ten miles from Serbia proper. Muslims normally made up about 75 percent of the population of 37,000, mostly well-paid miners and factory workers. Serbian paramilitary forces had captured Srebrenica in April 1992, but Muslim defenders soon retook it. For another year, Serbians lay siege to the town, to which Muslims from the countryside flocked for protection. The population swelled to 60,000. Under constant sniping by surrounding troops, residents ran out of gasoline, ammunition, tobacco, sugar, and anything else that could not be grown or made in the village. Finally, in mid-1993, the intrepid French commander in charge of UN troops in Bosnia ignored instructions from headquarters and broke through the lines. "I will never abandon you," Philippe Morillon declared, though it cost him his job. Under worldwide scrutiny now, the UN raised its flag over Srebrenica and declared the town a "safe area" for Muslims. Canadian and Dutch Peacekeepers were deployed to monitor the cease-fire. They disarmed the Muslim militias and occupied the hilltop positions that local defenders had captured from the Serbs.[34]

The fragile peace of Srebrenica broke on July 6, 1995, when Serbian tanks started shelling the UN positions. Under fire for the first time, disbelieving Dutch soldiers hunkered down in their watchtowers. They immediately radioed for NATO air strikes against Serb artillery, but their request was denied. Following the hostage-taking incident several weeks earlier, the secretary-general of the UN had nearly eliminated air support. The UN "redefined their primary mission not as the protection of the people of Srebrenica, but as the safety of the U.N. forces themselves," as New Jersey congressman Christopher Smith later succinctly described the situation.[35]

Indeed, Smith's formulation echoed the guidelines issued by the supreme commander of UN Peacekeeping Forces in Bosnia, Lieutenant-General Bernard Janvier of France. Whenever directly threatened by Serb forces, the Peacekeepers were to abandon their positions. "The execution of the mandate is secondary to the security of UN personnel," Janvier told his multinational force. Therefore, following instructions, the Dutch Peacekeepers evacuated the "safe" zone, leaving disarmed civilians to defend themselves. As two scholars commented, "The safe-area policy failed because of a contradictory moralistic impulse and a lack of collective will to use (some) force on the part of the international community."[36]

Now unopposed, Serbian forces under Ratko Mladic entered Srebrenica on July 8. There they slaughtered some victims with knives and buried others alive in mass graves. Males of all ages were systematically separated from females, taken to open fields, and mowed down with machine-gun fire. Serbian soldiers with handguns followed behind to make sure that each victim was terminated. The best estimates for the number of Muslim civilians murdered over a four-day period surpasses 8,000, mostly males. From there, Serbian forces moved on to Zepa, another so-called safety zone abandoned by the UN. "I am Ratko Mladic!" the commander shouted into a megaphone aimed at civilians cowering in the woods around the small town. "Not Allah, not the United Nations, not anything can help you. I am your God."[37]

The Clinton administration finally decided it had no choice but to press for military action, long advocated by the chief U.S. negotiator for a Bosnian peace accord, Richard Holbrooke, a career diplomat who had once directed the Peace Corps in Morocco. Secretary of State Warren Christopher agreed with Holbrooke. They needed to take the decision-making power out of the hands of international bureaucrats and give it, if possible, to competent soldiers. State Department officials struggled to avoid offending European allies or violating international due process. At the end of August 1995, U.S. ambassador to the UN Madeleine Albright finally convinced Kofi Annan, a Ghanaian diplomat in charge of UN Peacekeeping Forces, to temporarily relinquish the UN veto over NATO operations and allow NATO to determine if and when to retaliate against Serbia. Other American negotiators, including Richard Holbrooke, then convinced NATO secretary-general Willy Claes of Belgium to delegate responsibility to NATO officers in the field—Americans—who had been holding lists of Serbian targets for months.

Massive air strikes began the next day, launched from bases in Italy and from the USS *Theodore Roosevelt* in the Adriatic. The long-dead President Roosevelt would undoubtedly have approved the use, at last, of a stick big enough to stop the Serb militias. The irregular units folded like a cheap paperback. Two weeks later, meeting at a villa outside Belgrade, Slobodan Milosevic and Ratko Mladic signed an initial peace treaty negotiated by Richard Holbrooke. "We are ready for peace," complained one Serbian official (later prosecuted for war crimes) as he signed his name. "Why did you bomb us?"

Holbrooke picked up the precious surrender document and answered, "I think you know."[38]

The four-year siege of Sarajevo was lifted that day. Genocide came to a stop. Final accords were drawn up two months later in the flat prairie town of Dayton, Ohio—the heartland of America—far from Brussels and the mountainous Balkans.

"The Western mistake over the previous four years had been to treat the Serbs as rational people with whom one could argue, negotiate, compromise, and agree," Holbrooke asserted. "In fact, they respected only force or an unambiguous and credible threat to use it." William Pfaff, the Paris-based correspondent for the *International Herald Tribune,* was even more blunt. Pfaff wrote the morning after NATO air strikes finally commenced, "The United States today is again Europe's leader; there is no other. Both the Bush and Clinton administrations tried, and failed, to convince the European governments to take over Europe's leadership."[39]

American hopes that the United States could transfer some of the burden of umpiring had not materialized. Once again, the country found itself sucked into a European problem in which it had been determined (and asked) to refrain from intervening. "Predictably," National Security staff member David Gompert observed ruefully, "the attempt to hold the Yugoslav crisis at arm's length did not spare the United States the effects of, or responsibility for, the failure that followed." Reliance on the fledgling European Union was a "grave mistake," Gompert believed, for which the people of Bosnia and Croatia paid dearly.[40]

America paid, too. When Osama bin Laden pronounced his homicidal fatwa against the United States a year later, in 1996, he listed its failure to act quickly enough in Bosnia as evidence that Americans considered Muslim blood "cheapest." In Bosnia-Herzegovina, "the dispossessed people were even prevented from obtaining arms to defend themselves," the terrorist accurately pointed out.[41] Of course, two presidents had futilely advocated lifting the arms embargo. Washington eventually insisted that NATO defend the Muslim civilians. Had the United States acted earlier, it would have alienated European allies. Intervening later, it alienated some Middle Easterners. An umpire can never please everyone. By definition, umpires cannot win.

In 2011, ten years after United Flight 93 tore a hole in the bucolic fields of Pennsylvania, the United States was still fighting in Afghanistan. British, American, and Australian forces had attacked Afghanistan the month after 9/11 to unseat the Taliban government that sheltered Osama bin Laden. Ten years after 9/11, American troops were also just leaving Iraq. U.S., British, Australian, and Polish forces had attacked Iraq in 2003 in order to topple Saddam Hussein, judged (incorrectly) to be in possession of weapons of mass destruction and prepared to use them. Like the Serbians, but for a longer period, Hussein had defied UN attempts to make him heed Security Council demands. More than 4,500 Americans died in combat in the two Middle Eastern wars aimed primarily at defeating the imperial ambitions of Islamic fundamentalists. Their deaths might reasonably call to mind the ancient Chinese proverb, "He who seeks revenge should remember to dig two graves."

These wars have not yet receded into history. They bridge past, present, and future, where only fools, angels, and journalists dare to tread. Perhaps the best one can say about the ongoing conflicts, speaking from a historical rather than partisan point of view, is that the first, Afghanistan, was a defensive war. The second, in Iraq, was a preemptive one, based on a mistaken premise. The umpire, hit by a hard pitch, his eye swollen, did not correctly evaluate what was going on in Iraq. He pointed his finger and threw Saddam Hussein out of the game. It was probably a bad call, though time will be the best judge.

More precisely, the United States had led its allies into another dangerous, opaque battle—this time to alleviate the misery of the Middle East and the terrorist threats it generated. Those allies that followed did so for their own reasons, based on their own perceptions of risk. More misery resulted, the threat seemed unabated, and the end results would not be apparent for at least a generation. As in Europe in 1946, it was anyone's guess whether conflict would continue indefinitely or the subcontinent would finally achieve peace. Although democracy spread in North Africa and the Middle East in the "Arab Spring" of 2011, violence followed close behind. Ethnic and religious nationalism, complicated by al-Qaeda's imperialism, were locked in a titanic contest whose conclusion could not be foreseen.

The Islamic fundamentalists were bucking the trend of the preceding three hundred years. They hoped to restore precisely the kind of religious empire that Europeans had rejected in the Treaty of Westphalia. Their goals and methods seemed medieval because they were. Time might march forward, but human experience can always loop back. The fall of ancient Rome initiated a Dark Age across Europe. Nuclear weapons have the power to turn the light out on civilization once again, which was the best reason for caring whether Saddam Hussein possessed weapons of mass destruction.

True to its historical pattern, however, the United States withdrew from Iraq after helping to establish an elected government, supremely uninterested in creating a colony. Even when disappointed in themselves, American citizens tried to contribute toward nation-building and a safer world for all. While some allies objected strenuously to the war against Hussein (particularly Germany and France), civility prevailed. The long-term coalition held because of the larger value it had for participants on almost every continent.

Ten years after 9/11, the United States also found itself buffeted by recession. The causes were mostly endogamous—that is, the bust originated in the United States. Although the costs of umpiring certainly placed an incalculable strain on the American economy, bad lending practices and consumer speculation (on real estate rather than securities this time) tipped the nation over, much as in the Great Depression. Similar conditions in Europe led to a severe downturn there, where real estate was also grossly overvalued. Federal reserves and international coordination softened the effects on both continents. This may have averted the type of democratic meltdown that led to World War II, though it is still not possible to know.

In all regions of the world, national policies proved the surest predictors of how well or poorly a country endured the gale. Canada, for example, showed great probity in banking, the sector that precipitated collapse. There, neither the public nor private sectors required bailout funds.[42] Poverty rates actually fell worldwide, partly because of the strong performance of China and India, populous developing nations that had recently come to embrace free and accessible markets.[43] Nonetheless, to some extent the international integration of jobs and goods meant that the two hundred or so countries of the world ultimately stood or fell together.

In the centuries following the American Revolution, the position of the United States in the world changed dramatically, but its core values proved stable. Between 1776 and the present, Americans continued to believe passionately in the equality of states. They might dislike or disrespect other polities, and compete strenuously against them, but they defended the principle of juridical equality with their very lives. This transcendent ideal explains why new territories were allowed to join the union on a basis of strict parity with the founding members after 1787. It accounts for why the United States entered the imperial game late and quit early. It illuminates American leadership after both world wars in constructing global democratic organizations. It clarifies America's support for a postwar economic system in which it claimed no imperial primacy and had to run hard to stay up with the competition. It tells us why, in the words of journalist Thomas Friedman, "The world is flat." Although the metaphor of an "American Empire" has shown enormous persistence, it has little basis in fact.[44]

Does this mean that the United States instead became an objective, bona fide "umpire," with no stake in outcomes, akin to the blue-uniformed professionals on a National League baseball diamond?

To make the analogy as precise as possible, the United States bears more similarity to a player-umpire: a member of a contending team drawn into the role on an impromptu basis, as when amateur players on a community field don't have the resources for a "real" ump. A player-umpire may strive for objectivity, and be the preferred candidate for the task, but his interests are never truly apart—especially whenever a teammate slides into second base under the fielder's glove. The arrangement is not completely fair to anyone, the umpire or the other players. But it is often better than having no ump at all.

Imperialism itself came to an end in the course of the twentieth century, as the world collectively abolished it. *Access* to political power and economic opportunity, *arbitration* of conflict, and *transparency* in government became leitmotifs of national policy and global history, even though they were never the only pertinent descriptors of democratic capitalism or human society more generally. Dictatorships, warfare, and secrecy thrived as well. What changed most completely was that the majority of people, worldwide, came to believe that these older ways were wrong. They showed this in their daily demands and practices. Global systems approached the new norms asymptotically.

The founder with the least personal attachment to any particular state in the federation created by the Constitutional Convention of 1787 was Alexander Hamilton, an orphaned immigrant from the British West Indies. Perhaps for this reason, he perceived more clearly than anyone other than George Washington the necessity of forming and funding a central government to coordinate the interests of the states, create a strong economy, and prevent family disintegration. Thomas Jefferson and James Madison, privileged sons of proud Virginia, wanted to preserve the right of states to act unilaterally as well. Indeed, the ability to act unilaterally is the essence of sovereignty. These tensions—between multilateralism and unilateralism—have helped define American politics for almost three hundred years. They produced many things, but not an empire.

Notes

Introduction

1. Scholars and commentators occasionally object to appropriation of the term "American" by the citizens of the United States, arguing that all peoples in the Western Hemisphere have equal right to the name. They suggest alternative appellations, such as United Statesers, for those inhabiting the Union. This book rejects that nomenclature. Names reasonably belong to those who claim them or wish to use them. So, for example, citizens of Mexico call themselves "Mexicans," a name of far more ancient provenance in this hemisphere than "American," which is an Italian import. Nonetheless, there is nothing to prevent them, or Peruvians or Brazilians, for that matter, from adopting the moniker "American" should they choose to—but they have not. Additionally, several nations have employed the term "United States of ———." Thus, by the aforementioned logic, it would be just as presumptuous for citizens in this country to call themselves "United Statesers" as "Americans." What's in a name? Not much, except a handy identifier generally associated with the first group to use it. It is hardly surprising, or egregiously arrogant, that the first autonomous nation-state in the Western Hemisphere would call itself America.

2. D. C. Watt, ed., *Documents on the Suez Crisis* (London, 1957), 26, 29, 44, 49.

3. Diane Kunz, *The Economic Diplomacy of the Suez Crisis* (Chapel Hill, N.C., 1991).

4. David Armitage, *The Declaration of Independence: A Global History* (Cambridge, Mass., 2007), 3; Burke quoted on 87.

5. Dipesh Chakrabarty, *Provincializing Europe: Postcolonial Thought and Historical Difference* (Princeton, 2000), 16, 41.

6. David A. Moss, *When All Else Fails: Government as the Ultimate Risk Manager* (Cambridge, Mass., 2002), 56.

7. Francis Fukuyama, *The End of History and the Last Man* (New York, 1992).

8. George Kennan, *American Diplomacy* (New York, 1951).

9. Richard Dawkins, *The Selfish Gene* (Oxford, 2006), 192.

10. Robert Kagan, *The World America Made* (New York, 2012), 22–25.

11. Yun-Wing Sun, *The China–Hong Kong Connection: The Key to China's Open Door Policy* (Cambridge, U.K., 1992).

12. Federalist 85, in *The Debate on the Constitution,* v. 2 (New York, 1993), 504.

13. Yaron Ezrahi, "Technology and the Civil Epistemology of Democracy," in *Technology and the Politics of Knowledge,* ed. Andrew Feenberg and Alastair Hannay (Bloomington, Ind., 1995), 162. John Meyer's pioneering work in sociology underscores the globalization of values and practices like transparency. In a volume that elucidates Meyer's oeuvre, Yong Suk Jang discusses modern corporate accounting as a good example of the phenomenon: "Accountability involves social relations in which actors are required to provide explanations for their actions. In its simplest sense, accountability can be seen as a relationship invoking 'the giving and demanding of reasons for conduct' . . . [demonstrating] the global expansion of accounting activities and the worldwide development of the transparency model." Yong Suk Jang, "Transparent Accounting as a World Societal Rule," in *Globalization and Organization: World Society and Organizational Change,* ed. Gili Drori, John Meyer, and Hokyu Hwang (Oxford, 2006), 167–168.

14. "Web Sites Shine Light on Petty Bribery Worldwide," *New York Times,* March 7, 2012, B1.

15. Historian Dennis Bark was one of the first to make this observation. Bark, *Professor Bark's Amazing Digital Adventure: Five Faces of the Internet* (Emeryville, Calif., 2000).

16. The routine publication of British parliamentary debates began as a private enterprise by the Hansard Company, only reluctantly accepted by the legislature. See *The Parliamentary Debates from the Year 1803 to the Present Time,* ed. T. C. Hansard et al., later known simply as *Hansard's Parliamentary Debates* (after 1829). As of 2000, eleven countries routinely declassified secret diplomatic correspondence: in chronological order, the United States (1861), France (1910), the United Kingdom (1926), Japan (1936), Italy (1946), Canada (1967), Australia (1967), Netherlands (1971), Israel (1974), Germany (1990), and Ireland (1997).

17. United Nations Development Programme, *Human Development Report 2002: Deepening Democracy in a Fragmented World* (New York, 2002); Agnus Maddison, *The World Economy: A Millennial Perspective* (Paris, 2001), 30, 126; Jonathan Margolis, *A Brief History of Tomorrow: The Future, Past and Present* (London, 2000), 74; Gary M. Walton, "A Long-term Economic Perspective on Human Progress," Foundation for Teaching Economics, Davis, Calif., http://www.fte.org/capitalism/introduction/index.html (accessed 4/2/2011).

18. On the rights of territories and dependencies, see Tim Hillier, *Sourcebook on Public International Law* (London, 1998), 196.

19. It is reasonable to ask whether its relationship to Puerto Rico, the Northern Mariana Islands, or Guam makes the United States an empire still. Without going

into the considerable detail required to explain each example, it seems reasonable to assert that these cases alone are not sufficient to qualify the United States as an empire. Consistent with various UN resolutions since the 1960s, any of these territories could cancel its relationship with the United States. There is scant evidence to suggest the move would encounter significant resistance from Washington or the American public. In the case of Puerto Rico, the U.S. government has repeatedly urged it to either apply for statehood or give up its territorial status. However, in three plebiscites since 1967, Puerto Rican voters have elected to retain the ambiguous status of a U.S. commonwealth.

20. William Appleman Williams, *The Tragedy of American Diplomacy*, rev. and enl. ed. (New York, 1962), 47, 60. For Williams in full stride, see his later (and more apoplectic) work, *Empire as a Way of Life* (New York, 1980). For an overview of Williams and his legacy at the fifty-year anniversary of *The Tragedy of American Diplomacy*, see *Passport: The Newsletter of the Society for Historians of American Foreign Relations* 40, no. 3 (September 2009). For an early critique of Williams, see Arthur Schlesinger, Jr., *The Cycles of American History* (Boston, 1986), 125, 148, 161; and James A. Field, Jr., "American Imperialism: The Worst Chapter in Almost Any Book," *American Historical Review* 83, no. 3 (June 1978): 644–668.

21. Chalmers Johnson blazed this path in his best-selling series that began with *Blowback: The Costs and Consequences of American Empire* (New York, 2000).

22. The term "American empire" is commonplace but loosely defined in much of this new literature. See, for example: Barbara Bush, *Imperialism and Postcolonialism* (London, 2006); John Lewis Gaddis, *We Now Know: Rethinking Cold War History* (New York, 1997); Amy Greenberg, *Manifest Manhood and the Antebellum American Empire* (New York, 2005); Richard H. Immerman, *Empire for Liberty: A History of American Imperialism from Benjamin Franklin to Paul Wolfowitz* (Princeton, N.J., 2010); Amy Kaplan, *The Anarchy of Empire in the Making of U.S. Culture* (Cambridge, Mass., 2002); Paul A. Kramer, *The Blood of Government: Race, Empire, the United States, and the Philippines* (Chapel Hill, N.C., 2006); Geir Lundestad, *Empire by Integration: The United States and European Integration, 1945–1997* (Oxford, 1998); Charles Maier, *Among Empires* (Cambridge, Mass., 2005); Michael Mann, *Incoherent Empire* (New York, 2004); Dennis Merrill, *Negotiating Paradise: U.S. Tourism and Empire in Twentieth-Century Latin America* (Chapel Hill, N.C., 2009); Antonio Negri and Michael Hardt, *Empire* (Cambridge, Mass., 2000). Some scholars, such as Andrew Bacevich in *American Empire: The Realities and Consequences of U.S. Diplomacy* (Cambridge, Mass., 2002) and Walter Nugent in *Habits of Empire: A History of American Expansion* (New York, 2008), specifically cite William Appleman Williams as their starting point. Kathryn Statler's book on Vietnam also utilizes "the interpretation established by William Appleman Williams that the United States, as an advanced industrial nation, was . . . controlling and one-sided" and thus "imperialistic." Statler, *Replacing France: The Origins of American Intervention in Vietnam* (Lexington, Ky., 2007), 8.

23. World Development Indicators Database, World Bank, "Gross National Income per Capita 2010, Atlas Method and PPP," http://data.worldbank.org/data -catalog. On life expectancy in 2012, see Central Intelligence Agency, "The World Factbook," https://www.cia.gov/library/publications/the-world-factbook /rankorder/2102rank.html (accessed 2/21/12).

24. See, especially, Robert Kagan, *Dangerous Nation* (New York, 2006); William Earl Weeks, *John Quincy Adams and American Global Empire* (Lexington, Ky., 1992); and Nugent, *Habits of Empire.*

25. Scholars today recognize that Amerindians were as prone to coercive empire building as most other peoples around the globe, and often just as successful. See, for example, Pekka Hämäläinen, *The Comanche Empire* (New Haven, Conn., 2008), and James Gump, *The Dust Rose Like Smoke: The Subjugation of the Zulu and the Sioux* (Lincoln, Nebr., 1994).

26. Quote from Clinton Rossiter, introduction to *The Federalist Papers,* ed. Rossiter (New York, 1960), viii. The first fifteen of these essays focus persistently on the contentious question of whether or not it was possible to maintain a republican government over a territory as large as the combined thirteen original states—an area the size of "Poland before the late dismemberment," as James Madison pointed out (102).

27. Valerie Reed, "U.S. Military Bases in Foreign Nations: A Summary of the Pentagon's Data," Center for Defense Information, November 16, 2007. These data are incomplete because they do not take into account the temporary occupation forces in Iraq and Afghanistan, only bases established by treaty; see http://www.cdi .org/program/document.cfm?documentid=4140&programID=37&from_page =../friendlyversion/printversion.cfm (accessed 9/7/11).

28. Raymond Aron, *The Imperial Republic: The United States and the World, 1945–1973* (Englewood Cliffs, N.J., 1974), 257. The important exception is Guantanamo Bay in Cuba, where the United States has maintained a base for more than fifty years, against the wishes of the local government, citing the legal terms of the treaty that allowed it to establish the base in the first place. This is questionable policy, but it certainly has not made communist Cuba into a colony.

29. Alexander Hamilton, "Federalist 7," in Alexander Hamilton, James Madison, and John Jay, *The Federalist Papers,* ed. Clinton Rossiter (New York, 1961), 61. Also, John Jay, "Federalist 4," ibid., 49.

30. Author's interview with Peter MacKay, Stanford University, February 22, 2012. Also see "Invocation of Article 5: Five Years On," NATO Review, http://www .nato.int/docu/review/2006/issue2/english/art1.html (accessed 2/29/12).

31. "France and Britain Lead Military Push on Libya," *New York Times,* March 19, 2011, A9.

32. Geir Lundestad, "Empire by Invitation? The United States and Western Europe, 1945–1952," *Journal of Peace Research* 23, no. 3 (September 1986): 263–277. Thomas McCormick, *America's Half-Century: United States Foreign Policy in the Cold War and After* (Baltimore, 1995), 5.

33. Kyrgyzstan hosted both Russian and American bases. Neither superpower could claim it as an exclusive dependency, which is perhaps the best test of imperial authority. For Kyrgyzstan, foreign military bases were a way of generating cash and boosting influence, akin to oil leases. "Russia May Face Higher Rent for Kyrgyzstan Military Sites," *New York Times*, September 17, 2010, A6.

34. Mark Bowden, *Guests of the Ayatollah: The First Battle in America's War with Islam* (New York, 2006), 86.

35. Philip Zelikow, "The Transformation of National Security: Five Redefinitions," *The National Interest* (Spring 2003): 18.

1. To Compel Acquiescence

1. Even one region's deportment seemed strange to another, like the manners of a Londoner to a Parisian. As New Englander John Adams complained of New Yorkers, "I have not seen one real Gentleman, one well bred Man since I came to Town. . . . They talk very loud, very fast, and alltogether. If they ask you a Question, before you can utter 3 Words of your Answer, they will break out upon you, again— and talk away." *The Adams Papers: Digital Edition,* ed. C. James Taylor (Charlottesville, Va., 2008), Diary, August 23, 1774.

2. Daniel T. Rodgers, *Atlantic Crossings: Social Politics in a Progressive Age* (Cambridge, Mass., 1998), 1.

3. Jerome, Letter 60, reproduced in *Consoling Heliodorus: A Commentary on Jerome, Letter 60,* ed. J. H. D. Scourfield (Oxford, 1993), 69.

4. For a catalog of the Danes' remarkable pillaging, see *The Anglo Saxon Chronicle,* trans. M. J. Swanton (London, 1996), 55–198. For the quote by the monk Alcuin to the effect that the Danes trampled the holy men of Lindisfarne in 793 like "dung," see Floyd Collins, *Seamus Heaney: Crisis of Identity* (Cranbury, N.J., 2003), 80.

5. Marcilus of Padua, *The Defender of the Peace,* trans. Annabel Brett (Cambridge, U.K., 2005), 5.

6. Robert Folz, *The Concept of Empire in Western Europe from the Fifth to the Fourteenth Century* (New York, 1969), 4–7.

7. Although Rome is the focus here, there were similar precedents elsewhere around the globe, from the Han Dynasty of China to the Gupta Empire of India, where emperors imposed a general peace over competing warlords and kingdoms for which the populace was often grateful. On feudal Europe and the limits of papal authority, see Stéphane Beaulac, *The Power of Language in the Making of International Law: The Word "Sovereignty" in Bodin and Vattel and the Myth of Westphalia* (Leiden, 2004), 57–76.

8. Folz, *Concept of Empire,* xiii. According to Raymond Aron, the nostalgia for the coherence of the Roman Empire "lasted for centuries." Aron, *The Imperial Republic: The United States and the World, 1945–1973* (Englewood Cliffs, N.J., 1974), 259. Henry Kissinger notes that it was the Reformation that finally killed "the medieval

aspiration to universality" and a common world order ruled by one emperor. Kissinger, *Diplomacy* (New York, 1994), 56.

9. Richard Koebner and Helmut Dan Schmidt, *Imperialism: The Story and Significance of a Political Word, 1840–1960* (Cambridge, U.K., 1964), 45–46, 295.

10. There were some exceptions to this rule, as to all rules. In imperial cities, Charles V gave inhabitants a choice of either Catholicism or Lutheranism, allowing for individual conscience. For the sake of clarity, however, I will resist adding too many qualifications of this sort. In a more circumscribed history, fine details are important to absolute accuracy, but they can detract from a clear overview of broad trends. This account will fell a few trees to make the forest easier to see, for which I ask the reader's indulgence.

11. Quoted in Helmut Georg Koenigsberger, *Politicians and Virtuosi: Essays in Early Modern History* (London, 1986), 87.

12. "Act of Abjuration," July 26, 1581, http://www.let.rug.nl/usa/D/1501-1600 /plakkaat/plakkaaten.htm, (accessed 5/27/12).

13. Herbert Langer, *Thirty Years' War*, trans. C. S. V. Salt (New York, 1980), 58.

14. Ibid., 8 and plate 31.

15. Raymond Birn, *Crisis, Absolutism, Revolution: Europe and the World, 1648–1789*, 3rd ed. (Toronto, 2005), 3–7. Peter H. Wilson, *Europe's Tragedy: A History of the Thirty Years' War* (New York, 2009), 792.

16. Wilson, *Europe's Tragedy*, 672.

17. Deepak Lal maintains that the Westphalian system was so unprecedented as to be aberrant. He asserts that human society is best organized along imperial lines, to prevent anarchic competition and create large common markets. Lal, *In Praise of Empires: Globalization and Order* (New York, 2004), 19.

18. Ron Chernow, *Alexander Hamilton* (New York, 2005), 52.

19. Emer de Vattel, *The Law of Nations; or, The Principles of the Law of Nature applied to the Conduct and Affairs of Nations and Sovereigns,* ed. Joseph Chitty, electronic ed. (Philadelphia, 1852), xiii. Vattel assumed that the law of nations could be derived from "natural law," which was God-given. In the nineteenth century, natural law was replaced by the concept of "positive law": laws arising from specific international agreements, ratified by domestic legislatures, that created legal commitments between nations that international courts created for that purpose could adjudicate. See Tim Hillier, *Sourcebook on Public International Law* (London, 1998), 196, 2–11, and David Armitage, *The Declaration of Independence: A Global History* (Cambridge, Mass., 2007), 80.

20. Quoted in David C. Hendrickson, *Peace Pact: The Lost World of the American Founding* (Lawrence, Kans., 2003), 170.

21. Aron, *Imperial Republic*, 2.

22. For literary purposes, I occasionally use "England" as a synonym for Britain or the United Kingdom. I recognize that it is not actually synonymous, as the United Kingdom also encompasses Northern Ireland, Scotland, and Wales.

23. John Locke, "Of Monarchy, by Inheritance from Adam," in *Two Treatises of Government*, Book 1, chapter 9, paragraph 81, http://www.lonang.com/exlibris /locke/loc-109a.htm (accessed 4/2/12).

24. Barbara Tuchman, *The First Salute: A View of the American Revolution* (New York, 1988), 37.

25. Chris Cook and Jon Stevenson, *The Longman Handbook of Modern British History, 1714–2001*, 4th ed. (Harlow, U.K., 2001), 81.

26. William Bradford, *History of Plymouth Plantation*, ed. Samuel Eliot Morison (New York, 1952), 77, 443.

27. William Appleman Williams makes particularly scathing use of Winthrop's phrase, which he equates with a U.S. imperium. Williams, *Empire as a Way of Life* (New York, 1980), viii–vix.

28. John Winthrop, "A Model of Christian Charity" (1630), reprinted in *The Winthrop Papers, Volume 2, 1623–1630*, ed. Stewart Mitchell, Massachusetts Historical Society (Boston, 1931), 295.

29. "Resolutions," October 19, 1765, in *Collections of Interesting, Authentic Papers Relative to the Dispute between Great Britain and North America*, ed. John Almon (London, 1777), 27.

30. Thomas Paine, *Common Sense and Other Writings* (New York, 2005), 39. Prior to the Revolution, the English system was believed to be, as Samuel Adams put it, "the best model of Government that can be framed by Mortals." Quoted in Gordon Wood, *Creation of the American Republic, 1776–1787* (New York, 1972), 11.

31. Jeremy Bentham quoted in Armitage, *Declaration of Independence*, 79. Bentham spoke for a variety of observers, both sympathetic and unsympathetic, who dismissed the legal claims of the Americans as specious.

32. Articles of Confederation and Perpetual Union, 1777, Article III: "The said States hereby severally enter into a firm league of friendship with each other, for their common defense, the security of their liberties, and their mutual and general welfare, binding themselves to assist each other, against all force offered to, or attacks made upon them, or any of them, on account of religion, sovereignty, trade, or any other pretense whatever."

33. David Hendrickson, "The First Union: Nationalism versus Internationalism in the American Revolution," in *Empire and Nation: The American Revolution in the Atlantic World*, ed. Eliga Gould and Peter Onuf (Baltimore, 2005), 46.

34. See, for example, Jefferson's comments on "this country's" prior intolerance of religious differences and on architecture in "our country," both clear references to Virginia itself. Jefferson, *Notes on the State of Virginia* (Richmond, Va., 1853), 164, 168. Also see, even more famously, in his comments on slavery: "Indeed I tremble for my country when I realize that God is just: that his justice cannot sleep forever" (174–175). Joseph Ellis makes the same point in *American Creation: Triumphs and Tragedies at the Founding of the Republic* (New York, 2007), 88–89.

35. Hendrickson, "The First Union," 38.

36. Articles of Confederation and Perpetual Union, Article V: "In determining questions in the United States in Congress assembled, each State shall have one vote."

37. James Madison, Federalist 10, in Alexander Hamilton, James Madison, and John Jay, *The Federalist Papers*, ed. Clinton Rossiter (New York, 1961), 81, hereafter cited as *Federalist Papers*. Also see Arthur Schlesinger, Jr., *The Cycles of American History* (Boston, 1986), 5–7.

38. James Madison, "Notes on Ancient and Modern Confederacies," April–June? 1786, in *The Papers of James Madison: Digital Edition*, ed. J. C. A. Stagg (Charlottesville, Va., 2010), 16; hereafter cited as *Madison Papers*.

39. David Walter Brown, *The Commercial Power of Congress, Considered in Light of Its Origin* (New York, 1910), 19.

40. Washington to James McHenry, August 22, 1785, in *The Papers of George Washington: Digital Edition*, ed. Theodore Crackel (Charlottesville, Va., 2008); hereafter, cited as *Washington Papers*.

41. David McCullough, *John Adams* (New York, 2001), 337, 351. On the lack of diplomatic reciprocity, see Charles R. Ritcheson, *Aftermath of Revolution: British Policy toward the United States, 1783–1795* (Dallas, 1969), viii, 127, 140–141. Only after the election of George Washington and "the creation of a respectable central government" did Britain consider sending a diplomatic representative, effective in the spring of 1791.

42. Chernow, *Hamilton*, 225.

43. Thomas Jefferson to James Madison, January 30, 1787, in *The Papers of Thomas Jefferson: Digital Edition*, ed. Barbara B. Oberg and J. Jefferson Looney (Charlottesville, Va., 2009); hereafter cited as *Jefferson Papers*.

44. Leonard L. Richards, *Shays's Rebellion: The American Revolution's Final Battle* (Philadelphia, 2002), 63.

45. Ibid., 8, 15–16, 59.

46. Jefferson to Madison, January 30, 1787, *Jefferson Papers*.

47. Washington to David Humphreys, October 22, 1786; Washington to Henry Lee, October 31, 1786; Washington to Knox, December 26, 1786, *Washington Papers*. On Samuel Adams see Richards, *Shays's Rebellion*, 16.

48. Jack Rakove, *The Beginnings of National Politics: An Interpretive History of the Continental Congress* (Baltimore, 1979), 216, 335, 341. For Washington's complaint, see Washington to Jefferson, March 29, 1784, *Washington Papers*. On the Treaty of Paris, see Ellis, *American Creation*, 88.

49. Madison, "Vices of the Political System of the United States," April 1787, *Madison Papers*.

50. Rakove, *The Beginnings of National Politics*, 365, 339–340.

51. Washington to David Humphreys, October 22, 1786, *Washington Papers*. On Burke, see Jack Rakove, *Revolutionaries: A New History of the Invention of America* (New York, 2010), 69.

52. Mercy Otis Warren, *History of the Rise, Progress and Termination of the American Revolution,* excerpted in *The Essential Antifederalist,* ed. W. B. Allen and Gordon Lloyd, 2nd ed. (Lanham, Md., 2002), 288–289.

53. Robert Yates and Robert Lansing, Jr., to Governor George Clinton, quoted in Catherine Drinker Bowen, *Miracle at Philadelphia* (Boston, 1966), 311–312. Alexander Hamilton was the only member of New York's three-person delegation to support the Constitution.

54. Madison to Washington, April 16, 1787; Madison to Randolph, April 8, 1787, *Madison Papers.*

55. Jack Rakove makes the point that the founders grasped and accepted the idea of judicial review, even though the principle would be more fully articulated in *Marbury v. Madison.* Rakove, *Revolutionaries,* 377.

56. John Austin Stevens, *Albert Gallatin,* 6th ed., American Statesmen (Boston, 1888), 40. For a recent treatment, see Pauline Maier, *Ratification: The People Debate the Constitution, 1787–1788* (New York, 2010).

57. Alexander Hamilton, Federalist 1, *Federalist Papers,* 33.

58. Alison LaCroix, *The Ideological Origins of American Federalism* (Cambridge, Mass., 2010), 22–23.

59. Peter and Nicholas Onuf, *Federal Union, Modern World: The Law of Nations in an Age of Revolutions, 1776–1814* (Madison, Wis., 1993), 55–56, 68.

60. Washington to "Officials of the City of Richmond," November 15, 1784, and to William Grayson, June 22, 1785, *Washington Papers.* New York, incidentally, traces the origin of its nickname, the Empire State, to Washington's reputed reference to it in December 1784 as "at present the seat of the Empire": http://www.nyhistory.com/empire.htm (accessed 12/7/11).

61. Madison to Monroe, June 21, 1786, *Madison Papers.*

62. Hamilton, Federalist 1, 33. On the Constitutional Convention's dismissal of the proposal to ensure a permanent voting majority for the original thirteen colonies, see Rakove, *Revolutionaries,* 373. Haitian Declaration of Independence, January 1, 1804, reprinted in Armitage, *Declaration of Independence,* 193.

63. "Draft of Report of the Harrisburg Conference," September 3, 1788, *Writings of Albert Gallatin,* vol. 1, ed. Henry Adams (Philadelphia, 1879), 1. For the final report see: http://www.constitution.org/bor/amdpacon.htm (accessed 3/12/11).

64. Lowe quoted in *Oxford English Dictionary Online,* 2nd ed. (Oxford, 1989), "Umpire, *n,*" from the translation of *Lucan's Pharsalia.* Madison, Federalist 43, *Federalist Papers,* 277.

65. Patrick Henry at the Virginia Ratifying Convention, June 4 and 5, 1788, quoted in Allen, *Essential Antifederalist,* 129.

66. Ibid., 135, 130.

67. John Jay, Federalist, *Federalist Papers,* 49.

68. Alexander Hamilton, Federalist 9, *Federalist Papers,* 71–73.

69. Alexander Hamilton, Federalist 6, *Federalist Papers,* 59.

70. James Madison and Alexander Hamilton, Federalist 18, *Federalist Papers,* 124.

71. Hamilton, Federalist 1, 33, and Federalist 7, *Federalist Papers,* 61, 66.

72. Hamilton, Federalist 1, 36.

73. John Jay, Federalist 5, *Federalist Papers,* 51.

74. W. B. Allen and Gordon Lloyd, "Interpretive Essay," in Allen, *Essential Antifederalist,* xvi.

75. William Appleman Williams is somewhat unclear on this point, but he implies that the founders had a genuinely imperialistic—not democratic—outlook. He notes that they "used the word [empire] regularly . . . in speaking of their own condition, policies, and aspirations," and that "later generations became steadily less candid about their imperial attitudes and practices." Williams, *Empire as a Way of Life,* viii. Robert Kazan claims that imperialist, territorial expansionism was a deeply held goal of those of the founders' generation, "who were convinced their new nation was destined for a greatness approaching that of Rome and Athens." Robert Kagan, *Dangerous Nation* (New York, 2006), 67. Richard Immerman bases his book on the same assumption: that colonial Americans hoped to create an imperialistic empire akin to Great Britain, though paradoxically, one more committed to liberty. Immerman, *Empire for Liberty: A History of American Imperialism from Benjamin Franklin to Paul Wolfowitz* (Princeton, N.J., 2010).

76. Maryland Farmer, Essay III, Part One, March 7, 1788, in Allen, *Essential Antifederalist,* 127.

77. Rakove, *Beginnings of National Politics,* 350.

78. James Madison, "Federalist No. 14," *Federalist Papers,* 101–102.

79. Jay, "Federalist No. 5," 50–51; "Federalist No. 4," 48.

80. Gordon Wood, *Revolutionary Characters: What Made the Founders Different* (New York, 2006), 49.

81. Rakove, *Beginnings of National Politics,* 393.

82. Madison, "Federalist No. 10," 78, 81, 84; also see "Federalist No. 14," 100.

83. *Poughkeepsie Country Journal,* October 3, 1787, in *The Documentary History of the Ratification of the Constitution: Digital Edition,* ed. John P. Kaminski et al. (Charlottesville, Va., 2009).

84. Vattel, *The Law of Nations,* xiii.

85. Ellis, *American Creation,* 90–91.

86. Immerman, *Empire for Liberty,* 8. Even Ellis, normally a painstaking analyst of the founders' rhetoric, glosses over Washington's meaning of "empire." Ellis, *American Creation,* 87–89.

87. Hendrickson, *Peace Pact,* 176.

2. Umpire Attacked

1. "Expedition to the Ohio, 1754: Narrative," letter from Washington to his brother John Augustine, May 31, 1754, *The Papers of George Washington: Digital Edition,* ed. Theodore Crackel (Charlottesville, Va., 2008); hereafter, *Washington Papers.*

2. Washington to Knox, April 1, 1789; diary entry, April 16, 1789, *Washington Papers.*

3. Aaron Burr famously shot Alexander Hamilton in 1804. Less well known is that Hamilton's eldest son also lost a fatal duel against one of his father's political critics, or that New York mayor Dewitt Clinton put two bullets in the leg of one of his opponents. As Ron Chernow observes, there were many such affairs of honor in the early republic, when dueling became "fashionable for settling political quarrels." These were personal affairs, however, not government policy, as during the French Reign of Terror. Ron Chernow, *Alexander Hamilton* (New York, 2004), 662. Nor was dueling limited to the United States in this period, as shown in the infamous clash between British minister of war Lord Castlereagh and Foreign Secretary George Canning in 1809. Also see Richard Hofstadter, *The Idea of a Party System; The Rise of Legitimate Opposition in the United States, 1780–1840* (Berkeley, Calif., 1969), 86–102; and, Paul Varg, *Foreign Policy of the Founding Fathers* (East Lansing, Mich., 1963), chapter 5, "Credit versus Markets: The Origin of Party Conflict over Foreign Policy." The works of Joseph Ellis, especially *Founding Brothers: The Revolutionary Generation* (New York, 2000), best illuminate the divisive rivalry that erupted after 1789.

4. Washington quoted in Felix Gilbert, *To the Farewell Address: Ideas of Early American Foreign Policy* (Princeton, N.J., 1961), Appendix, 138. Gilbert's book remains the best short monograph on the foreign policy ideas of the revolutionary generation. On their integration of realism and idealism, see David Hendrickson, *Union, Nation, or Empire: The American Debate over International Relations, 1789–1941* (Lawrence, Kans., 2009), 32.

5. Jefferson to Madison, March 24, 1793, *The Papers of Thomas Jefferson: Digital Edition,* ed. Barbara B. Oberg and J. Jefferson Looney (Charlottesville, Va., 2009); hereafter, *Jefferson Papers.*

6. Gilbert, *Farewell Address,* chapter 3: "Novus Ordo Seculorum."

7. Guillame-François Le Trosne, quoted in Gilbert, *Farewell Address,* 61.

8. On the anti-imperialism of the Enlightenment, also see Sankar Muthu, *Enlightenment against Empire* (Princeton, N.J., 2003).

9. Gilbert, *Farewell Address,* 57.

10. F. W. Hirst, *From Adam Smith to Philip Snowden: A History of Free Trade in Great Britain* (New York, 1925), 4, 8–9.

11. David Hume, "Of the Jealousy of Trade," *Essays and Treatises on Several Subjects* (Dublin, 1779), 351; available online from Electronic Text Center, University of Virginia Library, http://etext.lib.virginia.edu/images/modeng/public/HumJeal /HumJe351.jpg.

12. On the middle class, see Gilbert, *Farewell Address*, 64.

13. Thomas Paine, *Common Sense and Other Writings* (New York, 2005), 34.

14. David McCullough, *John Adams* (New York, 2001), 161; Adams quoted in Gilbert, *Farewell Address*, 49.

15. *Journals of the Continental Congress, 1774–1789* (July 18, 1776), ed. Worthington C. Ford et al. (Washington, D.C., 1904–37), 5:576–577; available online from Library of Congress.

16. Gilbert, *Farewell Address*, 51.

17. *Journals of the Continental Congress*, September 24, 1776, 5:813.

18. Gilbert, *Farewell Address*, 53, 54.

19. Jonathan R. Dull, *A Diplomatic History of the American Revolution* (New Haven, Conn., 1985), 92.

20. *The Papers of Robert Morris, 1781–1784: January 1–October 30, 1784* (Pittsburgh, 1999), 486f.

21. James Breck Perkins, *France in the American Revolution* (Williamstown, Mass., 1970), 382, 386–387.

22. Peter Onuf and Nicholas Onuf, *Federal Union, Modern World: The Law of Nations in the Age of Revolutions, 1776–1814* (Madison, Wis., 1993), 15.

23. Charles Ritcheson, *Aftermath of Revolution: British Policy toward the United States, 1783–1795* (Dallas, 1969), 6.

24. James Madison, May 4, 1789, "Tonnage Duties," *The Papers of James Madison: Digital Edition*, ed. J. C. A. Stagg (Charlottesville, Va., 2010); hereafter, *Madison Papers*.

25. Quotes from Madison in ibid. Also see Ritcheson, *Aftermath of Revolution*, 13, 92, and Drew McCoy, *The Elusive Republic: Political Economy in Jeffersonian America* (Chapel Hill, N.C., 1980), 138, 140–147. On "gee gaws," Jefferson quoted in Burton Spivak, *Jefferson's English Crisis: Commerce, Embargo, and the Republican Revolution* (Charlottesville, Va., 1979), 4, 39.

26. C. J. Bartlett and Gene A. Smith, "A 'Species of Milito-Nautico-Guerilla-Plundering Warfare,'" *Britain and America Go to War: The Impact of War and Warfare in Anglo-America, 1754–1815*, ed. Julie Flavell and Stephen Conway (Gainesville, Fla., 2004), 174.

27. James Madison, "Notes for Speech in Congress," April 9, 1789, *Madison Papers*.

28. McCoy, *Elusive Republic*, 143.

29. Madison, "Notes for Speech in Congress."

30. Garry Wills, *James Madison* (New York, 2002), 44.

31. Lawrence quoted in McCoy, *Elusive Republic*, 144.

32. Alexander Hamilton, Federalist 11, Avalon Project, Yale University, http://avalon.law.yale.edu/18th_century/fed11.asp (accessed 4/3/12).

33. Thomas Jefferson, "Final State of the Report on Commerce," December 16, 1793, *Jefferson Papers*.

34. Jefferson to Lafayette, November 3, 1786, *Jefferson Papers.*

35. McCoy, *Elusive Republic,* 151.

36. Chernow, *Hamilton,* 374.

37. Ibid., 294. Spivak, *Jefferson's English Crisis,* 5.

38. McCoy, *Elusive Republic,* chap. 1.

39. Jefferson to Madison, October 1, 1792, *Jefferson Papers* (italics added).

40. Abigail Adams quoted in Chernow, *Hamilton,* 383.

41. Hamilton to Edward Carrington, May 26, 1792, *Papers of Alexander Hamilton,* 27 vols. (New York, 1961–1987), 11:429, 438–439; hereafter cited as *Hamilton Papers.*

42. Washington to Jefferson, July 6, 1796, and Jefferson to Edward Rutledge, June 24, 1797, *Jefferson Papers.*

43. Hamilton to Henry Lee, June 22, 1793, *Hamilton Papers,* 15:15, 16; also see Doina Pasca Harsanyi, *Lessons from America: Liberal French Nobles in Exile, 1793–1798* (University Park, Pa., 2010), 83.

44. Morris to Jefferson, September 10, 1792, *Jefferson Papers.*

45. William Short to Jefferson, July 20 and August 15, 1792, *Jefferson Papers.*

46. Jefferson to Short, January 3, 1793, *Jefferson Papers.* Jefferson later appealed to Congress to assist Lafayette in his imprisonment by retroactively paying the marquis for service in the Continental Army, for which Lafayette had previously refused compensation. Count de Rochambeau escaped execution by an accident of timing. The cart that came to take him to his rendezvous with the guillotine was full. By the time of the next scheduled execution, "Robespierre had been sent to the block and the prisoners were liberated." Jefferson to Washington, December 30, 1793, *Jefferson Papers;* Perkins, *France,* 411.

47. Jefferson to Washington, September 9, 1792, *Jefferson Papers.*

48. Quoted in Chernow, *Hamilton,* 434.

49. Ibid., 433.

50. Jefferson to Madison, March 24, 1793, *Jefferson Papers.*

51. Alexander Hamilton, *Hamilton Papers,* 14:372.

52. Thomas Jefferson, "Final State of the Report on Commerce."

53. Ritcheson, *Aftermath of Revolution,* 299–301.

54. David Walter Brown, *Commercial Power of Congress* (New York, 1910), 185–187. Also see the president's correspondence from March through April 1794 for numerous references to enforcement of the embargo, *Washington Papers.*

55. Ritcheson, *Aftermath of Revolution,* 309.

56. George Herring, *From Colony to Superpower: U.S. Foreign Relations since 1776* (New York, 2008), 77. On British reparations, see Greg H. Williams, *The French Assault on American Shipping, 1793–1813: A History and Comprehensive Record of Merchant Marine Losses* (Jefferson, N.C., 2009), 19.

57. Herring, *From Colony,* 78–79.

58. Jefferson to Mann Page, August 30, 1795, *Jefferson Papers.*

59. "Jefferson's Fair Copy," before October 4, 1798, *Jefferson Papers*.

60. "Virginia Resolutions," December 21, 1798, *Madison Papers*.

61. Williams, *French Assault*, 2.

62. Ron Chernow, *Washington: A Life* (New York, 2010), 780, 816.

63. Stoddert quoted in Spencer Tucker, *The Jeffersonian Gunboat Navy* (Columbia, S.C., 1993), 9. Also see ibid., 6, and Williams, *French Assault*, 25, 31. Robert G. Albion, *The Makers of Naval Policy: 1798–1947* (Annapolis, Md., 1980), 184. Statistics on British naval strength obtained from National Museum of the Royal Navy, December 16, 2010 (courtesy of Allison Wareham, librarian).

3. Another Umpire than Arms

1. Jefferson to George Logan, March 21, 1801, *The Papers of Thomas Jefferson: Digital Edition*, ed. Barbara B. Oberg and J. Jefferson Looney (Charlottesville, Va., 2009); hereafter, *Jefferson Papers*.

2. For an overview, see David Armitage and Sanjay Subrahmanyam, eds., *The Age of Revolutions in Global Context, c. 1760–1840*, (London, 2010).

3. Burton Spivak, *Jefferson's English Crisis: Commerce, Embargo, and the Republican Revolution* (Charlottesville, Va., 1979), 5, 15. Drew McCoy, *The Elusive Republic: Political Economy in Jeffersonian America* (Chapel Hill, N.C., 1980), 187.

4. Jefferson to Robert J. Livingston, September 9, 1801, quoted in Spivak, *Jefferson's English Crisis*, 7. Jefferson to George Logan March 21, 1801, *Jefferson Papers*.

5. Napoleon quoted (October 18, 1797) by Philip Dwyer, *Napoleon: The Path to Power* (London, 2007), 334.

6. Geoffrey Ellis, *The Napoleonic Empire* (Atlantic Highlands, N.J., 1991), 109.

7. Jefferson to Livingston, April 18, 1802, cited in *Major Problems in American Foreign Relations*, ed. Dennis Merrill and Thomas Paterson, vol. 1, 5th ed. (Boston, 2000), 96.

8. Spivak, *Jefferson's English Crisis*, 86.

9. Jefferson to Madison, December 20, 1787, *Jefferson Papers*.

10. Napoleon's March 1821 comment is quoted in Emilio Ocampo, *The Emperor's Last Campaign: A Napoleonic Empire in America* (Tuscaloosa, Ala., 2009), xiv–xv.

11. Napoleon quoted in François Barbé-Marbois, *The History of Louisiana, Particularly of the Cession of That Colony to the United States of America*, trans. E. Wilson Lyon (1830; repr., Baton Rouge, La., 1977), 276, 312.

12. "Foreign Trade—Value of Exports and Imports: 1790–1945," *Historical Statistics of the United States* (Washington, D.C., 1949), 245.

13. Spivak, *Jefferson's English Crisis*, 39.

14. Louis Bergernon, *France under Napoleon*, trans. R. R. Palmer (Princeton, N.J., 1981), 173. Ellis, *Napoleonic Empire*, 99–101.

15. James Fulton Zimmerman, *Impressment of American Seamen* (1925; repr., Port Washington, N.Y., 1966), 267.

16. Quoted in Charles R. Ritcheson, *Aftermath of Revolution: British Policy toward the United States, 1783–1795* (Dallas, 1969), 380.

17. Ibid. Monthly pay was six pounds sterling on average. The prevailing exchange rate was roughly $4.44 per English pound. See "Weights and Measures," April 7, 1821, *Niles' Weekly Register: Documents, Essays, and Facts* (Baltimore, 1821), 91.

18. Spivak, *Jefferson's English Crisis*, 22.

19. Albert Gallatin to Jefferson, April 13, 1807, *The Writings of Albert Gallatin*, ed. Henry Adams, 3 vols. (Philadelphia, 1879), 1:332–333. See also Bradford Perkins, *The Creation of a Republican Empire*, excerpted in Merrill and Paterson, *Major Problems*, 140.

20. Tammany Society quoted in Spivak, *Jefferson's English Crisis*, 71.

21. Spivak, *Jefferson's English Crisis*, 29, 71.

22. Jefferson to G. K. van Hogendorp, October 13, 1785, *Jefferson Papers*.

23. Robert E. Cray, Jr., "Remembering the USS *Chesapeake*: The Politics of Maritime Death and Impressment," *Journal of the Early Republic* 25, no. 3 (Fall 2005): 452–464.

24. Ibid. Madison to James Monroe, July 6, 1807, reproduced in Merrill and Paterson, *Major Problems*, 129.

25. Jefferson to William Duane, July 20, 1807, quoted in Spivak, *Jefferson's English Crisis*, 73.

26. Albert Gallatin to Joseph Nicholson, July 17, 1807, in *Writings of Gallatin*, 1:339. See also Spivak, *Jefferson's English Crisis*, 83 and 97.

27. Gallatin to Jefferson, October 21, 1807, in Spivak, *Jefferson's English Crisis*, 97.

28. Gerry to Madison, March 12, 1806, in Spivak, *Jefferson's English Crisis*, 69.

29. Jefferson first recommended embargo in 1774, when he penned the resolution of Albemarle County to put "an immediate stop to . . . all commercial intercourse with every part of the British Empire." In this, Virginia was united with other rebellious colonies. Quoted in Louis M. Sears, *Jefferson and the Embargo* (1927; repr., New York, 1966), 47–48.

30. J. Barnes to Jefferson, quoted in Sears, *Jefferson and the Embargo*, 55.

31. Spivak, *Jefferson's English Crisis*, 104.

32. Gallatin to Jefferson, December 18, 1807, *Writings of Gallatin*, 1:368.

33. "Alexander Hamilton's Letter of Instructions to the Commanding Officers of the Revenue Cutter," June 4, 1791; available on the U.S. Coast Guard website: http://www.uscg.mil/history/faqs/hamiltonletter.pdf (accessed 7/18/12).

34. New Hampshire legislature quoted in Sears, *Jefferson and the Embargo*, 104. "Message from the President of the United States, inclosing certain resolutions of the

Senate and House of Representatives of the state of Pennsylvania," December 30, 1808, *Early American Imprints,* Series 2, no. 18961.

35. Sears, *Jefferson and the Embargo,* 89.

36. Gallatin to Jefferson, August 17, 1808, *Writings of Gallatin,* 1:406. Sears, *Jefferson and the Embargo,* 75.

37. Gallatin to Jefferson, August 6, 1808, *Writings of Gallatin,* 1:401. See also Sears, *Jefferson and the Embargo,* 84, 91, 134.

38. "Remonstrance of the Massachusetts Legislature against the Embargo Laws," February 27, 1809, 10th Congress, 2d Session, "Commerce and Navigation," no. 142, 776.

39. *Historical Statistics,* 245.

40. Jack McLaughlin, *To His Excellency Thomas Jefferson: Letters to a President* (New York, 1991), 27, 35, 36, 38.

41. Jefferson to Gallatin, May 16, 1808, *Writings of Gallatin,* 1:389.

42. "Embargo," communicated to the House of Representatives, February 6, 1809, 10th Congress, 2d Session, no. 139, 744–745. James M. Banner, Jr., *To the Hartford Convention* (New York, 1970), 299–300.

43. Perkins, *Creation of a Republican Empire,* 142.

44. See Bartlett and Smith, "A Species of Warfare," for an account of the atrocities and anger on both sides.

45. *Historical Statistics of the United States,* 245.

46. See J. C. A. Stagg, *Mr. Madison's War: Politics, Diplomacy, and Warfare in the Early American Republic, 1783–1830* (Princeton, N.J., 1983), x. Also, Samuel Eliot Morison, "America's Most Unpopular War," *Proceedings of the Massachusetts Historical Society,* 3rd ser., 80 (1968): 42; Otis quoted on 39.

47. Theodore Dwight, *History of the Hartford Convention* (New York, 1833), 332.

48. Wirt to Mrs. Wirt, October 15, 1814, in Stagg, *Mr. Madison's War,* 472–473.

49. Lowell and others quoted in Morison, "America's Most Unpopular War," 48, 50–51, 54. Stagg, *Madison's War,* 473.

50. Quoted in Banner, *Hartford Convention,* 316–317, 322. Noah Webster claimed that ferment was stronger in rural towns than in Boston—similar to the earlier topography of Shays's Rebellion.

51. *Historical Statistics of the United States,* 245, 335.

52. Sears, *Jefferson and the Embargo,* 278–279.

53. Ibid., 31.

54. Jefferson, "Final State of the Report on Commerce," December 16, 1793, *Jefferson Papers.*

55. Ocampo, *Emperor's Last Campaign,* 56, 63. Napoleon called America a place "where you can enjoy a very special kind of freedom. If you are sad, you can get on your carriage and travel a thousand miles enjoying the pleasures of a simpler traveler.

In America you are everybody's equal; you can get lost in the crowd without difficulty, with your customs, your language, your religion, etc."

4. A Rowboat in the Wake of a Battleship

1. Robert P. Broadwater, "William B. Mumford Became a Southern Hero for Defying Union Soldiers in New Orleans," *America's Civil War* 18, no. 5 (November 2005): 20, 60. See also Chester G. Hearn, *The Capture of New Orleans, 1862* (Baton Rouge, 1995), 244–246.

2. Richard Horowitz, "International Law and State Transformation in China, Siam, and the Ottoman Empire during the Nineteenth Century," *Journal of World History* 15, no. 4 (December 2004): 475. M. S. Anderson, *The Rise of Modern Diplomacy, 1450–1919* (London, 1993), 99. Daniel Headrick, *The Tools of Empire: Technology and European Imperialism in the Nineteenth Century* (Oxford, 1981).

3. Nelson Reed, *The Caste War of Yucatán*, rev. ed. (Stanford, Calif., 2001).

4. Mill quoted in Thomas Bender, *A Nation among Nations: America's Place in World History* (New York, 2006), 127. Benedict Anderson, *Imagined Communities: Reflections on the Origin and Spread of Nationalism* (London, 1991).

5. Scholars today recognize that Amerindians were as prone to coercive empire building as other peoples around the globe, and often just as successful. See, for example, Pekka Hämäläinen, *The Comanche Empire* (New Haven, Conn., 2008), and James Gump, *The Dust Rose Like Smoke: The Subjugation of the Zulu and the Sioux* (Lincoln, Nebr., 1994).

6. Reginald Horsman, *Race and Manifest Destiny* (Cambridge, Mass., 1981), 14, 48, 152.

7. The United States negotiated acquisition of the Ohio Valley, Louisiana, Florida, Oregon, Arizona (Gadsden Purchase), and Alaska. It conquered the territory of California/New Mexico. For a characterization of American policy as exceptionally violent, see Walter Hixson in *The Myth of American Diplomacy: National Identity and U.S. Foreign Policy* (New Haven, Conn., 2008). Richard Immerman says that Americans obtained the continent by "combining force (primarily) and diplomacy (secondarily)." Immerman, *Empire for Liberty: A History of American Imperialism from Benjamin Franklin to Paul Wolfowitz* (Princeton, N.J., 2010), 7.

8. Charles Gibson, "Conquest, Capitulation, and Indian Treaties," *American Historical Review* 83, no. 1 (February 1978): 1–15. "Report of the Royal Commission on Aboriginal peoples," Government of Canada, updated February 8, 2006, www.collectionscanada.gc.ca/webarchives/2007 (accessed 1/31/11).

9. Stuart Banner, "Why Terra Nullius? Anthropology and Property Law in Early Australia," *Law and History Review* 23, no. 1 (Spring 2005). Australian policy changed only in 1992, in the landmark decision *Mabo v. Queensland.*

10. Simon Collier, "Nationality, Nationalism, and Supranationalism in the Writings of Simón Bolívar," *Hispanic American Historical Review* 63, no. 1 (February 1983): 37–64.

11. Like the United States, Britain often acted from a combination of motives. It sometimes acted against self-interest, such as by prohibiting the export of slaves to the Americas after 1807 (a profitable international trade that it had dominated) and freeing all slaves in its own colonies in the 1830s. Seymour Drescher, *Econocide: British Slavery in the Era of Abolition* (Chapel Hill, N.C., 2010), 27.

12. Bender, *A Nation among Nations,* 127–128.

13. Adams quoted in Walter LaFeber, *The American Age: United States Foreign Policy at Home and Abroad since 1750* (New York, 1989), 82.

14. Adams, November 7, 1823, *Diary of John Quincy Adams, 1794–1845,* ed. Allan Nevins (New York, 1951), 303; hereafter cited as *Diary of JQA.*

15. On Monroe's attitude, see *Diary of JQA,* 178, 186. In the War of 1812, the United States suffered an estimated 2,260 killed, 4,505 wounded. Donald R. Hickey, *The War of 1812: A Forgotten Conflict* (Chicago, 1989), 302.

16. Edward J. Renehan, Jr., *The Monroe Doctrine: The Cornerstone of American Foreign Policy* (New York, 2007), 83.

17. Lord Castlereagh, "State Paper of 5 May 1820; or the Foundation of British Foreign Policy," in Harold Temperley and Lillian Penson, *Foundations of British Foreign Policy: From Pitt (1792) to Salisbury (1902)* (London, 1966), 54.

18. Lord Byron quoted in George Austin Test, *Satire: Spirit and Art* (Gainesville, Fla., 1991), 141. Shelley, *Complete Works,* ed. Nathan Dole (London, 1905), 193.

19. Quoted in Norman Lowe, *Mastering Modern British History,* 4th ed. (London, 2009), 44.

20. Felix Gilbert expertly charts this genealogy in *To the Farewell Address* (Princeton, N.J., 1971).

21. Castlereagh quoted in Temperley and Penson, *Foundations of British Foreign Policy,* 61, 52.

22. George Herring, *From Colony to Superpower* (New York, 2008), 143–144.

23. George Canning to the Chevalier de Los Rios, Minister Plenipotentiary of His Most Catholic Majesty, March 25, 1825, in Temperley and Penson, *Foundations of British Foreign Policy,* 78–79. Also see G. A. Gooch and J. H. B. Masterman, *A Century of British Foreign Policy* (1917; repr., London, 1971), 4–5.

24. Congressional Committee on Foreign Affairs (1822), quoted in Gregory Weeks, "Almost Jeffersonian: U.S. Recognition Policy toward Latin America," *Presidential Studies Quarterly* 31, no. 3 (September 2001): 493.

25. Temperley and Penson, *Foundations of British Foreign Policy,* 70, 75.

26. Adams, November 7, 1823, *Diary of JQA,* 304–305.

27. Ukase quoted in Irby C. Nichols, Jr., "The Russian Ukase and the Monroe Doctrine: A Re-Evaluation," *Pacific Historical Review* 36, no. 1 (February 1967): 13.

28. Adams, November 15, 1823, *Diary of JQA*, 305.

29. Adams, February 16, 1821, *Diary of JQA*, 254.

30. It was President James K. Polk who coined the phrase, "Monroe Doctrine." Renehan, *Monroe Doctrine*, 89.

31. Washington, "The Farewell Address," Transcript of the Final Manuscript, from *The Papers of George Washington: Digital Edition*, ed. Theodore Crackel (Charlottesville, Va., 2008), 25, 27.

32. Canning quoted in Gooch and Masterman, *A Century*, 5. Also see the "Polignac Memorandum" and related comments in Temperley and Penson, *Foundations of British Foreign Policy*, 70–77. On casualties in the wars of independence, see Timothy Anna, "The Independence of Mexico and Central America," in *The Independence of Latin America*, ed. Leslie Bethell (Cambridge, U.K., 1987), 91.

33. Quoted in Armin Rappaport, *A History of American Diplomacy* (New York, 1975), 92.

34. Bolívar to Francisco de Paula Santander, April 7, 1825, quoted in David Sowell, "The Mirror of Public Opinion Bolívar, Republicanism and the United States Press, 1821–1831," *Revista de Historia de América* 134 (2004): 169.

35. Tang-i Li, *A History of Modern China*, trans. L. Bennett and Hsüeh-feng Yang (Dartmouth, N.H., 1970), 26.

36. Herman Melville, *Moby Dick: Or, The White Whale* (Boston, 1892), 107.

37. Adam Smith, *Inquiry into the Nature and Causes of the Wealth of Nations* (1776), book I, chap. 11, 129; see online at Library of Economics and Liberty, www.econlib.org.

38. Li, *Modern China*, 26.

39. Peter Ward Fay, *The Opium War, 1840–1842* (Chapel Hill, N.C., 1975), 20.

40. Peter Booth Wiley, *Yankees in the Lands of the Gods: Commodore Perry and the Opening of Japan* (New York, 1990), 24–25, 30. Samuel Eliot Morison, *"Old Bruin": Commodore Matthew C. Perry, 1794–1858* (Boston, 1967), 263.

41. Fay, *Opium War*, 54.

42. Carl A. Trocki, *Opium, Empire, and the Global Political Economy: A Study of the Asian Opium Trade, 1750–1950* (London, 1999), 54, 73–74, 83.

43. E. H. Parker, trans., *Chinese Account of the Opium War* (Shanghai, 1888), 1–10.

44. "American Merchants in Canton Plead for Protection during the Opium Crisis, 1839," U.S. House of Representatives, January 9, 1840, reprinted in Dennis Merrill and Thomas Paterson, eds. *Major Problems in American Foreign Relations*, vol. 1, 5th ed. (Boston, 2000), 272–273.

45. Headrick, *Tools of Empire*, 52. For the quote of the Chinese emperor, see Li, *Modern China*, 60.

46. Parker, *Chinese Account of the Opium War*, 73–74.

47. Horowitz, "International Law," 460–461.

48. Immanuel C. Y. Hsü, *The Rise of Modern China* (New York, 1995), 192.

49. G. Zay Wood, "The Genesis of the Open Door Policy in China," thesis, Columbia University, 1921, 1–3. Also see comments on the Open Door Policy by Stephen Barker, "The Harding Administration and the Open Door Policy," in *The Chinese Students' Monthly*, v. 17 (November 1921–June 1922), 137–141; available online at Google Books.

50. "A Chinese Official Recommends Pitting American Barbarians against British Barbarians, 1841," quoted in Merrill and Paterson, *Major Problems*, 73.

51. Jeffrey R. Biggs, "The Origins of American Diplomacy with China: The Cushing Mission of 1844 and the Treaty of Wang-Hsia," thesis, Harvard University, 1975, xi. Also see Article XVIII of the Treaty of Wanghia.

52. Li, *Modern China*, 63, 67. "Secretary of State Daniel Webster Instructs Caleb Cushing on Negotiating with China, 1843," in Merrill and Paterson, *Major Problems*, 274–275.

53. Daniel Yergin, *Oil: The Epic Quest for Oil, Money, and Power* (New York, 1991), 34.

54. Wiley, *Yankees in the Lands of the Gods*, 25–28. Also see Frederic Trautmann, trans., *With Perry in Japan: A Memoir by William Heine* (Honolulu, 1990), 1.

55. Morison, *"Old Bruin,"* 263–266. Also see Stephen Mansfield, *Tokyo: A Cultural History* (Oxford, 2009), 19.

56. Morison, *"Old Bruin,"* 127. Trautmann, *With Perry*, 4. "Instructions to Commodore Matthew C. Perry for His Expedition to Japan, 1852," in Merrill and Paterson, *Major Problems*, 276–278.

57. "Instructions," in Merrill and Paterson, *Major Problems*, 277–278.

58. Morison, *"Old Bruin,"* 270, 276–280. Trautmann, *With Perry*, 6.

59. Trautmann, *With Perry*, 68.

60. Ibid., 72–73. Also see Matthew C. Perry, *The Japan Expedition, 1852–1854: The Personal Journal of Matthew C. Perry* (Washington, D.C., 1968), 98. Morison notes that Perry "wished citizens of color to take part." Morison, *"Old Bruin,"* 332. For a Japanese watercolor of Perry and his flag-bearers, see Wiley, *Yankees in the Lands of the Gods*, 319.

61. Trautmann, *With Perry*, 104–105.

62. Ii Naosuke to Bakufu, October 1, 1853, in W. G. Beasley, ed. and trans., *Select Documents on Japanese Foreign Policy, 1853–1868* (London, 1955), 117–118.

63. Tokugawa Nariaki to Bakufu, August 14, 1853, in Beasley, *Select Documents*, 103.

64. Quoted in Herring, *From Colony to Superpower*, 213.

65. Casualty figures have recently been revised upward from the original 620,000, though these numbers are all estimates. "New Estimates Raise Civil War Death Toll," *New York Times*, April 2, 2012.

66. "Acquisition of the Public Domain, 1781–1867," U.S. Department of the Interior, Bureau of Land Management, www.blm.gov/public_land_statistics/pls02

/plsi-1_02.pdf (accessed 3/15/11). For size comparisons with other countries of Europe, see Edward Bicknell, *Territorial Acquisitions of the United States* (Boston, 1899), appendix.

67. Peter Onuf, "The Importance of the Northwest Ordinance," *Liberty's Legacy: Our Celebration of the Northwest Ordinance and the United States Constitution* (Columbus, Ohio, 1987), 9.

68. Paul Finkelman, "The Northwest Ordinance: A Constitution for an Empire of Liberty," in *Pathways to the Old Northwest* (Indianapolis, 1988), 4–5. Also see Peter Onuf, *Statehood and Union: A History of the Northwest Ordinance* (Bloomington, Ind., 1987), 24–25, 33.

69. Paul Finkelman, "Slavery and Bondage in the 'Empire of Liberty,' " in *The Northwest Ordinance,* ed. Frederick D. Williams (East Lansing, Mich., 1989), 68.

70. Joseph Ellis, *American Sphinx: The Character of Thomas Jefferson* (New York, 1999), 68.

71. Finkelman, "Slavery and Bondage," 62, 86–87.

72. William Weeks, *John Quincy Adams and American Global Empire* (Lexington, Ky., 1992).

73. Jefferson quoted in *Diary of JQA,* 195.

74. Onís quoted in Rappaport, *History of American Diplomacy,* 84.

75. Adams in *Diary of JQA,* 226.

76. Tallmadge in Rufus King, *Papers Relative to the Restriction of Slavery: Speeches of Mr. King in the Senate and of Messrs. Taylor & Talmadge in the House of Representatives of the United States* (Philadelphia, 1819), 21. Cobb and Tallmadge are also quoted in Daniel Walker Howe, "Missouri, Slave or Free?" *American Heritage Magazine* 60, no. 2 (Summer 2010); www.americanheritage.com.

77. Quoted by Adams, February 13, 1820, *Diary of JQA,* 227.

78. Adams, April 13, 1820, *Memoirs of John Quincy Adams: Comprising Portions of His Diary From 1795 to 1848,* ed. Charles Francis Adams, vol. 5 (Philadelphia, 1875), 68. Thomas Jefferson, in *Memoirs, Correspondence, and Private Papers of Thomas Jefferson,* ed. Thomas Jefferson Randolph, vol. 4 (London, 1829), 323–333.

79. Charles Pinckney quoted in Gary J. Kornblith, *Slavery and Sectional Strife in the Early American Republic, 1776–1821* (Lanham, Va., 2010), 60.

80. Jackson quoted in Daniel Farber, *Lincoln's Constitution* (Chicago, 2003), 61.

81. "Andrew Jackson Makes His Case for Removal, 1830," in Merrill and Paterson, *Major Problems,* 198.

82. Hämäläinen, *Comanche Empire,* 199. Brian DeLay, *War of a Thousand Deserts: Indian Raids and the U.S.-Mexican War* (New Haven, Conn., 2008), 18.

83. Peter Grayson, "The Release of Stephen F. Austin from Prison," *The Quarterly of the Texas State Historical Association* 14, no. 2 (October 1910): 156–157.

84. Reed, *Caste War of Yucatán.*

85. Editorial, *El Tiempo*, February 5, 1846, in *Origins of the Mexican War: A Documentary Source Book*, comp. Ward McAfee and Joy Cordell Robinson, vol. 2 (Salisbury, N.C., 1882), 54.

86. U.S. Minister Waddy Thompson quoted in Sam W. Haynes, "'But What Will England Say?' Great Britain, the United States, and the War with Mexico," in *Dueling Eagles: Reinterpreting the Mexican-American War, 1846–1848*, ed. Richard Francaviglia and Douglas Richmond (Fort Worth, Tx., 2000), 26, 33–34. Also see Tomás Murphy, Mexican minister to Great Britain, to Manuel de la Peña y Peña, October 1, 1845, in *Origins of the Mexican War*, vol. 1, 41–42.

87. Trist quoted by Josefina Zoraida Vázquez, "Causes of the War with the United States," and Grant quoted by Miguel A. Gonzalez-Quiroga, "The War between the United States and Mexico," in *Dueling Eagles*, 60 and 93.

88. DeLay, *War of a Thousand Deserts*, xiii, 294–295. Douglas Richmond notes that American willingness to confront Comanche raiders "undoubtedly encouraged collaboration on every level of society" with the American invasion of Mexico. Richmond, "A View of the Periphery: Regional Factors and Collaboration during the U.S.-Mexico Conflict, 1845–1848," in *Dueling Eagles*, 141. Also see Julia O'Hara, "'The Slayer of Victoria Bears His Honors Quietly': Tarahumaras and the Apache Wars in Nineteenth-Century Mexico," in *Military Struggle and Identity Formation in Latin America: Race, Nation, and Community during the Liberal Period*, ed. Nicola Foote and René Harder Horst (Gainesville, Fla., 2010), 224–242.

89. Miguel A. Centeno, ed., *Warfare in Latin America*, vol. 1 (Aldershot, U.K., 2007), xiii, xvi.

90. F. J. McLynn, "Consequences for Argentina of the War of the Triple Alliance, 1865–1870," in ibid., 352; and Thomas Whigham and Barbara Potthast, "The Paraguayan Rosetta Stone: New Insights into the Demographics of the Paraguayan War, 1864–1870," ibid., 380.

91. Quote on gunpowder from *Los Tiempos*, February 1879, cited by Luis Ortega, "Nitrates, Chilean Entrepreneurs and the Origins of the War in the Pacific," in ibid., 402; for quote of Chilean foreign minister, see 420. See also William F. Sater, *Chile and the War of the Pacific* (Lincoln, Nebr., 1986).

92. René Harder Horst, "Crossfire, Cactus, and Racial Construction: The Chaco War and Indigenous People in Paraguay," in *Military Struggle and Identity Formation in Latin America: Race, Nation, and Community during the Liberal Period*, ed. Nicola Foote and René Harder Horst (Gainesville, Fla., 2010), 286.

93. Nicola Foote and René D. Harder Horst, "Introduction: Decentering War: Military Struggle, Nationalism, and Black and Indigenous Populations in Latin America, 1850–1950," in ibid., 3–4. For an overview of the connections between Manifest Destiny and American notions of masculinity, see Amy S.

Greenberg, *Manifest Manhood and the Antebellum American Empire* (Cambridge, U.K., 2005).

94. Horsman, *Race and Manifest Destiny,* 211.

95. Corwin quoted in Rappaport, *History of American Diplomacy,* 107.

96. Quoted in ibid., 99.

97. *Charleston Mercury,* August 11, 1847, in *The Greenwood Library of American War Reporting,* vol. 2, ed. David Copeland (Westport, Conn., 2005), 474.

98. Lincoln and Calhoun quoted in Farber, *Lincoln's Constitution,* 30–31.

99. Farber, *Lincoln's Constitution,* 42.

100. Lincoln quoted in James McPherson, *Battle Cry Freedom: The Civil War Era* (New York, 1988), 309.

101. For Lincoln pictured as a 'coon, see "Up a Tree," *Punch* 42 (January 11, 1862): 15.

102. Ambassador Baron de Brunnow, January 1, 1861, quoted in Ephraim D. Adams, *Great Britain and the American Civil War,* vol. 2 (Gloucester, Mass., 1957), 50–51. Also see *Services Rendered by Russia to the American People during the War of the Rebellion* (Saint Petersburg, Russia, 1904), 5.

103. Stephen R. Wise, *Lifeline of the Confederacy: Blockade Running during the Civil War* (Columbia, S.C., 1988).

104. George Cornewall Lewis to Sir Edmund Head, May 13, 1861, *Letters of the Right Hon. Sir George Cornewall Lewis, Bart.* (London, 1870), 395.

105. "When Extremes Meet," *Punch* 45 (October 24, 1863): 169.

106. Karl Marx, "The North American Civil War," *Die Presse,* October 20, 1861, in *Marx/Engels Collected Works,* vol. 19 (Moscow, 1964); http://www.marxists.org /archive/marx/works/cw/volume19/index.htm (accessed 3/15/11).

107. David Blight, *Race and Reunion: The Civil War in American Memory* (Cambridge, Mass., 2001).

108. Lincoln's Cooper Union speech of February 27, 1860, quoted in Gary J. Bass, *Freedom's Battle: The Origins of Humanitarian Intervention* (New York, 2008), 354–355. *Morning Herald* quoted in Howard Jones, *Blue and Grey Diplomacy: A History of Union and Confederate Foreign Relations* (Chapel Hill, N.C., 2010), 215.

109. Bass, *Freedom's Battle,* 162, 23, 236.

110. The website of the International Court of Justice states that Jay's Treaty prompted the first international arbitration—although only American and British nationals participated. The Alabama Claims were unprecedented for submitting a matter of national interest to foreign judges: http://www.icj-cij.org/court/index.php ?p1=1&p2=1. Also see C. Roland Marchand, *The American Peace Movement and Social Reform, 1898–1918* (Princeton, N.J., 1972), 42.

111. *Pittsburgh Post,* April 15, 1861, and *Chicago Daily Journal,* April 17, 1861, in Howard C. Perkins, ed., *Northern Editorials on Secession,* vol. 1 (New York, 1942), 739 and 808; also, McPherson, *Battle Cry Freedom,* 308.

112. Whitney Smith, *Flags through the Ages and around the World* (New York, 1975), 56, 195–196.

5. Territorial Expansion versus Saltwater Imperialism

1. The Belle Époque is conventionally defined as ending with World War I, but for the purposes of U.S. history I am stretching the timeline to include the Treaty of Versailles.

2. Robert Pastor makes the same point in *A Century's Journey: How the Great Powers Shape the World*, ed. Robert Pastor (New York, 1999), 5.

3. Donald Puchala and Raymond Hopkins, "International Regimes: Lessons from Inductive Analysis," *International Organization* 36, no. 2 (Spring 1982): 246, 255.

4. Fareed Zakaria, *From Wealth to Power: The Unusual Origins of America's World Role* (Princeton, N.J., 1998), 43, 47.

5. David Strang, "Global Patterns of Decolonization, 1500–1987," in *International Studies Quarterly* 35, no. 4 (December 1991): 435, 439–440; also see Strang, "From Dependency to Sovereignty: An Event History Analysis of Decolonization, 1870–1987," *American Sociological Review* 55 (December 1990): 846. On the cross-cultural comparison of democracies and nondemocracies, see Strang, "The Inner Incompatibility of Empire and Nation: Popular Sovereignty and Decolonization," *Sociological Perspectives* 35, no. 2 (Summer 1992): 367–384.

6. Strang, "Global Patterns of Decolonization," 436.

7. DeAlva Stanwood Alexander, *History and Procedure of the House of Representatives* (Boston, 1916), 4.

8. Ramsden quoted in Howard Jones, *Blue and Gray Diplomacy: A History of Union and Confederate Foreign Relations* (Chapel Hill, N.C., 2010), 51.

9. Churchill, November 11, 1947, in *Hansard, The Official Report of Debates in Parliament,* 207; http://hansard.millbanksystems.com/commons/1947/nov/11/parliament-bill#column_207 (accessed 5/21/11).

10. See *The Statesman's Year-Book: Statistical and Historical Annual of the States of the World,* for the years 1870, 1880, 1900, and 1920 (London, 1870, 1800, 1900, 1920). In 1870 and 1880, the subtitle of this series was *Statistical and Historical Annual of the States of the Civilised World.* There was no separate list of "uncivilized" states, perhaps considered too amorphous to name. By 1900, the series had dropped this distinction. As David Strang notes, "In many cases, European states regarded non-European lands as unoccupied or unclaimed by a legitimate ruler. Western states therefore created many dependencies without reference to existing polities." Strang, "Global Patterns of Decolonization," 433.

11. W. T. Stead, *The United States of Europe on the Eve of the Parliament of Peace* (London, 1899), 14.

12. French diplomat François Barbé-Marbois commented in 1830 that it was still "obstinately predicted [in Europe] that the states will soon separate and make war upon one another," in Barbé-Marbois, *The History of Louisiana, Particularly of the Cession of That Colony to the United States of America,* trans. E. Wilson Lyon (1830; repr., Baton Rouge, La., 1977), 40.

13. Quote and statistics from George Herring, *From Colony to Superpower: U.S. Foreign Relations since 1776* (Oxford, 2008), 285–286. Also see Zakaria, *From Wealth to Power,* 131–133, and *Historical Statistics of the United States, 1789–1945* (Washington, D.C., 1949), 242.

14. Edward Lillie Pierce, ed., *Memoir and Letters of Charles Sumner* (Boston, 1877–1893), vol. 4, 323, 318.

15. Quoted in Paul S. Holbo, *Tarnished Expansion: The Alaska Scandal, The Press, and Congress* (Knoxville, Tenn., 1983), 10–11. On Sumner's proposed name for the territory, see "Sumner's Speech" in Archie Shiels, *The Purchase of Alaska* (Fairbanks, Ala., 1967), 125.

16. "Acquisition of the Public Domain, 1781–1867," U.S. Department of the Interior, Bureau of Land Management; www.blm.gov/public_land_statistics/pls02/pls1-1_02.pdf (accessed 4/5/12).

17. Confidential memorandum of Edouard de Stoeckl quoted in Shiels, *Purchase of Alaska,* 9, 15.

18. Holbo, *Tarnished Expansion,* 7.

19. Seward quoted by Stoeckl in his confidential dispatch of March 18, 1867, to Saint Petersburg, in Shiels, *Purchase of Alaska,* 17.

20. Holbo, *Tarnished Expansion,* 10.

21. Sumner, *Memoir,* 318–319, 325.

22. Holbo, *Tarnished Expansion,* 13; "The Russian Slice," *New York Tribune,* April 1, 1867, 4; *London Dispatch* (June 22, 1867) and *London Spectator* (April 6, 1867) quoted in Virginia Hancock Reid, *The Purchase of Alaska: Contemporary Opinion* (Long Beach, Calif., 1939), 46–47. On the debt, see Sumner, *Memoir,* 453, and *Historical Statistics of the United States,* 306.

23. "The Treaty with Russia—Acquisition of Territory on the Pacific," *New York Times,* April 1, 1867, 4.

24. On the vote, see Shiels, *Purchase of Alaska,* 189. See Zakaria, *From Wealth to Power,* 66, on Thaddeus Stevens. On the feeling toward Russia, see Ernest May, *American Imperialism: A Speculative Essay* (New York, 1968), 99.

25. Seward quoted in Zakaria, *From Wealth to Power,* 44.

26. Sumner, *Memoir,* 328.

27. Quote of historians Hugh Keenleyside and Gerald Brown, *Canada and the United States: Some Aspects of Their Historical Relations* (New York, 1952), 130, 131–136.

28. Bright was not the only one. Goldwin Smith, Regius professor of modern history at Oxford, made the same suggestion in 1863, as did many Tories. May, *American Imperialism*, 96–98, 120.

29. Sumner, *Memoir*, 426. On French recognition of Haiti, see Mary Treudley, "The United States and Santo Domingo 1789–1866," *Journal of Race Development* 7, no. 2 (October 1916): 228.

30. Captain Stockton quoted in Richard Challener, *Admirals, Generals, and American Foreign Policy, 1898–1914* (Princeton, N.J., 1973), 87.

31. See, for example, James W. Cortada, "A Case of International Rivalry in Latin America: Spain's Occupation of Santo Domingo, 1853–1865," *Revista de Historia de América* 82 (July–December 1976): 53–82. Also, Luis Martinez-Fernandez, "The Sword and the Crucifix: Church-State Relations and Nationality in the Nineteenth-Century Dominican Republic," *Latin American Research Review* 30, no. 1 (1995): 69–93.

32. On the terms of the proposed treaty, see Harold T. Pinkett, "Efforts to Annex Santo Domingo to the United States, 1866–1871," *Journal of Negro History* 26, no. 1 (January 1941): 29. Also see Eric T. Love, *Race over Empire: Racism and U.S. Imperialism* (Chapel Hill, N.C., 2004), 41.

33. Historian Eric Love believes that Sumner actually had racist reasons for opposing annexation, though Douglass would have found that surprising. Love, *Race over Empire*, 56–58.

34. Douglass quoted in Merline Pitre, "Frederick Douglass and the Annexation of Santo Domingo," *Journal of Negro History* 62, no. 4 (October 1977): 301–391, 395, 397.

35. See Frederick Douglass, *Autobiographies: Narrative of Frederick Douglass, an American Slave; My Bondage and My Freedom; Life and Times of Frederick Douglass*, ed. Henry Louis Gates, Jr. (New York, 1994), 846, 1029.

36. On American imperialism, see Pitre, "Frederick Douglass." For Grant's quote, see Douglass, *Autobiographies*, 846. For the characterization of Grant as a dupe, see Pinkett, "Efforts to Annex Santo Domingo," 23. See also Daniel Brantley, "Black Diplomacy and Frederick Douglass' Caribbean Experiences, 1871 and 1889–1891: The Untold History," *Phylon* 45, no. 3 (1984): 197–209. Douglass himself commented that before the Civil War he had fought any "extension of American power and influence." But once slavery was abolished, he welcomed the acquisition of additional territory if other peoples "wished to come to us." Douglass, *Autobiographies*, 1029.

37. Douglass, *Autobiographies*, 847.

38. Love, *Race over Empire*, chapter 2.

39. Michael L. Krenn, *The Color of Empire: Race and American Foreign Relations* (Dulles, Va., 2006), 103–107.

40. "The Treaty with Russia—Acquisition of Territory on the Pacific," *NYT,* April 1, 1867, 4.

41. Stead, *United States of Europe,* 9.

42. Seward believed that warfare itself would never be overcome "until mankind learn and feel the simple truth, that . . . all mankind are brethren . . . equal in endowments, equal in nature and political rights." William H. Seward, *The Works of William H. Seward,* ed. George Baker (Boston, 1884), vol. 3: 498. Grant quoted in Love, *Race over Empire,* 45.

43. Charles Sumner, "Naboth's Vineyard," in *Charles Sumner: His Complete Works* (Boston, 1880), 261.

44. Love, *Race over Empire,* 28. Fareed Zakaria says the United States had a severe case of "imperial understretch." Zakaria, *From Wealth to Power,* 54–55.

45. On the critique of "imperialism," see Richard Koebner and Helmut Dan Schmidt, *Imperialism: The Story and Significance of a Political Word* (Cambridge, U.K., 1964).

46. Arthur Schlesinger, Jr., *The Cycles of American History* (Boston, 1986), 150–151. Zakaria sees the American failure to expand territorially or imperially in the last third of the nineteenth century as one of the great puzzles of American history. For a list of the multiple opportunities forsworn, see Zakaria, *From Wealth to Power,* 88.

47. Quote and texts of earlier Hawaiian treaties in Lorrin Thurston, *Hand-Book on the Annexation of Hawaii* (Saint Joseph, Mich., 1897), 77. Also see William Adam Russ, Jr., *The Hawaiian Revolution: 1893–1894* (Selinsgrove, Pa., 1959), 6–12.

48. Stead, *United States of Europe,* 5.

49. Adams quoted in Walter LaFeber, *The American Age: United States Foreign Policy at Home and Abroad since 1750* (New York: 1989), 80. On the early nineteenth-century origins of humanitarian intervention, beginning with the Greek struggle for independence from the Ottoman Empire, see Gary Bass, *Freedom's Battle: The Origins of Humanitarian Intervention* (New York, 2008).

50. Clifford Staten, *The History of Cuba* (Westport, Conn., 2005), 33.

51. Antonio Luna quoted in Paul Kramer, *The Blood of Government: Race, Empire, the United States, and the Philippines* (Chapel Hill, N.C., 2006), 41, 48. European disdain for "mere colonials" stung Americans, too. Thomas Jefferson wrote *Notes on the State of Virginia* in 1781 partly to counter European assumptions that animals native to the New World were smaller than those in the old and that, when imported, European animals "degenerated in America." Jefferson, *Notes on the State of Virginia,* 2nd ed. (Philadelphia, 1794), 63.

52. John Lawrence, *War and Genocide in Cuba, 1895* (Chapel Hill, N.C., 2006), 151, 193, 197–200.

53. Ernest May, *Imperial Democracy: The Emergence of America As a Great Power* (New York, 1961), 68, 73.

54. Talented Walter LaFeber is the dean of this school of thought. See LaFeber, *The New Empire: An Interpretation of American Expansion, 1860–1898* (Ithaca, N.Y., 1963), vii.

55. William Allen quoted in the *Congressional Record*, 55th Congress, 4107 (April 20, 1898).

56. S. M. Weld quoted in Armin Rappaport, *A History of American Diplomacy* (New York, 1975), 195. *Commercial Advertiser* and *Harper's Weekly* quoted in Piero Gleijeses, "1898: The Opposition to the Spanish-American War," *Journal of Latin American Studies* 35 (2003): 705–706. On business opposition also see Zakaria, *From Wealth to Power*, 155.

57. May, *Imperial Democracy*, 82. Newspaper quotes from Gleijeses, "1898: The Opposition," 707. Moore quoted in Benjamin Coates, "Transatlantic Advocates: International Law and U.S. Foreign Relations, 1898–1919," PhD diss., Columbia University, 2010, 60. On Reed, see William Stanco, "Speaker Thomas Brackett Reed and the Will of the Majority," *Capitol Dome* (Fall 2007): 13. Also see May, *American Imperialism*, 189–191, in which the author concludes that the public had a greater, though more transient interest in intervention than politicians or corporations. On grassroots enthusiasm, see Zakaria, *From Wealth to Power*, 158–161. For a contrasting interpretation of business interest, see LaFeber, *The New Empire*. On gender, see Gail Bederman, *Manliness and Civilization: A Cultural History of Race and Gender in the United States, 1880–1917* (Chicago, 1995).

58. *Times* quoted in Lawrence, *War and Genocide*, 200.

59. Queen Victoria quoted in Bass, *Freedom's Battle*, 260.

60. Gladstone speech, December 29, 1894, quoted in Bass, *Freedom's Battle*, 316. On Gladstone's and the Liberal Party's critique of imperialism, see May, *American Imperialism*, 116–117, and Jonathan Schell, *Unconquerable World: Power, Nonviolence, and the Will of the People* (New York, 2003), 267–268. On business opposition to intervention, see Rappaport, *History of American Diplomacy*, 195.

61. *San Francisco Examiner*, August 1895, quoted in David Nasaw, *The Chief: The Life of William Randolph Hearst* (Boston, 2000), 125–126. Also see Bass, *Freedom's Battle*, 316–317. Quote from *Literary Digest* in Rappaport, *History of American Diplomacy*, 196.

62. William McKinley, Inaugural Address, March 4, 1897, http://millercenter .org/scripps/archive/speeches/detail/3562 (accessed 5/16/11).

63. Quentin R. Skrabec, *William McKinley, Apostle of Protectionism* (New York, 2008), 106. McKinley quoted in LaFeber, *The New Empire*, 329.

64. Rappaport, *History of American Diplomacy*, 193; Herring, *From Colony to Superpower*, 312. LaFeber portrays McKinley as militant, but he also points out that for more than a year McKinley (and the Republican Party) staunchly opposed recognizing Cuban independence, acknowledging a state of belligerency, or annexing the island, because "by our code of morality [such an action] would be criminal aggression." McKinley quoted in LaFeber, *The New Empire*, 341.

65. The Naval Heritage and History Command is the best source for nearly every fact on the American Navy: http://www.history.navy.mil/faqs/faq71-1.htm (accessed 5/18/11). For the quote, see Herring, *From Colony to Superpower*, 313. Such a candy dish is in the author's personal collection. Others are widely available online today, more than one hundred years later, in both clear and milk glass.

66. David Brady, *Congressional Voting in a Partisan Era: A Study of the McKinley Houses and a Comparison to the Modern House of Representatives* (Lawrence, Ks., 1973), 5. Also see roll-call data for the 55th Congress, House of Representatives roll calls 20 (May 25, 1897), 32 (July 7, 1897), and 45 (January 19, 1898), on VoteView.com.

67. McKinley quoted in H. H. Kohlsaat, *From McKinley to Harding: Personal Recollections of Our Presidents* (New York, 1923), 67. Gleijeses, "1898: The Opposition," 681.

68. Redfield Proctor in *CR*, 55th Congress, 2916–2917 (March 17, 1898).

69. Ibid. On Barton and Armenia, see "Aid for the Armenians; Miss Clara Barton Talks of the Red Cross's Undertaking," *NYT*, December 20, 1895.

70. Philip Dimare, ed., *Movies in American History: An Encyclopedia*, (Santa Barbara, Calif., 2011), 1114.

71. Herring, *From Colony to Superpower*, 311. Senator Clay quoted in *CR*, 55th Congress, 3150 (February 27, 1901). On the last-minute shenanigans to evade recognition of the rebels, see ibid., 4062–4064. (The record gives the date as April 18, but Congress did not conclude its business until 2:45 A.M. on the April 19.) I am grateful to David Brady and Colin McCubbins of Stanford University for assisting me with analyzing the partisan divide.

72. Brady, *Congressional Voting*, 5.

73. Senators Edmund Pettus, John Morgan, Benjamin Tillman, and Orville Platt quoted in *CR*, 56th Congress, 3025, 3148–3150 (February 27, 1901).

74. J. Fred Rippy, "A Century of British Investments in Chile," *Pacific Historical Review* 21, no. 4 (November 1952): 343. The period from 1873 to 1913 saw the highest-ever levels of foreign direct investment. The United States absorbed significant foreign capital, but larger consumers of loans were Argentina, Australia, Brazil, and Canada. Britain and France were the primary lenders. See Albert Fishlow, "Lessons from the Past: Capital Markets during the 19th Century and the Interwar Period," *International Organization* 39, no. 1 (Summer 1985): 385.

75. Sven Beckert, "Emancipation and Empire: Reconstructing the Worldwide Web of Cotton Production in the Age of the American Civil War," *American Historical Review* 109, no. 5 (December 2004): 1414. Marshall Hodgson, *The Venture of Islam*, vol. 3 (Chicago, 1974), 240–241. On debt figures, see "Ismail Pasha," Encyclopædia Britannica Online, http://www.britannica.com/EBchecked/topic/296116/Ismail-Pasha (accessed 6/2/11).

76. Tillman quoted in *CR*, 55th Congress, 3891 (April 15, 1898).

77. For example, see Stead, *United States of Europe*, 54–55.

78. Richard Horowitz, "International Law and State Transformation in China, Siam, and the Ottoman Empire during the Nineteenth Century," *Journal of World History* 15, no. 4 (December 2004): 448.

79. "Experts Busy with Finances of China," *New York Herald*, November 25, 1921. Notably, the United States instigated a series of treaties in 1928 to give China autonomy in setting tariff levels, which soon tripled China's income. See Nicholas Clifford, "Sir Frederick Maze and the Chinese Maritime Customs, 1937–1941," *Journal of Modern History* 37, no. 1 (March 1965): 19.

80. Jones, *Blue and Gray Diplomacy*, 78–79. LaFeber, *The New Empire*, 248.

81. Theodore Roosevelt, Annual Message to Congress, *CR*, 58th Congress, 19 (December 6, 1904).

82. John Blassingame, "The Press and American Intervention in Haiti and the Dominican Republic, 1904–1920," *Caribbean Studies* 9, no. 2 (July 1969): 27.

83. "U.S. Direct Investment in Foreign Countries, By Region and Industry: 1929–1998," *Historical Statistics of the United States, Earliest Times to the Present: Millennial Edition Online*, ed. Susan B. Carter et al. (Cambridge, U.K., 2006), Table Ee72-131.

84. Paul Drake, *Money Doctor in the Andes: The Kemmerer Missions, 1923–1933* (Durham, N.C., 1989), 1–2, 7.

85. Quoted in Walter Russell Mead, *Special Providence: American Foreign Policy and How It Changed the World* (New York, 2002), 16.

86. One provision that remained, however, was the ongoing leasing of Guantanamo Bay (negotiated under the Platt Amendment) for a U.S. naval base. The new treaty signed in 1934 granted this lease to the United States in perpetuity, unless both governments agreed to its abrogation. Cuba has refused since the early 1960s to cash the annual rental payments sent by the United States.

87. First quotation by Gleijeses, "1898: The Opposition," 718; Cuban quotation in Herring, *From Colony*, 325.

88. See Gleijeses's examination of the newspaper records, in "1898: The Opposition," 717. McKinley quoted in Kohlsaat, *From McKinley to Harding*, 68.

89. "The Teller Amendment, 1898," reprinted in *Major Problems in American Foreign Relations*, ed. Dennis Merrill and Thomas Paterson, 5th ed. (Boston, 2000), 356.

90. McKinley quoted in Rappaport, *History of American Diplomacy*, 200.

91. Michael Kazin, *A Godly Hero: The Life of William Jennings Bryan* (New York, 2006), 86–87. The author possesses one such pin in her personal collection.

92. *CR*, 55th Congress, 3rd Session, 96 (December 12, 1898), and 526, 530–531 (January 10, 1899).

93. Ibid., 733–734 (January 18, 1899).

94. Robert Beisner, *Twelve against Empire: The Anti-Imperialists, 1898–1900* (New York, 1968), xii. Roland Marchand similarly argues that anti-imperialists represented

the wider consensus. C. Roland Marchand, *The American Peace Movement and Social Reform, 1898–1918* (Princeton, N.J., 1972), 23.

95. Orville Platt, in *CR,* 55th Congress, 288 (December 19, 1898).

96. Ibid., 292.

97. LaFeber, *The New Empire,* 92.

98. Challener, *Admirals, Generals,* 13. LaFeber, *The New Empire,* 85.

99. Alfred Thayer Mahan, *The Influence of Sea Power upon History, 1660–1783,* 5th ed. (Boston, 1894), 83. May notes that proponents of imperialism were a "minority." May, *Imperial Democracy,* 186.

100. On the navy's feckless quest for bases, see Challener, *Admirals, Generals,* 81–110.

101. Reed quoted in Stanco, "Speaker Thomas Brackett Reed," 10, 13.

102. Lt. John Hood, "The Pacific Submarine Cable," September 1900, quoted in Challener, *Admirals, Generals,* 12. Oscar Straus quoted in "Root Heads New Body on International Law," *NYT,* January 13, 1906, 4. For additional context see Coates, "Transatlantic Advocates," 2, who talks about the choice between pith helmets and legal robes. Frank Ninkovich similarly concludes that the most cogent explanation for U.S. behavior was an "identity crisis." Ninkovich, *The Wilsonian Century: U.S. Foreign Policy since 1900* (Chicago, 1999), 19.

103. May, *American Imperialism,* 215.

104. Frank Ninkovich, *The United States and Imperialism* (Malden, Mass., 2001), 247. On racist arguments, see Love, *Race over Empire,* 181–195.

105. Ken DeBevoise, *Agents of Apocalypse: Epidemic Disease in the Colonial Philippines* (Princeton, N.J., 1995), 13. David Silbey, *A War of Frontier and Empire: The Philippine-American War, 1899–1902* (New York, 2007), xvi.

106. Brian McAllister Linn, *The U.S. Army and Counterinsurgency in the Philippine War, 1899–1902* (Chapel Hill, N.C., 1989), 145. Ninkovich, *United States and Imperialism,* 50–54.

107. *Report of the Philippine Commission to the President,* vol. 1 (Washington, D.C., 1900), 5, 8.

108. Ibid., 12, 108–109.

109. Lakshmi Iyer and Noel Mauer, "The Cost of Property Rights: Establishing Institutions on the Philippine Frontier under American Rule, 1898–1918," Harvard Business School Working Paper 11. On the transitory character of U.S. imperialism, also see Challener, *Admirals, Generals,* 82.

110. T. R. quoted in Ninkovich, *United States and Imperialism,* 75.

111. Woodrow Wilson, "First Annual Message," December 2, 1913. Online by Gerhard Peters and John T. Woolley, *The American Presidency Project,* http://www.presidency.ucsb.edu/ws/?pid=29554 (accessed 5/26/11).

112. Wilson and the Roosevelts quoted in Ninkovich, *United States and Imperialism,* 67, 72, 75.

113. Ninkovich, *United States and Imperialism*, 61, 74–75.

114. Kramer, *Blood of Government*, 350–352.

115. Erez Manela, *The Wilsonian Moment: Self-Determination and the International Origins of Anticolonial Nationalism* (New York, 2007), 31, 219.

6. The Open Door and the First International Rules

1. *Congressional Record*, 65th Congress, Part I, 680–682 (January 8, 1918).

2. Robert Pastor, ed., *A Century's Journey: How the Great Powers Shape the World* (New York, 1999), 192. Also see Arthur Link, *The Higher Realism of Woodrow Wilson and Other Essays* (Nashville, Tenn., 1971), and Tony Smith, *America's Mission: The United States and the Worldwide Struggle for Democracy in the Twentieth Century* (Princeton, N.J., 1994).

3. Jan Schulte-Nordhult, *Woodrow Wilson: A Life for Peace*, trans. Herbert Rowen, excerpted in *Major Problems in American History*, 2nd ed., ed. Elizabeth Cobbs Hoffman (Boston, 2002), 167.

4. Henry Kissinger, *Diplomacy* (New York, 1994), 224, 222.

5. William Pfaff, *The Irony of Manifest Destiny: The Tragedy of America's Foreign Policy* (New York, 2010), 73. Sigmund Freud, "Introduction," in Sigmund Freud and William C. Bullitt, *Woodrow Wilson: A Psychological Study* (Boston, 1966), xii. Peter Beinert, *The Icarus Syndrome: A History of American Hubris* (New York, 2010), 36, 38, 46, 51. Jim Powell, *Wilson's War: How Woodrow Wilson's Great Blunder Led to Hitler, Lenin, Stalin, and WWII* (New York, 2005), 1.

6. Labouchère quoted in Christopher Howse, "Why Gladstone Had God Up His Sleeve," *Telegraph*, November 24, 2007; http://www.telegraph.co.uk/comment /columnists/christopherhowse/3644258/Why-Gladstone-had-God-up-his-sleeve. html (accessed 8/22/11).

7. Pastor, *Century's Journey*, 209.

8. Arthur C. F. Beales, *The History of Peace: A Short Account of the Organised Movements for International Peace* (London, 1931; New York, 1971), 24. J. Jiří, *The Universal Peace Organization of King George of Bohemia: A Fifteenth Century Plan for World Peace, 1462–1464* (Prague, 1964).

9. Beales, *History of Peace*, 31. Emer de Vattel, *The Law of Nations: Or, Principles of the Law of Nature, Applied to The Conduct and Affairs of Nations and Sovereigns*, trans. Joseph Chitty (Philadelphia, 1844), 277.

10. Beales, *History of Peace*, 35. Also see Bentham's "Plan for a Universal and Perpetual Peace," in *The Works of Jeremy Bentham*, ed. John Bowring, vol. 2, (Edinburgh, 1839), 546–547, 555.

11. Sankar Muthu, *Enlightenment against Empire* (Princeton, N.J., 2003), 4. Kant's "Perpetual Peace: A Philosophical Sketch" (1795), has been reprinted and digitized extensively. See, for example: http://www.constitution.org/kant/perpeace.htm.

12. United States Constitution, Article III, Section 2.

13. François Barbé-Marbois, *The History of Louisiana, Particularly of the Cession of That Colony to the United States of America,* trans. E. Wilson Lyon (1830; repr., Baton Rouge, La., 1977), 27–28.

14. Beales, *History of Peace,* remains the most complete source on the international character of the arbitration and disarmament movement from the eighteenth century through 1930. Also see W. T. Stead, *The United States of Europe on the Eve of the Parliament of Peace* (New York, 1899).

15. Hugo quoted in Beales, *History of Peace,* 79, and Merle Curti, *The American Peace Crusade, 1815–1860* (Durham, N.C., 1929), 174. Also see Graham Robb, *Victor Hugo: A Biography* (New York, 1997), 111, 434, and Arthur Eyffinger, *The 1899 Hague Peace Conference: "The Parliament of Man, The Federation of the World"* (The Hague, 2000), 48.

16. Beales, *History of Peace,* 76, 242.

17. Calvin Davis, *The United States and the Second Hague Peace Conference* (Durham, N.C., 1975), 17–19. Beales, *History of Peace,* 205. *Bering Sea Arbitration, Award of the Tribunal of Arbitration, Presented to Both Houses of Parliament by Command of Her Majesty* (London, 1893): http://www.archive.org/stream/behringseaarbitooberi uoft#page/n3/mode/2up (accessed 8/28/11).

18. Beales, *History of Peace,* 190–191.

19. Ibid., 205, 222, 250. Davis, *Second Hague Peace Conference,* 43. The records of the Asociación Americana La Paz are in the National Teacher's Library of Argentina, http://www.bnm.me.gov.ar/.

20. Tennyson, *The Early Poems of Alfred, Lord Tennyson,* ed. John Churton Collins (London, 1900), 199, 203–204.

21. Eyffinger, *The 1899 Hague Peace,* 16. On the personality of Count Muraviev, also spelled Mouravieff (or Muravyov), see W. T. Stead, "The Late Count Mouravieff and His Successors," *Review of Reviews* 22 (July 16, 1900): 32–33.

22. "Czar Nicholas' Rescript," quoted in Eyffinger, *The 1899 Hague Peace,* 17.

23. Nicholas quoted in Princess Catherine Radziwill, *Nicholas II: The Last of the Czars* (London, 1931), 100.

24. Gertrude Henderson, "Czar Nicholas, The Peacemaker: Autocrat of All the Russias and His Dream of Peace," *Los Angeles Times,* September 4, 1898, 8.

25. Baroness Bertha von Suttner, quoted in Eyffinger, *The 1899 Hague Peace,* 24. Beales, *History of Peace,* 231.

26. See Klaus Schlictmann, "Japan, Germany and the Idea of the Hague Peace Conferences," *Journal of Peace Research* 40, no. 4, Special Issue on Peace History (July 2003): 381.

27. Beales, *History of Peace,* 201.

28. Bertha von Suttner, *Lay Down Your Arms: The Autobiography of Martha von Tilling,* trans. T. Holmes (London, 1894), 425.

29. See Bertha von Suttner's biography online at Nobelprize.org.

30. Kaiser Wilhelm II in Effinger, 26. Edward VII and McKinley in Davis, *Second Hague Peace Conference,* 6–7.

31. William Stead, "Letter From Russia," *New York Times,* October 3, 1898, A4. Nicholas II in Beales, *History of Peace,* 232–233.

32. Davis, *Second Hague Peace Conference,* 23.

33. Schlictmann, "Japan, Germany, and the Idea of the Hague Peace," 391, 379.

34. Schwarzhoff quoted in Davis, *Second Hague Peace Conference,* 25.

35. Davis, *Second Hague Peace Conference,* 25.

36. Philipp Zorn, German delegate, quoted in ibid., 30–32.

37. Ibid., 36. Quotation from "1899 Convention for the Pacific Settlement of International Disputes," 8–10, available from the Permanent Court: http://www.pca -cpa.org/showpage.asp?pag_id=1067.

38. The nine pioneers were Argentina, Bolivia, the Dominican Republic, Guatemala, El Salvador, Mexico, Paraguay, Peru, and Uruguay. Davis, *Second Hague Peace Conference,* 49.

39. Ibid., 58.

40. Ibid., 85. Jerald Combs, *History of American Foreign Policy: To 1920* (New York, 2008), 184–185. "Preferential Treatment of Claims of Blockading Powers Against Venezuela: *Germany, Great Britain and Italy v. Venezuela,*" 1903. Available from the court at: http://www.pca-cpa.org/showpage.asp?pag_id=1029.

41. *Historical Statistics of the United States: Colonial Times to 1970* (Washington, D.C., 1975), vol. 1, 117, and vol. 2, 903, 906.

42. Michael Hunt, *Frontier Defense and the Open Door: Manchuria in Chinese-American Relations, 1895–1911* (New Haven, Conn., 1973), 21, 34–35, 43. James Reed, *The Missionary Mind and American East Asia* (Cambridge, Mass., 1983), 18, 42, 46.

43. Paul Varg, "The Myth of the China Market, 1890–1914," *American Historical Review* 73, no. 3 (February 1968): 751.

44. John Gallagher and Ronald Robinson, "The Imperialism of Free Trade," *Economic History Review,* n.s., 6, no. 1 (1953): 5–6, 9–10, 12.

45. Williams introduced the general concept in his 1959 book and employed the specific phrase beginning with the 1962 edition. See Williams, *Tragedy of American Diplomacy,* rev. ed. (New York, 1962), 90.

46. Frank Trentmann, *Free Trade Nation: Commerce, Consumption, and Civil Society in Modern Britain* (Oxford, 2008), 6, 90–91.

47. Trentmann, *Free Trade Nation,* 6. Also see Douglas Irwin, "Free Trade and Protection in Nineteenth-Century Britain and France Revisited," *Journal of Economic History* 53, no. 1 (March 1993): 148–150.

48. Henry Campbell-Bannerman quoted in Trentmann, *Free Trade Nation,* 1.

49. McKinley, September 5, 1901, quotation available online in "Document: William McKinley: Reciprocal Trade Agreements," *Encyclopædia Britannica* online,

http://www.britannica.com/bps/additionalcontent/8/116940/Document-William-McKinley-Reciprocal-Trade-Agreements (accessed 8/2/2012).

50. Theodore Roosevelt, "The Strenuous Life and Other Essays," excerpted in *Major Problems in American Foreign Relations,* ed. Dennis Merrill and Thomas Paterson, 5th ed., vol. 1 (Boston, 2000), 99.

51. Over time, the open door was extended to West Africa and the Ottoman Empire as well. F. A. Edwards, "The French on the Niger: The 'Open Door' in West Africa," *Fortnightly Review* 69 (1898): 576–591; "Minister Straus Returns . . . 'Open Door' for Americans in Turkey," *New York Times,* February 9, 1900.

52. McKinley quoted in Michael Hunt, *The Making of a Special Relationship: The United States and China to 1914* (New York, 1983), 181–182.

53. Hunt, *Frontier Defense,* 25. " 'The Break-up of China'; Lord Charles Beresford's Report on His Recent Tour Published, The Open Door a Necessity," *New York Times,* May 14, 1899. Ge-Zay Wood, *The Genesis of the Open Door Policy in China* (New York, 1921), 142–143. Paul Varg, "William Woodville Rockhill and the Open Door Notes," *Journal of Modern History,* 24, no. 4 (December 1952): 377–378.

54. Jonathan Spence, *The Search for Modern China* (New York, 1990), 232.

55. Ibid., 135.

56. Bob Nichols, *Bluejackets and Boxers: Australia's Naval Expedition to the Boxer Uprising* (Sydney, 1986), 55.

57. Hunt, *Special Relationship,* 194.

58. Quote from ibid., 34. Also see Spence, *Search for Modern China,* 231.

59. Robert H. Wiebe, *The Search for Order: 1877–1920* (New York, 1967).

60. Quotes from John Milton Cooper, *The Warrior and the Priest: Woodrow Wilson and Theodore Roosevelt* (Cambridge, Mass., 1983), 273, and Philip Dimare, ed., *Movies in American History: An Encyclopedia,* (Santa Barbara, Calif., 2011), 1114.

61. Oscar Straus quoted in League to Enforce Peace (U.S.), *Enforced Peace: Proceedings of the First Annual National Assemblage of the League to Enforce Peace, May 26–27, 1916* (New York, 1916), 31.

62. John Mez, *Peace Literature of the War: Material for the Study of International Polity, International Conciliation, Special Bulletin* (New York, 1916), 3–4. Hoover Institution Archives (hereafter, HIA), Peace Subject Collection (hereafter, PSC), Box 14, File: General 1915–1916.

63. Mez, *Peace Literature of the War,* 4.

64. "Prospectus, The United Nations," HIA, PSC, Box 14, File: General 1908–1960.

65. Letter of William O'Dowell, United Nations of the World, League of Peace, attached to H.J. Res. 335, Joint Resolution, House of Representatives, July 9, 1912. HIA, Papers of David Starr Jordan (hereafter, DSJ), Box 41, File: League of Peace.

66. Lucia Mead Ames, "International Police," *The Outlook* 74 (July 18, 1903), reprinted in *The Eagle and the Dove: The American Peace Movement and the United*

States, ed. John W. Chambers (Syracuse, N.Y., 1991), 8. Also see "The Practical Program for World Organization," undated, ca. 1904, HIA, PSC, Box 17, File: General, 1904–1938.

67. Theodore Roosevelt, "International Peace," reprinted in *Advocate of Peace* 72, no. 6 (June 1910): 146–147.

68. George Shibley to Wilson, December 14, 1915, see also attached memorandum, HIA, DSJ, Box 41, File: League for World Peace. "Wilson Watching Europe for a Sign," *New York Times,* December 21, 1915.

69. Beales, *History of Peace,* 296–297.

70. Jane Addams et al., *Women at The Hague* (New York, 1915), 8–9.

71. Ibid., 13, 152–153, 155. Christopher McKnight Nichols, *Promise and Peril: America at the Dawn of a Global Age* (Cambridge, Mass., 2011), 279.

72. Martin David Dubin, "Toward the Concept of Collective Security: The Bryce Group's 'Proposals for the Avoidance of War,' 1914–1917," *International Organization* 24, no. 2 (Spring 1970): 288–289.

73. Edward House, *The Intimate Papers of Colonel House,* ed. Charles Seymour (Boston, 1926), 114, 361, 365, 425. Jonathan Schell, *Unconquerable World: Power, Nonviolence, and the Will of the People* (New York, 2003), 270.

74. Kissinger, *Diplomacy,* 223.

75. It is sometimes hard to tell who more desired a closer relationship, Grey or House, an Anglophile. Grey certainly had the greater need. John Milton Cooper, *Woodrow Wilson: A Biography* (New York, 2009), 276–277, 315–316.

76. Dubin, "Toward the Concept of Collective Security," 304–305. "The Committee on the League of Nations: Interim Report," March 20, 1918, National Archives of Great Britain (hereafter, NAGB), Kew, CAB/24/50. Also see "Summary of Some of the Early Criticisms of Proposals for a League of Nations System of Collective Security Prior to the Peace Conference, 1919," August 25, 1936, NAGB, CAB/24/263.

77. Keith Robbins, *The Abolition of War: The 'Peace Movement' in Britain, 1914–1919* (Cardiff, U.K., 1976), 49–53. See the American Peace Society journal *Advocate of Peace* 80, no. 3 (March 1918): 93; available online at Google Books. [http://books.google.com/books?id=4FMOAQAAMAAJ&pg=RA1-PA94&lpg=RA1-PA94&dq =american+peace+society+journal,+advocate+of+peace,+March+1918&source =bl&ots=tZX2JGgQlg&sig=C9jbWhErl2TaEoFqh4gXcE2bw6I&hl=en&sa=X&ei =jxk4UPiFCofY2QWChYHIDg&ved=0CCoQ6AEwAA#v=onepage&q=ameri can%20peace%20society%20journal%2C%20advocate%20of%20peace%2C%20 March%201918&f=false] (accessed 8/24/12).

78. League to Enforce Peace, *Enforced Peace,* 7, 9–11. "Taft's League to Enforce Peace Is Formally Launched at Philadelphia," *Los Angeles Times,* June 18, 1915, 12. "Taft Outlines Plan for a Lasting Peace: Asks Cooperation of Commercial Orga-

nizations Representing 400,000 Business Men," *New York Times*, December 11, 1915.

79. Doris Eaton Travis, *The Days We Danced: The Story of My Theatrical Family* (Norman, Okla., 2003), 55–56.

80. Wilson quoted in Erez Manela, *The Wilsonian Moment: Self-Determination and the International Origins of Anticolonial Nationalism* (New York, 2007), 22. Alexander and Juliette George, *Woodrow Wilson and Colonel House* (New York, 1956), 159.

81. "$378,343 for Work of Enforced Peace," *New York Times*, May 28, 1916.

82. C. Roland Marchand, *The American Peace Movement and Social Reform, 1898–1918* (Princeton, N.J., 1972), 157. Taft quoted in "Favor League of Nations: Twelve States Have Indorsed Plan to Enforce Peace," *New York Times*, February 24, 1918.

83. "Influenza Pandemic," in *The European Powers in the First World War: An Encyclopedia*, ed. Spencer C. Tucker (New York, 1999), 360. Woodrow Wilson, "Address to a Joint Session of Congress Requesting a Declaration of War against Germany," April 2, 1917. Online by Gerhard Peters and John T. Woolley, *The American Presidency Project*, http://www.presidency.ucsb.edu/ws/?pid=65366.

84. Susan Pedersen, "The Meaning of the Mandate System: An Argument," *Geschichte und Gesellschaft* 32 (2006): 15. Also see Peter Sluglett, *Britain in Iraq: Contriving King and Country, 1914–1932* (New York, 2007).

85. Deepak Lal, *In Praise of Empires: Globalization and Order* (New York, 2004), 58, 65.

86. Manela, *Wilsonian Moment*, 219. Arthur Upham Pope (League of Oppressed Peoples) to David Starr Jordan, November 11, 1919, HIA, DSJ, Box 41, File: League of Oppressed Peoples.

87. Robert Dallek, *Franklin D. Roosevelt and American Foreign Policy, 1932–1945* (New York, 1979), 11.

88. Quoted in Marlee Richards, *America in the 1910s* (Minneapolis, 2010), 39.

89. Fritz Fischer, *Germany's Aims in the First World War* (New York, 1967).

90. See, for example, John Milton Cooper, Jr., *Breaking the Heart of the World: Woodrow Wilson and the Fight for the League of Nations* (New York, 2011).

91. Henry Cabot Lodge, "Great Work of the League to Enforce Peace," in League to Enforce Peace, *Enforced Peace*, 164, 166.

92. Lodge quoted in Nichols, *Promise and Peril*, 261, 265. David Fromkin, "Rival Internationalisms: Lodge, Wilson, and the Two Roosevelts," *World Policy Journal* 13, no. 2 (Summer 1996): 76–77.

93. Lodge quoted in Rappaport, *History of American Diplomacy*, 275, 276.

94. Borah quoted in Nichols, *Promise and Peril*, 265.

95. Wilson quoted in Frank Ninkovich, *The Wilsonian Century: U.S. Foreign Policy since 1900* (Chicago, 1999), 72, 75.

7. War against War

1. "Japan Scraps a Few Ships," *Los Angeles Times*, September 9, 1923, VIII4; "American-Japan Club Appeal for Warship," *Los Angeles Times*, May 16, 1924, 9; "Will Drop Bombs Two Miles in Air," *New York Times*, September 5, 1923, 19; "Begin to Scrap Two Hulls," *New York Times*, November 29, 1923, 14; "Navy Puts 21 Warships on Sale in Compliance with Arms Treaty," *New York Times*, October 14, 1923, XX13; "Last Battleship Is Built," *Los Angeles Times*, December 2, 1923, 11. "Australia to Sink Battleship," *New York Times*, May 5, 1922, 35. David Stevens and John Reeve, *The Navy and the Nation: The Influence of the Navy on Modern Australia* (Crows Nest, Australia, 2005), 165, 182–183.

2. Victoria DiGrazia, *Irresistible Empire: America's Advance through Twentieth-Century Europe* (Cambridge, Mass., 2005), 41. Robert Baden-Powell, *Scouting for Boys: A Handbook for Instruction in Good Citizenship* (1908; repr., Oxford, 2004).

3. George Washington and American Legion quotes from Evaline Dowling et al., *World Friendship: A Series of Articles Written by Some Teachers in the Los Angeles Schools* (Los Angeles, 1931), 33, 38–39, 62, 143. Maine quote is from *Maine State School Bulletin* 2, no. 1 (September 1932): 7. Also see Carnegie Endowment for International Peace, *Year Book, 1932,* (Washington, D.C., 1932), 70.

4. Benito Mussolini, "What Is Fascism, 1932," reprinted online in *Modern History Sourcebook,* http://www.fordham.edu/halsall/mod/mussolini-fascism.asp (accessed 9/7/11).

5. Adolf Hitler, *My Battle (Mein Kampf),* trans. E. T. S. Dugdale (Boston, 1933), 121–127, 136–137.

6. Martin Ceadel, "The 'King and Country' Debate, 1933: Student Politics, Pacifism and the Dictators," *Historical Journal* 22, no. 2 (June 1979): 397–422. A. A. Milne, *Peace with Honor* (New York, 1934), 20, 28.

7. David Anderson, "British Rearmament and the 'Merchants of Death': The 1935–36 Royal Commission on the Manufacture of and Trade in Armaments, *Journal of Contemporary History* 29, no. 1 (January 1994): 5–37. United States Senate, *Report of the Special Committee on Investigation of the Munitions Industry,* 73rd Congress (Washington, D.C., 1936).

8. Chamberlain quoted in *Sources of European History since 1900,* ed. Martin Perry et al. (Boston, 2011), 206.

9. "Inky" Stephensen quoted in E. M. Andrews, *Isolation and Appeasement in Australia: Reactions to the European Crises, 1935–1939* (Canberra, 1970), 7.

10. Theodore Roosevelt quoted in Armin Rappaport, *A History of American Diplomacy* (New York, 1975), 211.

11. Arthur Tiedemann, "The London Naval Treaty," in *Japan Erupts: The London Naval Conference and the Manchurian Incident, 1928–1932,* ed. James William Morely (New York, 1984), 6.

12. "Borah Offers Plan to Reduce Navies," *New York Times,* December 15, 1920, 1.

13. Rappaport, *History of American Diplomacy,* 289; William Reynolds Braisted, *The United States Navy in the Pacific, 1909–1922* (Austin, 1971), 562–564. "Lloyd George Endorses Harding Plan," *New York Times,* July 11, 1921, 1.

14. Harding quoted in Braisted, *United States Navy,* 597.

15. Lee quoted in ibid., 599.

16. Ibid., 631–637.

17. George Quester, "Bargaining and Bombing during World War II in Europe," *World Politics* 15, no. 3 (April 1963): 420.

18. Lodge speech in *Conference on the Limitation of Armament* (Washington, D.C., 1922), 106.

19. *Conference on the Limitation of Armament,* 96–97. Braisted, *United States Navy,* 651. On the "internationalization" of the Open Door Policy, see Frank Ninkovich, *The Wilsonian Century: U.S. Foreign Policy since 1900* (Chicago, 1999), 88. On the tariff, see Marc Gallicchio, *The African-American Encounter with Japan and China* (Chapel Hill, N.C., 2000), 64.

20. Lodge speech in *Conference on the Limitation of Armament,* 105–106.

21. Elihu Root speech in ibid., 160–161.

22. Ibid.

23. Jordan quoted in *Advocate of Peace* 80, no. 3 (March 1918): 93. Root is still quoted today in self-help books, an American mania. For example, see Annette Geffert and Diane Brown, *A Toolbox for Our Daughters: Building Strength, Confidence, and Integrity* (Novato, Calif., 2000), 214; Steve Klein, *Sell When You See the Whites of Their Eyes!* (Dallas, 2002), 149.

24. Braisted, *United States Navy,* 669.

25. Ibid., 598–599. Stevens and Reeve, *The Navy and the Nation,* 183.

26. Coolidge and Hoover quoted in Robert C. Byrd, *The Senate, 1789–1989: Addresses on the History of the United States Senate,* vol. 1 (Washington, D.C., 1988), 483.

27. Edward Filene quoted in League to Enforce Peace (U.S.), *Enforced Peace: Proceedings of the First Annual National Assemblage of the League to Enforce Peace, May 26–27, 1916* (New York, 1916), 46.

28. Édouard Herriot, *The United States of Europe,* trans. Reginald Dingle (New York, 1930). Kevin Wilson and Jan van der Dussen, eds., *The History of the Idea of Europe* (London, 1993), 77–79.

29. Christopher McKnight Nichols, *Promise and Peril: America at the Dawn of a Global Age* (Cambridge, Mass., 2011), 313–315, 322.

30. Nichols, *Promise and Peril,* 303. Also see Byrd, *The Senate,* 483. On Aristide Briand, see his biography online at Nobelprize.org, www.nobelprize.org/nobel _prizes/peace/laureates/1926/briand.html (accessed 9/14/11).

31. Elizabeth Borgwardt, *A New Deal for the World: America's Vision for Human Rights* (Cambridge, Mass., 2005), 197. Senator Reed, who appended the reservations to U.S. ratification, called Kellogg-Briand a "sort of international kiss." Quoted in Nichols, *Promise and Peril,* 308.

32. Ninkovich, *Wilsonian Century,* 81.

33. C. B. Schedvin, *Australia and the Great Depression: A Study of Economic Development and Policy in the 1920s and 1930s* (Sydney, 1988), 27–28, 149. Zara Steiner, *The Lights That Failed: European International History: 1919–1933* (Oxford, 2005), 277. Moses Ochonu, *Colonial Meltdown: Northern Nigeria in the Great Depression* (Athens, Ohio, 2009), 55–56.

34. Steiner, *Lights That Failed,* 25, 38. Hans-Joachim Braun, *The German Economy in the Twentieth Century* (London, 1990), 34–35, 45.

35. David Epstein and Sharyn O'Halloran, "The Partisan Paradox and the U.S. Tariff, 1877–1934," *International Organization* 50, no. 2 (Spring 1996): 303, 306, 319.

36. Coolidge quoted in Steiner, *Lights That Failed,* 38.

37. David M. Kennedy, *Freedom from Fear: The American People in War and Depression* (New York, 2001), 66.

38. Ibid., 67, 77. Lester Chandler, *America's Greatest Depression, 1929–1941* (New York, 1970), 5, 45. Timothy Tregarthen et al., *Economics* (New York, 2000), 28.

39. B. L. Turner et al., eds., *The Earth as Transformed by Human Action: Global and Regional Changes in the Biosphere over the Past 300 Years* (New York, 1990), 59.

40. Braun, *The German Economy,* 68–69.

41. Kennedy, *Freedom from Fear,* 390. Michael J. Hogan, *The Marshall Plan: America, Britain, and the Reconstruction of Western Europe, 1947–1952* (New York, 1987), 16–17.

42. George Herring, *From Colony to Superpower: U.S. Foreign Relations since 1776* (New York, 2008), 142. Ron Chernow, *Alexander Hamilton* (New York, 2004), 377, 458.

43. Frank Trentmann, *Free Trade Nation: Commerce, Consumption, and Civil Society in Modern Britain* (Oxford, 2008), 354.

44. Ibid., 1–2, 75, 318–319, 346.

45. Kennedy, *Freedom from Fear,* 77.

46. J. A. S. Grenville, *A History of the World in the Twentieth Century,* enl. ed. (Cambridge, Mass., 2000), 164; Thomas Skidmore and Peter Smith, *Modern Latin America,* 2nd ed. (New York, 1989), 53; Michael Crowder, *Colonial West Africa: Collected Essays* (London, 1978), 321.

47. Skidmore and Smith, *Modern Latin America,* 53.

48. Albert Michaels, "Fascism and *Sinarquismo*: Popular Nationalisms against the Mexican Revolution," *Journal of Church and State* 8, no. 2 (1966): 234–250.

49. Grenville, *History of the World,* 165. For slogan, see "Léon Blum" in *Encyclopædia Britannica* online, www.britannica.com. Also see Paul Mazgaj, "The Origins of the French Radical Right: A Historiographical Essay," *French Historical Studies* 15, no. 2 (Autumn 1987), 287–315.

50. Grenville, *History of the World,* 193.

51. Braun, *German Economy,* 67. Also see Winston Churchill, *Memoirs of the Second World War* (Boston, 1987), 30.

52. Grenville, *History of the World,* 194, 198.

53. Quester, "Bargaining and Bombing," 421.

54. Hitler quoted in Churchill, *Memoirs,* 36.

55. Elizabeth Anne Cobbs, *The Rich Neighbor Policy: Rockefeller and Kaiser in Brazil* (New Haven, Conn., 1992), 36–37; Joseph Smith, *Brazil and the United States: Convergence and Divergence* (Athens, Ga., 2010), 108.

56. On the White Australia Policy, see Naoko Shimazu, *Japan, Race, and Equality: The Racial Equality Proposal of 1919* (London, 1998), 126–130; John Fitzgerald, *Big White Lie: Chinese Australians in White Australia* (Sydney, 2007), 229; and Brian Hodge and Allen Whitehurst, *Nation and People: An Introduction to Australia in a Changing World* (Sydney, 1967), 69. On Canadian immigration, see David J. Wishart, *Encyclopedia of the Great Plains* (Lincoln, Nebr., 2004), 140.

57. Matsuoka quoted in Grenville, *History of the World,* 207.

58. Kenneth B. Pyle, "Japan: Opportunism in Pursuit of Power," in *A Century's Journey: How the Great Powers Shape the World,* ed. Robert Pastor (New York, 1999), 261, 269.

59. Akira Iriye, "The Extension of Hostilities, 1931–1932, Introduction," in *Japan Erupts: The London Naval Conference and the Manchurian Incident, 1928–1932,* ed. James William Morley (New York, 1984), 237.

60. Shimada Toshihiko, "The Extension of Hostilities," in *Japan Erupts,* ed. Morley, 332, 334.

61. "Economic Sanctions against Japan," March 9, 1932, 5–6. National Archives of Great Britain, Kew, CAB/24/228.

62. Walter LaFeber, *The American Age: United States Foreign Policy at Home and Abroad since 1750* (New York, 1989), 338. Quote in Armin Rappaport, *A History of American Diplomacy* (New York, 1975), 310.

63. Quotes in Gallicchio, *African-American Encounter,* 65, 77.

64. Iris Chang, *Rape of Nanking* (New York, 1997). James McCallum to his family, and John Magee to his wife, December 19, 1937, in *American Missionary Eyewitnesses to the Nanking Massacre, 1937–1938,* ed. Martha Lund Smalley (New Haven, Conn., 1997), 21–24.

65. Takashi Yoshida, *The Making of the "Rape of Nanking": History and Memory in Japan, China, and the United States* (New York, 2006), 12–13. Also see Philip

Towle, "The Japanese Army and Prisoners of War," in *Japanese Prisoners of War,* ed. Philip Towle, Margaret Kosuge, and Yoichi Kibata (London, 2000), 11.

66. Churchill, *Memoirs,* 123, 140, 145–147, 150, 153–154.

67. Haile Selassie quoted in William Safire, ed., *Lend Me Your Ears: Great Speeches in History* (New York, 2004), 320.

68. Kennedy, *Freedom from Fear,* 482.

69. Norman Davies, *Europe: A History* (New York, 1996), 1002, 1004; Grenville, *History of the World,* 247.

70. Chamberlain quoted in Joseph P. Lash, *Roosevelt and Churchill, 1939–1941: The Partnership That Saved the West* (New York, 1976), 199.

71. Churchill, *Memoirs,* 284–285.

72. Ibid., 326.

73. Quester, "Bargaining and Bombing," 427.

8. Up to the Neck and in to the Death

1. Philip E. Jacob, "Influences of World Events on U.S. 'Neutrality Opinion,'" *Public Opinion Quarterly* 4 (March 1940): 53, 58, 107. Gallup quote from H. Schuyler Foster, *Activism Replaces Isolationism: U.S. Public Attitudes, 1940–1975* (Washington, D.C., 1983), 19.

2. Franklin D. Roosevelt, "Address at Chicago," October 5, 1937. Online by Gerhard Peters and John T. Woolley, *The American Presidency Project,* http://www .presidency.ucsb.edu/index.php (hereafter APP/UCSB).

3. Franklin D. Roosevelt, "Message to Congress Urging Repeal of the Embargo Provisions of the Neutrality Law," September 21, 1939, APP/UCSB.

4. *Congressional Record,* 76th Congress, 2d Session, HR, 75.

5. Another way of stating these figures, as polling analyst Philip Jacob does, is that 57 percent still "agreed with Senator Borah" in August 1939 that the statutes should not be changed. Jacob, "Influences of World Events," 55 and 57. Gallup Poll (October 22, 1939), *Public Opinion Quarterly* 4 (March 1940): 102.

6. Justus D. Doenecke, ed., *In Danger Undaunted: The Anti-Interventionist Movement of 1940–1941 as Revealed in the Papers of the America First Committee* (Stanford, Calif., 1990), 2. For film footage on wooden rifles and pretend tanks, see the TV documentary *George Marshall and the American Century* (1994). Journalist Eric Sevareid was one of the draftees.

7. Doenecke, *In Danger Undaunted,* 7, 127.

8. Quotes and figures in ibid., 6, 17, 18. Borgwardt gives 800,000 as the number of America First members. See Elizabeth Borgwardt, *A New Deal for the World: America's Vision for Human Rights* (Cambridge, Mass., 2005), 24.

9. Doenecke, *In Danger Undaunted*, 51. David Hendrickson, *Union, Nation, or Empire: The American Debate over International Relations, 1789–1941* (Lawrence, Kans., 2009), 373.

10. Joseph P. Lash, *Roosevelt and Churchill, 1939–1941: The Partnership That Saved the West* (New York, 1976), 395.

11. David M. Kennedy, *Freedom from Fear: The American People in War and Depression* (New York, 2001), 522.

12. Franklin D. Roosevelt, "Message to Congress on Landing Troops in Iceland, Trinidad, and British Guiana," July 7, 1941, APP/UCSB.

13. Franklin D. Roosevelt, "Transmittal to Congress of a Message from the Prime Minister of Iceland," July 7, 1941, APP/UCSB.

14. Hugh Johnson, quoted in Kennedy, *Freedom from Fear*, 448, 451.

15. Franklin D. Roosevelt, "Fireside Chat," December 29, 1940, APP/UCSB.

16. Norman Davies, *Europe: A History* (New York, 1996), 1015.

17. Lash, *Roosevelt and Churchill*, 392, 398.

18. Davies, *Europe*, 1068.

19. Churchill quoted in Steven F. Hayward, *Greatness: Reagan, Churchill, and the Making of Extraordinary Leaders* (New York, 2005), 150–151.

20. Felix Frankfurter quoted in Lash, *Roosevelt and Churchill*, 396.

21. Winston Churchill, *Memoirs of the Second World War* (Boston, 1987), 490–491.

22. Quotes in Lash, *Roosevelt and Churchill*, 391, and Borgwardt, *New Deal for the World*, 2, 17.

23. Lash, *Roosevelt and Churchill*, 398.

24. Borgwardt, *New Deal for the World*, 1–2.

25. For "The Atlantic Charter," August 14, 1941, see Churchill, *Memoirs*, 491–492.

26. Roosevelt in Borgwardt, *New Deal for the World*, 25.

27. Nelson Mandela, *Long Walk to Freedom: The Autobiography of Nelson Mandela* (New York, 1994), 83–84.

28. Churchill quote in Borgwardt, *New Deal for the World*, 45. For an example of the literature on American global leadership and the end of segregation, see Mary Dudziak, *Cold War Civil Rights: Race and the Image of American Democracy* (Princeton, N.J., 2000).

29. Churchill, *Memoirs*, 488–489, 492.

30. Jeremi Suri, *Liberty's Surest Guardian: American Nation-Building from the Founders to Obama* (New York, 2011), 90–93.

31. Kenneth Pyle, "Japan: Opportunism in the Pursuit of Power," in *A Century's Journey: How the Great Powers Shape the World*, ed. Robert Pastor (New York, 1999), 267. Also see Takashi Shiraishi, and Motoo Furuta, eds., *Indochina in the 1940s and 1950s* (Ithaca, N.Y., 1992), 90–91.

32. Churchill, *Memoirs,* 492–493. Lash, *Roosevelt and Churchill,* 400.

33. Matsuoka quoted in Marius B. Jansen, *Japan and China: From War to Peace: 1894–1972* (New York, 1975), 404; Hideki in Maruyama Masao, *Thought and Behavior in Modern Japanese Politics,* ed. Ivan Morris (Oxford, 1969), 85. Also quoted in Pyle, "Japan: Opportunism in the Pursuit of Power," 269.

34. Diane Burke Fessler, ed., *No Time for Fear: Voices of American Military Nurses in World War II* (Ann Arbor, Mich., 1996), 14–16.

35. Franklin D. Roosevelt, "Address to Congress Requesting a Declaration of War with Japan," December 8, 1941; "Fireside Chat," December 9, 1941; and "Message to Congress Requesting War Declarations with Germany and Italy," December 11, 1941, APP/UCSB.

36. Han Suyin, *Birdless Summer* (New York, 1968), 235–236. Also see Michael Schaller, *The U.S. Crusade in China, 1938–1945* (New York, 1979), 88.

37. Churchill, *Memoirs,* 507.

38. Ibid.

39. U.S. Department of State, *Foreign Relations of the United States, Diplomatic Papers, The Conferences at Cairo and Tehran, 1943* (Washington, D.C., 1961), 530–532.

40. Foster, *Activism Replaces Isolationism,* 19, 22, 25.

41. Borgwardt, *New Deal for the World,* 162.

42. Joe Alex Morris, *Nelson Rockefeller: A Biography* (New York, 1960), 252. Also see Cobbs, *Rich Neighbor,* 40–50.

43. Roosevelt in Borgwardt, *New Deal for the World,* 136.

44. Quoted in Kennedy, *Freedom from Fear,* 845. On casualty estimates, also see Robert Ferrell, *Harry S. Truman: A Life* (Columbia, Mo., 1994), 213.

45. J. A. S. Grenville, *A History of the World in the Twentieth Century* (Cambridge, Mass., 2000), 320. Iris Chang, *The Rape of Nanking: The Forgotten Holocaust of World War II* (New York, 1997), 167.

46. Dwight D. Eisenhower, *The Papers of Dwight David Eisenhower,* vol. 4: *The War Years,* ed. Alfred D. Chandler, Jr. (Baltimore, 1970), 2615–2617.

47. David H. Burton, *Clara Barton: In the Service of Humanity* (Westport, Conn., 1995), 95.

48. Philip Towle, introduction to *Japanese Prisoners of War,* ed. Philip Towle, Margaret Kosuge, and Yoichi Kibata (London, 2000), xiii–xv.

49. Philip Towle, "The Japanese Army and Prisoners of War," in ibid., 7. Van Waterford, *Prisoners of the Japanese in World War II: Statistical History, Personal Narratives and Memorials concerning POWs in Camps and on Hellships, Civilian Internees, Asian Slave Laborers and Others Captured in the Pacific Theater* (Jefferson, N.C., 1994), 35, 43, 116, 146, 220. Also see Margaret Stetz and Bonnie B. C. Oh, eds., *Legacies of the Comfort Women of World War II* (London, 2001), and Chang, *Rape of Nanking,* 173.

50. "The How of an Internment, But Not All the Whys," *New York Times,* December 9, 2011. "Ottawa Will Pay Compensation to Uprooted Japanese-Canadians," ibid., September 23, 1988.

51. Action Reconciliation for Peace website, https://www.asf-ev.de/en/about-us/history.html (accessed 10/4/11).

52. Ibid., https://www.asf-ev.de/uk/about-us/history/uk.html (accessed 10/4/11). Elizabeth Cobbs Hoffman, *All You Need Is Love: The Peace Corps and the Spirit of the 1960s* (Cambridge, Mass., 1998), 149.

53. Chang, *Rape of Nanking,* 12, 205–209, 221–223.

54. Stephen J. Lee, *Europe, 1890–1945* (London, 2003), 298.

55. U.S. Department of State, *Foreign Relations of the United States,* 532. Ferrell, *Harry S. Truman,* 246.

9. The Buck Stops Here

1. "Khrushchev Bangs Shoe on Desk," *New York Times*, October 13, 1960, 1, 14.

2. "Boland Angered: Chairman Acts after Colonialism Debate Causes an Uproar," *New York Times,* October 12, 1960, 1, 14. "Philippine Group Unruffled by Khrushchev," *New York Times,* October 14, 1960, 5.

3. Khrushchev in "Khrushchev Rampage Routs General Assembly: Premier Waves His Shoe in Air in Wild Uproar on Colonials," *Los Angeles Times*, October 13, 1960, 7.

4. Wilcox and Boland in "Khrushchev Rampage Routs General Assembly," *Los Angeles Times,* October 13, 1960, 1, 7.

5. "Angry Farewell: Soviet Loses Vote on U.S. 'Aggression' but Gains One Victory," *New York Times,* October 14, 1960, 1.

6. "Declaration on the Granting of Independence to Colonial Countries and Peoples," December 14, 1960, Resolution 1514, UN General Assembly, Fifteenth Session; http://untreaty.un.org/cod/avl/ha/dicc/dicc.html (accessed 12/10/11).

7. James Feron, "U.N. Urges Steps to Free Colonies," *New York Times,* December 15, 1960, 1, 15.

8. John Springhall, *Decolonization since 1945: The Collapse of European Overseas Empires* (London, 2001), 143.

9. Tony Chafer notes that French decolonization was "largely peaceful" in sub-Saharan Africa compared with Algeria. Tony Chafer, *The End of Empire in French West Africa: France's Successful Decolonization?* (Oxford, 2002), 12. Also see David Strang, "The Inner Incompatibility of Empire and Nation: Popular Sovereignty and Decolonization, *Sociological Perspectives* 35, no. 2 (Summer 1992): 367–384.

10. H. W. Brands, "The United States, Germany, and the Multilateralization of International Relations," in *The United States and Germany in the Era of the Cold War, 1968–1990,* ed. Detlef Junker, vol. 1: *1945–1968* (New York, 2004), 50.

11. Tony Judt, *Postwar: A History of Europe since 1945* (New York, 2005), 282.

12. William S. Triplet, *In the Philippines and Okinawa: A Memoir, 1945–1948,* ed. Robert H. Ferrell (Columbia, Mo., 2001), 124–125.

13. Ibid., 125. On American casualties in the thirty-day Battle of Manila, see Todd C. Helmus and Russell W. Glenn, *Steeling the Mind: Combat Stress Reactions and Their Implications for Urban Warfare* (Santa Monica, Calif., 2005), 49.

14. "Spain Holds Celebration: Madrid Program Marks Philippine Independence Day," *New York Times,* July 5, 1946, 5. In *Los Angeles Times,* July 4, 1946, see: "Birth of a Republic in the Orient," A4; "Independence Dawnes [*sic*] for the Philippines," 3; "Philippines Republic Born in Colorful Fete," 1; and "Truman Pledges Help to Philippines Republic," 5. Also see "Los Angeles Filipinos Hail Birth of Republic" and "Filipinos Raise National Flag in Washington," *Los Angeles Times,* July 5, 1946, 5; "Angeleno Recalls First Philippines Republic," *Los Angeles Times,* July 6, 1946, A3.

15. Vicente Villamin, "The New Island Republic," *Los Angeles Times,* July 4, 1946, A4.

16. "Nixon Aids Inauguration of New Nation, Ghana," *Los Angeles Times,* March 7, 1957, 11.

17. *Defender* quoted in James Hunter Meriweather, *Proudly We Can Be Africans: Black Americans and Africa, 1935–1961* (Chapel Hill, N.C., 2002), 159. Also see James T. Campbell, *Middle Passage: African American Journeys to Africa, 1787–2005* (New York, 2006), 318.

18. "Race Discrimination Hurts U.S. in Far East, Veep Says," *Fort Wayne News-Sentinel,* January 4, 1954.

19. On Indonesia, see Judt, *Postwar,* 281. Mitterrand quoted in "France: Suitcase or Coffin?" *Time,* November 15, 1954. On Algeria, see "French-Algerian War," *Time* Archive, http://www.time.com/time/archive/collections/0,21428,c_algerian_war,00 .shtml.

20. Charles R. Nixon, "Independence Comes in Africa," *Los Angeles Times,* March 7, 1957, B5.

21. Marilyn Young, *The Vietnam Wars, 1945–1990* (New York, 1991), 2.

22. Mark Atwood Lawrence, *Assuming the Burden: Europe and the American Commitment to War in Vietnam* (Berkeley, Calif., 2005), 24, 46, 55. See Memorandum by Roosevelt to Secretary of State Hull, January 24, 1944, reprinted in *Vietnam: The Definitive Documentation of Human Decisions,* ed. Gareth Porter, vol. 1 (Stanfordville, N.Y., 1979), 11.

23. Charles de Gaulle, *The War Memoirs of Charles de Gaulle: Salvation, 1944–1946,* trans. Richard Howard (New York, 1960), 187. Also see Michael Kelly, "The Reconstruction of Masculinity at Liberation," in *The Liberation of France: Image and Event,* ed. H. R. Kedward and Nancy Wood (Oxford, 1995), 117.

24. Lawrence, *Assuming the Burden,* 32–33.

25. Caffrey to Secretary of State Edward Stettinius, March 13, 1945, U.S. Department of State, *Foreign Relations of the United States* (hereafter, *FRUS*), 1945, vol. 6 (Washington, D.C., 1969), 300. Also see Lawrence, *Assuming the Burden*, 62.

26. Ho Chi Minh quoted in Mark Philip Bradley, *Imagining Vietnam and America: The Making of Postcolonial Vietnam, 1919–1950* (Chapel Hill, N.C., 2000), 123. Vietnamese Declaration of Independence quoted in Ross Marlay and Clark D. Neher, *Patriots and Tyrants: Ten Asian Leaders* (Lanham, Md., 1999), 102.

27. David Armitage, *The Declaration of Independence: A Global History* (Cambridge, Mass., 2007), 134–137. Ho Chi Minh quoted in Bradley, *Imagining Vietnam*, 127.

28. Judt, *Postwar*, 283.

29. Reports quoted in Lawrence, *Assuming the Burden*, 25–26, 90.

30. Ho Chi Minh to Harry Truman, February 16, 1946, reprinted in Porter, *Vietnam*, 1:95, 127. Also see Marlay and Neher, *Patriots and Tyrants*, 102–103.

31. Truman quoted in Lawrence, *Assuming the Burden*, 75, 78–79.

32. Truman quoted in Ralph Levering and Verena Botzenhart-Viehe, "The American Perspective," in *Debating the Origins of the Cold War: American and Russian Perspectives*, ed. Ralph Levering, et al. (Lanham, Md., 2001), 34.

33. Quotes in John Lewis Gaddis, *We Now Know: Rethinking Cold War History* (New York, 1997), 21–24.

34. Stalin quoted in Gaddis, *We Now Know*, 23.

35. Norman Naimark and Leonid Gibianskii, eds., *The Establishment of Communist Regimes in Eastern Europe, 1944–1949* (Boulder, Colo., 1997), 7. For the Yalta accord, see *FRUS*, 1945, *The Conferences at Malta and Yalta* (Washington, D.C., 1955), 975–982.

36. Donovan quoted in Terry H. Anderson, *The United States, Great Britain, and the Cold War, 1944–1947* (Columbia, Mo., 1981), 76. Norman Naimark, *Russians in Germany: A History of the Soviet Zone of Occupation, 1945–1949* (Cambridge, Mass., 1995), 88–89, 107. Also see Gaddis, *We Now Know*, 45, 286.

37. John Kent, *British Imperial Strategy and the Origins of the Cold War, 1944–1949* (London, 1993), 57.

38. Quotes from Anderson, *The United States, Great Britain*, 112, 115, 153. On Wallace, see Arthur H. Vandenberg, *The Private Papers of Senator Vandenberg* (Boston, 1952), 300.

39. Truman quoted in Anderson, *The United States, Great Britain*, 104. Kennan in *FRUS*, 1946, *Eastern Europe: The Soviet Union*, vol. 6, 706–707. Smith to the secretary of state, January 2, 1947, in *FRUS*, 1947, *The Near East and Africa*, vol. 5, 3. See letters from the U.S. ambassadors to Greece and Turkey conveying Greek and Turkish requests, January 11, 1947, and January 17, 1947, in *FRUS*, 1947, vol. 5, 5–8.

40. British quote in *FRUS*, 1947, vol. 5: "Chargé in the United Kingdom to Secretary of States," January 31, 1947, 13–14. On American stalling, see Anderson, *The United States, Great Britain*, 146–147.

41. British quotes in *FRUS*, 1947, vol. 5: "British Embassy to the Department of State," February 21, 1947, 34–37, and in John Balfour to George C. Marshall, July 30, 1947, Subject File "Foreign Affairs—British," President's Secretary Files, Harry S. Truman Library (hereafter, HTL). Also see Ina Zweiniger-Bargielowska, *Austerity in Britain: Rationing, Controls, and Consumption, 1939–1955* (Oxford, 2000), 10, 24, 30–31. On wartime destruction, see Anderson, *The United States, Great Britain*, 83. For polls taken in January 1947, see George H. Gallup, ed., *The Gallup International Public Opinion Polls: Great Britain, 1937–1975*, vol. 1 (New York, 1976), 148.

42. On force statistics, see Anderson, *The United States, Great Britain*, 152. "Demand Daddies Back: Young Toledo Mothers Will Ask Congress to Release Fathers," *New York Times*, November 10, 1945, 20.

43. Quoted in Anderson, *The United States, Great Britain*, 106, 149.

44. Ibid., 85, 165.

45. Attlee memorandum of February 22, 1946, quoted in Klaus Larres, *Churchill's Cold War: The Politics of Personal Diplomacy* (New Haven, Conn., 2002), 111.

46. Acheson quote in Anderson, *The United States, Great Britain*, 174. Vandenberg, *Private Papers*, 338–339. "Meeting Notes," ca. February 1947, 1–3, Subject File, Joseph M. Jones Papers, HTL; vailable online at www.trumanlibrary.org.

47. "Meeting Notes," ca. February 1947, 1–3, HTL. Vandenberg, *Private Papers*, 339.

48. "Meeting Notes," ca. February 1947, 1–3, HTL. Vandenberg, *Private Papers*, 339. Also see "Draft Suggestions for President's Message to Congress on Greek Situation," March 3, 1947, Subject File, Joseph M. Jones Papers, HTL.

49. "Draft Suggestions for President's Message," March 3, 1947, and "Chronology: Drafting of the President's Message of March 12, 1947," ca. March 1947. Both found in Subject File, Joseph M. Jones Papers, HTL. Clifford quoted in Anderson, *The United States, Great Britain*, 174.

50. "Address of the President to Congress, Recommending Assistance to Greece and Turkey," *Congressional Record*, 80th Congress, 1st Session, Doc. 171 (March 12, 1947).

51. Ibid.

52. Ibid.

53. For quotes in this paragraph and the one above, see *Congressional Record*, 80th Congress, vol. 93, part 3, 2993–2997, 3038, 3237–3239, 3279, 3283, 3289. "Chester Holifield, 91, Congressman for 32 Years," *New York Times*, February 9, 1995.

54. Quotations in this paragraph and the one above taken from *Congressional Record*, 80th Congress, vol. 93, part 3, 3137, 3139, 3379–3380.

55. Vandenberg, *Private Papers*, 334, 343–346. Also quoted in Julian Zelizer, *Arsenal of Democracy: The Politics of National Security—From World War II to the War on Terrorism* (New York, 2005), 5, and in Melvin Leffler, *Preponderance of Power:*

National Security, The Truman Administration, and the Cold War (Stanford, Calif., 1992), 146.

56. "Vote on Aid to Near East" and "The House Vote," *New York Times,* May 10, 1947, 2 and 12.

57. "Editorial Reaction to Current Issues," Greek Situation, Parts I and II, March 19, 1947, 1–2, President's Secretary's Files, HTL.

58. Robert Mann, *The Complete Idiot's Guide to the Cold War* (Indianapolis, 2002), 97. See Walter LaFeber, who largely pioneered this interpretation, in *The American Age: United States Foreign Policy at Home and Abroad since 1750* (New York, 1989), 453–454.

59. Quotes from "Meeting Notes," ca. February 1947, 3, HTL. Also see typed and handwritten references to communism in "Draft Suggestions for President's Message to Congress on Greek Situation," March 3, 1947. Both found in Subject File, Joseph M. Jones Papers, HTL.

60. George H. Gallup, ed., *The Gallup Poll: Public Opinion, 1935–1971,* vol. 1 (New York, 1972), 636–637, 666, 675; *The Gallup International Public Opinion Polls: Great Britain, 1937–1975,* vol. 1 (New York, 1976), 148; and *The Gallup International Public Opinion Polls: France, 1937–1975,* vol. 1 (New York, 1976), 79.

61. Elizabeth Borgwardt, *A New Deal for the World: America's Vision for Human Rights* (Cambridge, Mass., 2005), 6. Gallup, *Gallup Poll: Public Opinion,* 664. Gallup, *Gallup International: Great Britain,* 179.

62. Gallup, *Gallup Poll: Public Opinion,* 658.

63. Ron Kovic, *Born on the Fourth of July* (New York, 1976).

10. A Coercive Logic

1. Jimmy Carter, *Keeping Faith: Memoirs of a President* (Fayetteville, 1995), 5.

2. Scott Sigmund Gartner, "Military Personnel on Active Duty, by Branch of Service and Sex: 1789–1995" (Table Ed26–47), in *Historical Statistics of the United States, Earliest Times to the Present: Millennial Edition,* ed. Susan B. Carter et al. (New York, 2006).

3. United Nations Development Programme, *Human Development Report 2002: Deepening Democracy in a Fragmented World* (New York, 2002); Agnus Maddison, *The World Economy: A Millennial Perspective* (Paris, 2001), 30, 126; Jonathan Margolis, *A Brief History of Tomorrow: The Future, Past and Present* (London, 2000), 74. Also see Tony Judt, *Postwar: A History of Europe since 1945* (New York, 2005), 324–353.

4. Judt, *Postwar,* 325. Also see Bart van Ark, Mary O'Mahony, and Marcel Timmer, "The Productivity Gap between Europe and the United States: Trends and Causes," *Journal of Economic Perspectives* 22, no. 1 (Winter 2008): 28.

5. On Japan, see Kenneth Pyle, "Japan: Opportunism in the Pursuit of Power," in *A Century's Journey: How the Great Powers Shape the World,* ed. Robert Pastor

(New York, 1999), 275–277; Benigno Valdés, "An Application of Convergence Theory to Japan's Post-WWII Economic 'Miracle,'" *Journal of Economic Education* 34, no. 1 (Winter 2003): 61; also Aaron Forsberg, *America and the Japanese Miracle: The Cold War Context of Japan's Postwar Revival* (Chapel Hill, N.C., 2000). For the figures on China, see Frank Trentmann, *Free Trade Nation: Commerce, Consumption, and Civil Society in Modern Britain* (Oxford, 2008), 351. On the U.S. economy in 2011, see U.S. Department of Commerce, Bureau of Economic Analysis, "News Release on Gross Domestic Product and Corporate Profits," September 29, 2011, http://www.bea.gov/newsreleases/national/gdp/2011/gdp2q11_3rd.htm (accessed 10/11/11).

6. Michael J. Hogan, *The Marshall Plan: America, Britain, and the Reconstruction of Europe, 1947–1952* (Cambridge, UK, 1987), 35–39. On the UN budget, see John Allphin Moore and Jerry Pubantz, *Encyclopedia of the United Nations*, 2nd ed., vol. 2 (New York, 2008), 366–367.

7. Lord Ismay is quoted ubiquitously. See, for example, H. W. Brands, "The United States, Germany, and the Multilateralization of International Relations," in *The United States and Germany in the Era of the Cold War, 1968–1990*, ed. Detlef Junker, vol. 1 (New York, 2004), 50.

8. For one example of intracoalition competition see Klaus Schwabe, "Détente and Multipolarity: The Cold War and German-American Relations, 1968–1990," in *The United States and Germany in the Era of the Cold War, 1968–1990*, ed. Detlef Junker, vol. 1 (New York, 2004), 1–17.

9. Eugenie M. Blang, *Allies at Odds: America, Europe, and Vietnam, 1961–1968* (Lanham, Md., 2007), 105.

10. Quoted in Scott Sullivan, *From War to Wealth: Fifty Years of Innovation* (Paris, 1997), 12.

11. Barry Machado, *In Search of a Usable Past: The Marshall Plan and Postwar Construction Today* (Lexington, Va., 2000), 20–21.

12. George H. Gallup, ed., *The Gallup Poll: Public Opinion, 1935–1971*, vol. 1 (New York, 1972), 661.

13. Wolfgang J. Huschke, *The Candy Bombers: The Berlin Airlift 1948/49: The Technical Conditions and Their Successful Transformation* (Berlin, 2008), 93–94, 100, 250, 288, 119. Andrei Cherny, *The Candy Bombers: The Untold Story of the Berlin Airlift and America's Finest Hour* (New York, 2008), 409. "Air-Lift Santa Claus: Berlin Children Thank Pilot for 'Chute Candy,'" *Los Angeles Times*, October 4, 1948, 1.

14. Robert F. Kennedy quoted in Willy Brandt, *People and Politics: The Years 1960–1975* (Boston, 1976), 87. To hear Dwight Eisenhower's speech on the second Berlin crisis in 1959, go to http://www.history.com/audio/eisenhower-on-the-second-berlin-crisis#eisenhower-on-the-second-berlin-crisis (accessed 12/7/11).

15. John Kent, *British Imperial Strategy and the Origins of the Cold War, 1944–1949* (London, 1993), 171–172. Bertram Hulen, "Truman Supports 5-Country Treaty:

Calls for Full U.S. Assistance to 'Free Nations' in Efforts 'to Protect Themselves,'"
New York Times, March 18, 1948, 10. Also see "5 Western Nations Sign 50-Year Pact,"
New York Times, March 18, 1948, 1.

16. Bevin quoted in Kent, *British Imperial Strategy*, 172. On the September 1947
poll, see George H. Gallup, ed., *The Gallup International Public Opinion Polls: Great
Britain, 1937–1975*, vol. 1 (New York, 1976), 162.

17. Oswaldo Aranha to Rául Fernandes, March 18, 1947, 1–2, Fundação Getulio
Vargas, Rio de Janeiro, Centro de Pesquise e Documentação de História Contem-
porânea do Brasil, Oswaldo Aranha Papers 47.03.18. Also see Elizabeth Anne Cobbs,
The Rich Neighbor Policy: Rockefeller and Kaiser in Brazil (New Haven, Conn., 1992),
64–65, 68–69.

18. Stanley Sandler, *The Korean War: No Victors, No Vanquished* (London, 1999),
155, 16–165. Ross Gregory and Richard Balkin, *Cold War America, 1946–1990* (New
York, 2003), 270.

19. NSC-68, in U.S. Department of State, *Foreign Relations of the U.S.* (hereafter, *FRUS*), 1950, National Security Affairs; Foreign Economic Policy (Washington,
D.C., 1977), 1:237–290.

20. "Memorandum from the Director of the Office of Strategic Services (Donovan)" to President Truman, August 25, 1945, and "Memorandum from the Lovett
Committee to Secretary of War Patterson," November 3, 1945, in *FRUS*, 1945–1950,
Emergence of the Intelligence Establishment (Washington, D.C., 1996), http://www
.state.gov/www/about_state/history/intel/index.html (accessed 10/10/11).

21. John Lewis Gaddis, *George F. Kennan, An American Life* (New York, 2011), 318.

22. See, for example, Christopher Andrew and Vasili Mitrokhin, *The World Was
Going Our Way: The KGB and the Battle for the Third World* (New York, 2005); Piero
Gleijeses, *Conflicting Missions: Havana, Washington, and Africa, 1959–1976* (Chapel
Hill, N.C., 2002); and Merle Pribbenow, "E-Dossier No. 25: Vietnam Covertly Supplies Weapons to Revolutionaries in Algeria and Latin America," Cold War International History Project, Wilson Center, Washington, D.C.: http://www.wilsoncenter
.org / publication/e-dossier-no-25-vietnam-covertly-supplied-weapons-to-revolutiona
ries-algeria-and-latin (accessed 11/4/11).

23. On the Australian Secret Intelligence Service, see the official website: http://
www.asis.gov.au/About-Us/History.html. On Britain's, see text of the Intelligence Services Act, particularly Section 7: http://www.legislation.gov.uk/ukpga/1994/13
/crossheading/the-secret-intelligence-service. On immunity from the U.K. Freedom of
Information Act, https://www.sis.gov.uk/our-history/archive.html (accessed 11/4/11).

24. Daniel Yergin, *The Prize: The Epic Quest for Oil, Money, and Power* (New
York, 1991), 258–261, 417. Also see Francisco Parra, *Oil Politics: A Modern History of
Petroleum* (New York, 2005), 14–15, and Lee Stacy, ed., *Mexico and the United States*
(Tarrytown, N.Y., 2003), 604.

25. Yergin, *The Prize*, 429.

26. Mary Ann Heiss, *Empire and Nationhood: The United States, Great Britain, and Iranian Oil, 1950–1954* (New York, 1997), 223. Yergin, *The Prize,* 118–121.

27. Heiss, *Empire and Nationhood,* 20, 223.

28. Ibid., 53.

29. Mosaddeq quoted in ibid., 71.

30. Acheson quoted in Douglas Little, *American Orientalism: The United States and the Middle East since 1945* (Chapel Hill, N.C., 2008), 57. Also, Heiss, *Empire and Nationhood,* 56, 66.

31. W. Roger Louis, "Britain and the Overthrow of the Mosaddeq Government," in *Mohammad Mosaddeq and the 1953 Coup in Iran,* ed. Mark J. Gasiorowski and Malcolm Byrne (Syracuse, N.Y., 2004), 129.

32. Maziar Behrooz, "The 1953 Coup and the Legacy of the Tudeh," in Gasiorowski and Byrne, *Mohammad Mosaddeq,* 110. Heiss, *Empire and Nationhood,* 3, 136–137, 235.

33. Heiss, *Empire and Nationhood,* 172. Salim Yaqub, *Containing Arab Nationalism: The Eisenhower Doctrine and the Middle East* (Chapel Hill, N.C., 2004), 28–30.

34. Louis, "Britain and the Overthrow of the Mosaddeq Government," 129. Heiss, *Empire and Nationhood,* 186. For examples of this widespread tendency, see George Herring, *From Colony to Superpower: U.S. Foreign Relations since 1776* (New York, 2008), 672–673; Little, *American Orientalism;* and Stephen Kinzer, *All The Shah's Men: An American Coup and the Roots of Middle East Terror* (Hoboken, N.J., 2008).

35. Piero Gliejeses, *Shattered Hope: The Guatemalan Revolution and the United States, 1944–1954* (Princeton, N.J., 1991), 134, 282–283, 338, 363–365. In recent years, historians examining new archival evidence have tended to conclude that the government of Jacobo Arbenz was influenced by Communist ideology and fell largely because it lost the support of its original power base in the army, though American activities played a critical role. For an overview of this literature, see Stephen M. Streeter, "Interpreting the 1954 U.S. Intervention in Guatemala: Realist, Revisionist, and Postrevisionist Perspectives," *The History Teacher,* November 2000, http://www.historycooperative.org/journals/ht/34.1/streeter.html (accessed 11/9/11).

36. Louis, "Britain and the Overthrow of the Mosaddeq Government," 126, 307.

37. Fakhreddin Azimi, "Unseating Mosaddeq: The Configuration and Role of Domestic Forces," in Gasiorowski and Byrne, *Mohammad Mosaddeq,* 28–29. Heiss, *Empire and Nationhood,* 68, 179–180, 184, 208, 214–215.

38. Heiss, *Empire and Nationhood,* 204.

39. Andrew and Mitrokhin, *World Was Going Our Way,* 170–171.

40. General Jean de Lattre quoted in Kathryn Statler, *Replacing France: The Origins of American Intervention in Vietnam* (Lexington, Ky., 2007), 38.

41. Statler, *Replacing France,* 278.

42. Martin Windrow, *The Last Valley: Dien Bien Phu and the French Defeat in Vietnam* (London, 2004), 637.

43. Robert Schulzinger, *A Time for War: The United States and Vietnam, 1941–1975* (New York, 1997), 233. Nixon quoted in Patrick Hagopian, *The Vietnam War in American Memory: Veterans, Memorials, and the Politics of Healing* (Amherst, Mass., 2009), 28.

44. Michael Lind, *The Necessary War: A Reinterpretation of America's Most Disastrous Military Conflict* (New York, 1999), 137.

45. Kiem Do and Julia Kane, *Counterpart: A South Vietnamese Naval Officer's War* (Annapolis, Md., 1998).

46. Mark Cutts, *The State of the World's Refugees, 2000: Fifty Years of Humanitarian Action* (Oxford, 2000), 90.

47. Lind, *Necessary War,* 138. Joaquín Fermandois, "The Persistence of a Myth: Chile in the Hurricane of the Cold War: Books under Review," *World Affairs* 167, no. 3 (Winter 2005): 112.

48. Quoted in preface to *Foundations of Foreign Policy, FRUS, 1969–1976,* vol. 1 (Washington, D.C., 2003).

49. *European Security, FRUS,* 1969–1976, vol. 39 (Washington, D.C., 2008), 7.

50. Robert McNamara, *In Retrospect: The Tragedy and Lessons of Vietnam* (New York, 1995), xx.

51. F. Ugboaja Ohaegbulam, *A Culture of Deference: Congress, the President, and the Course of the U.S.-Led Invasion and Occupation of Iraq* (New York, 2007), 105–106.

52. King Fahd quoted in Alberto Bin, Richard Hill, and Archer Jones, *Desert Storm: A Forgotten War* (Westport, Conn., 1998), 26–28, 79. Kwai-Cheung Chan, *Operation Desert Storm: Evaluation of the Air Campaign* (Washington, D.C., 1997), 75, 194.

53. Vojtech Mastny, *Helsinki, Human Rights, and National Security* (Durham, N.C., 1986), 1.

54. John J. Maresca, *To Helsinki: The Conference on Security and Cooperation in Europe, 1973–1975* (Durham, N.C., 1985), 3.

55. Jon Lee, "Finland Walks Tightrope between 2 Trade Blocs: Tries to Remain Friendly with Russians While Dealing with the West," *New York Times,* December 16, 1968, 73.

56. Maresca, *To Helsinki,* 110; appendix, 236–237, 242.

57. Michael Mastanduno, *Economic Containment: CoCom and the Politics of East-West Trade* (Ithaca, N.Y., 1991), 1–2.

58. Mastny, *Helsinki, Human Rights,* 7–8.

59. Brezhnev Doctrine, November 12, 1968, reprinted in Mastny, *Helsinki, Human Rights,* 48. Also see Peter Kenez, *A History of the Soviet Union from the Beginning to the End* (New York, 1999), 239.

60. National Archives, RG 59, Transcripts of Secretary of State Kissinger's Staff Meetings, 1973–1977, Entry 5177, Box 5, Secretary's Staff Meetings. Reprinted in *FRUS*, 1969–76, vol. 39 (Washington, D.C., 2007), 779–780.

61. Andrew Downer Crain, *The Ford Presidency: A History* (Jefferson, N.C., 2009), 170. Also see Leonard R. Sussman, "Why Did We Go to Helsinki and Madrid?" in *Three Years at the East-West Divide* (New York, 1983), xv.

62. Kissinger quoted in Maresca, *To Helsinki*, 36. Kissinger made these comments in the context of another dispute, but they shed "light on his attitude toward the [Helsinki] Conference," Maresca asserts.

63. Helsinki Final Act, reprinted in Maresca, *To Helsinki*, 229, 231. James T. McHugh and James C. Pacy, *Diplomats without a Country: Baltic Diplomacy, International Law, and the Cold War* (Westport, Conn., 2001), 84, 111.

64. Mastny, *Helsinki, Human Rights*, 4.

65. McHugh and Pacy, *Diplomats without a Country*, 84. Mastanduno, *Economic Containment*, 2.

66. Mastny, *Helsinki, Human Rights*, 6.

67. Carter, 147, 149.

68. For a useful overview, see Silvio Pons and Frederico Romero, eds., *Reinterpreting the End of the Cold War: Issues, Interpretations, Periodizations* (Oxford, 2005).

69. Stephen F. Cohen and Katrina Vanden Heuvel, *Voices of Glasnost: Interviews with Gorbachev's Reformers* (New York, 1989), 313. Also see Adrian G. V. Hyde-Price, *The International Politics of East Central Europe* (Manchester, UK, 1996), 145–146, 172, and Ross Gregory and Richard Balkin, *Cold War America, 1946 to 1990* (New York, 2003), 303. On British and French objections and U.S. support for reunification, see Carsten Volkery, "The Iron Lady's Views on German Reunification: 'The Germans Are Back!'" *Spiegel Online*, September 11, 2009, http://www.spiegel.de /international/europe/0,1518,648364,00.html (accessed 4/17/12). Also see Richard Holbrooke, *To End a War* (New York, 1999), 28.

70. Peter Kenez, *A History of the Soviet Union from the Beginning to the End*, 2nd ed. (New York, 2006), 291.

71. Eisenhower quoted in Geir Lundestad, *"Empire by Integration": The United States and European Integration, 1945–1997* (Oxford, 1998), 17.

72. Lundestad, *"Empire by Integration,"* 1, 4.

73. Furio Cerutti and Sonia Lucarelli, *The Search for a European Identity: Values, Policies, and the Legitimacy of the European Union* (New York, 2008), 48.

74. By excluding cheap foreign food, one consequence of EEC agricultural policy was to drive up costs for urban consumers by approximately $1,600 per year, per family. Noel Malcolm, "The Case against 'Europe,'" *Foreign Affairs* 74, no. 254 (March/April 1995): 57–59.

75. Brown quoted in Klaus Larres and Elizabeth Meehan, *Uneasy Allies: British-German Relations and European Integration since 1945* (Oxford, 2000), 42.

76. William Fulbright, *Congressional Record*, 80th Congress, vol. 93, part 3 (April 7, 1947), 3138. On the State Department position see Randall Woods, *Fulbright: A Biography* (Cambridge, U.K., 1995), 142.

77. Hogan, *Marshall Plan*, 38–39; *Congressional Review*, 80th Congress, vol. 93, part 3, 3139–3140.

78. *Congressional Review*, 80th Congress, vol. 93, part 3, 3139–3140. Dulles also quoted in Pascaline Winand, *Eisenhower, Kennedy, and the United States of Europe* (New York, 1993), 34.

79. Hogan, *Marshall Plan*, 23.

80. Judt, *Postwar*, 281.

81. Lundestad, *Empire by Integration*, 132.

82. Roosevelt quoted in Borgwardt, *New Deal for the World*, 48. Aaron Forsberg, *America and the Japanese Miracle: The Cold War Context of Japan's Postwar Economic Revival, 1950–1960* (Chapel Hill, N.C., 2000), 3.

83. Dulles quoted in Forsberg, *America and the Japanese Miracle*, 43, 70–72, and 76–77.

84. Forsberg, *America and the Japanese Miracle*, 41.

85. "Four Asian Nations Support Draft of Japanese Treaty, Challenge Soviet Charges: U.S. Policy Backed," *New York Times*, September 7, 1951, 1, 6.

86. "Excerpts from Statements Made at the Japanese Treaty Conference on Its Third Day," *New York Times*, September 7, 1951, 1, 6.

87. Shigeru Yoshida, *Shigeru Yoshida: Last Meiji Man*, ed. Hiroshi Nara (Lanham, Md., 2007), 4. Yoshida also quoted in Pyle, "Opportunism in the Pursuit of Power," 276–277.

88. Forsberg, *America and the Japanese Miracle*, 10, 13–14, 22, 24, 77–79, 166–167, 243. Pyle, "Opportunism in the Pursuit of Power," 276.

89. Michael Spence, *The Next Convergence: The Future of Economic Growth in a Multi-Speed World* (New York, 2011), 26.

90. Richard Gardner, *Sterling-Dollar Diplomacy: The Origins and the Prospects of Our International Economic Order* (New York, 1969), lxiii.

91. Spence, *Next Convergence*, 13.

92. Thomas Leonard, *Encyclopedia of the Developing World*, vol. 1 (Hoboken, N.J., 2005), 328. "Rise of a Trading Power, in 10 Years," *New York Times*, December 9, 2011, B1, B4.

Conclusion

1. Jim Lacey, *The First Clash: The Miraculous Greek Victory at Marathon and Its Impact on Western Civilization* (New York, 2011), 23, 139.

2. National Commission on Terrorist Attacks upon the United States, *The 9/11 Commission Report* (Washington, D.C., 2004), 13–14.

3. Peter Ford, "'Why Do They Hate Us?'" *Christian Science Monitor,* September 27, 2001, http://www.csmonitor.com/2001/0927/p1s1-wogi.html (accessed 11/25/11).

4. National Commission, *9/11 Commission Report,* 57, 155.

5. Jane Corbin, *Al-Qaeda: In Search of the Terror Network that Threatens the World* (New York, 2002), 11, 23, 68, 131. Phillip Margulies, *Al Qaeda: Osama bin Laden's Army of Terrorists* (New York, 2003), 23. John Dower, *Cultures of War: Pearl Harbor, Hiroshima, 9–11, Iraq* (New York, 2010), 87. National Commission, *9/11 Commission Report,* 57, 155.

6. "Bin Laden's Fatwa," *PBS NewsHour,* August 1996, http://www.pbs.org/newshour/terrorism/international/fatwa_1996.html (accessed 11/25/11).

7. Frank Rich, preface to Joan Didion, *Fixed Ideas: America since 9.11* (New York, 2003), viii.

8. Chalmers Johnson wrote a trilogy of books that became bestsellers after 9/11, accusing the United States of a sustained and misguided campaign to rule the world. The first in the series is the best known; see Johnson, *Blowback: The Costs and Consequences of American Empire* (New York, 2000).

9. Didion, *Fixed Ideas,* 6. Also see John Leonard, "Who Stole Democracy?" *New York Times Book Review,* September 23, 2001, 14, and Andy Newman, "Irony Is Dead. Again. Yeah, Right," *New York Times,* November 21, 2008. Lev Grossman, "Why the 9/11 Conspiracy Theories Won't Go Away," *Time Magazine,* September 3, 2006. Noam Chomsky, *Nine-Eleven* (New York, 2001).

10. Amy Zegart, *Spying Blind: The CIA, the FBI, and the Origins of 9/11* (Princeton, N.J., 2007), 3.

11. For current statistics on defense spending across the globe, see the annual reports of the Stockholm International Peace Research Institute (SIPRI) Military Expenditure Database, http://www.sipri.org/databases/milex.

12. "Arbitration Award for Exxon Is Detailed," *New York Times,* January 3, 2010, B4.

13. Robert Kagan concludes that it would be catastrophic if the United States committed "preemptive superpower suicide." Kagan, *The World America Made* (New York, 2012), 7. Economists Benn Steil and Manuel Hinds similarly warn that unrestrained economic nationalism, especially in the United States, could damage the entire global economy. Steil and Hinds, *Money, Markets, and Sovereignty* (New Haven, Conn., 2009).

14. Ron Paul, "Ron Paul: Close Foreign Military Bases," Politico.com, November 20, 2011, http://www.politico.com/blogs/politicolive/1111/Ron_Paul_Close_foreign_military_bases.html (accessed 1/4/12). Also see Ron Paul, "Ron Paul: Let's Stop Bribing and Threatening North Korea," May 31, 2009, http://www.ronpaul.com/2009-05-31/ron-paul-lets-stop-bribing-and-threatening-north-korea/ (accessed 1/4/12).

15. Gillard quoted in "Gillard, Obama Detail U.S. Troop Deployment," Australian Broadcasting Corporation, November 16, 2011, http://www.abc.net.au/news /2011-11-16/gillard2c-obama-announce-darwin-troop-deployment/3675596 (accessed 11/25/11). Also see "U.S. Pivots Eastward to Address Uneasy Allies," October 25, 2011; "As U.S. Looks to Asia, It Sees China Everywhere," November 15, 2011; and "Obama Addresses Troops at Final Stop in Australia," November 17, 2011, all in *New York Times,* online edition (www.nytimes.com).

16. Quoted in Samuel Mitcham, *The Rise of the Wehrmacht: The German Armed Forces and World War II,* vol. 1 (Westport, Conn., 2008), 393.

17. Author's interview with George P. Shultz, Hoover Institution, Stanford University, April 18, 2011. Joshua Goldstein and Steven Pinker, "War Really Is Going Out of Style," *New York Times,* December 17, 2011.

18. On this subject, see Gene Lyons and Michael Mastanduno, eds., *Beyond Westphalia: State Sovereignty and International Intervention* (Baltimore, 1995).

19. Beatriz Escriña Cremades, "R2P and the UN," *UN Chronicle,* http://www .un.org/wcm/content/site/chronicle/home/archive/issues2011/pursuingpeace /r2pandtheun (accessed 5/31/12). Again, James Madison was explicit on this: see Madison to Washington, April 16, 1787, and Madison to Randolph, April 8, 1787, in *The Papers of James Madison: Digital Edition,* ed. J. C. A. Stagg (Charlottesville, Va., 2010).

20. "Indonesia: Dutch Apologize for 1947 Massacre of 430 Villagers," *New York Times,* December 9, 2011, A7. "President Signs Law to Redress Wartime Wrong," *New York Times,* August 11, 1988. "Ottawa Will Pay Compensation to Uprooted Japanese-Canadians," *New York Times,* September 23, 1988.

21. "Remarks to Genocide Survivors in Kigali, Rwanda," March 25, 1998. Online by Gerhard Peters and John T. Woolley, *The American Presidency Project,* http:// www.presidency.ucsb.edu/index.php. "Belgian Apology to Rwanda," BBC News, April 7, 2000, http://news.bbc.co.uk/2/hi/africa/705402.stm. "Canadian Government Apologizes for Rwandan Genocide Inaction," April 23, 2010, http://tj.facing history.org/resources/facingtoday/canadian-government-apologiz (accessed 11/30/11).

22. Author's interview with Condoleezza Rice, Hoover Institution, Stanford University, March 22, 2012.

23. Delors and Poos quoted in Noel Malcolm, "The Case against 'Europe,'" *Foreign Affairs* 74, no. 2 (March–April 1995), 68.

24. Richard C. Holbrooke, *To End a War* (New York, 1998), 26. David Rohde, *Endgame: The Betrayal and Fall of Srebrenica, Europe's Worst Massacre since World War II* (New York, 1997), xi.

25. Noel Malcolm, *Bosnia: A Short History* (New York, 1994), 252.

26. Michael Libal, *Limits of Persuasion: Germany and the Yugoslav Crisis, 1991–1992* (Westport, Conn., 1997), 11.

27. David Gompert quoted in Holbrooke, *To End a War,* 27.

28. James A. Baker III, with Thomas M. DeFrank, *The Politics of Diplomacy* (New York, 1995), 637. Baker also quoted in Holbrooke, *To End a War*, 27–28.

29. Rohde, *Endgame*, xii. Wolfowitz quoted in Holbrooke, *To End a War*, 30.

30. Holbrook, *To End a War*, 34. Beverley Allen, *Rape Warfare: The Hidden Genocide in Bosnia-Herzegovina and Croatia* (Minneapolis, 1996), 57, 100–101.

31. Rohde, *Endgame*, 23–25.

32. Holbrooke, *To End a War*, 39, 55, 61. Jan Willem Honig and Norbert Both, *Srebrenica: Record of a War Crime* (New York, 1996), 110–111.

33. Rohde, *Endgame*, 25–27. Holbrooke, *To End a War*, 64.

34. Morillon quoted in Rohde, *Endgame*, xv.

35. "The Betrayal of Srebrenica: Why Did the Massacre Happen? Will It Happen Again?" Hearings before the Subcommittee on International Operations, 105th Congress, 2d Session (March 31, 1998), 1. Rohde, *Endgame*, 27.

36. Janvier quoted in Rohde, *Endgame*, 23, 28, 290. Scholars quoted in Honig and Both, *Srebrenica*, xx.

37. Mladic quoted in Rohde, *Endgame*, 330. Also see "Betrayal of Srebrenica," 9–11.

38. Holbrooke, *To End a War*, 99–102, 152.

39. Pfaff quoted in Holbrooke, 103.

40. David Gompert, "The United States and Yugoslavia's Wars," in Richard H. Ullman, *The World and Yugoslavia's Wars* (New York, 1996), 127–128.

41. "Bin Laden's Fatwa," *PBS NewsHour*.

42. "Canada to Oppose International Bank Tax," *New York Times*, May 18, 2009, and "Canadian Banks Missed a Chance," *New York Times*, September 27, 2009.

43. "Extreme Poverty in Developing World Is Down Despite the Recession, Report Says," *New York Times*, March 7, 2012, A4.

44. Thomas L. Friedman, *The World Is Flat: A Brief History of the Twenty-First Century* (New York, 2005). Andrew Bacevich argues that scholarship and popular mythology collude "to deny the existence of an American Empire," but nearly the reverse seems true. Contemporary scholarship more typically presumes than denies a U.S. imperium. Bacevich, ed., *The Short American Century: A Postmortem* (Cambridge, Mass., 2012), 236.

Acknowledgments

My dear, deceased friend Barbara Jean Finberg, vice president of Carnegie Corporation of New York, encouraged me to write this book. I will be grateful all my life for the love, support, and inspiration she gave me from the age of twenty-two onward. She changed my life. Colleagues at two institutions made the book possible. Dean Paul Wong of San Diego State University facilitated an extended leave of absence and sabbatical, and the History Department there provided friendship and encouragement. I am especially grateful to the distinguished Edward Beasley for his extensive help in matters of world and British history. Professors Edward Blum, Ross Dunn, Mathew Kuefler, Thomas Passananti, and John Putman tolerated random questions with excellent humor. I wrote the book at Stanford University's Hoover Institution on War, Revolution, and Peace, where numerous colleagues gave generously of their time, advice, and insight, including Dennis Bart, Stephen Haber, Olivia Litz, Mandy MacCalla, Colin McCubbins, Condoleezza Rice, George Shultz, and Cheryl Weissbart. I owe a special debt to the brilliant and idiosyncratic David Brady, who pretends not to like people but invited me to Hoover, and then invited me back. To paraphrase Isaac Newton, we see farther by standing on the shoulders of giants. For their assiduous and learned feedback on the manuscript—which saved me from numerous errors and infelicities—I especially wish to thank Robert Kagan, David Kennedy, Erez Manela, Michael Mastanduno, Jack Rakove, Michael Schaller, and Salim Yaqub. Any remaining errors, especially typographical ones, are my own responsibility or those of my kitty cat, who refused to stay off the keys.

 Brian Balogh and Bruce Schulman remain my oldest, dearest friends in the historical profession. They light my way. Joyce Seltzer of Harvard University Press defines excellence in editing and makes a great dinner companion. The Miller Center for Public Affairs generously facilitated a final shakedown of the manuscript, to which many kind colleagues there contributed. The production crew associated with Harvard University Press was unfailingly helpful, especially Edward Wade and Julie Ericksen Hagen. Leon Nower, whom I have known since the age of fourteen, taught me much of what I know about writing and all I know in my heart about the sorrow of World War II. Lastly, I wish to acknowledge Daniel Hoffman for reading the *whole* thing, James Shelley for helping with promotion, and my children, Gregory and Victoria Shelby, whose willingness to stand by their mother's side throughout her adventures has been a precious gift. Thank you, one and all.

Index